Guide Library

Hillwood Museum
Washington, D.C.

SOVIET RUSSIAN LITERATURE

Soviet Russian Literature

Writers and Problems

1917-1977

SECOND REVISED EDITION

MARC SLONIM

New York
OXFORD UNIVERSITY PRESS
1977

Foreword

The title of this book defines both its scope and its limitations. Since it is a study of *Russian* post-revolutionary literature, it does not include writings in those languages of the different nations forming the USSR: and since it deals with Soviet writers, it omits the *émigrés*, who deserve a special survey of their own. Here I have followed the same method as in my *The Epic of Russian Literature* and *From Chekhov to the Revolution* of which this work is an organic sequel, even though each volume can be read separately. I have endeavored to combine portraits of the prominent writers with a description of the social and political background, and to alternate discussion of individual poets and novelists with analysis of the problems they have had to face in a totalitarian state.

It is obviously impossible at this time to offer a true history of Soviet literature. It is a commonplace to say that to evaluate our contemporaries is an uncertain, arduous task; literary critics, as is well known, feel much more at ease dealing with dead authors than with living ones. But in the case of Soviet literature we are confronted with peculiar difficulties. We lack data even about those writers who have suffered natural or violent death, and we do not know how many of their unpublished works may be locked up in some secret archives. We do not possess exact information of the circumstances in which the victims of Stalinist purges and terror were suppressed. Moreover, the majority of biographical and critical surveys published in Soviet Russia during the last sixty years present such falsification and re-arrangement of history, such a dark net of lies and pre-fabrications, such distortions and political deception, that the student of modern Russian literature is menaced by endless pitfalls. The constant shifts and twists in Party literary policy under Stalin and his heirs have provoked a series of changes in official evaluations of writers and their works, of factual omissions and deliberate silences—all to make literature fit into the latest patterns of Communist exegetics.

It is not easy for a researcher, who tries to the best of his ability, to find a safe path in this quicksand of contradictory evaluations, reticence, or outright mendacity. To see the true literary situation one has to plow through a staggering number of novels, poems, essays, articles, Party resolutions, and official commentaries—a task far from entertaining, requiring a great deal of time, patience, and a special flair for seeing the hidden meanings behind the printed word. I hope that, after having conducted such investigations for so many years, I am qualified to present a fairly accurate description of Soviet Russian literature, to separate true achievements from tendentious trash, and to assess the pressures of the State and the reigning literary dogma on current prose and poetry in the USSR. I also hope that I have judged fairly the major events of the last years—the renewal of literature in the post-Stalin era, the emergence of a new generation of writers, the ultimate downfall of the myth of "socialist realism," and all the zig-zags of government policy bent on stopping the artist's irreversible movement toward freedom and independence.

The general picture I offer is by no means exhaustive or definitive, and I am fully aware that my inclusion of some authors and omission of others can be debated, but I feel that my efforts may be helpful for the understanding of Soviet cultural life.

Sarah Lawrence College
Bronxville, New York—Geneva, Switzerland
Fall 1964   M.S.

The present volume of *Soviet Russian Literature* is a revised and amplified version of the 1964 and 1967 editions. There are new chapters on Mandelstam, Akhmatova, Tsvetayeva, Bulgakov, Platanov, Zabolotsky, and Solzhenitsyn, and on Samizdat and the Third Emigration.

Contents

1. The Transition, 3

2. Sergey Essenin: THE CONFUSED PEASANT, 11

3. Vladimir Mayakovsky: THE POET OF THE REVOLUTION, 19

4. The Proletcult, 33

5. The NEP and the 'Twenties, 41

6. Boris Pilnyak: THE UNTIMELY SYMBOLIST, 61

7. Isaac Babel: THE ROMANTIC STORYTELLER, 69

8. Vsevolod Ivanov: THE EXUBERANT SIBERIAN, 75

9. Evgeny Zamyatin: THE IRONIC DISSIDENT, 82

10. Mikhail Zoshchenko: THE CONDEMNED HUMORIST, 92

11. The Serapion Brethren, The Pass, and The Oberiuts, 99

12. Mikhail Prishvin: THE NATURE LOVER, 109

13. Soviet Romantics: FROM GRIN, PAUSTOVSKY, AND OLESHA TO TIKHONOV AND BAGRITSKY, 116

14. Konstantin Fedin: THE TRADITIONAL NOVELIST, 134

15. Alexey Tolstoy: THE MASTER OF THE ANECDOTE, 144

16. From the Five-Year Plan to Socialist Realism, 155

17. Literature of Communist Persuasion: FROM FURMANOV TO OSTROVSKY, 169

18. Mikhail Sholokhov: THE EPIC NARRATOR, 188

19. Leonid Leonov: THE PSYCHOLOGICAL NOVELIST, 198

20. Ilya Ehrenburg: THE MASTER JOURNALIST, 213

21. Boris Pasternak: THE VOICE OF THE OTHER RUSSIA, 223

22. The Era of Stabilization and Dictatorship, 236

23. The Fate of Poets: MANDELSTAM, AKHMATOVA, TSVETAYEVA, 248

24. The Historical Novel, 268

25. The Pre-War Years, 277

26. War Literature, 292

27. The Aftermath of War: THE ERA OF "ZHDANOVISM," 304

28. The Thaw, 320

29. The Unstable Equilibrium, 338

30. Posthumous revivals: BULGAKOV, PLATONOV, ZABOLOTSKY, 352

31. Alexander Solzhenitsyn: THE GREAT CHALLENGER, 363

32. Samizdat: THE UNDERGROUND PRESS, 376

33. The Newcomers, 383

34. Fluctuations and Trials, 394

35. The Third Emigration, 408

INDEX, 419

SOVIET RUSSIAN LITERATURE

1

The Transition

The fall of the Tsarist Empire in 1917, and the ascension to power of the Bolsheviks under Lenin and Trotsky, brought on the physical collapse of nineteenth-century Russian culture. From the moment when the Communist Revolution triumphed in Petrograd on November 7, 1917,* and began its struggle for total domination of the whole of Russia, the social and economic support of this culture, the privileged way of life that had favored its blossoming, and the very contradictions and conflicts that had kept it alive, started to disintegrate. To the intellectuals, whom the victors treated initially as potential enemies, the events of the Revolution were catastrophic. Alexander Blok's predictions had come true; overnight the intelligentsia found themselves at the bottom of the pit. The cruel upheaval had rejected them mercilessly. "The iron broom of history had swept them away together with other rubbish," said Trotsky. All they had loved and cherished—refinement, noble sentiments, gentle humanitarianism, repentance, sophistication, and the cult of beauty or of vague liberalism—suddenly had no value and seemed fantastically out of place during the rough, barren years of military Communism and civil war. What was happening bore no resemblance whatever to the magnificent prophecies of the symbolist seers or the mystical-minded radicals: it simply meant epidemics, starvation, prison, exile—physical as well as spiritual annihilation. Russia seemed to be in agony, and a large number of poets or novelists felt that the only thing they could do was to hold a funeral service for the land that was going to its doom. This mood is to be found in various

* The Bolshevik Revolt took place on October 23, Old Style, or November 7, New Style, which accounts for the fact that while Russians speak of the October Revolution, the rest of the world refers to it as the November Revolution.

works, from Remizov's prose ("The Lay of the Destruction of the Land of Russia") to Ehrenburg's verse ("Prayer for Russia"), as well as in many later works such as Shmelyov's *The Sun of the Dead* (1923), and Bunin's *Ungodly Days* or *Hippius' Diary*.

The material situation of men of letters after the October Revolution soon became impossible. Only a few writers, such as the symbolist poet Briussov and the aged storyteller Yeronim Yassinsky (1850-1930), joined the new regime at the beginning. A large group (of whom Gorky was the leading representative) remained hesitant and somewhat critical. The vast majority did not want to collaborate with the "usurpers of power," the "criminal utopians," and concentrated all their efforts on survival, on avoiding starvation, cold, and terror. Some members of the intelligentsia decided to "lose themselves among the people": they went into the country and lived like peasants until the end of the civil war, at which time they emerged as clerical workers, technicians, teachers, and librarians. Pasternak depicts such efforts in *Doctor Zhivago*. And, finally, a large number went over to the Whites and eventually settled abroad—deliberately or accidentally —as political *émigrés*. By 1922 the list of writers who had fled to European countries included Bunin, Balmont, Remizov, Merezhkovsky, Kuprin, Andreyev, Shmelyov, Alexis Tolstoy, Khodassevich, Tsvetayeva, Vyacheslav Ivanov, Severyanin, Minsky, and hundreds of other poets, novelists, essayists, and journalists. There was a time when it seemed that all the literary salons of Moscow and St. Petersburg had been reopened in Paris, Berlin, and Prague; Hippius wrote in the early 'twenties that the whole cup of Russian literature had overflown abroad.

Those who remained in Russia for various reasons, including patriotic ones as in the case of Anna Akhmatova, were confronted not only by a desperate material plight but also by tremendous ideological, moral, and artistic problems. The 1914-18 war with Germany and Austro-Hungary had already disrupted the normal current of literary life; Communism dealt it a well nigh mortal blow. In 1918-19 the arts were on the brink of annihilation. The break with the past had come with the first shots of the Bolshevik *coup d'état*. Old newspapers and magazines ceased publication or were banned; printing presses were confiscated and became state property; publishers closed their doors or led a pitiful, precarious existence trying to survive by their wits. By 1920 the annual output of books had fallen to 3260 titles—as compared with some 20,000 in the year preceding World War I (1913)—and the majority of these were of a political or propaganda nature. The scarcity of paper and printing facilities and the deterioration of all means of communication had reduced the size and circulation of even dailies and weeklies published by Soviet agencies.

The governmental decrees introducing the New Style calendar and the new orthography (both of which had been worked out and approved by academic bodies long before the Revolution) were received by intellectuals merely as symbols of a complete rejection of the past. Material difficulties and fear arising from insecurity and social dislocation made any sustained creative effort futile. The civil war was devastating two-thirds of Russian territory between 1918 and 1922; millions were uprooted; membership in the Red Army or the White forces had thinned the ranks of all literary and artistic groups. *Silent leges inter arma,* and what is true of laws was also true of the Muses: literature seemed superfluous. The writers, confused, depressed, and utterly incapable of coping with the situation, compared themselves to grains of sand whirled by a tornado. Their whole world of ideas and forms was engulfed in the vortex of the general catacylsm; most of the issues that had agitated or rocked generations of intellectuals suddenly lost all significance and turned into ashes. Traditional themes and characters dissolved as if by magic; recent controversies of literary schools appeared meaningless—and the habitual reader along with the familiar critic vanished as well. All intellectual and artistic relationships were tottering, all authorities had grown tarnished, all the statues in the garden of Russian letters had been smashed to smithereens. Everything had to be built anew—and to be built on the site of a conflagration. While the majority of the intelligentsia and of the bourgeoisie were shocked, discouraged, or completely absorbed by the daily search for food, fuel, and clothing, those who took an active part in the events or sympathized with the Revolution found a sort of intoxication in the frenzy of the storm. The Revolution represented a tremendous release of energy, at first untamed and destructive; the fury of the mass movement had something overwhelming, cruel, and heroic about it and life was fantastic and thrilling among ruins, dangers, primitive passions, and death. It was an era of pathos and dynamism, when all things were possible; whatever was written during those momentous years—regardless of its artistic value—reflected, to a greater or lesser degree, the Great Eruption.

The renewal of literary activity was slow and gradual. It was encouraged by three main factors. Pre-revolutionary groups or their individual members attempted, upon overcoming their shock and lethargy, to reform their lines and either to continue the trends they represented or to adapt these to new conditions. Young people, however, most of whom were involved in the fighting, felt the urge to respond creatively to their times and to express their personal experience—sometimes in a rudimentary way—thus forming a new literary corpus and initiating a new chapter in the history of Russian literature. In the 'twenties the newcomers greatly outnumbered the poets, novelists, and dramatists of the older generation. And, finally, Communist leaders of whom the majority had belonged to the old intelligentsia, were eager to promote literature that would express the ideology of the Revolution and portray the changed social order. They were also committed by their own theories to vast measures of mass education—and this involved literature as well as the theater and the other arts. The independent development and the interaction of these three factors during the first years determined the whole structure of Soviet letters. The relationship between the literary groups moved from bitter struggle to co-operation, the intervention of the Communist Party into literary life grew in strength and importance, and the replacement of the old ruling classes by the lower strata of society resulted in the emergence of new readers and spectators, whose demands and opinions became more insistent with the consolidation of the regime. (But the true pressure of the masses on all the arts as well as the systematic organization of Party controls belong to a later period at the end of the 'twenties.)

There is one fact that must be kept in mind by those who wish to understand the origin and the evolution of Soviet literature: despite the feeling among the intellectuals and semi-literate middle-class groups that the end of the world had come, pre-revolutionary literary trends showed an amazing vitality and they did survive, often co-existing with the new currents and influencing them. Many apparently contradictory phenomena in the extremely complex Soviet literary scene can be explained by this literary survival. Orthodox Marxist critics under Stalin tried to deny it, or simply ignored the facts, and so produced an extremely distorted picture of the 'twenties in Soviet historical and critical essays and treatises. But in reality literary tradition proved to be more persistent than many other "leftovers" of the old regime. Various early twentieth-century literary movements, such as symbolism or imagism, simply splashed over and across the post-revolutionary era and gradually exhausted themselves under the Soviets. Some became extinct; others blended into the new picture, while still others, such as futurism or the Tolstoyan brand of psychological realism, exerted a decisive influence on Soviet writers. In quite a few instances (for example, in the case of Gladkov), works of fiction published as new and original and bearing the "Made in the Soviet Union" stamp were actually nothing but imitations or adaptations of the old. Considered objectively the Russian literary tradition has never been disrupted; although the young writers of the 1918-20 period felt like pioneers hewing logs for new dwellings in the wilderness, they were really putting up walls and laying roofs with the bricks and shingles left behind by their pre-revolutionary predecessors.

Chronologically, the first group of writers who attempted to "hymn the Revolution" were the Scythians, for the most part left-wing intellectuals whose theoretician, Razumnik Ivanov-Razumnik (1878-1946), had won a reputation as critic and author with his *History of Russian Social Thought* (1906). In 1917-22 he exerted considerable influence on Blok, Essenin, Kluyev, and other poets and novelists, as he was then founder and theoretician of the Scythians group, marked by its populist and Slavophile leanings. Later he was often persecuted and imprisoned. He described his personal experiences as well as the plight of Russian writers under Stalin in his *Jails and Exile*, an impressive book published abroad in the forties. Politically the Scythians were close to the Populists and the socialist revolutionaries; in literature they

supported the symbolists and the modernists. They interpreted
the great upheaval as a rebellion of the masses, peasants for the
most part, whose aspirations for social justice had turned a bourgeois political revolution into a socialist movement bearing the
stamp of the Russian national spirit. The works of the Scythians,
lyrical in form and utopian in content, reflected the embryonic
stage of Soviet literature which seemed to flow directly from
religious and social symbolism. When early in 1918 Blok published "The Twelve," his poem provoked endless discussions
because it portrayed twelve Red soldiers plundering and mur-
dering in snow-bound Petrograd not only as bandits but also
as dreamers inspired by the hatred of the old world and a confused yearning for a better life. Christ himself appears at the
end of the poem as their invisible leader. Thus the twelve criminals become the twelve apostles, and out of the blood and filth
emerges the image of a new gospel that justifies the terror and
the destructiveness of Bolshevism. The poem sounds like a dirge
for the old Russia—and like an Easter Mass announcing the Resurrection; death and the hope for a happy future are blended in
this poem, and its form merges realistic descriptions with symbolic
imagery. The anti-Communists considered it a blasphemy, and
the Communists were not very happy with the vision of the
Crucified as the bearer of the innermost revolutionary truth. Nor
were they very satisfied with Blok's "Scythians," an ode that
reverted to Dostoevsky's concept of Russian universality but
stressed the uncouth primitive strength of the nation and threatened the West with an alliance between the hordes of Slavs and
Asians in case Europe refused to collaborate with the land of the
Revolution. The stir provoked by these poems was so profound
that even today they occasion highly biased and passionately contradictory evaluations among Soviet readers as well as among
Russian *émigrés*.

It should not seem strange that the first positive reactions to
the Bolshevik Revolution should have come from symbolists
who embodied a whole epoch of aristocratic culture. The symbolists had had a foreboding of the cataclysm, and they were well
qualified to express the belief that the flame kindled in Moscow
would set the whole world ablaze, "to bring all bourgeois to

ruination" as Blok put it in "The Twelve." Revolutionary messianism was in the air: in the cities and villages speakers were proclaiming Russia as the savior of humanity and the builder of a
new society. Poets expressed the same conviction—the old belief
of the Slavophiles and Populists. Andrey Bely in his "Christ is
Risen" (1918) spoke of sufferings and sacrifice for the redemption of mankind. A score of minor poets followed this religious
trend. Others emphasized the national idiosyncrasies of the popular movement. Maximilian Voloshin (1877-1932), a symbolist who
had once written about Paris and the Mediterranean, was now
flaunting a mystical patriotism. His poems about Stenka Razin,
the rebellious Volga river pirate, and other historical characters
represented the anarchical eruption of the masses as deeply national and searched for the historical roots of contemporary
events. At the same time he was horrified by the Red terror and
its blind destructiveness, and some of his most impressive poems
on that subject were not allowed to be printed in Russia for political reasons (he apparently stopped writing around 1925). But
despite his anti-Communist feelings, he maintained that "a Great
and Marvelous Sun" was rising and asked: "Why then does such
poignant faith overflow and bear me along?" Other symbolists or
acmeists, such as Anna Akhmatova, also sang of illumination and
spoke of the Revolution with messianic fervor.

But those who were young and had actually fought for the
triumph of the Soviets, had nothing to do with mystical or religious trends. Their romantic and heroic poems stressed the gran-
deur, the universal sweep of events, and were frankly utopian
and hyperbolic. A group of proletarian poets, calling themselves
Cosmists, predicted a conquest of space beyond our planet: "we
will first overthrow the earth then we shall stage the rebellion of
the stars . . . Its elbow rumpling the skies, the reign of the workers
steps into the sphere of another world."

Most of the young poets of 1918-20 were dizzy with hope and
thrilled beyond measure by what they called a social and political
earthquake. They expected the World Revolution to come at any
moment from just around the corner; they could hear the tread
of history. Consciously or unconsciously the people of Russia
welcomed the advent of a new era: the crumbling of Austro-

Hungary and the collapse of the Hohenzollern monarchy in Germany sounded like the clarion call to a world uprising. The messianic poems reflecting this mood were, however, merely emotional outbursts, and for the most part without much artistic merit. They were usually read aloud in halls, clubs, and taverns, since the scarcity of paper, ink, and printing facilities compelled the poets to address their audiences directly. This was the "café period" of Soviet literature, when all sorts of basement dens in Moscow and Petrograd (such as the Pegasus Manger or The Poets Café) served as platforms, particularly for the imagists and futurists. Poetry was the thing; it did not demand the lengthy preparation of a work of prose, it offered a spontaneous emotional response to changing reality. This explains in part why poets—primarily Essenin and Mayakovsky—emerged as the most popular figures of the early 'twenties and why poetic works prevailed during the first stage of Soviet literature.

2

Sergey Essenin

THE CONFUSED PEASANT

When Sergey Essenin (1895-1925), the son of a Ryazan *muzhik* and himself a former shepherd, made his appearance in the St. Petersburg literary salons in 1915, he was acclaimed as a true "Poet of the People." This young lad in a peasant blouse belted with a brightly colored silk cord recited (or rather chanted) poems on the harvest, cows, clouds, and meadows. In folk lyrics he sang of sweet Jesus and the melancholy landscapes of Central Russia; his stylized saints prayed to God the Father, who sat on a golden cloud, to His Son the Saviour walking across the fields with a pilgrim's staff, while the Virgin Mary covered her blond braids with the flowered kerchief of a peasant woman. There was something of Fra Angelico about the tender colors—blue, gold, and pink—of Essenin's bucolic and naïve visions of nature, humble huts, and silent villages, against which he contrasted the noisy bustle of the city.

Between 1913 and 1917 Essenin learnt from the symbolists advanced poetic techniques, which he added to his innate qualities. His first printed works were well received by the critics, and even the Empress listened with interest to his stanzas and asked the poet why they were so sad (a fact Essenin preferred not to mention after the Revolution). In 1917 Essenin became closely associated with the Populists and socialist revolutionaries. His first wife, Zinaida Reich, who divorced him and then married Vsevolod Meyerhold, had been a member of the Socialist Revolutionary Party. Under the influence of Ivanov-Razumnik and other Scythians, Essenin joined the dissident left wing of the party which at first collaborated with the Bolsheviks but later rebelled against them and was driven into opposition. "I was on the side of the

October Revolution, a most fiery fellow-traveler," he declared in his autobiography, "but I interpreted it in my own way—giving it a peasant slant." His was a revolutionary messianism of the Populist brand, his long, well-known poem "Inonia" depicts a rural paradise in an agricultural, anti-capitalist republic where life is in complete accord with Mother Nature. The city is not mentioned in this utopia of the Golden Age: for Essenin, the town was still the symbol of a mechanized civilization that enslaves man. The poet warns America not to "launch steel ships on the sea of unbelief," and prohesies the collapse of skyscrapers and industrial giants. Had he lived longer he would have been simply horrified by the five-year plans and the urbanization of the Soviet Union. The Revolution meant to Essenin a return to primitive democratic simplicity, to farmers' communities; he celebrated peasant life in poems that sound like religious chants: the Resurrection, Easter, the Nativity, the Transfiguration—these were his metaphors in 1918.

In the poem "Comrade," Jesus decends to earth to help the Russians in their struggle for freedom and equality—and a policeman's bullet kills Him; He is buried in a common grave with the other victims of the Tsarist resistance, while "the iron word Republic reverberates through the streets." There was, however, a basic contradiction between the spirit of such poetry and the Revolution. Russia was resounding with speeches about the dictatorship of the proletariat, dialectical materialism, and Marxist art while Essenin was glorifying the Revolution on his rustic dulcimer and enriching symbolist poetry with similes and words from spirituals, incantations, ballads, and other folk material. He was still writing about plowing, haymaking, kind saints, and mystically inclined vagabonds, although machine guns were clattering, the civil war was raging, and lyrical dreams of serenity and piety were utterly out of place. As the censors did not allow his use of "religious terminology," he had a very hard time publishing his poems; his friends—left-wing socialist revolutionaries—were ruthlessly persecuted by the Communists. For in fact the Revolution was no idyllic transfiguration; the city was waging war against the countryside and sending punitive expeditions into the villages to requisition grain which the peasants hid from the new masters. Lenin was envisioning factories, mills, electrification, and the Communists were eager to destroy the saintly Russia of humble farms and resigned peasants.

At first Essenin attempted to accept this harsh reality and to adapt his life and poetry to it. He gave free rein to the elements of challenge, revelry, and restlessness that had always lain dormant in the dreamy and bucolic side of his nature. He tried to kill in himself the church choirboy, and wrote poems about Pugachev, the eighteenth-century rebel and pretender, about the devil-may-care Vas'ka Buslayev, the adventurous hero of medieval songs, and about Martha, the woman leader of the turbulent city of Novgorod. He always had a bent for a colorful, somewhat bizarre imagery that stemmed from folklore and recalled popular woodcuts: "the moon—that ruddy goose," "clouds like pools," "the dawn like a she-wolf." Now, in 1918-19 when dozens of splinter groups, such as nothingists, cosmists, super-realists, and many others, were competing with each other in the search for new poetic forms, it did not take Essenin long to become the leader of the imagists. It must be stressed that Russian imagism had no connection with the imagist school founded by Ezra Pound and continued by Amy Lowell in 1914. Backed by minor but vociferous poets such as Anatoly Marienhof (b.1897), Rurik Ivnev (Mikhail Kovalev, b.1893), Vadim Shershenevich (b.1893), and Alexander Kusikov (b.1896), it proclaimed the supremacy of the image over all other elements of poetic creativeness, including sense and rhythm. A "broken string of images" was all that was needed for a poem, but each image had to be startling, striking, vivid and make an impact on the reader.

Stylistically, imagism was an outgrowth of symbolism and actually aimed at a poetry that would appeal to the subconscious by a concatenation of strange similes; for Essenin personally, it offered an escape from the social compulsion and political intent which were the order of the day. The imagists as a group never had a large following and disappeared from the literary scene with the death of their leader. Under the thin disguise of an innovation which he pretended was "congenial to the spirit of the Revolution," Essenin was defending his right to lyricism and to the expression of a non-rational, whimsical vision of the world.

At the start of the imagist movement Essenin played with metaphors: "I go about unkempt—my head is like a kerosene lamp
on my shoulders." In "Pugachev," a long narrative poem full of
tiresome hints and vague allegories, he used a succession of con-
trived images: "the pliers of sunrise yank the stars like teeth from
the maw of darkness"; "my eyes hungrily suck the udders of
dawn, that red skinned camel." His verbal eccentricities in 1920-22
were caused not only by the desire to break down old canons and
find new poetic devices, typical of the times, but also by his
mounting inner anxiety. The erstwhile rhapsodist of kindly saints
and peaceful sunsets now spent his days and nights in taverns in
the company of barflies, prostitutes, and drug addicts. Like Fran-
cois Villon he preferred tramps to the literati. The feeling of
dissatisfaction with himself, with his society and his century drove
him away from home and work. Drink and carousing were for
him the simplest means of escape.

A casual meeting with Isadora Duncan, the famous American
dancer who came to Moscow to convert revolutionaries to the
cult of Greek beauty, led Essenin into a whirlwind love affair
and marriage to her, a woman twice his age. They went abroad,
and the young Russian became the playboy of Europe and America. The scandal sheets of Berlin, Paris, and New York reported
extensively on his drinking bouts, rowdyism, and matrimonial
quarrels, which often ended in public fisticuffs. Upon his return
home and a new marriage (to a granddaughter of Leo Tolstoy)
he strutted through the nightclubs of Moscow as the prince of
literary bohemia and his extravagances were greater than ever.
This behavior was a clear indication of the complex crisis that
the man and poet were going through. During the civil war he
could not adjust himself to the atmosphere of cruelty and destruction, he did not get along with the fanatics who obeyed the
ruthless law of vengeance, and he could not accept the strait
jacket of Communism. Now he was disgusted with the vulgarity
and meanness of the NEP, Lenin's compromise economic program. This divorce from the political doctrines and the social
environment of his era was neither conscious nor cerebral—although he had written a few poems that could not be published

in Russia because of their anti-Soviet spirit. It was emotional incompatibility and he interpreted his inability to conform as a personal failure. Everybody was fighting, struggling, or building—he alone felt useless and a stranger in his own land.

Neither as an individual nor as a poet could he fit into his times —and he passed from spells of melancholy to outbursts of wild revelry. Occasionally he had the illusion that his hooliganism (as he called it himself) drew him closer to the elemental fury of the Revolution, that his drinking and blasphemous verse were akin to the people's rebellion; so he wrote such poems as "The Moscow of Taverns" (1923) and "The Confession of a Hooligan" (1924), informing readers that if he had not been born a poet he would have become a cut-throat or a thief. But this was wishful thinking, rather than true self-revelation. The trouble was that Essenin actually bore within himself the sense of guilt and the yearning of a prodigal son; what he desired above all was to return to the village, to the peaceful kindliness of his mother, to the healing bosom of nature; and in order to drown his sensitivity and his nostalgia, he drank, took drugs, indulged in cynical attitudes, changed wives and mistresses, and made all sorts of mischief. The "primordial purity" he longed for seemed to him the mark of Cain. The bar-room brawls, the street set-to's, the provocative poems, and harebrained exploits were simply morbid forms of self-punishment. His life from 1922 to the very end, in 1925, was a process of self-immolation, a drive to annihilation. All his outbursts were, however, of no avail and could not silence the inner voice: "A living soul cannot be changed in a century. No, I shall never make peace with myself, I am a stranger to my own self." Even as the wild stories of his escapades made the rounds of Moscow, his tragedy was deepening. He felt drained, tired, and frustrated; his attempts to behave like a wild Scythian or a dandified gallant were alike pitiful failures. All his poses were merely a blind; what he really loved and confessed to in his best lyrical poems were country roads, ponds shadowed by old birch trees, recollections of his happy youth, and his native land. Grief and resignation blended in his verse, which by now had shed all the exaggerations of imagism. His life passed away "like the white haze of apple blossoms"; all was lost, for there was no return to the peaceful fields. He told of his dreams and defeats in simple, poignant lines.

In 1924 the prodigal son came back to his native village but could scarcely recognize the land he had once glorified in his poems. Nothing reminded him of the compassion, gentleness, and saintliness of old Russia: the peasants were discussing battles and wars, and bands of Communist youth as they marched downhill were bawling the propaganda couplets of Demyan Bedny in lieu of folklore songs. "What a country! Why in hell did I caterwaul about my being a friend of the people? They have no need either of me or my poetry." Even if he stayed and died there, the grave-digger would merely say: "What a crackpot! During his lifetime he was almost frantically agitated, yet he could never make himself read even five pages of Marx's *Capital.*" In his famous poem "Soviet Russia" (1924) he complained that "the talk of the citizens sounds strange to my ear; I live an alien in my own land." Yet the attitude of resignation did not help him much. He talked himself into accepting everything and asserted that "the glow in the windows of the huts has been lit by a new generation," but he feared the industrial era and knew that the noise of tractors would soon drown out the songs of birds. He also felt apprehensive about his own songs: "I will surrender everything but my lyre." The last poet of the village, as he called himself, was the victim of a revolution that had not fulfilled his dreams of Natural Man or of a rural utopia. He remained an anachronism. "Why should I conceal it?" he said in one of his last poems. "I am not a New Man. With one foot in the past, I try with the other to catch up with the army of steel and I stumble and fall." Depressed by the awareness that his life was being wasted, torn by feelings of repentance and guilt, he soon came to the end of his tether. In "The Black Man," one of his most revealing poems, he engages in a dialogue with his demon, who enumerates all of the poet's sins and failings. This horrifying confession, and self-indictment, couched in sharp, terse lines and changing rhythms, shows the degree of tedium and despair he had reached by 1925. His nerves were frayed, he had a breakdown and was forced to enter a mental institution, but he came out only to acknowledge the irremediable tragedy of his situation. "My dear, my friend, only death shuts the eyes which had recovered sight." During the Christmas season of 1925 he felt his loneliness more than ever and wrote: "To die is no novelty—but neither is it novel to be alive." On December 27 he slashed his wrists and hanged himself in a hotel room.

There are two major aspects of Essenin's poetry. During the last years of his life the poet of the countryside, the lyricist of the village, the peasant bard was overshadowed by the author of "The Moscow of Taverns" and of "Soviet Russia," in which he expressed the torments of a gentle heart in search of love, purity, and humanity. Between 1923 and 1925 his melodious verse, liberated from artificial imagist tricks, became more direct and simple. He used again the rhythms, vocabulary, and similes of folklore—and these gave a strong national, even regional, character to his lyrics. Their charm, however, lay in the wistful musicality, and "the sweet poison of despondency" they insidiously distilled. He may be said to have sung of a whole generation that had been badly mauled by the Revolution. The contradictions that had ruined his life and led him to his tragic end were close to thousands of young men and women who had also been uprooted and trampled under during the cataclysm: they read their own lives, their own complaints into his poems of sorrow and discouragement.

At the time of his death he was extremely popular. Gorky declared that "this splendid and true poet reflected our epoch in his own way and enriched it with his songs." Voronsky, the critic, in speaking of Essenin's disintegration, called him a peasant bard who had been lured by and had perished in the morasses of the city. Trotsky praised his poetic gifts and regretted that the times had been "too catastrophic, epic, public" for Essenin's personal, lyrical, and solitary voice. It was not long, however, before the very popularity of Essenin, which overshadowed that of Mayakovsky, became politically suspect. "Essenism" was declared socially dangerous: it meant moral weakness and degradation, feminine softness, or a combination of despondent passivity and pathological bohemianism. Although in 1926-7 the State Publishing House brought out Essenin's collected works in four volumes, the printing was limited to 10,000 copies, and a great many poems were not included in this edition. Then, for twenty-two years, hardly any reprints of his works were allowed; only a few of his poems appeared in anthologies, and he was granted but passing mention in surveys of Soviet literature. Moscow Encyclopedia stated: "Essenism expressed itself in suicides." Nevertheless, when a volume of his selected poems was published in Moscow in 1948, it sold out immediately. It showed that the fight against Essenin conducted by the Communist critics had not impressed Soviet youth, who had continued to circulate his poems in manuscript copies and to memorize his doleful lines. The negative attitude of Communist bureaucrats, particularly under Stalin, was paralleled by that of older *émigrés*. In 1950, for example, Bunin wrote a vehement condemnation of Essenin's "barbershop poetry," denying any importance to this "sentimental hooligan," as he contemptuously dubbed him.

Without making any sensational comeback, however, Essenin's name has been taken off the scroll of the damned, and even before Stalin's death he was restored as one of the pre-eminent poets of the 'twenties. He is still widely read in the Soviet Union, and every reprint of his works in the 'fifties, 'sixties, and 'seventies has always been sold out in record time.

3

Vladimir Mayakovsky

THE POET OF THE REVOLUTION

While Essenin, the peasant poet, reflected the tragedy of the victims, Vladimir Mayakovsky expressed the aggressiveness and ·hopes of the masters. Essenin personified the spirit of loss and defeat; Mayakovsky sang of strength and victory. Yet their fate was similar: both ended as suicides. Vladimir Mayakovsky (1893-1930) was the son of an impoverished nobleman who held the post of forest ranger in the Caucasus; the future poet spent his childhood in Georgia, and the family moved to Moscow in 1906 after the father's death. Vladimir was more interested in revolutionary agitation than in studying and dropped out of school after only a year. His underground activities and early association with the Bolsheviks led to three arrests and eleven months in prison. Released because of his youth (he was fifteen), he entered a school of fine arts in 1910, but it did not take him very long to find poetry more attractive than draftsmanship.

David Burliuk, a painter who emigrated to the United States in 1922, brought him into the futurist movement, introducing him as "my friend Mayakovsky, a genius." At nineteen Mayakovsky emerged as the most turbulent of the militant cubo-futurists. He attacked "the academy and decrepit old literature," demanded a revolution in the arts in the name of modernity, speed, dynamism, and direct colloquial means of expression, and was ready to support avant-garde theories with his fists. A tall athletic-looking youth endowed with a violent temperament and the voice of a heckler, he loved to "shock the bourgeois," went around in a bright yellow blazer, and treated the stage where he read his poems as a boxing arena. He enjoyed "A Slap in the Public's Face" as the futurist manifesto was entitled in 1912, showered abuse on opponents in his public appearances, which often ended in free-for-

alls, and invented all sorts of stunts and hoaxes. It would be useless
to deny a great deal of exhibitionism and pose in the challenges
and extravagances of the futurists (who often went around with
carrots instead of flowers in their buttonholes), but their purpose
was serious, and they reflected the inner crisis in literature and
art. And the poems which Mayakovsky started publishing in 1915,
despite the provocative titles of his two booklets—*A Cloud in
Trousers, The Spine Flute*—were unusual in their form but sad and
almost tragic in their essence. Excerpts from his "War and Peace"
and "Man" appeared in Gorky's monthly *The Annals* which followed a mild line in poetry and fiction. In all these works of
exceptional vigor Mayakovsky used futuristic diction and eccentric, broken meters, *outré* near-rhymes, assonances, topiary ar-
rangements, and whimsical punctuation, while his vocabulary was
ostentatiously colloquial and crude. What made his poems highly
original was the combination of rebellion and lyricism, of force
approaching brutality of expression and hidden emotional sensitivity. He interwove in them the story of a tragic love with the
negation of art, of state, and of religion; intimate confession followed his thrusts against social conditions. He complained that
his sufferings and inner void came from "the loss of feelings on
the city pavements." His heart, he claimed, was like a bordello
on fire, and his words were the prostitutes leaping out of its blaz-
ing windows. He spoke incessantly of his torments: "I burned my
soul where tenderness was bred; it is more difficult than the storm-
ing of a thousand Bastilles." His stanzas, filled with extravagant
similes, aimed at a complete break with the tradition of the genteel,
the sublime, or the esoteric: Mayakovsky wanted to be loud,
coarse, impetuous, anti-aesthetic. He loathed the watery sentimentalism of patrician poets, and the verbal vagueness of the
symbolists. The debasement of language and metaphor, as well as
the ironical or grotesque twist in his verse and its conversational
tone, were intentionally directed against the "spirituality" and
"purity" of traditional poetry. A considerable part of Mayakovsky's work was inspired by poetical polemics. But the passion
and anger of *A Cloud in Trousers* and *The Spine Flute* make them
outstanding poems; they certainly belong to the best works of
Mayakovsky though Communist critics are reluctant to admit
this. In general, they prefer to underestimate Mayakovsky's fu-

turism and pass over in silence the fact that all his poetic characteristics were evident before 1917.

Even at that time he was extremely fond of reading his verse before large audiences, and displayed keen wit in controversy. He enjoyed the intoxication of struggle and challenge. His craving for hyperbolic images and theatrical effects matched his stentorian voice and uncouth manners. This gaunt lad with the muscles of a prizefighter hailed the fall of Tsarism not only on political grounds: it offered a release for his temperament. Here was a marvelous adventure in this complete renovation of Russia and mankind ("We trample on laws given us by Adam and Eve"), and he was delighted by the sweep and the perspectives of the Revolution; they made him forget the anxieties and torments of his early poems. He immediately joined the Bolsheviks. Now his tremendous energy and rebellious tendencies were channeled; he could storm the heights of Parnassus, from which the academicians and symbolists had fled in disorder; he could at last address his mass reader in the bold style he had forged before 1917 as the most adequate poetic idiom of the new era. And he could expand the satirical, revolutionary themes and moods of his early poems (particularly of his autobiographical parody "Man" and his verses against war and the bourgeoisie).

The futurists led by Mayakovsky came to the fore in 1918 claiming to be a school perfectly suited to the times. Their insolent declarations, in the spirit of the 1912 manifesto, resounded loudly amid the general silence, and Mayakovsky renewed his attacks against traditional art ("The White Guard is given over to a firing squad: why not Pushkin?"), and urged his fellow artists "onto the barricades of souls and hearts," asserting that "streets are our brushes, squares are our palettes."

In calling for an offensive against the classics, and waging war on aestheticism, lyricism, and other "similar bourgeois prejudices from the arsenal of the arts," Mayakovsky and his friends formulated a utilitarian and social theory of poetry and advised the poets "to spit upon the rhymes and arias, and the rose bush, and other such melancrockery." The new poetry was to celebrate the bustle of the city, the uprising of the people, the revolutionary battles, and the work of machine-conscious proletarians. The airiness, musicality, subtlety, and individuality of the symbolists, the perfectionism of the acmeists had to be supplanted by an art of the masses, of earth, of toil, and of daily efforts. Mayakovsky in finding a literary form for his ideas had become the herald and bard of all the hopes and strivings of the Revolution's initial, heroic years. The futurists, however, had more ambitious aims: regarding themselves as the vanguard of Communist culture, they wanted to reform literature and all the other arts, and promote an integral movement, the Left Front (LEF).

This group had scarcely any unity of doctrine, but it did possess a genuine revolutionary drive and showed inventiveness and linguistic daring. This is clearly expressed in its 1923 declaration: "We refuse to see any distinction between poetry, prose, and everyday speech. We recognize only one medium—the word —and we are using it in our immediate work. We are working for a phonetic organization of the language, for polyphony of rhythm, for the simplification of verbal construction, for the invention of new thematic devices. This work represents no purely aesthetic strivings, but rather a laboratory for the best rendition of contemporary facts. We are no pontificating creators but master agents of the social order." This declaration makes clear the connection between the formalists who were interested in craft and linguistics, and other literary leaders, who were pre-occupied with the role of literature in the new society. LEF's official spokesmen —Mayakovsky, Aseyev, and Brik—called for "the integration of literature into life" and asserted the principle of art's social utility. In 1922 a group of writers (including the young Ehrenburg) more or less connected with futurism started *The Thing*, a review which claimed that art should be functional and utilitarian: works of art should be produced in the same way that any other concrete object is produced. In general during these years, there was the tendency, deriving from Marxist ideology, to eliminate the difference between physical and intellectual labor. But Mayakovsky understood, of course, the specifics of literature and of creative effort; he called poetry "a ride into the unknown," and hailed the work of the poet: "it is like extracting radium—a year of work, a gram of profit, for one word you need a ton of verbal ore." But he was ready to forego his intimate convictions for the sake of the Revolution. And this was not an easy task.

Although most of the futurists rallied enthusiastically (and sincerely) round the new regime, only a few of them belonged to the Party or were Marxists. Most of the members of the LEF, including its subsidiary adherents, such as the followers of *The Thing* and the formalist professors and critics, were intellectuals for whom the Revolution held an emotional appeal: "the heart is on the left," was their familiar witticism. Yet for Mayakovsky the LEF had a momentous importance; his assumption was that "poetry begins where there is significance." Faithful to this dubious formula he demanded the end of "useless versification"; he prided himself that his work "merged with the work of the Republic." The value of poetry was to be judged by its service to the state. The masses were in need of a Communist education, of revolutionary songs, of uplifting slogans—and Mayakovsky felt it his duty to provide them; he called himself "the soldier poet of the Revolution."

There was a time when he declared that the newspapers satisfied all literary needs: leading articles and columns of verse and prose were to replace all existing genres of literature, thus completing the merger of art and reality. In this way the artist would be an organic and necessary part of the social whole: "All my poetic power have I given to you, the attacking class." One of his first works in this vein was *The Mystery Bouffe* (1918, revised in 1920-21), a comedy and a parody of the biblical legend of the flood, depicting in a farcical style the collapse of capitalism and the marvels of Communism, under which loaves of bread would grow on trees. The new ark of Noah makes a symbolic journey from the drowned world of the past to the firm land of the future, but it is not so much the meaning of the whole play as the separate scenes filled with puns, grotesques, and topical or satirical hints that give *The Mystery Bouffe* its provocative value. *The 150 Millions* (1920) had the same character of hyperbolic jest; in this poem Ivan is the symbol of the Russian Revolution, while Woodrow Wilson is the incarnation of world capitalism: the latter squats in his wondrous palace in Chicago—a city built on a gigantic screw and operated by a dynamo. At the end of this utopian and highly romantic epic written in a crude, highly pitched, half-surrealistic, half-slapstick style, America is being won over to Communism by 150,000,000 Ivans; a hundred years hence the centenary of this event is celebrated in a Sahara that by then is blooming. The play and the poem both belong to the utopian and grandiose prophecies of world Communism so typical of the times, but they bear the imprint of Mayakovsky's poetic personality and of his sharp, brittle diction.

In the years that followed Mayakovsky worked in the propaganda section of the Telegraphic Agency and turned out more than three thousand captions for posters and hundreds of jingles for commercial advertisements or for agitational purposes. Some of them sound almost ridiculous today ("Stop! Do you have a leather coat and pants? Shame on you! They freeze at the front line. Send them your coat and pants immediately"), but Mayakovsky was completely convinced that he was doing the right thing. He said later: "The force of a poet does not consist in the hiccup with which posterity will remember him; no, his rhyme today is a caress and a slogan, a bayonet and a whip." He launched slogans for all sorts of campaigns: for everything from the military draft to the effort to get people to drink boiled water in the struggle against epidemics. From 1922 on, he wrote a great deal of topical verse, for the most part pieces on industrial effort and new trade establishments, and also composed long propaganda poems which included "Vladimir Ilych Lenin" in four thousand lines (1924), and "All Right!" (1928), an enthusiastic picture of Soviet reconstruction.

A poet, he maintained, was not a fellow with long hair who goes about bleating of love and sorrow. A poet was one who devoted his pen to the service of the armed proletariat and fears no commission, avoids no theme:

> I don't want to be a wayside flower
> plucked after morning in an idle hour.

Mayakovsky did what he wanted to do, for he became a commentator in verse on current events; his was a kind of poetic journalism. He echoed all the topics of the day: the World Revolution, the Soviet Savings Bank, the price of wheat, the New Economic Policy, and lagging soap production. In his satirical portraits he presented the enemies of the regime—Pilsudski, Lloyd

George, Clemenceau—as grotesque monsters. He traveled extensively and excoriated what he saw: American capitalism, Mexican poverty, German smugness, and French pettiness. He fought against red tape and Moscow hoodlums; he debated problems of industrialization, exalted the successes of Soviet diplomats and engineers, launched appeals to Communist youth, and described the New Jerusalem of Socialism. He did it all in his pungent, shrill verse, filled with humor and anger. In his poems he fought civil wars and held party meetings. Hundreds of his stanzas, scattered in dailies and magazines, appear meaningless today without ample historical footnotes, but they did their job in their times, when the readers knew what he was talking about.

In Paris the *chansonniers* and *diseuses* of Montmartre, Montparnasse, and the Latin Quarter do approximately the same thing in cabarets and little theaters, and Mexico has its show-booths of topical satire: Mayakovsky's stage was Russian literature and the Communist Revolution, and his voice was heard throughout the land. Yet jingles, even though written by a great poet, remain jingles, and their short life is measured by the duration of events that brought them into being. Only a few of his propaganda poems have any lasting value: most of them are lyrico-epic narratives, such as "Lenin" and "All Right!" in which there are passages of great expressive force, of savage irony, and an effervescent love of life. In writing his poem about Lenin immediately after the leader's death, Mayakovsky admitted his fears that he might simply "sink into political periphrase"; this was a danger he could not escape and only a few lyrical parts of the poem remain alive. The rest falls short, as is usually the case with Mayakovsky's discursive works. But his emotional outbursts, his caustic humor, his striking formulas, his hope in the future, in the "remaking of the earth," his optimistic and heroic tone not unlike that of Whitman (whom he praised highly) give a peculiar vigor to many of his poems.

Mayakovsky considered his poetry a weapon. He served the Revolution with his word just as others served it with the sword. There is no doubt that he did it deliberately and wholeheartedly: he was the poet of the Kremlin by conviction and not by appointment. It is well known that Lenin, who had a very conservative taste in literature, did not like and did not understand his works. But Mayakovsky sang of the same Lenin and taxes and government bonds not because he expected a reward but because his civic and poetic credo demanded it; he was convinced that modern poets had to "turn themselves inside out" and "rush into the morrow, strain forward so that their pants would split." It is easy to mock such tropes and object that splitting one's trousers is not exactly the best way to write good verse, but the point remains that despite all his excessive energy Mayakovsky was a true poet. Some critics have compared him with Nekrassov, the popular bard of the 1860's, who also wanted to merge poetry with life and who wrote topical poems, but despite this similarity, the two poets are far apart. Nekrassov's muse is one of grief, tears, and repentance; Mayakovsky's is active, dynamic, and displays a vibrant acceptance of life. His motto was "To shine like the sun," as he affirmed in one of his best poems "A Most Extraordinary Adventure" (1920), which depicts a visit paid by the Sun to the poet's country house.

While psychological and ideological motives predominate in Nekrassov, Mayakovsky's poems are for the most part satirical descriptions, ardent appeals, or oratorical formulations of Communist aims. It would be futile to look for complex ideas in Mayakovsky. He is forceful rather than deep. His philosophy is quite primitive; it can be summed up as revolutionary materialism, based on the superiority of reason and social service over idealistic romanticism or inertia.

His poems, with their obvious and simple meaning, were aimed at the mass reader. He addressed the multitudes in the naïve and crude language of broad hyperbole, lush sarcasm, and coarse humor; he resorted to sensuous metaphors, and stressed the visual, the palpable, the earthy. This anti-metaphysical poet captured the imagination of his audiences by evoking the notions of mass and quantity: Woodrow Wilson's silk topper is as high as the Eiffel Tower, Chicago has 12,000 streets, the army of the proletariat numbers 150,000,000 Ivans. He shouts at the top of his voice, his sentences roll like drums, and he plays masterfully the complex keyboard of assonances, changing rhythms, unusual rhymes, and rollicking jests. His virtuosity in sounds, meters, and the integration of colloquialisms into the brittle pace of his lines give his poems a unique verbal expressiveness. As loud (and effective) as circus posters, they are yet full-blooded and sonorous: they demand to be read from a rostrum; they have a thunderous declamatory quality that only the eighteenth-century poet Derzhavin—Mayakovsky's formal predecessor—had achieved previously. But Derzhavin glorified the splendors of the Empire under Catherine the Great in well ordered syllabic-tonic odes, while Mayakovsky sang revolutionary passions in words that marched in military step. Mayakovsky's manner is oratorical and rhetorical, and consists of short, broken lines, printed in staircase fashion; single words and sentences are heavily accented, the stress is on intonation and meaning, the emphasis on syllabic variations of rhymes and the auditory effect of intentionally "difficult" words. He aimed at the "de-poetization" of the language and also "corrected" the current prosody by adopting a meter in which primarily accents (or stresses) in each line were counted. He thus initiated a whole school in Russian poetry, which will be linked with his name regardless of the fate of his individual poems or of the ideas he tried to put across. Toward the end of the 1920's Mayakovsky was convinced that his style truly represented the spirit of the Revolution. With his usual boastfulness (like many people basically unsure of themselves, he despised humility and designated modesty as stupidity or hypocrisy), he claimed that he and his friends were "carrying the literary load." He had a strong sense of responsibility and often chose a topic because he felt it to be a social and political obligation and not any spontaneous choice prompted by preference or attraction. In an unfinished poem written just before his tragic death he remarked:

> I am also fed up
> with the agit-prop; *
> I too could compose
> ballads about you—
> it is pleasanter and pays more—
> but I forced myself
> by planting my foot on the throat of my own song.

In "A Cloud in Trousers" he spoke of "the blood-stained rag of my heart," of the "scream which is my crucified soul," and chal-

* Department of Agitation and Propaganda.

lenged the skies, reproaching them for the torments of his love. He led an intense and turbulent life of emotions—and love lyrics have as important a part in his works as the songs of Revolution. He was the poet of the first decade of Russian Communism with all its exaggerations, wild hopes, and tempestuousness, but he was also a tender, ironical, and sensitive sufferer of the "high disease" compounded of sentiment and imagination—and the two opposing drives within him and in his poetry were not always reconciled.

The New Man he portrayed did not give a rap for "lyrical nonsense," in fact Mayakovsky bragged about strength, rationality, and a revolutionary approach to personal matters. Yet so many of his poems, such as "A Letter from Paris Concerning Love" (1927) and his beautiful "At the Top of My Voice," are confessions of wistfulness and amorous longing. And others contain poignant notes of solitude and inner dissension. He was unable to get rid of that romantic "melancrockery" he condemned so dashingly in his didactic verse. As a revolutionist he banned "individualistic emotions" and rejected the lyricist in his literature. But, in an uncanny act of revenge, the lyricist killed Mayakovsky in real life. The drives, dreams, and doubts the poet had tried to chain and imprison escaped and tore their jailer to shreds. Mayakovsky, who jeered at sentimental lovers and announced the replacement of the soul by steam and electricity, fell victim to erotic and emotional failure: he committed suicide mainly because of unrequited love.

By 1930 this trumpeting poet of loud optimism felt lonely and frustrated. He no longer had any illusions about the drawbacks of the regime he was serving, and his satirical plays, *The Bedbug* (1928) and *The Bathhouse* (1930), were bold denunciations of the red tape and triviality that were undermining the heroic dreams of the Revolution. *The Bedbug* depicts the pseudo-Communist Prisypkin, a stupid and vulgar parasite who survives by anabiosis; future generations keep him and put him in a zoo as a curious specimen of some savage tribe—together with the bedbug they find on his collar. In *The Bathhouse* a fierce attack against the smugness of petty leaders is combined with an exposé of Communist bureaucracy. Meyerhold produced both plays in his theater with brilliant inventiveness, but they were dubbed subversive by the Party press, and disappeared from the Soviet stage.

It took almost three decades before they made a comeback in the late 'fifties after the death of Stalin.

Criticism of the plays was not the only conflict between Mayakovsky and the rigid Party line. It should not be forgotten that Lenin disliked Mayakovsky and rejected futurism and all forms of revolutionary art. In his *Reminiscences* Gorky writes: "Lenin distrusted Mayakovsky and was irritated by his works. In his opinion the poet was shouting, invented crooked words, and made difficult reading. Lenin never changed this negative attitude. In 1921 he called Mayakovsky's *150 Millions* "stupid, pretentious junk." When Lunacharsky attempted to explain that the "futurists supported Communism," Lenin answered that "theirs was hooliganism not Communism."

When these and other statements by Lenin on Mayakovsky and contemporary poetry were published in the sixty-fifth volume of the series "Literary Heritage" in 1958, the Party Central Committee forbade the sale of the book. The 630-page volume also included articles from various Communist periodicals which had launched a vicious campaign against the poet in the late 'twenties. The enthusiasm of the initial stage of the Revolution was over by this time; a grim police state with a large bureaucratic machine was being built up by methods that seemed dangerously similar to those of the Tsarist regime; in literature the so-called proletarian writers were on top not through their own literary merits but because public officials were insensitive. And the newcomers attacked Mayakovsky: Was he not a free-lancer who did not even carry a Party card? Was not his fantastic poetry suspect from the point of view of good old realism patronized by Lenin? And was he not out of step with all his romantic notions about the Revolution, when all the Soviets needed now were administrators, engineers, tradesmen, and obedient civil servants?

At the age of thirty-seven, after a long career of struggle and sacrifice Mayakovsky felt himself isolated and doomed; all the pangs of unhappy love, unsatisfied sex, and of practical and emotional instability added to his ennui. Thus the irrational, non-utilitarian aspirations he had wanted to eliminate gripped him irresistibly—and he must have felt humiliated and baffled by this discrepancy between his real emotions and the principles he had proclaimed in poems.

As a young man he had written:

> The heart longs for a bullet:
> the throat craves for a razor;
> the soul trembles between walls of ice—
> and it will never escape the ice.

Suicide seemed the only way out of this glacial prison: on April 14, 1930, Mayakovsky shot himself.

The impact of his poetry and personality on Soviet literature was tremendous. Not only did he enjoy the love of vast audiences who acclaimed him as the poet of the Revolution and of the working class, but a whole generation of poets recognized him as their leader and imitated him. Even those who did not want to jettison all the themes and traditions of the past felt Mayakovsky's influence and evinced an intention to transform literature into an active means for changing reality. This latter tendency became prevalent in Soviet poetry, and it was accepted as indisputable truth by all Communist poets and many fellow-travelers; thus Mayakovsky promoted a literary trend which is fundamental to the aesthetic credo of the USSR: to approach a work of art as a social phenomenon and to evaluate it in terms of the contribution it makes to the common cause.

Several young poets became his disciples. Nikolay Aseyev (1889-1963), the most gifted and faithful among them, wrote in the master's style and paid sincere tribute to him in the long poem, "Vladimir Mayakovsky." But Mayakovsky's verse always marched impetuously to the sound of drums and trumpets whereas Aseyev preferred a much slower pace and softer rhythms. He is a good romantic poet in his own right, and the collection of his works published around his seventieth birthday disclosed the genuine qualities of an imaginative and cultured craftsman. Next in stature stands Semyon Kirsanov (b. 1906), author of political poems in Mayakovsky's vein ("The Five Year Plan," 1931, and "Comrade Marx," 1933), but also a good lyricist whose love songs, the charming long poem "Cinderella" (1935) and "Seven Days" (1957), reveal considerable poetic freshness. Less original is Alexander Bezymensky (1898-1973), whom Mayakovsky did not rate highly. He wrote about the Party, Communist youth, and other topics of the day in a somewhat simplified manner, without ever attaining the wit and forcefulness of his model. Next to numerous second- and third-rate followers, a whole generation of poets imitated the staccato of Mayakovsky's rhythm, the broken lines of his accented verse, the intonations of his declamatory manner. He was after Blok the first Russian poet to exert such a powerful and wide influence.

Although Mayakovsky was recognized as the greatest poet of the Revolution and his fame throughout the Soviet Union grew steadily, his official canonization did not really begin until the end of the 1930's (following his suicide there was a definite reluctance in higher circles to glorify his work). But from the moment Stalin called him "the best and most gifted poet of our Soviet epoch," his work was treated as a classic and the study of Mayakovsky became an obligatory part of every school program and textbook. The latter mostly distorted his image and deliberately ignored some of his controversial pieces (*The Bedbug* and *The Bathhouse*, for instance). Pasternak said in his *An Essay in Autobiography* that Mayakovsky "began to be introduced forcibly, like potatoes under Catherine the Great. This was his second death, but he had nothing to do with it." In 1940 the tenth anniversary of his death furnished an occasion for pontification from the press, who hailed the consistency of his political and aesthetic convictions. His futurism and his connections with the formalists were either disregarded or minimized, and scarcely any mention was made of his suicide. This attitude continued through the next decade. In fact, the reader of the 57-page introduction to a two-volume collection of his poems brought out in a popular edition in 1950 will find no hint whatsoever that the poet took his own life.

Statistics show that after Pushkin, Lermontov, and Nekrassov, Mayakovsky is the most widely read poet in the Soviet Union. Between 1917 and 1954 more than 23 million copies of his works were sold in Russian and in 51 languages of the Republic. Villages, streets, and squares were named after him, and so were *sovkhozes*, *kolhozes*, schools, libraries, theaters, steamships, and a station of the Moscow subway. M. Maslin, one of his biographers, offers a typical explanation of this popularity: "The Soviet people love

and appreciate Mayakovsky for the ideological strength and popular spirit of his verse, for the novelty and monumental scope of
his images, for his humanity and for the moving intensity of his
emotions." When the series "Literary Heritage" published in 1958
new materials on Mayakovsky, bringing out his contradictory
nature and his personal tragedy as well as unknown details of his
love life, the Central Committee of the Communist Party deemed
it necessary to approve a special resolution against this publication
as being "dangerous and offering arguments for *émigré* critics."
It shows the extent to which Mayakovsky is today considered the
official bard of the Communist Revolution.

4

The Proletcult

In 1918-20 the futurists placed themselves at the service of the Communist regime, but demanded in return a privileged position in arts and letters as exclusive interpreters of the revolutionary spirit. A considerable number of Party leaders, including the Commissar of Education Anatoly Lunacharsky (1875-1933), himself a playwright and essayist with a weakness for the avant-garde, were inclined to grant the title of poet laureate to some of the futurists; for together with various splinter groups of the artistic left, they were firmly entrenched in the theater and graphic arts. In the early part of the Soviet era, bold innovations on the stage were made by Meyerhold, Tairov, and other directors who collaborated with the members of the LEF movement. The attempts to organize performances in the streets and on public squares were made mostly by painters, architects, and theatrical producers drafted from the ranks of the futurist or functionalist avant-garde. For example, Meyerhold staged *Mystery Bouffe* as a huge mass spectacle. In the theater and in the visual arts the first years of the Revolution were marked by a definite predominance of the advanced groups, which, by the way, had their Western counterparts in post-symbolist currents in art, including dadaism and surrealism.

The peak of the LEF movement was attained around 1923. Later on it met with increasing difficulties: it was assailed by the Marxists for its "ideological inconsistencies," criticized by proletarian writers as "a fanciful vestige of bourgeois trickery," abandoned by Party officials who found the futurists "too undisciplined," and was badly treated by fellow-travelers who did not want literature to become the "bond maid" of politics. The LEF split into factions, which either continued a precarious existence or were absorbed by other groups. In 1927 Mayakovsky renamed his review the *New LEF*, but this did not help. At the time of his death in 1930 LEF had ceased to play an active role, and its later adherents were labeled simply as Mayakovsky's pupils. This process corresponded to the general elimination of the artistic avant-garde and the adoption by the Party of a conservative line in arts and letters.

The strongest opposition to the LEF was offered by the proletarian writers, who denounced its "decadent" roots and its "intellectual-bourgeois" personnel. In the struggle for hegemony the proletarians showed themselves formidable rivals; they actually fought for power and behaved like contenders in a civil war, transferring its ruthlessness and intransigence to the literary field.

They inaugurated methods and a polemical style that remained one of the most peculiar features of the arts in the Soviet Union. The theoretical foundations of the Proletarian Writers movement were contained in the Marxist formula "being determines consciousness," which meant that every culture is the expression of a given socio-economic order and the product of a definite class. Literature, the arts, and the sciences were considered superstructures on the main edifice of the economic regime. With the proletariat as the victorious class in the Communist Revolution in Russia, they were bound to produce a new culture. Thenceforth literature, the arts, and the sciences were in the hands of proletarians and had to be permeated by proletarian ideology, just as they had once been created by noblemen, aristocrats, and burghers whose ideologies they reflected. The leaders of the movement hoped that their work would revolutionize literature as radically as the Bolsheviks had changed the political system and the social structure of Russia. The analogy was pushed further: the same war had to be waged against bourgeois tendencies and counter-revolution on the literary front as on the battlefront —and the same measures of coercion, terror, compulsion, and punishment had to be employed in art as in life. Some of the proletarian writers argued that post-revolutionary literature had to start from scratch, without bothering about traditions: "We do not need to fill the gap between the past and the present," wrote the novelist Bessalko. "Let us simply reject the past." A policy of persecution was applied to old and politically suspect writers, interdiction, censorship, abuse, denunciation, and strong-arm tactics were used agains these "class enemies."

Once the aim—the creation of a proletarian culture—had been clearly defined, the next problem had to do with the ways and means of attaining it as speedily as possible. At first it seemed that it would be sufficient to awaken the latent creative possibilities of the proletariat by educational measures. The attempt was made through the Proletcult (Proletarian Cultural Educational Organizations). At its first convention in September 1918, Alexander Bogdanov, the pen name of A. Malinovsky (1873-1928), one of the promoters of the movement and the author of *Art and the Working Classes*, formulated the objectives of the Proletcult in a unanimously approved resolution: "Art by means of living images organizes social experience not only in the sphere of knowledge but also in that of the emotions and aspirations. Consequently, it is one of the most powerful implements for the organization of collective and class forces in a class society. A class-art of its own is indispensable to the proletariat for the organization of its forces for social work, struggle, and construction. Labor collectivism—this is the spirit of this art, which ought to reflect the world from the point of view of the labor collective, expressing the complex of its sentiments and its militant and creative will." The resolution also warned the working class not to absorb the treasures of ancient art passively, but to examine them in the light of proletarian critical doctrine. The Proletcult obtained large subsidies from central and local government agencies, and declared in its review *The Days to Come*, that "while bourgeois culture was disintegrating, the proletariat was creating a new culture." It concentrated its efforts on establishing studios or workshops throughout the country. The members of these workshops were for the most part young workers and artisans (only men and women of proletarian origin with "the class point of view" were admitted); they were encouraged to write poems and stories and produce plays in "workers' clubs" and similar organizations.

In 1920 the Proletcult, backed by the Commissariat of Education and by a few Marxist critics, was operating 300 workshops with 84,000 members, and was publishing a review, *Proletarian*

Culture. It practically controlled many thousands of amateur companies and theaters in small towns and villages. In some instances there were curious relations between the Proletcult and some groups of the avant-garde, because young proletarians were often attracted by formal innovations, mistaking them for signs of a new Communist art. It was not long, however, before it became obvious that the attempt to nurse a literary movement by laboratory and hot-house methods was doomed to failure. It was possible to drill an army of Red Guards but it did not pay to train a regiment of poets. In the more successful cases the members of the Proletcult learned how to read, but their writings seldom reached even the level of freshman compositions. No less discouraging was the fact that the most articulate of the workshop students simply produced bad imitations of Gorky or of the very bourgeois writers they were supposed not only to supplant but to excel. By the end of 1920, Lenin dealt a mortal blow to the Proletcult by declaring that "Proletarian culture must be a legitimate development of all reserves of knowledge mankind has accumulated under the pressure of capitalist society, of landlord society, of bureaucrat society." By 1922 the number of active Proletcult units had dwindled to twenty, and by 1924 to seven, with a total enrollment of less than 500. This marked the end of the Proletcult crusade for a speedy mass production of "class conscious" writers.

The failure of the Proletcult did not, however, prevent other efforts in the same direction—this time by various groups of writers of proletarian extraction. They all agreed on the necessity of building a new culture that would reflect the revolutionary changes, but they disagreed on the methods and techniques for achieving this end. They incorporated the best elements of the defunct Proletcult; most of the proletarian groups were interested in poetry—here again the lyrical form seemed most appropriate as an instantaneous response to rapid events. The prevailing mood in all these groups was one of pride and joyous exultation. The Bolshevik Revolution was officially labeled "Proletarian," and was described as having been consummated by the toiling masses under the leadership of the urban proletariat; the representatives of the victorious class were hailed as "the rulers of the day," "they who had been nothing and now become everything," thus fulfilling the prophecy of the "Internationale," the nineteenth-century revolutionary anthem. Particularly in the first decade of the Soviet regime it was as great a privilege to belong to the working class as it had been to be a member of an aristocratic society previously.

Proletarian writers who came to the fore in the early 'twenties were young newcomers. Vladimir Kirillov (1890-1943) sang of "the innumerable legions of labor who had conquered land and sea and had become their own God, Judge, and Law"; he promised to find "a new, dazzling path for our planet" and wrote in 1918: "In the name of our morrow, let us burn Raphael, destroy museums and trample on the flowers of art." The bio-cosmist Ilya Sadofyev (1889-1965), in his "Dynamo Poems," spoke of his friends as the "forerunners of future ages"; the universe, according to him, was "aflame like a bride awaiting her bridegroom—the new class." Most of these aggressive and grandiloquent poems were patterned after those of the Belgian Emile Verhaeren, who enjoyed great popularity in pre-revolutionary Russia; some bore a faint resemblance to Whitman's verse. The two most important groups of the early 1920's were the Smithy and the October. The members of the Smithy—Vassily Kazin (b. 1898), Mikhail Gerasimov (1889-1939), Alexey Gastev (1882-1941), Alexander Sannikov (1899-1969)—were attracted by the ode and the epic, but in their attempts to create "true proletarian art," they revealed their indebtedness to symbolism and futurism. Under Whitman's influence, Gastev hailed the machine, "that Iron Messiah," and the Iron Blossoms of the Foundry, wrote hymns to physical labor, and represented the universe as "a huge factory." The titles of his books clearly indicate their character: *Poems of the Workers' Strike, We Grow from Iron, Hymn of Industrial Might* and *Proletarian Victories*. He was deeply interested in all achievements of modern technology and idolized science. Arrested in 1938, he perished in a labor camp. Some Smithy poets imitated Valery Briussov, the symbolist master who had joined the Communists and extolled the city and the machine. Quite a few of the Smithy members had begun their literary careers before World War I (Gastev was born in 1882, the novelist Liashko in 1884), and were more traditional than they were willing to admit. Most of them belonged to the Communist Party, but this did not prevent them from being imprisoned, executed, or exiled in the late 'thirties as "left extremists." The members of the October group were much younger, most of them were in their twenties, and despite the lack of class homogeneity, this group which included writers from the middle bourgeoisie and the intelligentsia presented more of an ideological unity. Most of them belonged to the Communist Party, they were militant and aggressive, asserted the priority of content over form, and hoped that the young Communists would create a literature inspired by the new social order. They also felt that they should fight against "bourgeois attitudes" in poetry and prose. The leading poets of the group, Alexander Zharov (b. 1904), Joseph Utkin (1903-44), Mikhail Svetlov (1903-49), Ivan Doronin (b. 1900), Mikhail Golodny (1903-64), and Alexander Bezymensky wrote social poems in narrative style, and throughout the 'twenties filled Soviet periodicals with their works. Some of these, such as poems by Utkin and Svetlov, have a certain historical interest. The role of the October grew, however, when it began publishing its magazine *On Guard* (1923) and a monthly *October* (1924) which became one of Moscow's leading literary periodicals. It also aimed at leadership of the united front of proletarian literature, and in order to achieve this purpose crushed its rivals (like the Smithy) or conquered the existing writers' organizations (the Association of Proletarian Writers in its heyday had more than 3000 members). In this second phase of its activity, the October was led by Bezymensky, the novelist Yury Libedinsky (1898-1960), and the critics Semyon Rodov, Labory Kalmanson-Lelevich, and later Ilya Vardin (Mgeladze). In the 'thirties Smithy (and partly October) writers were classified as "decadent" or lacking in socialist realism.

Despite all the efforts, declarations, and official support, not a single poet of distinction has emerged from the proletariat since the beginning of the Soviet regime. As a matter of fact all the leading poets of the Revolution came from the nobility (Blok, Mayakovsky), or the intelligentsia (Pasternak), or the peasantry (Essenin). The same is true of the poet who was acclaimed in the 1920's as the "true herald of the victorious class." Yefim Pridvorov (1883-1945), the natural son of a grand duke wrote under the pen name of Demyan Bedny (Damian the Poor) and enjoyed tremendous popularity as a satirist between 1917 and 1930. Even Boris Pasternak thought he had discovered in him "the spirit of the people" and praised his verse. Demyan Bedny contributed to the Socialist press long before the Revolution, and his witty political fables were the despair of Tsarist censorship. As a friend of prominent Party members and a trusted bard of the new regime, he acquired a unique and prominent position. His squibs, fables, and propaganda jingles, in which he commented on current events and Party slogans, in the simple accessible style of popular songs and factory couplets, were the delight of Red soldiers and workmen. Their crude directness, slapstick wit, satirical exaggerations, and attacks against Western capitalists and statesmen found a wide response among the masses. Their vogue diminished, however, and by the beginning of the 1930's they appeared too coarse and vulgar. When patriotic and nationalistic tendencies prevailed under Stalin, Demyan Bedny made a blunder by writing a satirical comedy *Men of Might* (Bogatyri), ridiculing Russian history, and was severely reprimanded by the dictator for his disrespect and cynicism. This marked his downfall, and even the highly patriotic verse he offered during World War II against Hitler could not restore his position in the Party. The score and a half of books published by this poetic journalist are useful as historical documents and interesting as a political performance, but on the whole they have little literary value. An attempt to resurrect Demyan Bedny by Party officials in 1963, as a move against the "formalists," failed to arouse any interest in his poetry.

It is highly significant that Demyan Bedny wrote in the tradition of Ivan Krylov and other Russian fabulists. The proletarian poets who came from the working masses and introduced the new topics of manual labor and class enthusiasm, also followed models from the past—mostly the symbolists and even the patrician poets. In no sense can they be termed stylistic innovators. The futurists, led by Mayakovsky, the constructivists, and a few single poets influenced by Khlebnikov (Tikhonov, for instance) were the only ones to combine loyalty to the new order with an originality of meter, rhythm and poetic structure, but they could not retain their hegemony in Soviet literature.

These facts are of utmost importance: the Revolution did not

create a new revolutionary style, and its most staunch defenders—
the representatives of the working classes and the members of
the Communist Party—preferred to express themselves in traditional, almost conservative ways. This trend became even stronger
with the consolidation of the Soviet government, and between
the 'thirties and the 'sixties, the land that claimed to lead mankind
in all fields nursed and favored an artistic school which can be
called the most provincial and reactionary in twentieth-century
world literature.

5

The NEP and the 'Twenties

By 1921 the civil war period had ended with the Communist triumph over the Whites and foreign interventionists. The victory on the firing line, however, was not matched by equivalent success on the home front. The methods of military compulsion and terror used in this era of struggle failed to revitalize the economy of the Soviet Union. With only 13 per cent of Russia's pre-war industry operating, with a catastrophic decline of agriculture, yielding only 40 per cent of 1913 foodstuffs, with famine reigning in towns and villages, Russia seemed doomed to perish from starvation and labor paralysis. During the drought that hit the Volga region in 1920-21, five million peasants died in southeastern Russia. Throughout the rest of the country epidemics and malnutrition took a larger toll than the war had. The problem of supply and demand and of the exchange of produce and goods between the village and the city could not be solved by requisitions and confiscation, and angry farmers, weary of privations and valueless money which did not buy anything, often resorted to uprisings. The mutiny of sailors in Kronstadt in 1921 was a typical manifestation of discontent among the masses.

Lenin had no illusions about the situation, and in March 1921 he announced at the Tenth Convention of the Communist Party that the poverty, the exhaustion, and the ruin of workers and peasants had made the increase of industrial and agricultural output the basic problem of the Revolution. He overcame the opposition of the left wing and laid the foundations of the NEP (New Economic Policy). This tactical retreat comprised an abandonment of military, intransigent Communism, a partial restoration of free trade, and many concessions to the peasantry, including the right to sell surplus products in the open market, the abolition of the levy in kind, and so forth. The "Dictatorship of the Proletariat" could not exist without the consent of the peasants, or at least without their tolerance. The Revolution, which Marxian theoreticians considered proletarian, had been basically a peasant revolution, and NEP was merely a recognition of this fact.

This recognition was not, however, expressed in political terms: the non-proletarian classes either were denied political rights (as was the case with the former aristocracy, the bourgeoisie, and the clergy, who together formed the disfranchised group) or were granted limited rights only. While the disfranchised had no right to vote, and their access to positions of responsibility (or even to higher learning) was made extremely difficult, the peasants were underprivileged in comparison with urban workers.

For Lenin and his disciples the NEP was a breathing spell, a period of coasting with the brakes on, without which the Party would have been unable to retain power. For the thousands of Communists who had fought in the civil war and were ready to impose collectivism by shock methods, the NEP was almost a betrayal or—to put it mildly—an ignominious retreat; for the non-partisan population it was a hopeful beginning of peaceful work and reconstruction. Of course, this reconstruction was bound to be of a socialistic nature, and even the "NEP men," who were making a great deal of money between 1921 and 1928, were perfectly aware that they were profiting from a temporary interlude. But in the meantime the loosening of controls in all branches of national life led to an economic revival, and it created a feeling of relief, a new psychological atmosphere. The NEP diminished the gap between Russia's isolation and the West which dated actually from 1914, when the war against Germany, Austro-Hungary, and Turkey had closed all the routes to Europe save the narrow and dangerous North Sea passage; also, from 1917 on, Soviet Russia had been practically blockaded. Between 1924 and 1927 the gradual recognition of the Soviet government by Great Britain, Italy, Norway, France and other countries, was followed by trade and travel thus marking the return of Russia to Europe. During the same period, the first Constitution of the Soviet Union was finally adopted, and by 1928 the eleven Republics of the new federation covered almost the same territory as the former Empire of the Tsars (with the exception of Finland, Poland, Lithuania, Latvia, and Estonia, which had proclaimed their independence, and of Bessarabia, taken over by Rumania, and certain regions of Caucasus annexed by Turkey). The transformation of Russia into a multi-national federation was a fact of primary importance; so were the emancipation of women and the vast measures of mass education. It was during the period of the NEP that the foundations of all these great reforms were laid.

The NEP also meant a substantial change for the Party itself. Revolutionists, partison fighters, passionate orators, and utopians were gradually supplanted by business men, factory managers, diplomats, and accountants. The Communist bureaucrat made his appearance next to the Communist idealist—and usurped a constantly increasing sphere. Although the crack-unit morality and military bearing (including Stalin's uniform) remained firmly entrenched in the Party mores as the heritage of the civil war, the Bolshevik leaders were becoming more used to the attitudes of cautious administrators confronted with tremendous practical problems. The Party had to train a ruling class, and it gradually took on the strangely mixed character of a business concern and an educational institution, that also was in charge of working out an infallible credo. And this task was not easy, because in the 1920's the Party was far from achieving homogeneity or reaching the final formulation of its doctrine. The NEP was a turbulent period of struggle and controversy—and in contrast to the following decades when the regime had become more stabilized and controlled, these controversies were out in the open. Various groups and factions, including the "workers opposition," were clashing so violently that the din of the battle could not be muffled. After the death of Lenin in 1924, the ensuing rift among the candidates for succession— Stalin, Trotsky, Kamenev, Zinoviev, and some minor contenders —was coupled with much theoretical discussion and lengthy exposition of the different points of view. Trotsky was defending "pure Communism" and the idea of permanent revolution, which presumed an outright support of revolutionary movements in other countries, and laid emphasis on the activities of the Comintern— the new central organization of the world Communist parties led by Moscow; other groups were opposing the concessions to the peasants and were criticizing the NEP as a dangerous "deviation."

And while the debates raged, Stalin was gaining control over the Party machine; as soon as he felt strong enough he dealt a resounding blow to his foes by formulating the doctrine of "building socialism in one country." This meant that Stalin and his followers voiced strong sentiments within the country and insisted on national reconstruction without· waiting for the collapse of capitalism outside of Russia. As Krassin, Commissar of Trade, put it, the Communist government was ready "to lower the banner of world revolution," and concentrate on domestic affairs—despite the "bourgeois encirclement" which Trotsky, for example, considered a mortal threat to the young Soviet State. Stalin's doctrine was a prelude to the change from utopian internationalism to down-to-earth nationalism. It also meant that the party of proletarian dictatorship was resolved to assume two tasks that stemmed from Russia's special socio-economic structure: socialization of agriculture in a country where the peasants formed an enormous majority, and industrialization in a country where it had been retarded because of general backwardness, Tsarist inertia, and a slow and inefficient development of capitalism. By 1926 Trotsky had lost the battle with Stalin, although his exile to Turkestan did not come until 1928, and his banishment to Turkey took place only the year after. Stalin's victory opened a new chapter in Russian history: the collectivization of the villages and the industrialization of national resources through the controlled economy of the five-year plans. This new, second phase of the Revolution had begun as soon as the NEP had shown such an increase in economic activity that agriculture and industry had almost attained their 1913 levels. The recovery was indisputable, and the NEP could be safely abandoned. By 1928 the NEP was brought to a close, and new factors began to shape life in the Soviet Union. Collectivization and industrialization were two aspects of a new Communist offensive which during the 1930's unfolded its dramatic contradictions—its tragedies and achievements, its defeats and victories.

In the 1920's the New Economic Policy was matched by developments on the "front of culture." In this highly sensitive area, "a literary NEP" as contemporaries called it, reflected all the dislocations and shifts within the Party. Though it took a relatively moderate attitude toward writers and artists, the new policy failed to solve numerous literary and aesthetic problems of the revolutionary period. The crucial issue was that of Communism as an ideocracy. Since the Bolsheviks did not limit its aims to establish a new economic, social, and political regime, but wanted to impose its philosophy, encompassing all the fields of human knowledge, on all fields of Russian life, the intellectual and spiritual activities of Soviet citizens were submitted to the same system of controlled planning as was their work in producing food and machines. Dialectical materialism was supposed to offer an infallible approach to science, to education, to poetry, and to painting. The question was, however, how to replace the decadent capitalist culture by the progressive and healthy achievements of the emerging new class. And this, as we shall see later, raised many puzzling issues. To what extent was the new culture to absorb the heritage of the past? What could be taken from bourgeois literature, for example, without compromising Communist theory and practice? Who were to be called the true exponents of the new culture—only the artists and scientists of proletarian extraction, or also the scions of other social groups, provided they accepted the Revolution? Most embarrassing of all was the question of the relation between the ideological (and presumably revolutionary) content of the new arts and their form, or means of expression.

In order to promote the cultural revolution, restrictive measures were taken under military Communism. These included preventive, such as censorship, as well as disciplinary ones. No printed matter could (or can today) be published in the Soviet Union without the rubber stamp of the censor, and each book had (and still has) to carry on its back leaf the number under which the legal authorization has been issued. The same system was (and still is) applied to plays, movies, exhibitions, radio, and all other communication media. Disciplinary measures—arrest, prison, exile, death—were meted out to authors whose works revealed counter-revolutionary tendencies, real or imaginary. Indications are that between 1921 and 1928 the number of such victims was relatively small. Much larger, however, was the category of writers who were simply expelled from professional organizations, ostracized, condemned to silence, or deprived of the possibility of making a living at their craft. And, of course, quite a few writers paid dearly for their association with political parties: the famous poet Gumilev was executed by a firing squad in 1921 for being a member of an anti-Soviet conspiracy, and others were sentenced to capital punishment as "enemies of the people." Later, under Stalin, this label was pinned on "Trotskyites," "Western spies," and "inner deviationists."

Other measures were aimed at the control of printing presses, paper mills, and subsequently of all dailies, magazines, and book publishing ventures. In 1921 the establishment of the State Publishing House and its chain of bookshops laid the foundation for a total nationalization of the book trade. By 1925, however, this had still not been achieved. At the beginning of the NEP there were 220 private publishing enterprises in Moscow, and some of them became co-operative or group publishing ventures. They were all supervised by state or Party representatives. Their activity was curtailed when the NEP was liquidated, and by 1930 only a few of them, owned by large organizations, were still functioning (the publishing house The Soviet Writer, controlled by the Writers' Union, for example). Monthlies were published by various organizations, which elected or appointed their editorial boards, but a representative of Glavlit (Central Committee for Literary Affairs) was invariably assigned to each such publication. The editorial staff of the dailies was usually appointed by Party authorities.

A further body of measures dealt with education. They encompassed a series of reforms (some of them originating in the Empire), from the introduction of a new orthography and the Gregorian calendar to the adoption of a metric system of measurements, an attack on illiteracy, and the reorganization of the entire school system. Compulsory elementary education, a tremendous expansion of secondary and graduate schools, and the promotion of cultural activities among various nationalities and peoples of the Soviet Union (a considerable number of which had not possessed even an alphabet) must be cited among the many achievements of the new regime in the field of education. Protection was set up for monuments, art treasures, and for scientific and artistic institutes which had passed through all kind of ordeals under military Communism; an effort to win over specialists, scholars, artists, and intellectuals, as well as measures to promote the theater, music, and ballet and bring them to the masses, must also be numbered among the highly creditable efforts of the Soviet government during the NEP period.

Repressive measures were a part of the "class struggle" and the fight against the opposition. Control over all means of communication was an organic part of an ideocracy, as well as a necessary item in the general blue print of socialization. Educational expansion and the struggle against ignorance (including even the campaign against religion, which was considered an "opiate for the people") were taken over, lock, stock, and barrel, from the programs of all Russian socialists.

All these activities could be expected from the Bolshevik government. Much more difficult and controversial was the problem of a positive policy in literature and the arts. What kind of art and, particularly, of prose and poetry was suitable for the new culture? The resumption of literary life under the favorable conditions of the NEP brought forward an embarassing number of literary schools. Which was the Party to support and which dismiss? The problem had been debated since 1918, but it was not until 1925, after several years of indecision owing to divergences of opinion, that the Party took a firm stand. Lenin and most of his friends were not only enemies of Proletcult and rejected the artificial breeding of Communist writers, but also favored the preservation of old intellectuals whose energy could be harnessed to the Revolution. Gorky was a staunch supporter of this view, and advocated a benevolent attitude toward writers, artists, and scholars. In prose and poetry this meant that room had to be made not only for Communists and those who were shouting from the housetops about their devotion to the cause, but also for all those motley elements who, for various reasons, were accepting the regime and were ready to collaborate with it. They were designated broadly as fellow-travelers—a term coined by Trotsky. In 1921 *The Red Virgin Soil* (Krasnaya Nov'), the first important Soviet monthly, was founded as the meeting place for Communists, fellow-travelers, and writers of the old generation; Lenin, again at the solicitation of Gorky, gave his blessings to the critic

Alexander Voronsky (1884-1943) as editor-in-chief of the new venture. Gorky himself received funds for his huge publishing project of *International Literature* which provided work and subsistence for hundreds of old and young literati drafted for translations, annotations, introductions, and so on. These two enterprises were considered a victory for the moderate wing of the Party led by Lunacharsky and supported by Lenin.

The literary NEP, or the loosening of controls, brought about a considerable freedom of expression for fellow-travelers. The novels, short stories, poems, and essays published between 1921 and 1928 presented more variety and contained more independent opinions and even criticisms of the current conditions than Soviet writers were allowed to display later on, with the possible exception of short periods during World War II and the post-Stalin thaw. The situation in general improved in comparison with the sombre years of military Communism. The literary NEP aimed at the reconstruction of artistic life; it opened the doors to the initiative shown by individual writers. The parallel with the reconstruction in the economy was amazingly complete, with the sole difference that the "socialized" sector—the proletarian writers —was much weaker artistically than the "private" sector—the fellow-travelers. On the relationship between these two factions depended the whole situation in Soviet letters during the NEP period. Another important feature in those years was the appearance of many literary organizations. Dozens of groups and units mushroomed throughout Russia, all of them striving desperately to expand and gain influence. They demanded authorization to publish magazines and books, they held meetings and conventions, made declarations, signed manifestoes, solicited grants from local Soviets, and tried to take a hand in shaping the cultural policy of governmental agencies. The rivalry of large organizations, such as the Union of Proletarian Writers with its Moscow and Leningrad branches, the League of Writers, and the Futurist Left Center, had repercussions within the Party. Each organization, to the extent that it had backers among the prominent Communist leaders, exercised an influence upon the course of official literary policy. On the other hand, the government utilized these groups for carrying out the decisions arrived at in the Kremlin.

The proletarian writers did not produce great works but they were well organized and disciplined, and, despite the failure of the Proletcult, they aspired to a commanding position. They had the support of some influential Marxist critics, such as Peter Kogan (1872-1932), President of the Academy of Literary Science, and Vladimir Fritche (1870-1929), who wanted proletarian poetry to be written only by workmen and claimed that "Socialist and industrialist culture must be thoroughly rationalistic." Such periodicals as *On Guard, October,* and *The Young Guard* (the organ of the League of Communist Youth) represented the "ideologically pure," and their editorial boards played a prominent role in the All-Union Association of Proletarian Writers (VAPP). Led by Sosnovsky, Lelevich, and Rodov, the On Guardists made furious attacks against the fellow-travelers (those "petty bourgeois") and "complacency in literature." Ilya Vardin, one of their leading exponents, declared that "all writers ought to pass through the school of political literacy." "Communists are too kind," wrote Lelevich, "we must demand and impose the party line in literature." From the heights of their ideological intransigence they rejected all works that did not serve the Party purpose. Gorky was to them "the darling of the Western bourgeoisie"; they reproached the State Publishing House for bringing out books by such "pseudo-Revolutionary writers as Alexey Tolstoy and Ehrenburg"; they besmirched Mayakovsky, Essenin, Pilnyak, and the Serapion Brethren, and sneered at Voronsky, Polonsky, and other "liberals who pamper oldtimers and NEP-men." Their efforts, however, could not convince the Party leaders. Bukharin told them that they had to build before they could hope to gain recognition. In his polemical and highly influential book, *Literature and Revolution,* Trotsky parried the attacks of the On Guardists: "if we should eliminate Pilnyak, the Serapion Brethren, Mayakovsky and Essenin, what will remain of a future proletarian literature except a few defaulted promissory notes?" The proletarian writers had "to win hegemony by high-grade productiveness rather than by manifestoes"; for "the issue between the bourgeois and proletarian literature depends on quality." This common-sense attitude did not, however, prevent Trotsky from advocating "a watchful revolutionary censorship and a broad and flexible policy

in the fields of art." He recommended the hand of iron for "open
or secret enemies" and the velvet glove "for sympathizers or the
faint-hearted." As a matter of fact his vicious articles, under the
pretentious title "Dictatorship, Where Is Thy Whip" (directed
against the critic Yuli Aikhenwald who "dared to write eulogies
to Gumilev") resulted in the arrest and banishment, in 1922, of
Aikhenwald and several other well-known literary figures, such
as the philosophers Berdiaev and Bulgakov, the novelist Ossorghin,
the journalist Kuskova, and many others. But the general attitude
formulated by Trotsky coincided with the point of view of the
Communist leaders, and in 1925 it was definitely adopted by the
Central Committee in a resolution that sounded like a Magna
Charta:

> The hegemony of proletarian writers is, as yet, non-
> existent, and the Party ought to help those writers to earn
> for themselves the historical right to such a hegemony ...
> tact and care are essential in dealing with the fellow-trav-
> elers. The Party must evince tolerance toward transitional
> ideological forms. They must vigorously oppose any frivo-
> lous and contemptuous treatment of the old cultural herit-
> age, as well as of literary specialists. Communist criticism
> ought to dispense with any tone of literary command—the
> Party cannot bind itself to support any particular tendency
> in the sphere of literary form ... The new style will be
> created by other methods, and the solution of this problem
> is not yet pressing—the Party should, therefore, encourage
> the free competition of various groups and tendencies in
> any given field. The Party cannot allow, by decree or proc-
> lamation, any legal monopoly of literary production on the
> part of one group or literary organization, and cannot grant
> this monopoly to any group—not even to the proletarian
> group itself.

Some three decades later the Chinese Communists, in proclaiming the value of cultivating "many flowers" in the field of art and
culture, must have had this resolution as a model. In the 'sixties,
however, they rejected it as "harmful revisionism."

This statement of the Central Committee gave a legal status

to the work of all fellow-travelers and even to "neutral" writers, as long as the latter could be classified as "exponents of transitional ideologies," a vague term that could be—and was—interpreted very loosely. It also signified an official rejection of the On Guard position. The leaders of that group acknowledged their defeat: some of them resigned, and the less aggressive (such as the novelist Yury Libedinsky) took over and renamed their magazine *On Literary Guard*. They had to wait three years, until the end of the NEP and the promulgation of the first Five-Year Plan, before they could resume their bid for power and succeed in imposing their militant policy. For the moment the fellow-travelers seemed to have won all along the line, and the Party was compelled to recognize that the revival of literature was due mainly to their efforts. Later, from the end of the 'thirties to the death of Stalin, Soviet critics denied this fact in their efforts to "correct history," and simply ignored what had actually happened in the first decade of Communist rule. With a few insignificant exceptions, a true assessment of the 'twenties, and its role in the development of Russian letters, has never been made in the press of the USSR. Communist theoreticians always reproach American and other Western critics and literary historians, including this writer, for "exaggerating the importance of the 'twenties." They forget that a complex and manifold renaissance did take place in Russia under the NEP and that a series of most interesting works in prose and poetry saw light precisely in those fateful years.

The physical manifestation of this renaissance was a tremendous upsurge in the publishing business, and included many ventures owned by co-operative groups and organizations, such as the Soviet Writer, Academia, the Moscow Worker, Land and Factory, the Young Guard, and dozens of others. The range of publishing was amazingly wide—reprints of classics, translations of old and modern European and American poets and novelists (from Alexander Dumas to John Dos Passos), the works of contemporary Soviet authors, collections of poetry, and a fair number of memoirs and criticism. The growth of book production was so rapid that by 1927 it almost reached the pre-war level and the following year exceeded it. New magazines and literary monthlies replaced the old ones: *Red Virgin Soil* (Krasnaya Nov'), *New World*

(Novy Mir), *October*, *The Banner* (Znamia), founded in 1930, *The Star* (Zvezda), *The Press and Revolution*. The circulation of newspapers trebled in 1928 in comparison with 1921.

The improved living conditions, the relief the country felt after the end of the civil war, and the resumption of normal academic life promoted literary research. Museums, archives, universities, scholarly and artistic societies emerged as powerful agents of cultural expansion. It could be argued that this expansion was mainly quantitative and that whatever had been gained in breadth and vigor was lost in depth and refinement, but such a casual statement would not cover the whole issue. Although the so-called "democratization and popularization" of Russian culture was accompanied by all sorts of inevitable abuses and simplifications, many excellent, imaginative, and valuable works of art and scholarship were produced in the Soviet Union during the decade 1920-30. It is unfair to point out that to meet the requirements of half-ignorant and coarse multitudes art and science had to lower their standards: the "vulgarization" was but one aspect of the huge process of cultural revolution which took place in the former Empire of the Romanovs. Another was the atmosphere of excitement and novelty among the newcomers, the "youth of the Revolution," whose romantic intensity gave a unique flavor to the period and made literature vibrant with a zestful and creative spirit.

An important factor was also the resumption of relations with the West; writers and artists were allowed to go abroad and to stay in Berlin, Paris, and Prague, where they met the *émigrés* and where some of their work were published. The exchange between Moscow and European capitals in artistic and intellectual fields was reflected in abundant translations from various European languages. Publishing houses founded by the *émigrés* printed novels and poems by Soviet authors and to some extent exported them to Russia. The authorities soon put an end to such a dangerous practice, but travelers along with a number of expatriates who had decided to return to their native land brought back with them not only books but also vivid reports of what was going on in Western literature, music, theater, and painting. Many Soviet writers, such as Ehrenburg, Alexey Tolstoy, Pilnyak, Lidin, and others, either wrote travelogues or located the action of their stories and novels in Europe and America—and all these works reveal a broadening attitude toward the West.

The literary movement of the mid-'twenties had several striking characteristics: in comparison with the years of the civil war, a reversal in style had occurred and in quantity prose now out-stripped poetry; stylistic innovations and a bent toward "ornamental" devices were widespread; and both prose and poetry followed pre-revolutionary tendencies and schools.

It came as no surprise that old writers such as Serafimovich, Veressayev, and the whole Gorky group continued in their usual realistic manner, or that Briussov and Sologub remained faithful to symbolism, and Mandelstam and Kuzmin still adhered in their poetry to the principle of acmeistic precision or "beautiful clarity." More extraordinary was the fact that young writers—whether fellow-travelers or Communists—fell under the impact of symbolism and expressionism. "Russian prose at the start of the NEP," the Communist critic Gorbachev was compelled to acknowledge in 1928, "advanced under the sign of Bely's *Petersburg* and partly under that of Remizov and of *The Islanders* of Zamyatin." Bely's novel was the highest prose achievement of symbolism, and its impress can easily be perceived in the fragmentary, emotional compositions of Pilnyak, with his involved system of images and rhythmic style; in the descriptions of the civil war in the Crimea by Alexander Malyshkin (*The Fall of Dair*, 1923); in the scenes of revolutionary struggle in Yury Libedinsky's *The Week* (1922); and, subsequently, in the sprawling panoramas of Artyom Vesyoly (*My Native Land* and *Russia Washed in Blood*, 1926).* Dozens of minor works of the period also bear the unmistakable imprint of Bely. The glow of symbolism was bright in the first years of Soviet prose, but it gradually faded, and by the 'thirties had all but disappeared. Between the 1917 Revolution and his death in 1934 Bely wrote and published a number of important works, among them *Recollections on Blok* (1922), the autobiographical novel *Kotik Letayev*, the historical chronicle *Moskva* in three volumes (*A Moscow Eccentric*, 1926; *Moscow under the Blow*,

---

* Vesyoly was "liquidated" in the 'thirties.

1926; *Masks*, 1932), and a series of highly interesting and valuable
memoirs (*At the Turn of the Century*, 1930; *The Beginning of a
Century*, 1933; *Between Two Revolutions*, 1934) offering a colorful picture of the Russian intelligentsia and its artistic and ideological currents during the past fifty years.

The influence of Remizov* and Zamyatin,** two remarkable craftsmen, expressed itself in a number of works by young
writers who followed the older masters in their contrapuntal composition, in the blending of the lyrical with the expository, in
various linguistic devices, and in the use of irony. Remizov's face-
tiousness and Zamyatin's sense of humor determined the whole
satirical trend of the 'twenties. The stories of Zoshchenko, *The
Embezzlers* by Valentin Katayev, *The Twelve Chairs* and *The
Little Golden Calf*, those incomparable picaresques by Ilf and
Petrov, as well as tales and plays by many other Soviet young
men, created the best comic literature that the new regime ever
produced. Never again did Communist Russia see such a flowering of humor and satire. The group of Serapion Brethren who
contributed greatly to this current, Venyamin Kaverin, Vsevolod
Ivanov, Nikolay Nikitin, also dwelt on the fantastic tale, emphasizing the grotesque and the bizarre, which had a counterpart in plays by Erdman, Bulgakov, and Tretyakov, and, of course,
by Mayakovsky. The symbolists, the futurists, the Serapion Brethren, as well as many others who did not belong to any definite
faction, were all driven by an irresistible desire for experimentation. Just as Mayakovsky, Essenin, or Pasternak experimented in
poetry, and Meyerhold, Tairov, and dozens of other directors
did the same in the theater, Pilnyak, Fedin, Kaverin, Leonov,
Babel, Ehrenburg, and Vesyoly, all tried out new techniques in
the composition, characterization, and verbal treatment of fictional material. This spirit of inventiveness and exploration, which
permeated so much of the literature of the NEP era, was killed
in the 'thirties, and up to the present time Soviet letters have not
known such richness and diversity of formal attainments. Later

---

* See *From Chekhov to the Revolution* by Marc Slonim (New York:
Oxford University Press, 1962).
** See Chapter 9 below.

Communist critics dubbed this whole movement as "decadent formalism," without conceding that all the "tricks and bizarre games" of the 1920's reflected the basic yearning for a rejuvenation of the arts and were a natural consequence of the Revolution, while also allied to the larger framework of Western avant-garde literature. The sons of a new epoch were striving for new forms of expression, and in their search they started where the pre-revolutionary innovators and rebels had left off.

This effort coincided with attempts to renew the language, which, despite all the differences, also stemmed from Remizov, Bely, and the futurists. These attempts followed two courses: linguistic play, which included all sorts of neologisms, twists of syntax, and grammatical structure; and colloquial and vernacular speech. The former exhausted itself and faded out by the 1930's; the second, however, showed more resistance. The first current gave rise to "ornamental" prose, in which writers indulged in all kinds of verbal vignettes and embellishments, mainly borrowed from the modes of poetic language. This runs through most outstanding writers of the 1920's, from Vsevolod Ivanov to Leonov, but thins out in the era of the five-year plans and loses its vigor— spontaneously or under blows from the outside. On the other hand, beginning with Mayakovsky's verse, written in the idiom of the streets and the mass meeting, Russian literature felt the tremendous impact of the vernacular. Many works of Soviet fiction are so profusely larded with peasant speech and regional locutions that they become untranslatable. This is true of works usually considered in the Communist press as the highest achievements of Soviet literature, such as the novels by Sholokhov. Frequently the regionalistic trend was combined with "ornamentalism," creating such curious effects as are found in certain tales by Vsevolod Ivanov, Vesyoly, or minor Siberian writers. Of course the insistence on reproducing the true peasant speech has its roots in the Populist literature of the 1880's, but the literary renaissance of local idiom (including dialects) and of the vernacular was linked with the entry of the lower strata of the population into cultural life. Political factors—union of art with the people—also played some part in this almost general phenomenon. For the novelists of the NEP period, the use of common speech and regional locutions represented a new medium for expressing their art in the language of the masses. Some critics were so enthusiastic about this idea that they savored the "abolition of the literary language of the upper classes" and the "creation of a unique Soviet idiom." It is not necessary to say that those who held such an opinion simply failed to understand the basic difference between the spoken and written language and the necessity of linguistic as well as other conventions for a normal development of fictional literature. Moreover the desire, on the part of young authors in the 1930's and 1940's, to render as closely as possible the spoken idiom of the masses, resulted in pat, coarse, or altogether incorrect style. Millions of half-educated Russians now speak a vulgar and colorless lower-middle-class dialect, choked with foul clichés and bureaucratic terms.

In the 1920's, however, the influx of regional and popular elements was partly due to what may be called a replacement of literary personnel. Between 1920 and 1926 more than 150 writers made their debut in literature, and they accounted for the bulk of Soviet prose and poetry. The great majority of them were young men and women who had matured during the storm and were now turning to literature. And they came from all strata of society and all parts of the country. These two facts led to a complete breakdown of the social and geographical framework of Russian literature. Until 1917 it had been created basically by the nobility and the intelligentsia, mostly of noble extraction, and some representatives of the middle class. Russia's greatest poets and novelists of the nineteenth-century were for the most part born in the central districts of Great Russia. Now all the regions, even the most remote, had their sons and daughters among the literati, and the number of writers of peasant and proletarian origin was steadily increasing. This process of social and geographical expansion was enhanced by the efforts made by the Soviet government to develop the arts and letters of various nationalities of the Union. Although some of them, such as the Ukrainians, Byelorussians, the Armenians, the Georgians, the Tartars, had a long and strong literary tradition, others, such as the peoples of Central Asia (Kirghiz, Turkmens) or of Siberia (Yakuts, Buriato-Mongols), had only oral folklore, and were for the first time in their history introduced to the written word. It is obvious that the impact of prose and poetry in the Russian language was enormous for the literary development of all these nationalities, and that the range of Russian artistic influence expanded greatly after the Revolution. Later all the satellite countries were included in the sphere of Russian literary predominance.

The experimentation in new forms led first to a certain disintegration of established genres and to a marked transference of poetic devices into prose. The works of 1921-25 were more often than not extravagant, bizarre, either loose in construction or put together in a most sophisticated and frequently forced manner, highly emotional in style, and filled with pathos. From 1924 on there was, however, a distinct return to well-defined genres. Babel's short stories were tightly knit and compact; the comeback of the "well-made" novel began with Fedin's complex *Cities and Years*, the first full-length narrative of importance since Pilnyak's *The Naked Year* and Furmanov's *Chapayev*; it was followed by Leonov's *The Badgers*, Gladkov's *Cement*, Fadeyev's *The Rout*, Ehrenburg's *The Racketeer*—each of which had a definite plot and a well-told story.

Genres reappeared in other provinces of the literature as well: the playwrights abandoned the morality play done in the manner of Mayakovsky's *Mystery Bouffe*, or strictly propagandistic shows such as Tretyakov's *Roar China*, and returned to realistic drama. *Lyubov Yarovaya* by Trenyov, *Armored Train 14-69* by Ivanov, *The Days of Turbins* by Bulgakov, *Revolt* and *The Break* by Lavrenyov, were all devoted to the civil war and were strongly colored (with the exception of Bulgakov's work) by a heroic-romantic spirit. The general mood shared by the symbolists, the neo-realists, and many of the proletarian writers was definitely romantic; Babel, Leonov, and Olesha stressed it to such an extent that one may well speak of an extensive romantic-psychological trend. The mood expressed itself, among other things, in an interpretation of the Revolution in terms of natural rebellion and man's irrational urges, in various anti-rational attitudes, and in an emotional style that bristled with exaggerations, harsh chiaroscuro, and glaring contrasts. This romantic current runs through the poems of Pasternak, the ballads of Tikhonov and Bagritsky, the lyrics of the futurists, and the tales and novels by Pilnyak, Babel, Fedin, Leonov, Olesha, Kaverin, Tynyanov, Lavrenyov, and many others. The romantic tendency was expressed most fully by Alexander Grinevsky (1880-1932) who, under the pen name of Grin, wrote stories of love, adventure, and mystery, revealing the influence of Western masters, and by Konstantin Paustovsky (b.1892) who gained an important place in Soviet letters. Strong romantic characteristics are found in the works of Mikhail Prishvin (1873-1954), one of the most popular post-revolutionary novelists. The romantic mood took a different course in the writings of proletarian and Communist authors whose ideology was definitely rationalistic and who shied away from "idealistic nonsense" and "lifeless fantasy." But although their interpretation of events followed the pattern of Marxian dialectical materialism and was expressed in terms of the class struggle (Gladkov, Panfyorov, Ostrovsky, Libedinsky), they utilized romantic devices in building up their heroic protagonists. This is particularly obvious in the impressionistic *Cement* by Gladkov and in *The Fall of Dair* by Malyshkin.

The realistic tradition was followed by numerous writers, ranging from the factualism of a Furmanov to the naturalism of such peasant novelists as Neverov and Seifullina, or the candid-camera shots that made Romanov so popular around 1925. Alexey Tolstoy, the master of the anecdotal tale, and Ehrenburg, the eclectic who had started out as the disciple of the innovators and wound up by becoming almost a conformist, as well as dozens of minor middle-of-the-road writers, showed a definite hankering after traditional realism. On the whole, most of the old and new Communist and proletarian writers remained faithful to the nineteenth-century representational, realistic style, particularly that of Gorky, even though they were frequently influenced by the stylistic innovations of symbolism and neo-realism.

By the end of the 1920's the psychological realism of Fadeyev, Libedinsky, and some minor novelists had smoothed the way for Sholokhov, the leader of the Tolstoyan school in Soviet letters, and for the entire group that was destined to attain a prominent position and to receive, in 1934, the official stamp of Socialist Realism. Under the NEP, however, their influence was not too strong. Literature was dominated by the experimenters, the romantics, the Serapion Brethren, and other fellow-travelers. In poetry Mayakovsky and the futurists, Pasternak and the surrealists, Tikhonov and the post-acmeists, Essenin and the imagists, Bagritsky and the constructivists were holding the center of the stage, while Pilnyak, Babel, Zamyatin, Ivanov, Fedin, Kaverin, Olesha, Leonov, and a host of other storytellers were carrying on their experiments in prose.

All these writers, although highly differentiated and frequently antagonistic to each other, had something in common despite their political allegiances and aesthetic preferences: they all wrote about the Revolution. There is a surprising uniformity of subject matter in all this motley output of the 1920's, which chronologically was still so close to the old Russia of intellectuals, ignorant peasants, and aesthetic patricians. The topics that were to reign during the following decades—the socialist reconstruction, the religion of work and effort, the new man in the new society, the clash between the builders of the future and the remnants of the past, the role of the Party in the Great Change—were merely foreshadowed under the NEP. It is little wonder that most Soviet writers dealt with the Revolution and contemporary reality. They did not do so because of any social demand or political pressure, as some critics have wrongly intimated (although both factors did exist and were certainly instrumental); theirs was a perfectly natural desire to express the exciting, harrowing, and often stupefying experience of their generation. The fellow-travelers interpreted those experiences in the light of their own opinions and attitudes. They were not Communists—or even Marxists—like the enormous majority of the Russian people. They were, by a historical paradox, the voice of that non-Communist population which was ready to follow the Party without subscribing to all its tenets. At the same time they were close to the ideas and emotions of the old intelligentsia or bourgeoisie and, in one way or another, directly or obliquely, reflected their ideologies. They also mirrored the feelings and ideas of the new masses who were about to build a new Russia.

But the diversity of points of view and of artistic methods could flourish only in the 1920's. Later they narrowed down, becoming curtailed and reduced by the pressure of the expanding Communist and proletarian literary factions and by the stultification of the whole state machine. The complete triumph of the Communist ideocracy and hierarchy resulted in greater uniformity, introduced along with stylistic and methodological rigidity, and in the next decade most of the colorful variety and excitement of the transitional 'twenties was definitely gone. Literature became disciplined, planned, well controlled, strait-jacketed. By that time some of the prominent fellow-travelers, like Babel, Pilnyak, or Zamyatin, had been silenced, while others had had to change their tune in order to survive.

6

Boris Pilnyak

THE UNTIMELY SYMBOLIST

Chronologically, the first significant panorama of the Great Upheaval was presented in *The Naked Year* (1922), a novel consisting of a series of flashbacks and close-ups of an aristocratic family, an anarchist's bohemian colony, peasants, uprisings, fratricidal strife, and various episodes of cruelty, lust, famine, physical frenzy, and mental exaltation. The author of this strange yet attractive novel, which blended crude naturalistic descriptions with complex philosophical flights and extravagant stylistic devices, was 28-year-old Boris Pilnyak (1894-1938?), one of the most discussed Soviet writers of the NEP period. In his autobiography he says: "My true name is Vogau. My father—a country veterinarian—comes from German settlers of the Volga region; and my mother from an ancient now extinguished family of Saratov merchants. She graduated from Moscow Teachers' College. Both father and mother were close to the Populists of the 1880's and 1890's. On my paternal side I had German and a tiny bit of Jewish blood in my veins, on my maternal side, Slavic and Mongolian (Tartar). I spent my childhood in the provincial towns of the Moscow region—Mozhaisk, Bogorodsk, Kolomna, and in the homeland of my parents—in Saratov, and the village of Katerinenstadt (or Baronsk) on the Volga. I graduated from the High School in Nizhni Novgorod in 1913, and from the Moscow Commercial Institute (now the Marx Institute of People's Economy) in 1920. I started writing at the age of 9." What Pilnyak published before the Revolution had little value. He came to the fore only after 1918, and particularly when *The Naked Year* struck readers by its originality. His career, after this spectacular success, was a very peculiar one: it included sudden popularity

and humiliation, fame and oblivion, and ended tragically and
mysteriously with imprisonment and exile—or, perhaps, with execution. His attempts at establishing symbolist-Populist prose have
often been identified with that boldness of style which derives
from the revolutionary spirit of his times, and his whims, mannerisms, and stylistic fancies were regarded as typical of a whole
generation. For many conservatives he was the symbol of "cultural disintegration." The *émigré* critics showed especial hostility
toward this "incomprehensible, chaotic, and altogether horrid
scion of Bolshevism."

The truth was that basically Pilnyak did not represent the revolutionary mentality, and he was not a Communist. His literary
style was inspired by the decadents and the symbolists, and his
ideas and political leanings by the Slavophiles and Populists. He
lived for years among the peasants and humble folk of what was
called "the heart of Russia"—the Moscow region—and he had first-
hand contact with the genuine country people. But in his family
he was surrounded by radical intellectuals of a non-Marxian brand
and by a devotion to the Russian classics. As an adolescent and
a young man he was greatly influenced by Gogol and Dostoevsky,
by Rozanov, the sensuous mystic, and by Remizov and Bely. His
fragmentary composition, his lack of plots, his "blizzard of words"
deliberately let loose in a disorderly way, the use of characters
as bearers of concepts, and his philosophizing—all linked him with
the pre-revolutionary tradition.

Until about 1928 Pilnyak followed the model of Bely's "poetic
rhythmic prose." He wrote long, involved sentences, burdened
with incidental propositions, hints, allegorical turns, symbolic allusions, and all sorts of word play. The author's asides or divaga-
tions constantly broke the narrative; he conversed with the reader
or made disclosures about his own techniques; he often interrupted a highly emotional scene by wondering whether this part
of the novel really had come off as he had intended it to, or
placed quotations from historical documents in the midst of a
love dialogue. Like Dos Passos he obstructed his exposition with
"newsreels"—excerpts from the daily press, texts of law regulations and legal documents. *The Naked Year, Cow-Wheat*, and
Machines and Wolves (1925) look like literary jumble-shops—

poems in prose, reflections on Russian culture, and genealogical trees of the main characters alternating with coarse scenes of physical love and dramatic descriptions of violent happenings. Yet the attentive reader can easily discover a continuous thread through the fabric. Although the author assembles heterogeneous elements in order to shock and bewilder, the succession of seemingly unrelated episodes and irrelevant digressions falls into a pre-ordained pattern, and one even gets used to Pilnyak's vocabulary—a mixture of archaisms and colloquialisms with regional or local expressions, of sophisticated intellectual language and low vernacular. By the early 1930's Pilnyak had given up many of his artifices. Although his second great novel, *The Volga Flows into the Caspian Sea,* shows more directness and simplicity and is more readable, it still retains the basic features of his initial manner: his rejection of objective narrative, his insistence on the "conventionality" of art, and his own conventions of fragmentary composition, poetic technique, changing intonations, and mixed genres.

The underlying philosophy of his work was as eclectic as his style: it is a blend of the thought of Nietzsche, Rozanov, and Slavophile aspirations, with a peculiar flavor of nationalistic Bolshevism. Pilnyak welcomed the Revolution as the end of the artificial "Sanct Peter Burg period" and as the resurrection of seventeenth-century Moscow. "Moskva," he maintained, "meant dark water." The dark waters (the peasantry) were going to flood the city and engulf the intellectuals and the bureaucrats. The wild primitivism of revolutionary excesses was simply an outburst of national energies, proclaiming a resumption of a Scythian way of life. The whole system of symbols in *The Naked Year* indicates that famine and anarchy had been necessary to help the Russians rediscover themselves. The huts where bearded peasants live next to their cows, sheep, and pigs, the bonfires ignited by flint-lighters, the villages haunted in winter by hungry wolves, the exploits wherein lust and blood reign supreme—this is the true, savage Russia of anarchical peasant revolt, the Russia of Stenka Razin and Pugachev. Wars and epidemics fail to undermine the physical strength and animal vitality of the people, the pagan ritual of weddings and christenings go on throughout the country—and it does not make much difference whether the leaders believe in St. Nicholas or St. Marx. Pilnyak glorifies this bodily might of the Russians (Blok called it "burning love") in scenes of sexual passion or sheer erotic revelry, and contrasts them with impotent and hypocritical Europe. In *The Third Capital* (which is neither Petersburg nor Moscow) he writes: "a joyless dull sun rises over Russia, which had withdrawn into the steppes—but this is a sunrise, whereas in the West it is sunset, and the blood is thinning out."

A social emotionalist, Pilnyak had no precise political credo: sometimes he talked like a Slavophile of 1840, yet he interpreted the Revolution in terms of peasant anarchism, as a victory of the countryside over the city. This victory also meant the triumph of the subconscious and irrational over the conscious and rational in man and society. In his *Diary* for 1923 (published in 1924) he said: "Insofar as Communists are with Russia, I am with them. I realize that the destinies of the Communist Party interest me far less than the destinies of Russia. The Communist Party is for me but a link in the destiny of Russia." Yet *The Naked Year* he identified the Bolsheviks with the city dwellers who wanted to guide the peasants and to channel the anarchical elements of the rebellion; and he exalted the "men in leather jackets" (commonly worn by the Communists at that time), since they were the "steel-hard elite, the select from among the loose-sand Russians." They would rule because they had the will to power, the pluck and the strength to lead the primitive popular movement and give shape to inchoate aspirations.

Although Pilnyak had apparently accepted this situation, he often pointed out the rift between the anti-European Maximalism of the peasants and the planned Western inspired, efforts of the Communists. In *Mother Earth* (1926), one of his best short novels, he depicts a forlorn district beyond the Volga, a district as changeless and dark as the centuries-old forests bounding it. Time has stopped in these villages, and the Communist Nekluyev, who has come there with a group of comrades, finds medieval customs and troglodytic natives who reek of blood and raw pelts. All his efforts to draw closer to them and make them understand the ideas of the Revolution are doomed to failure; they represent the

Scythia of the seventeenth century, while he stands for the urban Communism of the twentieth. In none of his later works did Pilnyak answer the question he had raised in all his stories of primitive Russia. He seemed to have recognized the mission of the Communists as that of enlightening and organizing the peasants, but at the same time he could not hide his anti-European and anti-rational feelings. He frequently called the Communists "mechanical rationalists," and often exalted instinct and emotions as the basic elements of human behavior.

In *Spilled Time* (1927), a collection of stories that did not deal with revolutionary events, Pilnyak concentrated on what in his opinion were the psychological constants of the "game of life": birth, growth, the struggle for survival, sexual possession, death. Human beings are part of nature, and wisdom lies in obedience to cosmic rhythms, which govern both animal passions and the movement of the stars. Thus nature is opposed to culture; several tales resulting from Pilnyak's extensive travels in Europe, the Far East, and America reflect this point of view clearly. These tales, incidentally, have a strong anti-Western trait. Eurasia, or the union between Russia and Asia, particularly China, is envisioned by Pilnyak as a powerful primeval force that will overwhelm rationalistic and agnostic Occidental Europe.

Pilnyak's true beliefs found their best expression in *The Tale of the Unextinguished Moon* (1926), inspired by the death of Mikhail Frunze, the Commander-in-Chief of the Red Army. It alluded to Stalin as "the unbending man of steel" (*stal'* in Russian is steel). The story deals with one Gavrilov, a Red Army general, who falls ill and is ordered by the Central Committee of the Party to undergo an operation. Gavrilov feels instinctively that he ought to avoid the surgeon's knife. His thoughts on life and death are simple and profound; he reads Tolstoy with great delight and he likes children; fictional heroes and his own feelings appear to him most real and important. The Party machine, on the contrary, and the leaders who want Gavrilov to go on the operation table because "a useful worker ought to be repaired for further functioning," appear to him mechanical and futile. Gavrilov, despite all Party directives and medical science, dies under the knife—and life goes right on, triumphant over the smug trickery of poor reason. The high priests of the Kremlin, with all their control boards, telephones, radios, Red Guards standing at attention, and faultless aides-de-camp, had not treated Gavrilov as a human being; he had been no more than a tool to them.

The novella provoked a storm in the press, and Pilnyak was compelled to recant and acknowledge his "gross error." He wrote contrite letters; the monthly that had published the tale made public apologies, and the censor who let it pass was demoted.

The psychological and historical tales Pilnyak concentrated on after 1928, in the fallacious hope of avoiding the dangerous and slippery topics of Soviet actuality, did not save him from attacks. During the first Five-Year Plan he decided to prove his loyalty to the regime and wrote *The Volga Flows into the Caspian Sea* (1930). His intention was to show the building of a dam as a triumph of man's organized, purposeful activity in overcoming the traditional inertia of Russian life and in conquering nature—a typical article of faith in the Communist credo. He even succeeded in drawing a few portraits of Communist enthusiasts, and in exposing the conspiracy of counter-revolutionary wreckers. But many passages of the novel resumed Pilnyak's familiar theme of Russia's ambivalence, of the opposing Asiatic and European currents of her history and mentality, and the reader was often left with the impression that the author's sympathy was much more with the Asiatic past than with the European future of his country. Moreover, a significant part of the novel called "Mahogany" contained other heretical ideas.

As a separate novella *Mahogany* had been published in 1929 by an *émigré* publisher in Berlin and had provoked a violent campaign against Pilnyak in the Moscow press. He was expelled from all literary organizations, and his works were branded as examples of "reactionary philosophy." In its initial draft printed abroad, *Mahogany* depicted a somnolent provincial town deeply entangled in the ancient past. Pilnyak called it "Russian Bruges or Kamamura." Its inhabitants, even those who are Party members, live and act like Old Believers or the seventeenth-century "holy innocents." The two brothers Bezdetov who travel around in quest of antique mahogany furniture which they sell at a great profit, bear a resemblance to charac-

ters in Gogol's *Dead Souls*. They are, however, subsidiary to another, more complex and sophisticated couple of brothers: the old
Yakov who had survived two emperors and Lenin, and does not
believe in any changes, and Ivan, "a Communist of 1919," who
looks with contempt at the disintegration of revolutionary ideals
and at the NEP period when "Proletarians are being transformed
into engineers," and whose sole consolation is drinking. His son
is obviously a follower of Trotsky. The whole tone of *Mahogany*
betrayed Pilnyak's doubts about whether the Asiatic indolence,
the medieval way of life, could ever be redeemed. His old-
fashioned eccentrics did not hide their conviction that the succession of governments and regimes did not alter the substance of
Russia, and princes, tsars, or Communist bosses belonged to the
same category of temporary leaders. The Soviets were hailed
because they helped Muscovite isolationism from Europe, and the
Revolution was another means for national self-withdrawal.

Appalled and frightened by the reaction to *Mahogany*, Pilnyak
revised it before incorporating it into his novel, but this retreat
from previous positions was interpreted merely as a ruse. Communist ideologists could not forgive Pilnyak his anarchical spirit
and his anti-social, anti-historical attitude. Did he not speak
always about "the constants of human nature," implying that man
could not be changed by environment? He was concerned only
with the organic processes of birth, love, and death, and his best
pages dealt with solitude, sex, the torment and dread of annihilation, and the feeling of oneness with nature. He always intimated
that beyond social upheavals there was something fixed, something immutable in the human heart, and that the downfall of
empires, the tumult of mobs, and the reform of society could
not alter man's basic suffering or conflicts.

Whatever his leanings, Pilnyak, unlike Zamyatin, had not the
courage and moral stamina to withstand pressure. Attacks and
disfavor affected him deeply; he lacked backbone in life as in
literature; there was something flabby, almost equivocal about
him, and from 1929 on, under a barrage of harsh criticism, he
continued to go from repentance to recantation. He never regained his former position in Soviet letters; even the defeat of
his chief enemies in the On Guard group and the change in the

literary policy of the Party proved of no avail; his decline was complete. His last works, *OK* (his impressions of the United States, published in 1932) and *The Ripening of the Fruit*, a novel that appeared in a monthly but was never issued in book form, mirrored the curious instability of the writer's style and thought. He revised his books on Japan and on China, trying to make them more acceptable in Stalinist Russia. Since 1937 his name has not appeared in the Soviet press. We know now that he was arrested and accused of being a spy for the Japanese and a Trotskyite. There is no documentary evidence about his ultimate fate, but according to persistent rumors he was executed in 1937. His literary execution, however, decreed by the authorities, was beyond doubt: for two decades his name was simply obliterated from all surveys of Soviet literature. In the late 'fifties it reappeared in periodicals and special treatises, but even in such monumental editions as the three-volume *History of Soviet Literature* published in 1958-60, his works are either ignored or given perfunctory mention. The contemporary Soviet reader has no way of knowing how popular and influential they were and what violent polemics they provoked in the 'twenties.

7

Isaac Babel

THE ROMANTIC STORYTELLER

In 1924 a new writer suddenly rose to fame in Moscow. His name was Isaac Babel, a 30-year-old Jew from Odessa, and the stories he published in LEF and other periodicals were immediately recognized as outstanding. Later he collected them in several books; however, despite their stylistic and inner unity, they formed two distinct series. In the first, represented by *Red Cavalry* (1926), a classic of Soviet literature, Babel dealt with incidents of the civil war and the 1920 campaign against Poland led by Cossack riders under Budenny's command; the second included autobiographical reminiscences ("First Love" and "History of My Dovecote") and tales about Jewish toughs and eccentrics of Odessa.

Babel's works were spectacularly successful in the late 'twenties, but after that his production fell off. There were a few additions to previous collections, a couple of stories inspired by travels abroad ("Dante Street" and "Di Grasso"), two plays of Jewish life (*Sunset*, 1928, *Marie*, 1935), several film scenarios, and a chapter ("Gapa Guzhva") of an unfinished novel on *kolkhozes*, tentatively entitled *Velikaya Krinitsa*. "The Beginning," a four-page personal tribute to Gorky, published in the almanac year XXI (1938), was the last work of his to appear in the Soviet Union. At about the same time he was arrested and "illegally repressed," to use the term of the 1962 *Soviet Literary Encyclopedia*. The rumor was that he had been accused of "Trotskyite sympathies" and of friendship with other "repressed" persons. He died in a Siberian concentration camp in tragic circumstances on March 17, 1941, at the age of 47.

Isaac Babel was born in 1894 into the family of a Jewish shopkeeper of Moldavanka, a poor section of Odessa. His father forced him to study Hebrew, the Bible, and the Talmud until he was sixteen, but in the commercial school he attended, he read Russian classics, learnt foreign languages, and got so enthusiastic about Flaubert that he started writing stories in French. In 1915 he went to St. Petersburg, and the following year Gorky published his first stories in *Annals*, a literary and political monthly. The censors found their crude naturalism offensive, and Babel was sued for obscenity. Gorky, the young man's literary godfather, recommended that he go "into the world" before becoming a writer. Babel followed this advice, and for seven years led an adventurous existence. "I have been," says Babel in his autobiographical sketch, "a soldier on the Rumanian front, an employee in the Cheka (Extraordinary Commission for fighting against counter-revolution and speculation), in the Commissariat of Public Instruction, I took part in the food requisitions of 1918, served in the Northern army against General Yudenich, in the first Cavalry Army, and in the Odessa Regional Soviet, then worked as a newspaper reporter in Petersburg and Tiflis, and as a copy editor in the 7th Soviet Printing plant in Odessa, and so on." All these varied experiences changed the life of the dreamy youth from the Jewish Pale: he became realistic and tough. But they could not alter the mixture of pessimism, irony, romantic aspiration, and ardent faith he inherited as a descendant of persecuted generations. And he himself could not remold his sensitivity and renounce his morbid interest in man's cruelty. In his "History of My Dovecote" Babel tells of a Jewish pogrom in which as a child he witnessed the killing of defenseless people. Blood, murder, and destruction dominated his early impressions and they mark all his writing. When he joined the Cossacks in 1920, these professional dispensers of death looked with scorn at their bespectacled companion who did not know how to slay an enemy or tame a horse.

The clashes and ultimate reconciliation between the susceptible intellectual and the violent riders form one of the two main themes of *Red Cavalry*. Babel treats the subject with dry irony, but most dramatically. The other theme is the contradiction between the ruthless "soldiers of the Revolution" and their idealistic although inarticulate aspirations. In a terse manner, which often borders

on psychological naturalism, Babel tells of the inhuman element in
man. His turbulent companions not only despise his meekness
but consider themselves apostles of equality and the better life.
Their swords flash right and left to the war cry of "All hail to
the World Revolution!" They die for this slogan but they also
die shouting blasphemies, obscenities, or imbecile jests. Killing for
them is merely a daily chore. In a devastated village in Byelo-
russia, among corpses of gray-bearded men and pregnant women
with their bellies split by the retreating Poles, Babel sees his friend
Kudrya, a Red Cossack, cutting the throat of an old Jew accused
of espionage. Kudrya uses his dagger, going about his job with
the utmost care so as not to splatter his uniform with the blood
of the victim; he works as casually as a cook killing a fowl or
sticking a pig in his backyard. Afonky Bida, a young Cossack,
burns down Polish hamlets, shoots the old people, and loots the
peasants to avenge the death of a favorite horse destroyed during
a battle. Pavlishchenko, who had once been a shepherd, tramples
to death his former master, whom he hates. A soldier murders a
peasant woman because she has deceived him in order to sneak
into an overcrowded train. Kurdiukov's father joins the Whites
and captures one of his two sons, both of whom are in the Red
Army; the father tortures the boy all day long until the young
Cossack dies. To avenge his brother the other son hunts down his
father and puts him to death. Lieutenant Trunov rams his saber
down prisoners' throats or blows their heads off with a carbine.
When Shevelyov, a commanding officer, is wounded and lies
dying on the battlefield, Sashka, his mistress and the slut of the
squadron, gives herself to a coachman before Shevelyov's eyes.
But all these centaurs who pillage, ravish, and murder can turn
into heroes and give up their lives for their comrades. Occasionally they become romantic dreamers. After a retreat over roads
clogged with dead and wounded, Sidorov, a commander, is rest-
ing in a half-ruined hut. The air is heavy with the sickening odor
of corpses, yet by the flickering light of a tallow candle he is
writing a letter that evokes Italy, the Colosseum, the Capitol, the
fragrant fields of the Campagna. Alek, a young syphilitic, sings
to his depressed comrades-at-arms about a star shining over
meadows, near his old home, and sees his mother's "sad hand."

And Galkin, who has lost an eye, edits an army newspaper at the front line and envisions a beautiful future in which all the horrors of the present will be forgotten as if they had never been. Alek sings in a hovel crawling with lice, Sidorov surrounded by pestilential stench of death writes of Italy, Galkin talks of the glorious days to come while the shells explode and the wounded scream in agony—and Babel seems to enjoy this alternation of light and shade, this counterpoint of contrasts.

All of Babel's civil war stories are horrible, almost nightmarish, his revealing of physical savagery is brutal and at times painful, but these tragic vignettes are constantly relieved by sudden poetic revelations. This play on disparities is the very foundation of Babel's style and art: he shows tenderness next to coarseness, lofty aspirations next to savage cruelty, heroic sacrifice coming on the heels of debauchery and profanity. His descriptions, though laden with such repellent details that he was accused of sadism, pornography, and cynicism, are rendered in an exquisite rhythmic prose, in brief chiseled sentences; his poetic flashes have a lyrical quality, a moving poignancy. His whole technique is based on clashes of moods and contradictions in emotions, or on conflict between man and his environment. To describe the awakening of love and a child's erotic dreams, he chooses a background of illness, nausea, and a mob riot. In another story, his hero, the son of a rabbi, becomes a Communist and dies of typhoid: his dispatch case reveals portraits of Lenin and Maimonides, lying cheek by jowl; a girl's curly lock is nestling in the Resolutions of the Sixth Party Convention, and angular slanting lines of Hebrew poetry are penned on the margins of Russian propaganda leaflets. In the same way that his hero keeps cartridges as book-marks in "The Song of Songs," Babel mixes lyrical passages with naturalistic narration, and wistful flights of poetry with stark descriptions of bodily functions. The same counteraction of opposites gives a unique, romantic, and paradoxical quality to his Odessa tales. He is a master of the grotesque, and he presents a whole procession of cynical bums, pious rabbis, eccentric coachmen, and sly merchants "protected" by his beloved Benya the Yell, a gangster with flashy ties and flowery speech, not unlike some of the hold-up men in Damon Runyan. The cruel humor of these extravagant stories (such as the marriage of Benya's plain and sickly sister) is brittle and nonsensical; it unites the bitter humor of the Jews with the traditional Russian love for brightly colored, gay caricature. The grotesque prevails again in his dramas and European tales.

Babel's short stories are compact and terse. Maupassant and Chekhov are always mentioned as his teachers, but Babel's tales, unlike those of Chekhov who used the technique of "delayed action" and understatement, have dynamic, sharply developed plots, and dramatic, sometimes preposterous climaxes. The *Red Cavalry* sketches and Odessa stories are elegant and laconic, their structure is tightly balanced, the author's devices are perfectly controlled, and he insists on economy of artistic means. A disciple of Flaubert, he carefully polished his sentences and attached supreme importance to the swing and verbal modulations of each phrase. He formulated his aim very clearly: "There is no iron that can enter the human heart with the same stupefying effect as a period placed just at the right moment." As a true master of language, he was equally at home with refined speech and with that half-literate, half-popular idiom of the millions of men and women whom the Revolution had brought into contact with literary terms. A stylization of this speech gives an ironic or outright comic twist to his grimmest stories, which thus achieve an additional effect by their contrasts. For instance, in "The Death of Dolgushov," one of his best tales, a soldier's agony is emphasized by the irrelevant and ridiculous conversation of the people around him. As might be expected, Babel's style presents a formidable problem for his translators in any foreign tongue.

In *Odessa Tales* the verbal texture is even more complex. Odessa occupies a place in Russian literature similar to that of Marseilles in French. There is a complex of Odessa folklore, and Odessa anecdotes are repeated throughout Russia. Babel used this oral and written tradition, and he rendered the colorful local idiom, greatly influenced by Yiddish and Ukrainian, in a style that is as ironic as it is expressive. He has often been called the leader of the "Southern School" in Russian literature. Works produced by this group not only have a distinctive local flavor and easily recognizable linguistic particularities but also show a tendency toward the picaresque, a union of romanticism and humor, a swift pace of narrative, and a certain nonchalance and contempt for classical rules.

In the early 'thirties Babel was considered one of the leading Russian writers. Marshal Budenny, it is true, attacked him for having depicted the Red Cossacks as monsters and for thus having "defamed the heroism of the Revolution." The Soviet press debated whether or not Babel had represented reality faithfully. Then, too, what was he—a friend or an enemy of the regime? Could one call him a true fellow-traveler? There were too many misleading features in his naturalism and his romantic stylization, and Communist critics remained puzzled by them. Still, his books went through numerous reprints, hundreds of essays and even some books were written about his work, Gorky hailed him as "a great writer and a loyal Bolshevik," and it was rumored that Stalin enjoyed his stories.

A few years later Babel's voluntary silence became a forced silence, and he fell victim to Stalin's purges. The reasons for his arrest and downfall remain obscure, but one thing is certain—as a writer he was sentenced to oblivion. Communist surveys and histories of literature ignored Babel, for none of his stories was ever included in the numerous anthologies. His rehabilitation did not come until the late 'fifties when de-Stalinization permitted the rediscovery of the author of *Red Cavalry*. A selection of his works, a carefully censored and expurgated edition, was published in Moscow in 1957. The attitude of Communist critics toward Babel, however, remains rather cautious, and they talk of him with evident embarrassment. This does not diminish his stature: he is undoubtedly one of the most brilliant Russian storytellers of the twentieth-century and a Soviet prose-writer of the first magnitude.

8

Vsevolod Ivanov

THE EXUBERANT SIBERIAN

Vsevolod Ivanov's life (1895-1963) is quite as fantastic as some of his stories and yet extremely typical of his own era and generation. He was born on the border of Siberia and Turkestan, into an impoverished family. His mother was half-Polish and half-Mongolian, while his father, the natural son of the Turkestan governor general, dreamt of a university career (he knew seven Oriental languages) but ended up as a workman and village teacher, and an alcoholic too. Vsevolod, deeply affected by his father's misery, gave a pledge not to drink or smoke. As an adolescent, he ran away from the elementary school to perform as a clown in an itinerant circus. He then became a wanderer and was by turns laborer, "sword swallower" at the county fairs, actor, and for a time a traveling fakir Ben Ali Bey. This adventurous existence inspired his first stories, some of them published in local papers, some sent to Gorky who wrote a kind letter to the young author and recommended that he read and learn.

In 1917 Ivanov joined the Red Army, fought in the south-east and went through all sorts of frightening experiences. Later he wrote in his autobiography: "I have traveled the road of death and my only joy is that I am still alive." In 1920 he came to Petrograd and would have perished from cold and starvation had it not been for Gorky's help and encouragement. In the group of Serapion Brethren he found a congenial atmosphere, and met young poets and storytellers whose backgrounds were very similar to his own. His future as a writer was formed by this circle, in which Gorky played the role of literary benefactor and Zamyatin of literary teacher. In the tales he began publishing in 1921 he drew on personal experiences; most of his early works, which made him widely known as one of the pioneers of Soviet prose, dealt with guerrilla warfare—*Partisans* (1921), *Colored Winds* (1922), *Armored Train 14-69* (1922), *Skyblue Sands* (1923)—and various episodes of the civil war as shown in *The Child, The Return of Buddha* (1924), *Exotic Tales* (1925), and later the historical and biographical novels *The Iron Division* and *Parkhomenko* (1938). The first three books established his reputation as a writer. It was greatly enhanced when *Armored Train 14-69* was made into a play and performed with enormous success by the Moscow Art Theater and by numerous companies throughout Russia.

These tales are set in Siberia, Turkestan, and Mongolia, on the borders of China and India, and on the shores of the Pacific. Ivanov's heroes are Kirghiz, Buriats, Chinese, fishermen of the Amour river, nomads of various Turco-Tartar tribes, Russian settlers of the Altai mountains, and peasants of Trans-Baikal steppes. They all move amidst exotic landscapes and fantastic events. Their life is as cruel and primitive as the surrounding nature—"the skies close and warm as wolf pelts"—and all these men and women of unusual physical vigor and of strong but simple emotions are involved in the great drama of the civil war and of the struggle against the interventionists. The fighting is ruthless; the Whites plant a forest of gallows in the towns and villages they overrun, and the Reds slaughter their prisoners or bury them alive. The guerrilla chief, Seleznyov, explains why he kills with such abandon: "Man is dirt. It does not take much either to make him or to undo him." The commissar Vaska Zapus, who whips his wife, rejects all nonsense about the high value of the individual: "Man is like a plant—why feel pity for him?" And even though some of Ivanov's strong men are able to discuss the future of the Revolution and the problems of Communism, their basic philosophy is always the same: "Smite thy neighbor for the sake of the next generation." The intoxication of blood, the fury of annihilation sweep over millions of men, and the Revolution in Asiatic Russia is like a prairie fire. In Ivanov's tale "The Amulet," the Koreans, aroused by the Russians and rising up against the Japanese invaders, drive nails into the heads of enemy soldiers just as coldbloodedly as the latter torture the Koreans. But all this cruelty is thoughtless and elemental. The masses in revolt obey their instincts of hatred and revenge, their impulsive action is similar to an explosion. It is opposed to the calculated "pedagogical" cruelty of Nikitin, a dry logical Bolshevik, who gives orders for murder in a dogmatic inhuman manner. He operates like a tank, destroying men and women in his path as if they were inanimate obstacles.

Ivanov does not draw any conclusions from the scenes of annihilation and carnage. He merely records the revolutionary storm that in Asia had assumed particular violence, and treats the passions of the mob as natural phenomena. This attitude eliminates any trace of sadistic thrill from his descriptions of brutality. Besides, he does not limit the basic drives of his heroes to sheer lust of killing and destroying. He admires their strength and wholeness, their closeness to nature. His men are big and powerful, his women are wide-hipped and full-breasted, all of them are relentless in work, fighting, or love-making. They respect robustness and despise pallor, whether of skin or of passion. Znobov, a partisan leader, is disappointed when he encounters Peklevanov, the chairman of the Communist underground in Vladivostok; he distrusts this narrow-chested, bespectacled, low-voiced proletarian who subsists on dry herring and tea. Znobov's feelings reflect the instinctive antagonism of a peasant for a city dweller. Most of the Red guerrillas are farmers attached to the soil. Earth is their loving mother, they are nourished by her fruits, they get from her all their vigor and wisdom, and when they die "they kiss the earth with the last mortal kiss." In the *Armored Train 14-69*, one of the most representative works of the writer, this philosophy is expressed in the very plot of the short novel (as well as in its dramatic adaptation). Bands of peasant guerrillas encircle the engine of war led by the half-degenerate Nezelasov, a White officer. The train becomes the symbol of the counter-revolution and the hordes of muzhiks represent the movement of popular forces awakened by the march of history. They cannot rationalize or explain their struggle but they feel its universal appeal. The Chinese Sin Bin, who had joined their ranks earlier, sacrifices himself for the cause: he lies across the rails to stop the armored train. And when Vershinin, the patriarchal chief of guerrillas, hears about foreign intervention, he wonders why "the English muzhiks do not stop the sending of arms to the Whites."

In the same way that Ivanov portrays the elemental in the Revolution, he also depicts the mechanism of basic human drives. With the prodigality of a Rubens, he enjoys dealing with the flesh. His most expressive pages are devoted to lust, hunger, revelry, and feasts; his handling of physical elation, as well as of fatigue and illness, is excellent. He is, as a rule, naturalistically vivid in evoking the sensuous aspects of existence; this is an essential part of his originality. He introduced a strident and almost harsh note of sensuality into a literature that, shortly before 1917, had been rather aesthetic and precious. After so many flutes, harps, and violins accompanying tenor arias, his virile basso sounded in counterpoint. His heroes were typical of the new religion of force and resoluteness which was about to become the official credo of the Soviet State. From 1921 to 1927 psychology, introspection, gentility were all scoffed at as the heritage of sloppy intellectualism, and the Communist man was supposed to spurn all this decadent pre-revolutionary culture, and to stress activity, will-power, devotion to the earthly life, and combative spirit. Ivanov's trouble was, however, that he did not accept the ascetic and dogmatic tendencies of intransigent Communists, and glorified carnality instead of rationality, seeing in the Revolution the triumph of instincts rather than of ideology—and this made him suspect.

Ivanov's style went well with his basic tendencies. He wrote in a sweeping, highly ornate manner, wishing to use words and similes that were as emotional as his heroes. His winds are "the wind of meadows, green and flagrant, the wind of the North, icy and blue, the red-bearded angry Russian wind, the purple bronze, tense wind of the battle, the wind in a golden tunic, sleepy, tired wind of the sunset." His soul is like "a carriage at a turn," the hunted armored train is running around, "tossing about like a Chinese dragon." The idiom of his Siberian peasants is filled with arresting regional locutions. His plots are dramatic, the development of action in his tales is surprising, and his descriptions have bright hues. In general, the pattern of Ivanov's prose is as fanciful and vivid as those of a Persian rug. The lyrical often interrupts the narrative, the naturalistic detail is employed as a stylistic device, the Serapion Brethren precept of "making the image fresh and strange" is followed faithfully; all this adds to the general exotic character of Ivanov's tales and novels.

Ivanov was one of the first to write about Asiatic Russia; he was followed by Fadeyev, Leonov, Paustovsky, and many others. His language was also typical of the general trend: in the effort to "democratize" literature and bring it closer to the idiom of the masses, young writers resorted to a host of localisms and regional forms. The proletarians and the fellow-travelers alike were responsible for a veritable eruption of dialectical phrases, of slang, of colloquialisms.

By the end of the 1920's, when Ivanov's reputation was firmly established, he began the unenviable job of revising his own novels and stories, thus yielding to the double pressure of changing times and Communist critics. In reprints (and later in new editions of his collected works) he expurgated most of his naturalistic descriptions of cruelty and physical love. Instead of improving his work, many of these cuts take away his freshness and vigor. It must be said, however, that this watering down of his own writing coincided with the change in Ivanov's literary manner. He felt that human beings ought not to be interpreted solely in terms of reflexes; the unsophisticated, functional men and women who he had, as he said, placed "between the beast and the forest" lost their attraction for him. His style also passed from ornate luxuriousness and impressionistic profusion of color to a more sober and restrained prose. He shifted from the affirmation of physical life and heroic deeds to psychological analysis. Fighters with iron muscles were replaced in his new stories by dreamers crushed by historical events, or by common men who question the meaning of their lives.

In the *Mystery of Mysteries* (1927), a collection of tales, Ivanov wondered whether all the victories for which his mighty partisans had slain and died were really worth all the sacrifices and crimes. He emphasized again the elemental, but from a new angle and pointed to the prevalence of higher human feelings over history and ideology. In one of his stories, a woman spy is captured in the desert of Tuub Koya by Red soldiers, who fall in love with her: they desire her so violently that passion leads all of them to death and perdition. In the same desert a Red commander meets an English agent, and they both discover their human closeness—above nations, parties, and politics. In a later story, "Michael of the Silver Gates" (1929), Ivanov dealt with the struggle between the Reds and the Basmachis (nationalist rebels) in Central Asia, and represented a Soviet officer who has become inordinately attached to Silver Gates, a beautiful horse he has received as a gift from a local khan. But his opposite number, the rebel chief, has a mad desire to own this steed. During an encounter the Red leader is killed; the horse—object of dreams and covetousness—runs away, and the rebel chief, caught in a sand storm, is lost in the desert. The sand blinds and deafens everybody, it buries foe and friend alike, and all things—struggle, passions, love, and hatred—become senseless and futile. The critics censured Ivanov for this note of gloom and he tried to return to an optimistic rendering of Soviet life, but he could never regain the spontaneity and the major key of his early work (except perhaps for *Adventures of a Fakir*, an unfinished autobiographical chronicle published in 1934-35 and hailed by Gorky).

It is obvious that whatever Ivanov wrote in the 'thirties and afterwards was much inferior to his tales and short novels of the civil war. He tried to depict the Five-Year Plan and economic reconstruction (*Tales of Brigadier Sinitzyn*, 1931, *Journey into Never-Never Land*, 1930) but achieved only partial success. His *Parkhomenko* (1937), a glorification of a Red cavalry commander, was much more a romantic legend than an historical narrative, and Ivanov's attempts to join the current school of obedience and conformity resulted in artificiality and false notes. His plays never again reached the level of *Armored Train 14-69* which became a classic in the Soviet repertory, and his war correspondence and the novel *The Seizure of Berlin* (1945) were mediocre. In the years of reaction after the Second World War Ivanov, faithful to the liberal ideals of his youth, remained silent and preserved his independence at the price of retirement from active literary life. Finally in 1953 he published his interesting reminiscences of Gorky, and then later some articles and travelogues. One of the latter, depicting his journey across Eastern Siberia is particularly well written ("Hops or To Meet The Autumn Birds"); it was published in 1962, a few months before his death. None of Ivanov's writings after the 'thirties added anything substantial to his reputation. What he brought into Soviet literature is definitely limited to his early tales and novels. Their physiological plenitude indicated the untapped sources of Russian national strength, and their brightly colored style expressed the initial vitality of post-revolutionary prose. They belong to the 'twenties and represent artistic tendencies that have later been muted or distorted by the impositions and pressures of socialist realism.

9

Evgeny Zamyatin

THE IRONIC DISSIDENT

Two writers exerted a strong influence on post-revolutionary literature between 1918 and 1925. One was Andrey Bely, the symbolist, whose imprint was so obvious in Pilnyak; and the other was Evgeny Zamyatin who spread Remizov's neo-realism and his own brand of expressionism among the younger generation. At the beginning of the Soviet regime Zamyatin occupied a unique position: in his early thirties, he could not be identified with the "fathers" who had been swept away or had emigrated, and at the same time he was above the "children" who looked up to him because of his artistic maturity, brilliant craftsmanship, critical integrity, and independence of judgment. He naturally acted as a master, and a combination of personal and literary qualities made him one of the most original figures of the civil war and NEP era.

Zamyatin was born in 1884 in Lebedyan, a seventeenth-century town of Central Russia. "Lebedyan," he says in his autobiographical sketch, "was famous for its card sharpers, gypsy horse-market fairs, and most forceful Russian language, and Tolstoy and Turgenev wrote about it." The thoroughly national environment of Lebedyan gave Zamyatin an intimate knowledge of provincial Russia. In 1902 he entered the Polytechnic in St. Petersburg, traveled as a student across the country and in the Near East, became involved in politics, joined the Bolshevik faction of the Social Democratic Party, was arrested and sentenced to exile, but succeeded in graduating as a naval engineer in 1908. By this time the designs of a torpedo boat and mathematical charts were mixed on his desk with the sheets of his poems and stories. In 1911 Zamyatin's *Tale of a District*, a description of life in a

Northern province, written in a new sharp manner, suddenly stirred readers and critics; in two months it was being discussed in some three hundred reviews. Three years later his *At the World's End*, a short novel, also attracted general attention. It dealt with the weird happenings in a military garrison located in a god-forsaken town in Eastern Sibéria, and its details were so realistic that nobody believed Zamyatin had never been in the army. The Tsarist authorities sued the author for anti-militarism and subversion.

The two novels, as well as the short stories that followed, were distinctly satirical and attacked the coarseness and brutishness of the lower and middle classes. But their originality lay in the union of a colorful style, ironic observation, and a particular system of images. In each work Zamyatin emphasized a key image, or a "Mother metaphor" (Mirsky), which is used as a visual leitmotif. In the tale "North," Kortoma, a fat, ignorant merchant drinks innumerable tumblers of tea at his samovar—and the curved sides of the copper utensil reflect his face, a distorted ludicrous image; in Kortoma's mind the world is like his own face as mirrored in the samovar: distorted and ugly, and this simile reappears throughout the story. The way Zamyatin treated images corresponded to his carefully planned composition. In his autobiography he mentions his literary beginnings: "In Nikolayev I constructed several bulldozers and a few short stories." A builder of ice-breakers and a professor of ship construction, Zamyatin went about his writing with the spirit of a skilled professional: just as he could not permit any miscalculations in his naval blueprints, he could not overlook any flaws in the composition of his novels, tales, and plays. Whatever he wrote was well-planned, well-proportioned, and smoothly finished. He believed that aesthetic forms were subject to laws—not unlike the laws of physics and hydraulics—and so he demanded thorough organization of material, full control of devices, and a "purposeful selection of words."

Some critics believe that this method imparted a certain detachment and a chilly brilliance to his writings. This could have been true with another writer, but Zamyatin, despite all his external dryness and tongue-in-cheek humor, was a warm and

sensitive person. During World War I he had gone to Great
Britain on a mission to build ice-breakers for Russia, and afterwards friends teased him, contending that English composure was
now added to his innate self-control. Alexander Blok called him
with friendly mockery "the Englishman from Moscow." Lean,
clean-shaven, with reddish hair parted on the side, always wearing
tweeds and with an "unextinguishable" pipe in his wide generous
mouth, he indeed resembled an Englishman. He spoke in an even
voice, hardly changing his inflections when throwing out a sarcastic hint or an ironic allusion; his manners were reserved, and
to those who knew him but little he seemed all "buttoned up," a
man who kept an "unmelting icicle" inside—some hard core of
perfect self-mastery, strong will, and keen intelligence. But this
gentleman was an independent artist and a fearless thinker. He
combined logic and imagination, precision and fantasy. The technician who preached "functional expressionism" and taught young
men how to write a compact, economical prose, was a man of
strong passions. Under his balanced exterior were national traits
of intensity and deep inner life. Like many people with a scientific background, he loved dreams and irrational flights, and
glorified man's desire to overcome all limitations. An enemy of
conventional rules and dogmatic structures he had a romantic
devotion to freedom and individualism and exposed whatever
endangered them. These qualities were expressed with particular
vigor in his *The Islanders* (1917) and "The Fisher of Men." The
first gave an image of provincial British people who are afraid
of Mrs. Grundy and want to exclude "surprising or unexpected
emotions" from a well-patterned routine of respectability. The
vicar Dewly, author of "Precepts of Compulsory Salvation,"
demands that everybody live according to a fixed schedule, which
would indicate days of prayer and repentance, and the precise
times for meals or copulation, for charity or the "intake of fresh
air." Lady Kemble finds the sun "shockingly impudent"; she is
moreover indignant when the faces and habits of the people she
meets are too uncommon. Her son, however, abandons the straight
road, falls in love with a show girl, Didi, and kills the gay unconventional Irishman O'Kelly when it turns out that he is Didi's
lover. The young man is hanged in the courtyard of the local

prison, and everything returns to calm and tradition in the little town. In "The Fisher of Men," Craggs, who speaks of his gains on the stock exchange, actually makes money blackmailing couples who make love in the parks of London. In both tales hypocrisy and mechanical rules are opposed by genuine impulses—open and therefore fatal in young Kemble, hidden and repressed in Lory, Cragg's wife. What made *The Islanders* (as well as other tales written in the 1917-22 period) a model of new literary technique, was not only its compactness and perfect composition, but also the device of significant details and symbolic central images. Young Kemble is like a tractor, he is square, he moves and thinks in straight lines; sudden passion ruins this simple machine. His mother has thin lips, like worms, and the repetition of this comparison serves to delineate her portrait. This stylization gave the works of Zamyatin a structural unity; there was something angular, almost cubistic, in their outlines, and the use of movie-like flashes, of grotesque and ironical dialogue enhanced their theatrical expressionism. In a way Zamyatin's devices were similar to those of modern painting: not only did he render the psychological through the visual, but he also utilized surrealist multiplane composition and symbolic representation of unconscious drives. In his *Flood* (1926), a short novel about a woman suddenly overcome by passion, the emotional awakening is made analogous to the Neva river inundating the banks and islands of Leningrad. The short story "Mamai" (1920) starts with the sentence: "In the evening and at night there are no more houses left in Petersburg: only six-storeyed stone ships." This image is then expanded: "The ships, solitary six-storeyed worlds, scud along the stone waves in the midst of other solitary, six-storeyed worlds; the ships gleam with the lights of numberless cabins into the agitated ocean of streets."

The Islanders was published in 1918, while other tales by Zamyatin, including "North," "The Fisher of Men," "Mamai," and "The Cave," appeared in 1922. In the two latter (as well as in his sketches "The Dragon," 1918, "The Eyes," 1918, and in "The Tale of the Most Essential," 1928), Zamyatin described the initial stage of the Communist regime. He portrayed intellectuals being caught up unaware by the revolutionary hurricane and perishing in the frozen cities like the passengers of a ship sinking at sea (the simile of "Mamai"). For Martin Martynovich, the hero of "The Cave," revolution meant a step backward into pre-history. He subsists in a cavernous icy cold room and sheds all his moral standards in the struggle for existence. He steals wood for his god—an ugly potbellied stove—but cannot endure his degradation, and prefers death to yielding and becoming a barbarian. Soviet critics attacked Zamyatin for concentrating only on the negative sides of contemporary actuality, but the rift between Zamyatin and the rulers of the day was much more profound. The censors were annoyed with every work published by the ironic writer. His *Impious Tales* (collected in a book form in 1927) or *Tales for Adult Children* were filled with malicious hints, as were his other stories which seemed to adhere to Anatole France's slogan: "Teach men to laugh at the stupid and the vicious, less we fall prey to the weakness of hating them." Zamyatin presented Soviet bureaucrats as narrow-minded replicas or Tsarist officials; they try to solve all problems, including disasters and epidemics, by posting decrees and regulations ("Famine is strictly forbidden," "Cholera is hereby officially proscribed"). One of Zamyatin's stories dealt with the adventures of a deacon who joined the Bolsheviks and wanted to study Marx, but since at the same time he was in love with a pretty girl called Martha, he was torn between Marthism and Marxism.

Communist critics found most irritating the fact that along with his satirical sketches Zamyatin wrote serious articles claiming that his verbal and compositional experiments were closer to the spirit of the Revolution than the naturalistic snapshots of proletarian writers. His concept of the Revolution did not coincide with current formulas. "When two extinguished stars collide with a deafening crash we do not hear and ignite a new star —that is revolution. When Lobachevsky [the Russian mathematical genius] crumbles with his book the walls of the millennial Euclidean world and opens a path into numberless non-Euclidean space, that is revolution. Revolution is everywhere, in everything; it is infinite; the last revolution, the last number does not exist. Social revolution is just one of innumerable numbers: its law is not a social law but an immeasurably greater one—

universal, cosmic, similar to that of entropy, of the conservation
and disintegration of energy." What he saw around him stirred
him to indignation: he could not call revolution the regimentation
and cruelty of a government that was becoming more and more
abusive. "Dogma," said Zamyatin, "is the hard crust which im-
prisons the fiery magma, that molten material from which the
hard rock is formed." A former Socialist, he saw Communists
becoming dogmatic authoritarians who ruled by oppression and
executions and as replacing Tsarist autocracy with Marxist ideocracy. Zamyatin could not accept despotism and pretense, and
with all the idealism of a humanitarian intellectual and the devastating irony of a temperamental artist, he fought for the rights
of freedom and reason. In his *Fires of St. Dominic* (1922), a historical drama probably inspired by Dostoevsky's *Legend of the
Grand Inquisitor*, he portrayed the Spanish Inquisition, and under
this thin disguise, attacked the Communist terror and the "righteous puritans of the Revolution" who were killing men in order
to save mankind.

Zamyatin's articles exposed what he called false art dominated
by frisky, sly individuals who knew when to sing hymns to the
Tsar and when to the hammer and sickle. "True literature," proclaimed Zamyatin, "can be created only by madmen, hermits,
heretics, dreamers, rebels, sceptics, and not by efficient and loyal
functionaries ... I am afraid we won't have true literature unless
we are cured of some kind of new catholicism which gets frightened by any heretical word. And if this illness is incurable, I am
afraid Russian literature will have but one future: its past" (1921).
He laughed at the attempts of proletarian writers to bring about
a "new literature" which he dubbed as a "retreat to the 'sixties of
the last century." When the extremists demanded "party art" and
threatened the non-conformists with repressive measures, Zamyatin defined *October*, the monthly which made the most vicious
attacks against "bourgeois writers," as "a periodical which has
to do only with one of all the arts: with the military art; its
writing is simply a new weapon, in addition to well known mines
and gas bombs." Obviously, such "repartees" created what Zamyatin called "negative popularity": he was singled out by the
Party press as a dangerous subversive. His dissonant voice, how-

ever, was heard far and wide. Zamyatin became a leading figure in Petrograd (and later Leningrad) literary circles; he founded various, and usually short-lived, periodicals, he gave courses and conferences, and he taught techniques of fiction in the "House of Art" to the group of Serapion Brethren. Among those who felt strongly his influence and were to a certain extent his disciples were Vsevolod Ivanov, Konstantin Fedin, Nikolay Nikitin, Mikhail Zoshchenko, Venyamin Kaverin, Yefim Zozulya, Mikhail Slonimsky, Yuri Olesha, and many others. Later Zamyatin said with his usual grin: "I taught them how to write with ninety proof ink." There was a moment when it looked as if Zamyatin would become the head of a whole literary school. He contended that literature was also subject to the laws of dialectics and that from the opposition of naturalism (thesis) and symbolism (antithesis) a new trend had been born, the synthesis of the first two. This neo-realism, or expressionism, he wrote, was legal heir of the past. But Zamyatin's own literary activity was soon curtailed. Branded as an enemy of the regime, Zamyatin endured arrest, persecution, and vituperation, particularly toward the end of the 'twenties. The Communist press offensive against him reached its peak in 1929 because of the publication abroad of his novel *We*.

In 1920 Zamyatin had felt that Communist society might degenerate into an ant heap, into a new, planned, and inescapable state slavery; in this mood he wrote *We*, a satirical picture of a collectivistic utopian city from which individuality and freedom are excluded. The city is roofed over with glass to avoid the intemperate freaks of weather and the insubordination of the climate; the inhabitants are designated by numerals and letters (vowels for females and consonants for males); they wear gray-blue uniforms; their work, thought, and leisure are regulated by the "wise authorities" headed by the Well-Doer or Benefactor; and they can make love only on days and at hours strictly prescribed and designated on special pink tickets issued by government agencies. The houses are of glass and therefore transparent, so the police can see what is going on in each dwelling; microphones pick up conversations; mechanical "eyes" and "ears" are erected in the streets, and the behavior and utterances of all citizens are watched and recorded from the cradle to the grave; electrocution takes care of the few rebels. One of these, D-503, a mathematician and builder of the Integral, a cosmic ship, dares to challenge the Bureau of Guardians and its Day of Unanimity: he commits the crimes of free thought and true love, at one point taking his mistress beyond the Green Wall that separates the city from unadulterated nature, from uncontrolled plants, animals, and menlike beings. But his attempt at revolt is duly liquidated: D-503 undergoes the Great Operation which makes him betray all other Enemies of Happiness and deliver his beloved to the Executors. Reason wins out, and the numbers are isolated from the world of chaos and improvisation by a new high-voltage fence. In *We* Zamyatin again emphasizes the opposition of mechanical rationalism and natural instincts of being. This is one of his main themes: the natural man, with all the variety of his emotions and capacities, with all his glow of imagination and thirst for infinity, is bound to clash with dogmatics, builders of robots and prisons, and with artifical regulations and limitations. Parenthetically, it may be mentioned that *We* was published in English in 1924, thus preceding a score of amazingly similar works by Aldous Huxley, George Orwell, and other social satirists.

Publication of *We* in the Soviet Union was, of course, impossible, but Zamyatin read it at one of the meetings of the Writers' Union in 1924. It went around in manuscript copies, and several Soviet authors referred to it as "one of the most earnest and jocular works Zamyatin ever wrote." In 1927 *We* was about to be translated into Czech, this writer who at that time was the literary editor of *Volia Rossii*, an *émigré* monthly in Prague, got hold of the Russian manuscript of the novel and printed it in his monthly. The introductory note preceding the text stated that this was a re-translation into Russian from the Czech, and to give weight to this assertion the editor had to change or distort Zamyatin's beautiful prose. The subterfuge, however, did not work. The Communist press, which had not paid much attention five years before to the appearance of *We* in English, this time accused its author of impudently challenging the authorities. Dubbed a counter-revolutionary, Zamyatin was compelled to resign from professional organizations and was completely ostracized. Soviet periodicals refused to print one line of the great criminal, the publication of his collected works in several volumes was suspended, and *The Fly*, a comedy Zamyatin adapted from a tale by Leskov, was banned from the theaters despite its huge success with hundreds of performances. As he said later, he became "the Devil of Soviet literature, and since to spit on the Devil is considered a good deed, all the critics did nothing but spit on me as viciously as they could." This sentence was part of a letter Zamyatin addressed to Stalin in 1931 asking for permission to go abroad and "to rest awhile from baiting and persecution." This message to the General Secretary of the Party (never divulged in the Soviet Union) reflected its author's rectitude, courage, and dignity. "I know," Zamyatin wrote, "that I have a very uncomfortable habit of saying not what seems most advantageous at this particular moment or that, but whatever I believe is the truth. Among other things I have never concealed what I think about literary servility, obsequiousness, and turning one's coat. I have always thought, and I continue to think, that such things are as humiliating to the writers as they are to the Revolution . . . I have been sentenced without trial to what amounts, for a writer, to capital punishment—silence . . . I beg that I be allowed to go abroad for a time—so that I may come home as soon as it is possible in our literature to express devotion to great ideas without crawling before small men, and as soon as our attitude toward the artist of the word changes." Thanks to Gorky's intervention, the authorization to leave Russia, was, to the general surprise, granted to Zamyatin and his wife five months later. In 1932 they settled in Paris. He wrote a few stories and scenarios, made a successful film with Jean Renoir of Gorky's *The Lower Depth*, and finished the first part of *Attila*, a historical novel in which the fall of the Roman Empire was described with many concealed references to the current European scene. His health, however, undermined by privations and by the nervous tension under which he lived for years, declined rapidly, and he died of a heart ailment in March 1937. No obituaries in the Soviet press marked his passing; his former friends and disciples were afraid to send their condolences to his widow. The official silence which isolated Zamyatin from Russian readers during his lifetime continued after his death. It lasted twenty-five years—and while it is being broken now in some critical circles, the works of this brilliant writer are still banned in his native land, and no surveys of Soviet literature dare to give a fair appraisal of the role he played in contemporary Russian prose.

The main impact of Zamyatin in the 'twenties was that of a master who had trained a new generation in craftsmanship. He also was a satirist and the head of that brand of neo-realism closest to European expressionism. His enemies called him a formalist: he actually was a literary professional who loved to experiment in words and plots but put above everything "a well-made story." The reason he provoked such deep antagonism in the Soviet press was due, probably, to the fact that he jeered and laughed when writers were required to sing "hosannah." Moreover, he was a liberal and a socialist, who maintained the best traditions of the Russian intelligentsia, and could not accept a new regime divorced from individual freedom. To a great extent Zamyatin and his friends carried on the ideology of the Russian non-Communist left, and this was why they were so badly treated. Communist dogmatics knew that monarchists and reactionaries represented a lost cause and that the real threat to the dictatorship could come only from traditional Russian socialism, which expressed the dreams of the masses. It was this potential danger that determined the intransigent attitude toward, and the ostracism of, Zamyatin. But the day is not far off, when, regardless of political struggle, new Russian readers will value Zamyatin as an excellent and truly independent writer.

10

Mikhail Zoshchenko

THE CONDEMNED HUMORIST

Mikhail Zoshchenko was born in 1895 into a noble family of Ukrainian extraction. His father was devoted to painting and passed on his artistic gift to his son. After the usual classical education, Zoshchenko joined the army in 1914, was wounded and gassed, won awards and medals, and finished the war as a lieutenant in the regiment of the Caucasian Grenadiers. He contended that by this time his health was completely ruined. One should not, however, put too much faith in this statement. Zoshchenko was suffering not only from real but also from imaginary illnesses and kept going to doctors and discovering in himself all sorts of ailments. Like many humorists, he had a sad countenance, was afflicted by fits of anxiety, and wandered around as if he were running away from his own shadow. Despite his reserved manners and slow, controlled speech, this small young man with regular features and dark thoughtful eyes was extremely nervous and impressionable.

Between 1917 and 1920 Zoshchenko lived in twelve different cities and took up ten different professions; he served in the Red Army and in the militia, was an employee of the telephone company and of the Police Criminal Investigation Department, hunted wild animals in the North, and worked on fruit plantations in the South. He used to say that his jobs ranged "from shoemaker's apprentice to stage actor." In 1921, however, he settled in Petrograd and devoted himself to writing. Member of the Serapion Brethren and a disciple of Zamyatin, he followed the humoristic and satirical trend so highly appreciated at that time by his literary companions. In a comparatively short while he had attained enormous popularity.

In *The Tales by Nazar Ilich Sinebryukhov* (1922), a book that launched Zoshchenko into fame, comic happenings continually verge on the grotesque. Corporal Sinebryukhov (Blue Belly), the narrator, is attracted by "high life," titled women, and refined manners—and when Communism does away with all this nonsense he becomes involved in most unbelievable situations. He undergoes privations and humiliations in order to amass paper money, which the Revolution makes completely valueless; he has a narrow escape from bandits, and in his turn becomes a highwayman—all for the sake of destitute aristocrats and of Victoria, the beautiful and noble Polish lady. Eventually, it comes out that she is neither noble nor virtuous, and not even as pretty as the corporal had imagined her.

In giving a full report of his bad luck, Sinebryukhov talks in the absurd idiom of the half-educated, mixing popular speech with journalese or mangled bookish terms. Zoshchenko, continuing Leskov's and Zamyatin's tradition, made this language his specialty. The *skaz* (colloquial tale in the first person) style which Zamyatin almost invariably used reproduced in an exaggerated fashion the slang of the lower-middle class and of the city periphery. Zoshchenko employed it in all his work, and it was tagged "Zoshchenko language." Essentially it is a combination of several linguistic levels, and its incongruity leads to comic effects, similar to those produced by Damon Runyon's Broadway guys and by certain characters of Ring Lardner. "It is usually maintained," Zoshchenko remarks in his *Letters to a Writer*, "that I am mutilating the beautiful Russian language, that I employ words not in their rightful meaning ... with the intention of provoking belly laughs, but all that is erroneous. I hardly twist anything: I write the same language in which the man in the street thinks and talks." Zoshchenko could add that the linguistic distortions of these men in the street simply reflected their mental confusion.

In the hundreds of short stories that Zoshchenko wrote in the 'twenties and 'thirties, the peculiarities of the idiom were matched by the grotesqueness of plot. The design of each story is clearly delineated and is almost on the verge of implausibility even though it is based on perfectly realistic incidents: for instance, members of a house committee deny the deficiency of the chimney flue and do not yield even when they collapse in the smoke-filled room. This technique of parallel incongruities in the language and in the subject matter forms the essence of Zoshchenko's humor. Its satirical intention is quite apparent: the writer wanted to castigate the negative aspects of Soviet life—by reflecting them in the convex mirror of exaggeration and absurdity. He reveals the ruts and rot of daily existence with its vulgarity and stupidity behind the facade of magnificent slogans. Reading his stories is like stepping from the orchestra of a theater from which the stage appears crowded with heroes and banners, into the wings where stage hands and spear-carriers curse and spit amid rubbish and coarsely daubed canvas. Zoshchenko's protagonist is the philistine, the ignorant citizen who uses a badly digested Communist phraseology but remains avaricious, competitive, and narrow-minded. He is entangled in a web of trivial mishaps to which he attaches great importance: the bus conductor has short-changed him, and the resultant squabble ends in a free-for-all; a pannikin of milk boils over in the communal kitchen, and half a dozen housewives go on the warpath; some office messengers hang about to watch a street fight, and an entire institution has to suspend work. All the characters in Zoshchenko's gallery are full of prejudices and superstitions: sentimental, guitar-strumming telegraph operators who try to speak in "elevated" style ("and from what ailment did she croak if I may ask such an indiscreet question?"); "progressive minded" bridegrooms who won't marry unless the beloved bride brings a good chest of drawers into the new household; the smug clerks whose clothes are stolen at the public bath; featherbrained girls who suddenly become quite resourceful when trying to hook a desirable bachelor. The dramatic personages of this Soviet comedy of manners are drowning in a swamp of poverty, fraud, selfishness, and vulgarity; one of their common traits is the complete lack of form and measure. They are aesthetically blind and deaf; and the incapacity to express what little humanity is hidden in them leads to a kind of dumbness. They do not speak, they mumble, their words are approximations, they can hardly express their fuzzy, often chaotic emotions, and their linguistic primitivism betrays their intellectual deficiency.

Zoshchenko's satire deals with the humdrum person, with that mean, narrow-minded, lower-middle-class citizen the Russians always called *meshchanin*: the derivative *meshchanstvo* designates a social phenomenon, a collection of all the negative traits that makes the philistine what he is. Alexander Herzen in the 1840's defined *meshchanstvo* as the "intellectual and moral scantiness and dullness of small folk, who are smug and ignorant, brutish and vulgar." From Gogol to Saltykov-Shchedrin and Chekhov, Russian writers kept exposing *meshchanstvo* in all its guises.

Zoshchenko's heroes are representative of the Soviet *meshchanstvo*. They prove that social and political changes have hardly touched the mind and soul of the *meshchanin*. The "average monstrosities" introduced in Zoshchenko's tales were not unusual, they were profoundly rooted in Russian reality. Thus despite all the exaggerations and the grotesqueness, readers of Zoshchenko's anecdotes never doubted their essential veracity. And this was the true reason for his rise and fall.

In 1922-25 when his stories were being read by thousands and were included in the repertory of all Soviet stage reciters, Zoshchenko was trying his hand at a different genre. Almost in a Chekhovian melancholy mood he wrote short novels about men crushed by life and history. The hero of his *Wisdom* (1924) talks enthusiastically about the splendor and charm of existence, but an absurd death cuts off his dreaming. Other tales, such as *Apollo and Tamara* (1923) and *Frightening Night* (1925), are definitely gloomy, and many later writings, despite their evident flavor of parody, are also pessimistic. It is clear that the author has a very poor opinion of his fellow men and is moreover convinced that our fate depends on chance and senseless coincidences. Zoshchenko's philosophy is quite simple: man's existence is regulated not by the laws of dialectical materialism, or by the balance of justice, or by divine recompense of virtues, but by accident and surprise, by the play of trial and error, by absurdity and silliness. We always fail and lose, or make fools of ourselves. All of Zoshchenko's best stories hinge on mistakes and frustration, and some of them are blunt parodies of the "happy endings" (*What the Nightingale Sang Of; Gay Adventure*, 1926).

Like so many storytellers who are reproached for the topical

and fragmentary nature of their work, Zoshchenko always aspired
to longer literary forms than the mere tale. In 1934, abandoning
all pretense of writing a novel, he collected in *The Pale-Blue
Book*, dedicated to Gorky, all sorts of historical, or rather pseudo-
historical, anecdotes about great events, famous figures, love,
money, and perfidy. In *Restored Youth*, which has more unity,
the hero is an old professor who has been successful in his attempts
at rejuvenation, but when he marries a young girl he has so much
trouble with her that he suffers a stroke and has to renounce any
restoration of youth. Zoshchenko was proud that some Soviet
scientists took his fantasy quite seriously, for he loved to talk
about physiology and gerontology; his *Restored Youth* was a
parody of science in the same way that *The Pale-Blue Book* was
a parody of history.

Zoshchenko's production was partially dictated by the needs of
self-defense. When the fellow-travelers were investigated by On
Guardists in the 'thirties, the question was raised about whether
Zoshchenko's satire was as innocent as it seemed. Did he not allow
himself too much leeway in depicting the average Soviet citizen
as a man of the past saddled with all the vices that, according
to the letter of the dogma, were the exclusive attributes of the
bourgeoisie? Was not his jeering actually directed against the
newly risen man of the people? After all, the Revolution was supposed to have swept away the lower middle class, and Zoshchenko
kept talking about its predominance in the new society. Moreover, the fact that he was enjoyed so much by the Russian *émigrés*
also appeared highly suspicious. For some time, Zoshchenko kept
on with his topical stories, creating new variants of his own protagonists. But Communist critics frowned on his humor: it lacked,
they declared, the social and ideological background. And when
in the middle 'thirties, with the compulsory introduction of socialist realism, writers were compelled to "portray positive heroes
and the progress of the movement toward Communism," his
laughter jarred in the "halleluia" chorus of obsequious conform-
ists. Zoshchenko was painfully affected by the criticisms which
came from the Party. He understood the warning and tried to
become "attuned to the current times." Although his political
convictions had never been very strong, he made a sincere at-

tempt to bring in new themes and to broaden the range of his satire. He wrote a pseudo-historical lampoon on Kerensky (1938), "Tales of Lenin" for adolescents, and a score of more neutral stories (such as *The Black Prince*—about the cargo of gold sunk in 1865 on the Crimean shores). But all these pledges of loyalty sounded false; the same is true of his stories about thieves morally regenerated by their work on the White Sea canal (constructed by inmates of camps and prisons), and of his later tales about anti-Hitler guerrillas.

None of these mediocre writings was of any help. His reputation, already undermined in the late 'thirties, declined in high Party circles during and immediately after the war with Germany. Even though he was awarded a medal for the defense of Leningrad, he was evacuated to Turkestan in 1943, and was accused by his foes of a "poor showing of patriotic feelings." The same year he started serializing in the monthly *October* his new work *Before the Sunrise,* which consisted of episodes, anecdotes, and reminiscences. It was an attempt at an autobigraphy or confession, in which he analyzed the hidden roots of his grief and melancholy. The aim of the book was partly therapeutic: by uncovering the true motivation of his complexes, Zoshchenko hoped to overcome them and to reach an inner harmony. The book had to show "how I got rid of many sorrows and became happy," as it was fitting for the life-affirming Soviet citizen to do. The readers, unfortunately, were not allowed to learn by what means the author attained happiness: after two installments publication of Zoshchenko's new work was suspended, and the editorial board of *October* made a public apology for having passed such "individualistic and petty bourgeois" fiction and thus having committed a "serious ideological error." Communist critics branded Zoshchenko as a "pernicious Freudian," for they were indignant that a writer dared to delve into his personal mannerisms while his companions were glorifying the heroic defense of the fatherland and helping to build up the morale of the people. Descriptions of fear, sex, shyness, and melancholy, which were the main topics of *Before the Sunrise,* were declared pathological and alien to the spirit of the epoch, and Zoshchenko's attempt to explain human conduct in terms of psychological motivation and unconscious drives, instead of social and economic conditioning, was dubbed "socially harmful." Some Communist critics called Zoshchenko "a brainless and pornographic scribbler."

Despite all these blows, immediately after the war Zoshchenko continued to play an important role in Leningrad literary organizations, and his popularity with the public was still very high. In 1946 a low-priced collection of his latest stories was issued in a first printing of 100,000 copies. It included "The Adventures of an Ape" which showed Soviet citizens as gossipy and vulgar half-wits. A few weeks later the Central Committee of the Communist Party voted a resolution against the monthlies *Zvezda* (Star) and *Leningrad*, in which it singled out poems of Akhmatova and stories by Zoshchenko as examples of "disintegration and decadence." Andrey Zhdanov, a member of the Politbureau, in announcing the tightening of controls over literature branded "The Adventures of an Ape" a "disgusting calumny on the Soviet People." As an enemy of the masses, a "cosmopolitan," a "lackey of reaction," an "apostate," and, finally, as a "corrupt literary bum," Zoshchenko was expelled from the Union of Soviet Writers. Later he was allowed to publish a few sketches in periodicals but they were pale and insignificant. Zoshchenko apparently never got over his literary execution. He was mortally wounded and ceased to exist as a writer and artist long before his physical end. He died in 1958, but there was no comment from the Soviet press. The same year, however, a censored selection of his stories was published in a printing of 30,000 copies; they sold out so quickly that a reprint had to be made in 1959. Those were the only editions of Zoshchenko's works in twelve years. He has not been rehabilitated officially probably because he was not "repressed" formally, and for some reason literary surveys of the late 'fifties and early 'sixties never devote more than a few perfunctory lines to his writing. Communist critics apparently refuse to acknowledge that with the exception of such writers as Ilf and Petrov and a few "guests," Zoshchenko is the only fully-fledged humorist of Soviet literature—from its beginning to the present day. His sketches still form a telling satirical document of the post-revolutionary era and a significant realistic exposé of Soviet society.

11

The Serapion Brethren, The Pass, and The Oberiuts

In the winter of 1921, when political pressures were very strong and debates about proletarian literature became rather heated, a few young men, most of them demobilized from the Red Army, gathered in Petrograd under the patronage of Zamyatin and Gorky. Petrograd (renamed Leningrad in 1924) was at that time a city of desolation, swept by blizzards and in the grip of sub-zero frosts; the trolleys were not running, and the young writers had to walk miles in order to attend meetings at the House of Art or in somebody's private quarters. Their shoes were usually broken, their coats torn or too light; most of them were chronically hungry and in poor health, but they would not have missed for anything the evening sessions where they could read their works and discuss aesthetic problems with a few craftsmen of the older generation.

These young men at last formed a group which called itself the Serapion Brethren: they were all great admirers of E.T.A. Hoffmann, the German Romantic (1776-1822), and took the vow of one of his heroes, a count and diplomat who renounces his career and, believing in the power of imagination to conquer time and space, asserts that he is Serapion, a saintly man who lived in Egypt under the Roman Emperors; then he himself became a hermit. When his contemporaries, several former schoolmates, decide to gather regularly to exchange strange stories in the atmosphere of artistic freedom and independence, they elect him as their patron and collectively assume his name. Their stories form six volumes entitled *The Serapion Brethren* in Hoffmann's collected works.

Most of the Russian Serapions were prose writers; of the founder-members, only two, Tikhonov and Polonskaya (the only Sister of the group), were poets, and Shklovsky and Gruzdev were literary critics. The majority of them were in their mid-twenties —Ivanov, Zoshchenko, Nikitin, Slonimsky; Kaverin and Lunz were 20, and Pozner was 18.* The novelist Fedin, the senior member of the group, was 30. This meant that, in general, they had received their education before the Revolution but had not had the time or opportunity to begin their literary careers. Other young men and women of approximately the same age gravitated toward the group. What united them was a common yearning for freedom of expression, a certain romantic mood, and a keen interest in stylistic and compositional experimentation. They all welcomed the Revolution and wrote about it, but they refused to be told what and how to write.

"In February 1921," a member of the group has written, "at a time of sumptuary legislation and barrack-room regimentation, when a single dreary and iron rule was applied to all, we decided to meet without rules and chairmen, without elections or votes. We came together in the days of great revolutionary and political tension. Whoever is not with us is against us: so we were told on all sides. On whose side are you, you Serapion Brethren? With the Communists or against the Communists? For or against the Revolution? On whose side are we, Serapion Brethren? We are on the side of the hermit Serapion."

The stress on the formal and technical aspects of art, the assertion of the poet's right to dreams and fancy, the resistance to vulgar social command—all were expressed in the manifesto of the group: "We have called ourselves the Serapion Brethren because we object to coercion and boredom, and because we object to everybody writing in the same way ... Each of us has his own drum. We think that present-day Russian literature is amazingly prim, smug, and monotonous. We are allowed to write stories, novels, and conforming dramas ... provided they are social in content and inevitably on contemporary themes. We demand but one thing: that a work of art be organic and authentic, and that it live its own peculiar life." And Nikitin added: "An artist should not be required to be a social seismograph, this is not the main aim of art, a writer has his own ear, his own particular form

*Vladimir Pozner later went to Paris, where he became a member of the French Communist Party, and wrote fiction and essays in French.

of play." The manifesto was signed by Lev Lunz (1901-24), a highly promising author of short stories and two interesting tragedies, whose works first appeared in the magazine *Literary Notes* and later in the *Serapion Brethren Anthology* (1922) to which Zoshchenko, Kaverin, Fedin, Slonimsky, and Nikitin contributed their stories, and Tikhonov and Polonskaya their poems.

Despite their rejection of political interference, all the Brethren were sons of the Revolution, who had accepted it and taken part in it. At the age of twenty-six, Zoshchenko summed up his experiences in these vital statistics: "Arrested six times, sentenced to death once, wounded three times, attempted suicide twice, beaten up three times." Others such as Vsevolod Ivanov and Tikhonov had also battled against the Whites, had endured privations, had been frequently exposed to death, and had followed dozens of trades in their desperate struggle for survival. All of them may be described as fellow-travelers and as sympathetic to the general aims of Communism—establishment of a classless, collectivistic society—although at that time none of them was a member of the Party. They all wrote about the civil war and the Revolution—it was they, in fact, who had disseminated these themes in Soviet prose—but they firmly believed that young writers ought to carry on pre-revolutionary aesthetic trends. Their opinions varied widely, and they favored and cherished this diversity. Some of them were staunch Westerners—Lunz called one of his articles "Go West"—and they were instrumental in making popularly known several European and American writers. Lunz (and to an extent Zamyatin) suggested that the Russians might learn from the West the art of plot construction and dynamic narrative, and he wanted to stress the elements of drama and suspense. Fedin also showed this Western influence, but other Serapion Brethren, such as Ivanov and Nikitin, were more inclined to follow the national tradition expressed in the Writers of the Soil group.

As disciples of Zamyatin, the Serapions had in common with him a concern for literary craftsmanship. Techniques and devices seemed to absorb them much more than problems of ideology. Their main contributions lay in stylistic inventiveness, fantasy, and the presentation of the happenings of the Revolution in an individual, often fanciful manner. Each of them occupied a unique place: Fedin was foremost in the revival of the novel, continuing in the nineteenth-century realistic tradition; Vsevolod Ivanov's ornamental prose represented the regional and Asiatic trend named "Eurasian" by the Russian *émigrés;* Zoshchenko as a humorist continued the satirical vein initiated by Zamyatin; Tikhonov, at first the poet of virility in Gumilev's vein, later came under Pasternak's influence yet, at the same time, was strongly attracted by the exotic. Most of the members of the group experimented with complex plots, story structure, and original endings (they found O. Henry's final twists to their liking). Fedin did it in his novels, Nikitin in his tales, Kaverin in all of his work.

Nikolay Nikitin (1897-1963) was close to Pilnyak in his interpretation of the Revolution. His tales dealing with the civil war in the north of Russia (*Fort Vomit,* 1922, *Stones,* 1923, *The Flight,* 1925, *Tales of Oboyansk,* 1926) combined romantic emotionalism, fragmentary composition, and an ornate rhythmic prose studded with lyrical digressions and folklore images. What happened to Nikitin is typical of many writers of his generation; under pressure from the outside, they gradually shed their bright colors and wrote more soberly, more conventionally, often trying to conform to the style and spirit of socialist realism. Nikitin's *Kirik Rudenko's Crime* (1927), a novel describing the ethical problems of the Communist youth, and the play *Baku* (1937) dealing with socialist reconstruction, were examples of his literary decline. His long novel *Aurora Borealis* (1951), a dramatic picture of the British intervention in Murmansk and Archangel in 1919 with some flashes reminiscent of his daring youth, and *The Third Alley* (1963), a novel of the post-war generation, did little to enhance his reputation.

Mikhail Slonimsky (1897-1972), less talented and less original than Nikitin, first wrote impressionistic stories, which had a freshness and promise ("The Actress," "Emery's Death Machine," 1924), and went on to old-fashioned, honest but plodding chronicles about intellectuals striving to adjust themselves to a socialist society (*The Lavrovs,* 1927, *Foma Kleshnyov,* 1931), and about Bolsheviks in administrative and industrial jobs (*The Chairman of the Town Soviet*, 1943). His *Engineers* (1950), an evocation of St. Petersburg in 1913, is marred by an artificial anti-Western bias.

More consistent was the career of Venyamin Kaverin (pen name of V. Zilberg, b.1902). His early stories—"Masters and Apprentices" (1923), "Nine Tenths of Fate" (1926), and "The End of Khasa," a colorful description of the underworld during the NEP period—all bore the imprint of romantic fantasy in Hoffmann's manner. Kaverin's interest in an exciting plot is fully shown in his novels devoted to Leningrad intellectuals: *The Brawler or The Evenings on Vassily Island* (1928), depicting academic circles; *Artist Unknown* (1931), a successful psychological exploration of the creative personality and its moral problems in a socialist society; and *The Fulfillment of Desires* (1936), which united an amusing intrigue with sketches of students and rather transparent portraits of well-known scholars. When writers were required to paint heroic canvases, Kaverin met the demand without sacrificing his artistic integrity and wrote *Two Captains* (1940-44), an exciting adventure tale of an Arctic pre-revolutionary sea expedition, full of plots, conspiracies, and secrets, and containing a post-revolutionary solution to all the riddles. Although it is one of the most beloved Soviet books for adolescents, it was also greatly enjoyed by adults. His war stories differed from the usual both in topic and tonality: in "The Seven Pairs of Impure" he tells of convicts' struggles to acquire the right to die for their country, and in "Oblique Rain" he renders the general atmosphere of diffidence and fear under Stalin. *In Front of the Mirror* (1971), a quite daring and unusual novel in the form of a correspondence between a Soviet scholar and a woman painter who emigrates to Paris and meets Russian expatriates (among them the poet Marina Tsvetayeva and the artist Natalia Goncharova), as she is searching for freedom of expression and genuine love. In his trilogy *The Open Book* (*The Open Book*, 1949, *Doctor Vlasenkova*, 1952, *Search and Hope*, 1957) Kaverin evoked the life of provincial Russia on the eve of the Revolution, and then led his heroine, the future Dr. Vlasenkova, through medical school to the feuds and intrigues of scholars and scientific bureaucrats. After this long chronicle Kaverin reverted to reminiscences and wrote amusing and moving pages on his own childhood and adolescence, particularly the autobiographical *The Illuminated Windows* (1974).

Kaverin personified the close connection between the Serapions and the formalistic current in literary criticism. In the same way, Victor Shklovsky (b.1893), a caustic and paradoxical critic, author of several controversial books of essays and memoirs (*A Sentimental Journey*, 1923; *Zoo or Letters not about Love*, 1923; *The Third Factory*, 1926; *Hamburg's Accounts*, 1928) was simultaneously a member of the Serapion fraternity and a promoter of the formalist theory which had been developed mostly by the founders of The Society for Study of Poetic Language (1914-23). This disciple of Laurence Sterne, Rozanov, and of St. Petersburg philologists contended that the use of new words and devices was an organic part of literary art; the aritist's aim was to rediscover reality by transforming familiar associations into strange and fresh ones. Only by this process of continuous rejuvenation of method and style could the reform of an old literature be achieved. In 1924 Boris Eichenbaum, one of the formalist theoreticians and a prominent literary scholar, wrote: "Marxism does not secure by itself a revolutionary position in astronomy or art. Within the limits of literary science, formalism is a revolutionary movement insofar as it liberates this discipline from old worn-out traditions and compels it to re-examine all the basic concepts and schemes." Shklovsky expressed the same point of view in his *About the Theory of Prose* (1925) and *The Technique of the Writer's Craft* (1928). Young fellow-travelers, and particularly the Serapion Brethren, were strongly attracted by Shklovsky's aggressive and highly challenging interpretation of literature. Later Shklovsky joined Mayakovsky's new LEF and fought for the elimination of any fiction except that "of facts." From what he called factography he went on to a revision of his former opinions, disowning them as "Youthful mistakes and exaggerations," and professed an unexpected interest in the sociological method (already indicated in his work on Tolstoy in the 'forties). His memoirs, serialized in 1962, are nevertheless written in his customary caustic style and give a vivid picture of the 'twenties.

The range of the Serapion's influence was not limited to the actual members of the fraternity. Such different writers as Yury Olesha and Yefim Zozulya, Leonid Leonov and Mikhail Bulgakov, Pyotr Pavlenko and Valentin Katayev were either close to the Brethren or felt the impact of their position. As a matter of fact almost all the leading Soviet novelists and short storytellers either belonged to the Brethren or were connected with them. This was more or less recognized in the 'twenties, but already in the 'thirties and particularly in the 'forties when the general attack against formalism, literary innovators, and, later on, against Westernism was launched, Communist critics declared that the Serapion Brethren had taken a sidetrack far removed from the main road of Soviet letters, that their role was grossly exaggerated, and that they represented a bourgeois mentality. The Serapions's claim to artistic independence was qualified as a mere "manifestation of a decadent theory of art for art's sake." When Fedin dared to write in his *Gorky in Our Midst* (1943) that "the Serapion Brethren are not going to be passed over in silence in the history of literature," his statement was challenged as "problematic and unwarranted." Official recognition of the fact that the Serapion Brethren stand at the very gates of Soviet literature, as its initiators and talented exponents, has not yet been made, and one would look for it in vain in the text books.

Another interesting group of the 'twenties was The Pass under the guidance of Alexander Voronsky, the prominent Communist critic and the editor of *Krasnaya Nov'*, the monthly that had become the meeting place of fellow-travelers. Voronsky shared Trotsky's thesis that there was no proletarian art in Russia and that its emergence was impossible until the creation of adequate material and cultural conditions was achieved. The present day's job was not to chase shadows but to absorb the literature of the past. Moreover, Voronsky questioned the role of ideology in art, and attached great importance to impressions, intuitions, and unconscious feelings as factors of the creative process. In his two volumes of literary portraits he analyzed the work of his contemporaries with sympathy and insight, revealing both understanding and a love of literature and his own talent as a writer. Arrested and exiled in 1927 as a partisan of Trotsky, he was expelled from the Party. A few years later he was allowed to return to the capital and to resume literary activities, but during the purges of the late 'thirties he again fell victim of the secret police—this time never to re-appear in Moscow.

The Pass, established in 1924, was formed by young writers, mostly veterans of the civil war, who believed in the ideals of the Revolution and the renovation of the world. At first the members of the group dreamed of a large organization but gradually under the influence of Voronsky and a few writers of the old generation, such as Prishvin, shifted their main interest to artistic qualifications. In 1927 The Pass published a declaration, written chiefly by Abram Lezhnyov and Dmitry Gorbov, the movement's principal theoreticians, in which they attacked plodding, "wingless descriptions of everyday life," the fiction of "social command," and criticized LEF and the Constructivists for their dry rationalism. They hailed the use of immediate impressions, sincerity, and the "Mozartian line" in art, and recommended to Soviet youth the masterpieces of Russian and world literature. These bold pronouncements were branded "inimical, idealistic, bourgeois, and counter-revolutionary" by orthodox Communist critics. The Pass, however, continued to publish its *Almanacs* with contributions by Platonov, Vesely, Bagritsky, Svetlov, Karavayeva, Golodny, and many others. But around 1930, under the pressure of a violent and unceasing campaign, a large number of the sixty original signers of the initial declaration preferred to abandon The Pass (Prishvin, Pavlenko, Malyshkin, and dozens of their friends). Still, for a couple of years the group preserved some activity under the leadership of a few good prose writers: Nikolay Zarudin (1899-1937), author of *Thirty Nights in a Vineyard* (1932), a sequence of eight tales filled with "cosmic" spirit but also with disguised political hints, and written in an ornate stylistic manner reminiscent of Pilnyak's stories; Ivan Katayev (1902-39) whose "Milk" and "The Poet" were moving and humane; Pyotr Sletov (1897-1948), whose sharp and amusing *Distant Republic*, a satirical picture of Soviet provincial routine, and *Mastership*, a defense of artistic freedom, were both published in 1930; and Boris Guber (1903-37) whose stories depicted the fate of "superfluous men" in a new society and furnished well-documented historical novels on Russia and France.

All of these writers were executed under Stalin, and by 1937 The Pass had ceased to exist as a group.

The Pass also included several poets and two talented critics: Dmitry Gorbov (b. 1894) and Abram Lezhnyov (1897-1938)— also executed during the purges of the late 'thirties (the latter is not to be confused with Isaiah Lezhnyov, a publicist with a checkered career).

Unjustly forgotten is another literary group which is now attracting the attention of historians of the 'twenties. It was established in Leningrad between 1926 and 1927 under the strange name of Oberiuts (from the Russian spelling of the first letters of the label "association for real art." They called themselves "a new vanguard of the revolutionary Left in fine arts, theater, cinema, music, and literature." They wanted to introduce a "new language, a new feeling of life," and emphasized the necessity of representing objects stripped of old meanings and cultural leftovers. In their works (mostly unpublished and preserved in manuscript copies) they experimented with illogical sequences of words and images, with simple but fantastic plots, and with dry satirical descriptions of current reality. In Nikolay Zabolotsky, one of the foremost Soviet poets (who soon broke away from Oberiuts), the movement's expressionistic tendencies turned to the grotesque. In fact, Oberiuts contained many disparate and often contradictory elements. For instance, Konstantin Vaghinov (1900-1934), an outstanding lyrical poet and the author of *The Song of the Goat*, a novel serialized in a periodical but never published in book form, had quite a following for a while but died ill, penniless, and dejected at the age of thirty-four. The fates of his friends were equally tragic. Daniel Harms (1905-42) used a sparse expressive idiom in his sophisticated stories (almost miniatures), some of which were published abroad in 1971. Exiled to a camp for several years, he later died of hunger in a Leningrad prison. Alexander Wvedensky (1904-41), whose plays (*Elizabeth Bom, The Christmas Tree at Ivanovs'*) today would be considered Theater of the Absurd, committed suicide in 1941 after his release from a concentration camp. Very few of the fifteen founders of the group escaped jail and exile. Zabolotsky spent eight years in a Siberian labor camp.

By the end of the 'twenties The Pass, Oberiuts, and other small literary groups, including the New LEF and the constructivists, were declining and finally disbanded. Their place was taken by large mass organizations, made up mainly of proletarian writers of various shades of political and literary intransigence. Their intrigues and struggle for power led in 1932 to their liquidation and to the establishment of a single, uniform Union of Soviet Writers under strict Party controls.

12

Mikhail Prishvin

THE NATURE LOVER

The main slogan of the industrial revolution promoted in Russia by the Communists was "the conquest of nature by man." The Party, repeating the statement of Bazarov, the nihilist hero of Turgenev's *Fathers and Sons*, that "nature is not a temple but a workshop, and man is a toiler in it," hailed the struggle against elemental forces, and saw mankind's historical aim as changing and shaping the face of the created world according to the rational designs of organized human beings. In an agricultural country such an ideology was bound to generate many contradictions. The conquerors of nature were linked to nature by a thousand bonds, they loved it and often felt that true happiness could be found only in its motherly womb. Though they built cities and power stations, harnessed rivers and bored through mountains, they frequently wondered whether supreme wisdom was not hidden in the serenity of the sky and the silence of the forest.

This contradiction was directly or obliquely reflected in fiction, and it explains the survival of a Rousseau-Tolstoy-back-to-nature trend in Soviet literature—even though such a tendency was condemned by official ideology. In the 'twenties and 'thirties its strength was proven by the growing popularity of Mikhail Prishvin. Acknowledged by Gorky as a first-rate writer, Prishvin was loved by millions of readers, and Communist critics had to make dialectical somersaults in order to explain why this "investigator of nature" was overshadowing the laudators of the Five-Year Plan and the social realists.

Prishvin was born in 1873 into a family of rich merchants. His father owned the estate Khrushchevo, near Elets, in Oryol province, and Mikhail's childhood was similar to that of the noblemen of Central Russia. His father died when he was seven. A few years later, while a student in Elets gymnasium he "escaped to America," but was duly caught and brought home. He had the typical upbringing of a radical intellectual, and since his family was connected with Populists, Mikhail became involved in revolutionary circles, was arrested, and subsequently went to Germany to finish his education. An agronomist by profession, he was an ethnographer, a folklorist, and a hunter by avocation, and began to write by the turn of the century. He wandered all over Russia, particularly in the north, with his rifle and notebook, listening "to the voice of forest, rock and water," talking to old peasants and young huntsmen, and gathering a tremendous amount of first-hand information about birds, beasts, plants, and human beings. Although his first books, such as *In the Land of Unfrightened Birds* (1907) and *The Little Round Loaf* (1908), which won him an award from the Geographical Society, were appreciated by nature lovers, he did not acquire a general public until after the Revolution, and he did not emerge as a mature and original artist until the 1920's. He was fifty when he began to play an important role in Soviet letters. His collections of tales, such as *The Springs of Berendey* (1925), and his vast autobiographical novel *The Chain of Kashchey*, serialized between 1923 and 1929 and published in book form in 1930, made him widely known, and his popularity kept growing. Other books, such as *Crane's Birthplace, The Calendar of Nature, Root of Life-Ginseng* (1932), *Forest Drip-Drop* (1940), *The Larder of the Sun* (1943), have been reprinted countless times.

Prishvin's work has a strong personal note: a wanderer and a sportsman, he wrote masterly sketches about nature which can be linked only with Aksakov's classic *Notes of a Rifle Hunter* (1852). "I do not know any other Russian writer," said Gorky, "in whom the knowledge and the love of the earth are so harmoniously united." For authors like Turgenev or Bunin nature is either a background or a frame and is conceived as a force hostile to man, but for Prishvin it is the main theme, and man's communion with it brings him wisdom and happiness. To him there is no rift between the "thinking reed" and the rest of the world; in contrast to Tiutchev, he affirms that man swims in the great cosmic stream, and that the life of the individual fits perfectly into the universal order of things. He speaks of animals, seasons, and men as equal manifestations of one and the same vital essence, but his outlook has no mystical vagueness, and his pantheism is free from overgeneralization. With the precision of a naturalist he gives the results of his observations; he has a horror of shallow talk about "the beauty of nature or the miracles of the creation," preferring to describe the exact coloring of a heathcock during mating time or the activity of bees on a summer day (*Honey from Beyond the Pale*, 1951). What makes the writing of this poet-scientist so captivating is his genuine love for everything that exists. He is forever making discoveries, and the thrill he feels in seeing and hearing, smelling and tasting, touching and thinking is infectious—it fills the reader with the joy of being alive and of detecting something new every moment. Fundamentally he is a moralist and a philosophical lyricist, and he talks of life with serenity and extraordinary insight. His own statement —"like autumn leaves, words of wisdom fall effortlessly"—can be fully applied to his writing. The wisdom of Prishvin derives from his "endless joy of constant discovery": beneath the phenomenal world he sees a "second world" of harmony and beauty, and his fiction becomes a poetization of nature. When readers and critics spoke of Prishvin's "spell and witchcraft," they actually meant his capacity to transform externals into meaningful images and to extract inner order from the diversity of impressions.

Gorky said to Prishvin: "You are a man's friend." And it is true that Prishvin's humanism is wholesome and simple, and devoid of sentimentality or sophistication. He has a delightful sense of humor and often chuckles over human foibles—the ridiculous grimaces of vanity and stupidity; the pretentious posturing of *Homo sapiens* are to him as funny as the caperings of monkeys. His approach, nevertheless, is not a purely biological one: he always looks for man's idealistic aspirations and tries to reveal in every individual that creative streak which, in his opinion, is "the essential thing in life." What is most important in man, he said, is the dream everyone keeps in his heart—be it the dream of a wood-cutter, a shoemaker, a hunter, or a famous scientist. In his peculiar and symbolic manner Prishvin gives the name of Berendey to those who are aware of this quality in themselves and have therefore found their own path and their own philosophy; most of them are doers and creators, from the simple peasants who display the wisdom of the earth and possess an infallible instinct of life, to artists and builders for whom every instant is a stimulus to creativeness. Those who search for the miraculous Ginseng or Gen Shen, the Chinese root of life which resembles the mandragora of the Renaissance, believe that this rare plant is a universal panacea; so does Louven, the hero of Prishvin's beautiful tale *Root of Life*. But their striving acquires a highly symbolic meaning, since men yearn for plenitude of being and for liberation from all the entanglements caused by social aberrations and false values.

This use of symbolism is Prishvin's usual device: his subject matter is strictly realistic and he is a student of concrete facts; but observation and inquiry lead him to general concepts and symbols that explain and hint at the secret order of the universe. As a writer he is akin to neo-realists like Remizov or Zamyatin, who absorbed and transformed in their work the heritage of Russian symbolism. What differentiates him from Remizov, however, is that his vocabulary is more simple, his sentence structure clearer, his syntax more condensed. One of the best post-revolutionary stylists, he declared that a good writer "has to use terms that are absolutely necessary and to compress words into units endowed with physical force." In fact his writing has a surprising quality of solidity. His prose is rhythmic and smooth, drawing from the sources of popular speech. He often makes use of miniatures that form some sort of literary mosaic, and his main themes are disclosed through metaphors which compare human feelings and social events with animal behavior. His images derive from a kind of animism that pervades his descriptions of seasons, plants, rocks, and rivers. It is more than anthropomorphism—he humanizes natural phenomena, but man in his work always belongs to the universal whole.

Although many Soviet writers learned a great deal from this "pagan rationalist," he refused to be considered a teacher. "It is useless to ask a writer about the mysteries of his creativeness,"

Prishvin answered when interviewed on "the secret of his art."
"One must put his question to life, one must live and stop asking
the artist who is in love with the world: 'how could I, too, fall
in love?' "

In *The Chain of Kashchey*, Prishvin tells how he became a lover
of life and nature and how his road went "from loneliness to
people." His hero Alpatov has heard in his childhood, which is
described in masterly fashion, the popular Russian fairy tale about
the evil sorcerer, deathless (and death-like) Kashchey, who cast
his chain about the earth and tangled all human beings in it.
When Alpatov grows up, he understands that Kashchey's chain
is forged of injustice, greed, malice, slavery, and poverty. It prevents men from leading decent, happy lives—so the chain must be
broken. In the same way that Tolstoy, as a child, had sought for
the little green magic wand that would unite all men in the great
Brotherhood of the Ant, Prishvin's young man searches for means
to break the chain. He does not quite understand what will bring
him closer to the great goal; he sympathizes with revolutionaries
and is arrested, yet at the same time feels that political activity is
not the whole answer. With experience he comes to understand
that each creative effort, each enterprise, each worthwhile deed is
a blow against the hateful chain.

Finally he gets absorbed in the practical task of draining swamps
in the Moscow region and discovers the formula of "blessed
work." To work for others is the highest achievement of mankind, since the fullest blossoming of the individual, of his creative
qualities, of his vital functions, is possible only in an activity that
fits into the general pattern of a common cause. The personal and
the collective efforts merge into a creative one; creativeness means
giving to others, it is an organic, natural part of life, as important
as mating and child-bearing, and it strengthens the ties among
human beings. It also brings man closer to the ever-producing,
generating, breeding, blossoming nature. To do, to build, to
work, to create, to give birth to somebody and something—these
are the primeval laws of life, and only in fulfilling them does man
attain satisfaction and inner peace. Thus Prishvin's religion of
nature and creative activity assumes moral overtones that are not
surprising in a writer whose ideological growth was determined in

its early stage by Tolstoy, and, in succeeding stages, by ethical and revolutionary Populists. Later, Prishvin said that he admired Lenin because the great leader talked about the "commune" which will always be the goal of mankind. But although Prishvin did not accept Tolstoy's "non-resistance to evil by violence" and his ascetic and religious preaching, he could not support the Bolshevik practice of terror and compulsion, and remained outside the political struggle of his era. He avoided taking part in social activities, lived in the country according to his heart's desire, and his way of life was in perfect accord with his convictions.

The Chain of Kashchey consists of ten separate tales, called links. The first or Kurumushka link, dealing with the hero's childhood, is still very popular in the Soviet Union (as are Prishvin's various books for children). The other links are filled with charm and wisdom, particularly those describing Alpatov's university years in Germany and his adventurous search for a girl who had visited him once in a Russian prison, pretending to be his betrothed so that she could see him. He pursues this unknown girl even as a male bird flies for miles after its mate, but when he finally overtakes her he realizes that there is no real hope for him, and his first love turns into his first great disillusionment. Alpatov is crushed and desperate, yet he is strong enough to sense that this is only the beginning in his long pursuit of happiness, and that passion and frustration, ecstasy and bitterness are still awaiting him on this marvelous and cruel earth.

This ending is, however, by no means sad or depressing. Prishvin's acceptance of life is unlimited and his optimism is never marred by melancholy. He does not complain about the brevity of earthly existence or the frailty of human illusions. His serenity in the face of death matches his consecration of vital instincts. His is not the primitive, biological optimism of brawn and bravado; he hails all the manifestations of being and the exuberance of the life force, but he also asserts the priority of an enlightened conscience that strives to unite reason and instinct, wisdom and intuition, man and nature. In one of his most meaningful books *Crane's Birthplace*, Prishvin wrote: "The world could be saved not by humanism, which degenerates into man's boasting about his civilization being superior to life, but by a harmonious accord of conscience and of creativeness of life through a single act of wedlock." To what extent this view expresses the mentality of an agricultural country is debatable. Some critics, at any rate, regard Prishvin as a typical representative of the peasant way of thinking. But even those, who find him old-fashioned and aloof from the issues of the day, concur in acknowledging "the deeply national characteristics of his writing." His whole outlook is so very Russian, his stories and fairy tales are so akin to folklore, his descriptions convey so strongly the smell of Russian fields and forests, and he gives his reader such a perfect image of the country's vastness and its inexhaustible vitality, that he must be ranked as high as his teachers Leskov and Remizov and be considered a worthy follower of Tolstoy.

In turn he became the head of a literary group. Several writers, such as Ivan Sokolov-Mikitov (1892-1975) author of *Tales of the Motherland* (1947), continued Prishvin's tradition and in their descriptions of the Russian landscape stressed the feeling of nature they inherited from their master. Others learned from him the art of the lyrical sketch, a genre that had and still has a tremendous vogue in Soviet literature. But they lacked Prishvin's "cosmic sense" and imitated only his technique. By stressing the proud role of man as conqueror and master of nature they betrayed the very essence of his philosophy. Much closer to Prishvin's spirit was Konstantin Paustovsky, but he overcame the influence of the master and achieved his own place in Soviet letters.

13

Soviet Romantics

Among the romantics of the Soviet period there was one writer who became an almost legendary figure. His strange stories and novels, his unhappy life, his engaging personality—all merged into the image of a poet who had failed in the real world but succeeded in the realm of fantasy. Alexander Grinevsky (1880-1932) who wrote under the pen name of Grin, son of a Pole exiled to the north of Russia for having taken part in the rebellion of 1863, spent a gloomy childhood of privation in the provincial town of Vyatka (now Kirov). Thrown out of school, beaten and persecuted at home, he left Vyatka at the age of fifteen and went to Odessa, lured by the south. He saw the sea—and became its passionate lover. Poverty and lack of a profession compelled him to try dozens of jobs: sailor, docker, wood-cutter, timber floater, miner, soldier, then he roamed as a hobo across European Russia and the Urals (where he went on foot with three rubles in his pocket). He read a great deal—and his favorite authors were Stevenson, Jules Verne, Kipling, Mérimée, and later the French symbolists. A portrait of Poe always hung over his bed. At the beginning of the century, in his early twenties, he met socialist revolutionaries, joined their party, and devoted himself to clandestine propaganda in the army and navy. Arrested twice, he spent two years in prison, escaped from his guards on the way to Siberia, used a false passport, was caught again, and this time could not avoid confinement in the extreme north. After release he published a story in a St. Petersburg paper and decided to sacrifice everything for writing. Neither poor health nor destitution could ever shatter his determination. War and revolution also failed to impress this unusually thin, tall, stooping man whose face was cut by thousands of wrinkles and scars and whose tired eyes shone only when he was listening to or telling himself some wondrous story.

With Gorky's help he lived in Petrograd in the 'twenties, and his tales and novels were accepted by periodicals and publishing houses. He found a large and appreciative audience for his works, and other writers became his friends. Since his heroes had Anglo-Saxon names, and the action of his stories took place in the fantastic country called "Grinland," in the cities of Lissa, Zurbagana, Ghertona, or Gel-Gyu, many of his readers took him for a foreigner whose writings were translated into Russian. The censors did not pay much attention to his fantasies of love, adventure, and mystery, in which there was not a word about current events. Grin, in fact, is one of the very rare Soviet writers who refused to deal with topical themes and to reflect current reality in his works. Only in the late 'twenties, when his novels such as *Red Sails* (1924) and *On the Slope of the Hill* (1927), and collections of his tales such as *Fire and Water* (1930), met with ever growing popularity, did some critics wonder about the social significance of an author who seemed to have completely ignored such facts as Communism, revolution, civil war, and industrialization. He obviously lived in the USSR with shut eyes —and listened only to his inner voice. From his childhood and throughout his checkered and painful existence he found escape from reality in dreams of beautiful isles, foaming oceans, sand dunes covered with heather, and white-walled cities on the shores of warm bays, where lovely women met captains and poets and where strange adventures awaited the traveler on marble-paved staircases, around ancient patrician houses, and in venerable offices of ship companies. Exotic skies, the search for love to the sound of guitars and violins, intrigues of evil wizards and violent robbers, miracles of faithfulness and coincidence, and above all the reverie of freedom, joy, and beauty—a hymn to hidden treasures of earth and sea—all these form the atmosphere of Grin's flights of imagination. Of course, externally his sea-side cities bear a strong resemblance to his beloved Sebastopol and other Crimean locales, but all these, like many other elements of

Grin's first-hand experience in this world, were transformed into pure fancy and mystery. It was another world, light and wonderful, freed from contingencies, misery, struggle, and death—a true leap from the "realm of necessity into the realm of liberty." But unlike the leap foretold by Marx this one was neither economic nor social: it was the unconditioned escape of art.

Was this the reason for Grin's popularity? Did his stories fulfill the intimate desire of his readers to get away from the dreariness of their environment through these fairy tales for adults? In any case, despite their vagueness and infrequent artistic short-comings (including a slightly "purple" style and wornout adventure plots), these stories of Grin, so unusual in the USSR of the 'thirties, appealed to a vast public and impressed many writers.

Grin died of cancer in the Crimea, at the age of 52, and his books enjoyed an even wider popularity after his death. But in 1950 the guardians of Communist purity suddenly discovered that this Westernizer was "a cosmopolitan and a militant reactionary"; he was accused of "decadentism," bourgeois mentality and "useless dreaming," and the printing of his books was temporarily suspended. The thaw of the 'fifties made his comeback possible, and his works reappeared in Russia from 1956 on.

A writer who was Grin's friend, who wrote about him, and greatly contributed to propagating his work and forming his legend, was himself a romantic and a storyteller whose importance increased with the years. Konstantin Paustovsky, a descendant of Ukrainian Cossacks, was born in Moscow in 1892. His father, a statistician, kept changing jobs and towns, and Konstantin inherited from him a passion for traveling. He studied in Kiev, then lived in Petrograd and in Odessa where he became associated with the whole group of poets and prose writers later known as the Southern school: Babel, Katayev, Ilf, Bagritsky, Shengeli, Slavin, and others. Like Grin he dreamt of wonderful exotic lands, adored the south, particularly the Crimea, and the Caucasus, and he read Poe, Stevenson, and Mérimée. But as a writer he was also influenced by Prishvin, the "investigator of nature," and by such different authors as Zamyatin, who taught him the art of a compact plot, and Bunin whom he admired for the purity and raciness of his language.

Paustovsky's first novel was entitled *Romantics* (1923) and its heroes were anarchically minded individuals and beautiful girls with strange destinies. His second novel *The Glittering Clouds* (1928) had a more complex plot of adventure and unrequited love, but again its characters consisted of bizarre eccentrics and lovely, unhappy women. Paustovsky also wrote a series of highly romantic stories, partly historical (*Charles Lonceville's Fate*, *The Northern Story*), and many of his topics were clearly inspired by Western literature. His exotic trait was rather bookish, but it expressed a genuine desire for new experiences and foreign skies. As Paustovsky had the opportunity to travel extensively in Russia and abroad, he accumulated a tremendous wealth of first-hand experiences. His interest in nature was equal to his curiosity about people, his memory capable of preserving thousands of details of both. His short novels presented innumerable episodes, each serving to illustrate a theme or a general concept. It is not so much the plot as the lyrical breath, the emotional consistency, the continuing sound of a note that give a unity to his fragmentary prose. It also has the brilliance some critics attributed to his fondness for the French; the finish of his stylizations and descriptions made him one of the best craftsmen among the young Soviet writers. Stories depicting imaginary adventures of Poe, Anderson, Grieg, and other Western poets and musicians, made him the master of "pastiche," a rare genre in the 'thirties. He also wrote about the painters Kiprensky and Levitan, the poet Shevchenko and the "Sorcerer" Grin, combining precise facts with fictional inventions.

It can be argued, as it has been done in Soviet criticism, that Paustovsky's romanticism and love of the exotic were merely a reaction to the dullness of life in provincial Russia, and that he felt sad and depressed because he could not actually reach the marvelous lands he dreamed of. But Paustovsky came of age at a period when his contemporaries found the fulfillment of their romantic aspirations in the Revolution. He did not join them but continued to glorify the beauty of nature and to idealize poets, rebels, and women. The latter, by the way, never acquire the reality of flesh and remain pale vignettes and sketchy profiles. The contention that Paustovsky's romanticism was of purely bookish origin and a youthful escape from an unsatisfactory environment is also refuted by his biography. In his late twenties he traveled and had adventures and led a very active existence. Before choosing writing as a profession, he worked as male nurse, tramway conductor, metallurgical worker, fisherman, reporter, and editor of a maritime newspaper. But direct contacts with life did not alter his romantic disposition. He wrote himself: "My life as a writer began from the desire of knowing everything and seeing everything, and of traveling." As late as 1954, he repeated the same point in *The Birth of a Story*, a tale in which the writer Muraviev comes to the conclusion that "the source of poetry and prose lies in two things—in knowledge and in mighty human imagination. Knowledge is the tuber from which grow the invisible, eternal flowers of imagination." The successful marriage of these two elements was achieved by Paustovsky in two short novels which brought him wide popularity: *Kara Bugaz* (1932) and *Kolchida* (1934).

The first told of various efforts in the past to utilize the sodium sulfate (Glauber salt) which covered the bottom of Kara Bugaz, an inhospitable bay of the Caspian sea on its desert Asiatic shores. Adventures of scientists and sailors, terrifying episodes of cruelty and death originated by the civil war, scenes of Asian backwardness, descriptions of storms blowing over the desolate south eastern steppes gave an exotic flavor to the story, which ended with Soviet pioneers transforming the whole area into an industrial center. *Kolchida* is a tale about a subtropical district in the Caucasus, which drainage and the growing of plants for technical purposes have turned into a new land of plenty. Nature here is as luxurious as it is bare in *Kara Bugaz*. Gorky, Krupskaya (Lenin's widow), and many others welcomed both books as a daring example of fiction integrated with science, but *Kara Bugaz* and *Kolchida* (as well as the ensuing *Black Sea,* 1936, and *The Tale of Forests,* 1948) were not the usual novels of industrialization based on data of botany, chemistry, geography, and history, but were adventure stories pervaded by a romantic spirit. What attracted Paustovsky to the Revolution and industrialization were the heroism of effort, the dream of change, and the creation of a "second nature" through the transformation of the physical world.

In the late 'thirties and early 'forties Paustovsky's stories acquired a stronger psychological bent, as he became more interested in the emotional and personal in man, and shifted from colorful strange heroes to ordinary people, in whom he tried to discover "the eternal light." Like Prishvin he portrayed small folk, laborers, and artisans, and stressed their closeness to nature, their simple virtues. At a time when Communist critics were pressing writers to show "the new Soviet man," Paustovsky retorted that "the magnificent world of freedom, justice, and culture" is still a dream, that in his opinion the new society begins where there is love of women, care of children, admiration for beauty and devotion to youth, and where goodness, humanity, and a feeling of solidarity are considered the highest values. He continued to follow Prishvin's "idealization of nature" and affirmed in one of his stories: "One cannot write books without knowing what kind of herbs grow on forest glades and on swamps; where is Sirius rising; what is the difference between the leaves of a birch and an aspen; whether blue bonnets migrate in winter; when the rye begins to flower, which winds bring the rain and when the drought . . . One cannot write books without having experienced the wind before the sunrise or the dark October night under open sky. The hands of a writer should not only be calloused from the pen but also hardened by the water of the river."

For a decade Paustovsky directed a seminar on prose in the Moscow Literary Institute and taught the craft and psychology of writing to hundreds of students. His influence on the new generation of writers was considerable and he had a large following. His views on the art of fiction are contained in a highly interesting collection of short stories *The Golden Rose* (1955).

Paustovsky's main work, entitled *The Tale of Life*, is in several volumes: *Distant Years* (1946), *The Restless Youth* (1955), *The Beginning of an Unknown Century* (1956), *The Time of Great Expectations* (1959), and *A Throw to the South* (1962). This autobiographical cycle presents a series of reminiscences, covering half a century of pre-revolutionary and Soviet life in a sequence of short novellas, and it unfolds an amazing variety of characters and incidents. This multiple and sectional composition, written in an excellent, compact style, is held together by its approach to reality. The author constantly and intentionally opposes two worlds: that of war, destruction, fear, and violence with that of joy, happiness, creativeness, enrichment, and love. His romantic vision is preserved throughout, and it apparently enchants many readers. Paustovsky's collected works, published in the 'fifties and 'sixties in two editions (300,000 copies each), and the numerous reprints of his tales and novels were sold out in record time. He died in 1968 but still is one of the most popular, beloved, and respected Soviet writers. His public image also remains high as it is common knowledge that he courageously defended the dissidents and protested against their arrests and exile. When I met him in Rome three years before his death, he strongly impressed me with his integrity, frankness, independent judgments, and the youthful enthusiasm with which he conversed on the primary role of imagination and fantasy in creative arts, particularly in literature. In 1965 Paustovsky was nominated for the Nobel Prize, but it was awarded to Sholokhov.

Perhaps the label of romantic does not do justice to the complexity of Yury Olesha, another representative of the Southern group, a novelist whose work and fate have a special place in Soviet literature. Born in 1899 into a middle-class family and brought up in Odessa, he served in the Red Army and then became a fellow-traveler and a journalist. His humoristic verse and sharp articles were published mainly in the *Steam Whistle*, the paper of the railroad workers' union. He suddenly came to the fore in 1927 when his *Envy* was hailed as a remarkable novel by both Soviet and *émigré* critics; Olesha's high reputation was established almost overnight. His other books—*The Three Fat Men*, a fantastic novel for children, *Love* (1928) and *Cherry Stone* (1929-30), two collections of short stories, *The List of Benefits* (1931), a play, *Excerpts from the Intimate Notes of Fellow Traveler Sand* (1932), and *A Strict Youth*, a scenario—were merely variations on the main themes of *Envy*: basically Olesha remains a man of one book.

Envy is a short novel about substantial issues that other writers often sought to formulate in a roundabout way; Olesha expressed them bluntly in a compact style, blending symbolism and psychological analysis. The issues all centered around the conflict between the individual and the collective. All Russian stories and novels of this period show evidence of an unending dialogue

between man and the epoch. The epoch commands man to become an active part of the gigantic process of social renovation
and construction, and demands from him the sacrifice of his
feelings and personal happiness. It also exacts obedience and
rationality, it imposes upon him the discipline of Communist
doctrine, it prescribes his behavior and morality, and it condemns
frivolity, daydreaming, and the yearning for transcendental values.
But man continues to defend his right to irrational impulses,
impetuous love, disarming tenderness, unaccountable passions. He
has vagaries of mind and heart, he dreams of freedom, he rebels
against the shackles of dogma, duty, social usefulness, and political
conformity. This conflict assumes tragic form because of the
necessity of adaptation to new conditions created by the Revolution. The lonely fate of the individual becomes a fate of suffering
and failure.

Envy is divided into two parts, each of which has its own
hero: both are rebels against the Soviet age. Kavalerov, the narrator of the first part, a drunkard and a good-for-nothing, is
given shelter by Andrey Babichev, a prominent Communist
and the director of a food trust. Andrey is strong, healthy, and
rationalistic, even though he allows himself to be moved by the
dejection of the intoxicated young stranger he has found in a
ditch. Kavalerov despises this self-confident man who has reached
a high echelon in the Soviet hierarchy simply because he knows
how to handle pork sausages and bacon; Kavalerov cannot accept the fact that his own unique individuality is not appreciated
by the new masters of Russian life, and dreams of winning glory
some day through his hidden talents. Yet he is assailed by doubts.
"It is possible that the nature of glory has changed? And if so,
has it changed throughout the world, or only here, in Russia?"
Kavalerov is a lonely man, in some way a modernized version of
Dostoevsky's "man from the underground"; he does not fit into
the society being built up around him, and he envies and hates
those who know what to do and stand on their own feet. The
trouble is that everybody is concerned with collective efforts,
whereas he wants to live as he wishes, "as an individual." Sometimes he feels he would like to hang himself just to prove that
he can do whatever he pleases with himself, that he is his own
master. At the age of twenty-seven he is a superfluous man, a lump

of human refuse; despite his extensive education he has no calling—
he has only daydreams, envy, and hatred.

Andrey, his benefactor, has a bitter enemy in his own brother
Ivan—a fantastic liar and a tosspot, who leads a precarious existence
and makes a living by performing card tricks, sketching portraits,
and playing the spontaneous wit for the entertainment of tavern
habitués. Kavalerov is simply a prey to his own feelings, a
victim of his lonely destiny; Ivan is a noisy and eloquent theoretician of anarchical freedom and an unbridled imagination. He believes that the new age has doomed "all sorts of feelings—such
as pity, tenderness, pride, jealousy, love; almost all feelings, in
short, which had been part of man's soul during the dying-out
era. In place of all these former feelings the epoch of socialism
is going to create a new series of states of the human soul." But
Ivan has nothing to do with this new series and he refuses to
surrender: he dreams of organizing a "conspiracy of feelings," a
phrase which was used as the title of the very successful stage
adaptation of *Envy*. He appeals to those who are still holding on
to the proscribed emotions and makes speeches in which fantasy,
rancor, and echoes of Nietzsche and Rozanov merge in an odd
amalgam. He calls himself "the king of trivial men" and rallies
"play-actors who dream of glory, unhappy lovers, old maids,
accountants, ambitious males, imbeciles, knights-errant, and cow-
ards." He even promises them the destruction of the new order,
pretending to have invented and constructed a miraculous and
mysterious machine which he has dubbed Ophelia. Lies and
whims are his weapons—and naturally he is not sure of ultimate
victory. He understands that the emotions he appeals to are
"decay, mold, phosphorescent fungi in a ditch"; and he is envious of the future which has no place for him: "The doomed
epoch is envious of its successor." There is but one choice left
to him: either to admit defeat or to disappear with a bang. The
latter alternative appeals to him, he loves the old order so much
that he would like to avenge its destruction: "If perish we must,
let us at least stab the present and rend it to pieces...My pains
and my offense," proclaims Ivan, "are those of the age itself."

But his Ophelia, which would blow sky-high Andrey's food
trusts and all the Communist enterprises and sports stadiums, is
nothing but sheer hallucination. Ivan and Kavalerov, who have

met by chance and have become friends, spend their time in impotent rage. Kavalerov is struck by the beauty of Valya, Ivan's young daughter, but she takes no notice of him—her heart belongs to one Makarov, a new and revised edition of Andrey. Makarov finds "too petty and restricted" all the feelings that Ivan makes so much fuss about. For this young man the basic emotion is the feeling of the times—it helps one to establish a division between the transitional and the essential, between the impermanent and the lasting. And the times demand engineers, inventors, teachers, workmen; the dreams are bound to come true and the strong healthy man is going to inherit the earth.

Kavalerov's attempt to assassinate Andrey ends in pitiful failure, and in this Ivan realizes his own defeat. He watches Makarov and Valya at a football match in the full triumph of youth and strength, and he exclaims to himself: "I ought to be struck blind. I made a mistake. I assumed that all feelings had perished—love, and devotion, and tenderness—but they are still there, though not for us: all that is left us is envy. Let's drink to our youth which is gone, to the conspiracy of feelings which miscarried, to the infernal machine which does not exist and never will." Frustration and loneliness overcome the two friends—and they share, by turns, the embraces of their ugly, old, and fat landlady.

The symbolic pattern of *Envy* and the expressionistic devices employed by Olesha made his work, despite its deceiving clarity of style, a complex and at times puzzling novel. It reflected not only Olesha's meditations on the changing values in a revolutionary era but also his own ambivalence which he was vainly trying to overcome by an act of faith. He felt strongly the line of demarcation between the old and the new, he did not hesitate to reject the past, but he was not sure whether the present was maintaining and affirming the humanistic values he was so fond of. And he could not hide his doubts about the new hero who was supposed to embody all the Communist virtues. The importance of *Envy* in Soviet literature depends precisely on the originality and vigor with which it formulated these fundamental problems.

The majority of Soviet critics interpreted *Envy* as an out-and-out condemnation of "bourgeois mentality" and hailed Olesha for his explicit attitude. There were some others, however, who felt uneasy: in their opinion, the author was too much concerned with the problem of the "isolated human destiny" and, despite the ending of the novel, did not seem fully convinced of what he said. The impression was due in some degree to the structure of *Envy*. The "positive" characters are presented directly through the eyes and words of their enemies; in the first part we have Kavalerov's confession written in the first person, and in the second part the description of Ivan is interpersed with ample quotations from his speeches. The ironic tone of the novel also contributes to a feeling of ambiguity. But even without these devices, Kavalerov and Ivan are much more alive than are the pork-butcher Andrey, the mechanically minded football player Makarov, or the shadowy, unreal Valya.

All these figures were only remotely related to Communism and are treated ironically: Andrey who whistles happily in the bathroom, resembles a Babbitt; Makarov is simple of heart and mind; and Valya is little more than a healthy bobby-soxer. Did this mean that they actually incarnated the practical, rational, and industrial spirit of the twentieth century, and that the conflict between the dreamers and the Communist managers and sportsmen was devoid of any specific social content, and could happen in capitalist America as easily as in Soviet Russia? As models of humanity neither Andrey nor Makarov are particularly attractive. Olesha had apparently paid but little attention to the strictly social and political implications of the Revolution. What had interested him most was the new soul, the new ethics, and the new pattern of behavior. His particular merit was that while taking for granted the social and economic changes brought about by the Bolshevik regime and not even discussing them, he did give real consideration to the new humanity and the new morality that were bound to emerge from a transformed environment. It can even be said that long before Silone, Malraux, Koestler, and other ex-Communists, Olesha had envisaged and interpreted Communism as a moral problem. What species of human beings was it trying to create? What new elements was it substituting for the old ethical norms of humanism and Christianity? Why was a rational business man such as Andrey Babichev a higher type of man than a Kavalerov? Only because he was a doer? These and other questions naturally arise in *Envy*, and its readers could not help sharing its author's perplexity and anxiety.

Sand, the fellow-traveler writer in Olesha's later story, wonders how he can "fuse with the masses," which is the remedy offered to him by a Communist, and how he can write on prescribed themes instead of those that come again and again to his mind. As long as all literary creation is based on personal experience, the "old feelings" can easily creep into a writer's work and provoke "untimely or reactionary themes" that are frowned upon. Here Olesha confessed his own inability to deal in his writing with industrialization, class struggle in the village, and other main topics of Communist novels. It was not that he did not want to devote his attention to them. He believed in the possibility of individual re-education, but he also emphasized to what extent such a process was difficult for men like himself, and other "heirs of the old order of things." Goncharova, the actress in his play *The List of Benefits,* evaluates the various measures of Soviet government and at the end draws up a favorable balance sheet: the benefits brought about by the new regime outweigh its evils. Yet not until she goes abroad does she reach this conclusion, which was that of many non-Communist intellectuals in the 'thirties. The comparison between Europe and Russia makes her reject the capitalist West. In Paris she is horrified by the corruption of the arts and the venality of the artists; she finally sees Communism as the great hope of the world, and dies in a demonstration, killed accidentally by a rightist Russian *émigré*.

Olesha's political stand in this play is unmistakable, despite all the inner dialogue his heroine is going through—with evocations of Hamlet and Charlie Chaplin, symbols of inner dispute and of the common man's plight. Yet he never has the courage to make the last step, or to conquer his incertitude. He is far removed from the official optimism of Communist literature, and he claims that man cannot exist without tragedies, suffering, and romantic aspirations. He also speaks of modesty, truth, altruism, sentimentality, and mercy. His doubts are as strong as his hopes. Sometimes he feels that a cherry stone tossed away on the site of an industrial building will grow into a magnificent tree in the center of the courtyard for the enjoyment of future generations;

yet he often despairs of integrating higher values into the new
world of Babichev and Makarov. In such moments he feels that
"old themes" are his blood and breath, that they remain in his
system, and he resents his own social futility, his incapacity to sing
with the chorus. At the Congress of Soviet Writers in 1934 he
spoke publicly of this inner strife and pointed out that impressions
of life must be strong and genuine before they can be transmuted
into images of art. And here again he called himself a beggar, an
unwanted man, a failure, because his dreams and emotions were
so far away from his epoch. He made, however, several attempts
at depicting a new hero as an idealized model of beauty, grace-
fulness, and nobility; but he did not go further than *A Strict
Youth,* a scenario of questionable literary quality. Apparently he
simply could not write "in accordance with the times." This was
his cross and the reason for his undoing. We do not know what
he left in the drawers of his desk, but as a novelist he ceased
publishing after 1934 on. He fell victim to his own ideological
and psychological complexes and died in 1960. Until the end he
kept his humor, his gift for brilliant similes and unusual poetic images, and his capacity for living in a reality created by his imagination. His friend Paustovsky wrote about him: "It always seemed to
me (or maybe it was the truth) that all his life Olesha talked inau-
dibly with geniuses and children, merry women and nice eccentrics."

A writer of great distinction, he was as subtle—and sometimes
as elusive—as the best representatives of that Western psychological school with which he had so many affinities. A consummate
dialectician and a poet, he expressed his psychological and intellectual anxiety, his doubts, and his queries in a clear, compact,
polished prose that flashed with striking metaphors; he was extremely economical, almost laconic, in his use of words, and
argued that when something can be said in one sentence, it is a
crime to expand it into two. His own lines had a resilient, nervous
quality; they were short, expressive, and reverberated with symbolic meaning. The ironic whimsicality and wistful romantic
nostalgia of his style were slightly akin to expressionism and perhaps to surrealism. What gave it charm was its purity, a perfection in simplicity which filled each phrase with almost material
energy.

Olesha wrote comparatively little (except for the journalistic work he continued after his rehabilitation), and when the volume of his collected works was published in 1934, it contained all his fiction. Yet his one novel and the several short stories and plays are a more remarkable and lasting phenomenon of modern Russian literature than the many bulky tomes of more fortunate and more popular Soviet writers.

The romantic mood was prevalent also in Soviet poetry of the 'twenties. It assumed various forms, from the heroic to the exotic, from the escape from current events to their glorification. Most of the poets were enchanted by the romantic spirit of revolutionary changes, and they extolled the advent of a new order and the struggle for its consolidation. First place among them must be given undoubtedly to Tikhonov and his popular ballads that sang of the supreme virtue of manhood and military bravery.

Nikolay Tikhonov, born in 1896 into a middle-class family, had poor schooling but read a great deal; he served in a hussar regiment in World War I and later in the Red Army. After years of adventures and dangers, including arrests, he settled down in his native Petrograd (or Leningrad) and joined the Serapion Brethren. His first two collections of poems (*The Horde*, 1922, and *Mead*, 1923) established him as one of the leading young poets. In the concreteness of his images, the pictorial details, the semantic precision, and the stress on masculine strength he revealed the influence of Gumilev; Tikhonov was in fact an heir of the acmeists. In this stage of his poetic development he saw the Revolution as a turbulent release of energy and as a school for courage. He belonged to the generation whom "life had trained with rifle and oar." "Fire and cord, bullet and axe bowed as servants and followed us ... It was then that we learned beautiful, bitter, and cruel words."

Fearlessness and fulfillment of duty form the main subject matter of Tikhonov's ballads. His heroes were the youth bled white from a wound but who brought an important message to Lenin, and the sailors on a doomed ship who faced death as an everyday job:

> One could make nails of such men;
> they would be the strongest nails in the world.

Some of his heroic ballads blended romantic narrative with a folk-lore vocabulary, as in the song about Makhno, the leader of the anarchical, anti-Red peasants in the Ukraine. The chief, and most effective features of Tikhonov's early style were the clarity and restraint with which he treated heroic action.

In the mid-1920's Tikhonov felt more and more the impact of Khlebnikov and, in particular, of Pasternak, and reverted to poetic experimentation: he used complex associations, abrupt shifts of meaning, "difficult" rhymes, and bizarre alliterations. This change coincided with his travels in the East, which wove a tre-mendous spell over him and supplied Oriental background for his poems. Unlike Kipling (whom he slightly resembled in the exalta-tion of soldierly virtues but whom he hated as a "colonialist") Tikhonov attempted to debunk exoticism and spoke with irony about "pineapples, tigers, sultans in armor, necklaces of skulls, and mirage palaces." Yet his landscapes of Turkestan and Persia (and later India and Central and Middle Asia) are exotic and romantically colorful. There is an aura of romanticism about his Caucasian poems as well: it would be interesting to compare them with Pushkin's and Lermontov's pieces in the same vein, and with Pasternak's visions of Georgia. For the Caucasus has always been and still remains the source of romantic inspiration for Russian poets. In the *Yurga* collection (1932) such poems as "A Gardener's Dream," or "A Saga About a Journalist," written in broken, nervous meters with bold tonal effects, are brilliant examples of Tikhonov's mature craftsmanship.

But formal experimentation did not prevent him from moving toward political conformism: by the early 1930's Tikhonov's acceptance of the regime became total, and since then he has often served as the bard and cultural ambassador of the Kremlin, equally dividing his time between writing and performing official func-tions. Paradoxically, while his narrative poems, despite their some-what abstruse form, were more and more concerned with broad social issues, his prose, which he had cultivated with success since 1927, remained thoroughly romantic in spirit and style. There is an atmosphere of mystery and wonder in his stories (the collec-tion *The Reckless Man*, 1927) and particularly in his picturesque and strange Caucasian tales (*An Oath in the Fog*, 1933).

Now that Tikhonov shared both the Communistic ideas and nationalistic leanings of the Soviet government and was active in various literary and political organizations, he praised "the romanticism of effort, the building of communism, and the struggle against the enemies." In *War* (1931), a second-rate novel, and in *The Shadow of a Friend* (1937), a collection of poems, Tikhonov summarized his impressions of extensive travels on the Continent: it was the time when Europe, already threatened by Hitler, was gripped by fear and foreboding of a catastrophe, and Tikhonov juxtaposed "the Western gloom and *taedium vitae*" to Russian faith in man's bright future. This was, however, different from the cheap pattern of a wholesale negation of the West frequently formulated at the time by Soviet publicists. The poet primarily extolled the USSR as the "land of hope and the cradle of new humanity." When the Germans invaded the Soviet Union, these general idealistic motifs were intensified by strong patriotic overtones, and the cause of Communism became for Tikhonov identical with the cause of Russia. His long poem "Kirov with Us" (1943), dealing with the Leningrad Party leader who was murdered in 1934, and his collections of stories, *Traits of the Soviet Man* (1943), stressed the moral stamina and the firmness of the young generation tempered by the Revolution and war. It is easy to recognize that Tikhonov was exalting the same virtues of courage, strength of character, and readiness for sacrifice he had sung twenty years earlier in his ballads.

After the war he wrote a collection of poems devoted to the Caucasus (*Georgian Spring*, 1948); and then "Sergo in the Mountains" (1958), a poem on Sergo Ordzhonikidze, a well-known Communist, comrade-in-arms of Lenin, and member of higher Party councils, whose activity in his native Georgia is presented by the poet as a heroic legend. A thoroughly political work, it repeats the intricate poetic gambits of Tikhonov's best period.

His literary work, as well as the part he took in the defense of Leningrad and the role he played in the Soviet international peace movement, brought Tikhonov honors and awards: he was decorated with the Order of Lenin, received a Stalin Prize, and was elected chairman of the Union of Soviet Writers. In 1946, when Zhdanov purged the arts, Tikhonov was demoted for not having opposed "with sufficient vigor the formalists and cosmopolitans in literature"; nevertheless he remained on the Executive Commit-

tee of the Union and his privileged position was not affected. In
the late 'fifties he was active in the campaign against Pasternak:
this was his way of showing his gratitude to the poet to whom
he owed so much. Tikhonov's disgraceful behavior has alienated
him from many Soviet writers, who feel that he has become a
"governmental poet" and who point out the artistic decline of his
latest poems and travelogues. It would be futile, however, to deny
Tikhonov's important place in Soviet poetry and his influence on
the young in the 'twenties and 'thirties.

Tikhonov's transition from romanticism to pseudo-realistic
propaganda was rather tortuous and complex. Much more simple
is the case of another romantic poet, Eduard Bagritsky (E.
Dziubin), born in Odessa in 1895 into a family of a poor Jewish
tradesman. He was graduated from a technical school as a land
surveyor but never practised his profession. He hailed the Revolution with enthusiasm and took part in the civil war as a member of
a Red guerrilla band and as a poet attached to a "propaganda
train" which had been sent to the southern front by proletarian
organizations. Later, however, he had to abstain from all activity
except writing; ill health made him an invalid, and in 1934 he
died at the age of thirty-nine.

Despite (or perhaps because of) his poor physical condition,
his poetry, eclectic in scope, impressed the readers by its exuberant
vitality. It is passionate, sensuous, and idealistic. Bagritsky quoted
Western romantic poets and Grin as his teachers. In a letter (1933)
he called Grin the favorite author of his youth from whom he
learned the meaning of virility and joy of life. The romantic trend
is manifest in Bagritsky's imagery and in his translations of Burns,
Coleridge, Scott, and English minor poets, in the ballad form he
liked so much, and in his beautified visions of the past. It was not
mere coincidence that one of his first collections bore a Dürer
drawing on its cover. He began in 1915 by imitating Gumilev, but
veered away from acmeism toward distinctly romantic verse. In
the first years of the Soviet regime his revolutionary activities
remained completely isolated from his poetry which was bookish
and curiously aloof to what was happening in real life. In "The
Fowler" Bagritsky proclaimed his love of "nature, wind, songs,
and freedom." His beloved heroes were Till Eulenspiegel, the
spirited Flemish folk-fool, and the Flying Dutchman. In *Southwest*

(1928), a collection of poems which had wide repercussions, Bagritsky turned to the colorful scenes and dramatic episodes of the civil war. At that time, settled in Moscow where he moved in 1925, Bagritsky discovered the romanticism of his own epoch. "All works of literature are nothing," he exclaimed, "in comparison with the biographies of those who witnessed the Revolution and took part in it." "The Lay of Opanas" (1926), which made him famous, was a ballad of Kogan, a Bolshevik Commissar and a Jew, who faced death without a flicker of an eyelash, and of his executioner, the peasant Opanas, who was strangely impressed by the moral courage of his victim and finally had to pay for his crime with his own life. The tradition of Tarass Shevchenko, the Ukraine's greatest poet, and folklore motifs as well as modern rhythms (akin to Gumilev and Tikhonov) were skillfully merged in this heroic lay. As a poetic narrative it was typical of the trend followed by Bagritsky in the last years of his life.

His later poems, mostly of the semi-epic narrative kind, were collected in *The Last Night* and *The Victors* (1932); in them Bagritsky identified himself with the socialist aims of the regime, but the romantic note rang in them passionately, almost wildly—quite different from Tikhonov's reserve and laconism.

Bagritsky's poetry, despite its great metric variety and the trace of many conflicting influences ranging from the classics to Maya-kovsky, has a basic unity: its positive attitude toward reality is enhanced by the dynamism of images, the sensuous ardor of descriptions, the emotional intensity of lyrical flights. When his collected works were published in two volumes in 1938, four years after his death, it became apparent that he had been one of the most remarkable poets of the period. Bagritsky's name is often associated with the constructivists, whom he joined mainly because they were his personal friends. Before that he belonged to The Pass; but his poetry did not express the spirit of either group. It remained with a rare consistency a joyful affirmation of romantic dreams and a glorification of the heroic and the wonderful. And since it could not be classified as anything even approaching socialist realism, Soviet critics have great trouble in finding a place for Bagritsky in their officially approved chart of post-revolutionary literature.

14

Konstantin Fedin

THE TRADITIONAL NOVELIST

Konstantin Fedin was born in 1892 in the Volga region. His mother was of noble extraction, while his father came from peasant stock. Konstantin attended the Commercial Institute in Moscow and his intellectual and artistic education was normal for a member of the radical intelligentsia. The outbreak of World War I found him in Bavaria, where he was interned until 1918. He enjoyed, however, various privileges because of his knowledge of German and was permitted to live for a certain time in different German provinces. On his return to Russia he served in the Red Army and worked in various Soviet institutions. His literary activities began before the Revolution but he devoted his full time to fiction only after the 'twenties when, on Gorky's recommendation, he joined the Serapion Brethren. A man of thirty, he was the oldest among them, and the first book he published *The Vacant Lot* (1932) contained seven stories of the past mostly about "the nameless drudge dragging the heavy cart of history from epoch to epoch." The best of them—"The Orchard" depicting the burning of a nobleman's manor by a former servant, and "Anna Timofeyevna" portraying an unhappy, self-effacing but very nice woman—were obviously inspired by Chekhov and Bunin, and appeared traditional and conservative. However, novelists of the older generation appreciated the assurance of Fedin's manner, and Gorky wrote that he was "a serious concentrated, cautiously working writer, he is not in a hurry to say his word but when he says it he says it well."

The publication of *Cities and Years* in 1924 confirmed this statement. In the post-revolutionary literature dominated by tales, fragmentary half-lyrical compositions, and ornate poetic prose,

Fedin's novel marked the beginning of the epic line, and the resumption of the monumental tradition. Although he said that he felt *Cities and Years* as an "emotional sequence" with frequent lyrical digressions, it was the first large canvas of current events. Much later in 1952, Fedin stated that the epic novel was a perfectly legitimate genre in times of Revolution because the latter "requires large generalization, the unfolding of vast pictures, of our history, of our heroic present, and demands great predictions." He attempted to fulfill all these requirements in his first long narrative which combined psychological realism of portraiture with a plot of adventure and suspense dealing with Germany and Russia and bridging the war of empires and the revolution.

Andrey Startsov, the hero of the novel, bears obvious autobiographical traits. A typical Russian intellectual, he is interned in a small town in Saxony at the outset of hostilities, and falls in love with Mary, the ex-fiancée of von Mühlen-Schoenau, a Prussian aristocrat. Andrey opens her eyes to the horrors of war, makes her understand the hypocrisy and stupidity of the Kaiser's regime, and, in general, awakens her revolutionary spirit. She helps him to escape, but the attempt fails and Andrey seeks sanctuary on the estate of von Mühlen-Schoenau. The German officer, without suspecting that he is saving his former fiancée's lover, sets Andrey free mainly because they have a mutual friend in Kurt Wahn, a painter whom they both admire. After the collapse of Germany, Mary joins the rebels, and Andrey returns to Russia with other war prisoners. The description of this journey and of the anxiety that grips the men, who find bloodshed, destruction, and fratricidal strife on their native soil, is one of the strongest parts of the book.

At home, Andrey becomes involved in civil war and Party activities, but is too weak and undecided to overcome his scruples. The years in Germany seem unreal to him; he forgets his promises to Mary and has an affair with a Russian girl, who bears him a child. His German friends in the meantime have been captured by the Russians; Kurt Wahn has turned Communist and is released, while von Mühlen-Schoenau sympathizes with the Whites and goes into hiding after an abortive uprising against the Soviets. Now it is Andrey's turn to save him and help him escape—even

though he is an avowed enemy. Mary has found her way to
Russia and joins Andrey—only to leave him as soon as she finds
out about his new love. Andrey, depressed, makes a full confession to Kurt Wahn, who kills him because Andrey is unworthy
of the cause he had wanted to serve. This last scene, with Andrey's
feverish speeches, his repentance and violent death, forms the
opening chapters of the novel. The narrative then unfolds the
preceding events, with flashbacks displacing the chronological
sequence of the tale. Some readers found the novel puzzling or
disturbing, yet they could not deny that as a whole, the complex
structure of *Cities and Years* was carefully planned.

This was the first novel of wide range and with a regular plot
to be published in the Soviet Union—and its impact was truly
enormous. The book attracted general attention and provoked
heated debate because the young writer had deliberately attempted
to restore methods of realistic narrative, and, at the same time,
used new stylistic devices, shifting from the ironical and lyrical
to the expository. Fedin had been brought up in the tradition of
the Westernizers, and knew and loved European culture and its
great ideas. His criticism of the West, like that of many Soviet
writers, was therefore directed only against capitalism, the bourgeois love of stasis, chauvinism, and militarism, particularly that
of Imperial Germany. Fedin hailed revolutionary individualism
as a true manifestation of the Russian spirit—this interpretation
was frequently offered during the first years of the Soviet regime.
As a fellow-traveler (he joined the Party in 1919 but abandoned
it two years later), Fedin acclaimed "the storm which creates
unrest, which breaks down the facades of respectability and replaces inertia by the sweep of creative change." These were his
reasons for accepting the Communist revolution—and they were
shared by thousands of non-Communist intellectuals who fought
in the Red Army, were swept by revolutionary romanticism, and
did not hesitate to sacrifice their lives for the consolidation of the
Soviet Republic.

Cities and Years had an almost kaleidoscopic variety of scenes
and settings; although it contained many overemphasized passages,
exaggerated similes, exclamatory remarks, and excessively drama-
tized incidents, yet it was much more restrained and sober than

most of the prose of the period. It was obvious that in writing this novel Fedin had in mind the models of nineteenth-century Russia and England: his vast work was definitely traditional, and even the motto of the book was borrowed from *A Tale of Two Cities*—"we had everything before us, we had nothing before us."

No less typical was Fedin's concern with moral problems. In this respect, the first Soviet novelist was a faithful disciple of the Russian classical writers. Andrey Startsov perishes because he is too sensitive to accept strife and cruelty. He is an intellectual who aspires to purity and moral integrity in an epoch when the frailty of glass is relentlessly shattered by the hardness of iron. Like many other "superfluous" men in Russian literature, he is crushed by pitiless reality, but the way the author condemns him reveals Fedin's ambivalent feelings toward his unfortunate hero. "If only he had taken one blemish," says Fedin, "and trampled one flower. Then our pity for him would have, perhaps, grown into love and we would not have let him disappear so painfully, so insignificantly." Although Fedin seems to admire the intransigent morality of the new hero who is strong and purposeful, his Kurt Wahn is hardly alive and too abstract while Andrey is vivid and convincing. All the work of Fedin discloses this peculiar conflict between his artistic incapacity to draw the image of a full-blooded Bolshevik and his success in portraying hesitant intellectuals and non-dogmatic fellow-travelers.

In 1927 Fedin published *Transvaal*, three stories of peasants, which resulted from his retirement to a village in the Smolensk region (1923-26). The title story portrays a hard Estonian of Boer extraction who exploits his fellow peasants. He has only contempt for them but succeeds in controlling their lives and becomes a leader of a whole region. *Transvaal* displeased the Communist critics who saw in it a defense of *kulaks*, completely missing the psychological insight with which the main character was drawn.

The Brothers (1928), Fedin's second long novel, questioned again the attitude of intellectuals confronted with the new ethics of struggle and ruthless action. This time, however, Fedin presented a more complex situation than in *Cities and Years*, because his hero, Nikita Karev, is a musician and a composer. His story is that of an artist who claims "an exemption from revolutionary service" and defends his right to unhampered individual creation, regardless of political passions. His younger brother Rostislav, an intransigent Bolshevik, meets him in tragic circumstances, and they argue bitterly. "You want to solve all problems by war," says Nikita. Perhaps mankind is better served by culture, art, and knowledge than it is by decrees, rifles, and bayonets. Man's highest virtues are not strength and violence but creativity and personal dignity. Nikita, however, is no preacher of oldfashioned individualism, and he wants to communicate with his contemporaries. Music is the medium through which, by expressing his own torments and dreams, he shows the feelings of a whole generation. At the end Nikita decides to join the cause for which Rostislav perished in a battle, and he believes he has overcome the contradiction between art and revolutionary activity. However, it does not change his conviction that the nature of art is essentially tragic, and that the true artist is forged only by suffering and retirement. Thus Fedin endeavors to blend the humanitarian heritage of the past with the demands of a new society. But here again, he fails to portray a convincing Communist. His Rostislav is too narrow-minded, the former sailor Rodion is too primitive, and only people beset by doubts and anxieties succeed as artistic achievements. The attempt to draw a "strong woman" in Varvara, Rodion's wife, who for a short time is Nikita's mistress, degenerates into an unconscious imitation of Dostoevsky's Nastasia Philippovna in *The Idiot*. But *The Brothers* had its importance as a novel because it raised the problem of the rapprochement between the intellectuals, particularly artists, and the Revolution. Its form, however, was more conservative than that of *Cities and Years*: it also utilized flashbacks but the pace of narration was more measured and better balanced, and the story of the three brothers Karev, descendants of Ural Cossacks, was given the structure of a family chronicle—with several charming side plots of love and amorous involvements.

Fedin, even as Gorky, belonged to the vast group of writers and scholars who had definitely rallied to the regime. Whatever their objections to certain practices of the government and the Party may have been (and these were often strong and numerous),

they maintained that Communism was historically an expression
of humanism, of the whole tradition of secular thought which
had stemmed from Christianity, undergone a transformation during the Renaissance, the age of Enlightenment, and the French
Revolution, and found its expression in our times in socialist doctrine. Russia was the champion of progressive ideas, representing
them today in the same way that Jacobin France had at the end
of the eighteenth century. In the 1930's this opinion was widely
held by European and American intellectuals impressed by the
Soviet experiment. Fedin was well aware of this through his personal contacts with the West; because he suffered from pul-
monary tuberculosis, he was permitted to spend a great deal of
time abroad at various resorts, mainly in Switzerland. His third
novel *The Rape of Europe* (1934-35) is devoted to the relations
between the West and the Soviets. It is certainly Fedin's weakest
novel; it is disjointed, its plot is slim, its motley episodes are not
well integrated, and the characters lack depth. Nevertheless, as a
political novel it is highly representative of the moods and hopes
of the early 1930's.

As in *Cities and Years* the locales of this novel are in Europe
as well as in Russia. The pivotal figure is Rogov, a Soviet journalist who travels in Germany and Norway and comes to Holland
to meet the van Rossums, a wealthy family of lumber dealers.
Claudia, the Russian wife of Franz van Rossum becomes Rogov's
mistress, and as usual Fedin's treatment of the love affair is poetic
and attractive. But the best pages of the book contrast the decline
of the capitalist West in the years of depression with the rise of
Russia. The dinner party at the house of the German millionnaire
Kaspar Krieg is described with the satirical sharpness of a grotesque. The scenes in Holland, particularly the descriptions of the
Rotterdam stock exchange, of Amsterdam jewelers, and of the
van Rossum household are brilliantly done. The portraits of
Lodovjik, the conservative head of the firm, and of Sir Justus
Eldeting-Meyser (obviously representing Sir Deterding, the
knighted petroleum magnate) are drawn in a lush and colorful
manner, reminiscent, to a certain extent, of Mann's *Buddenbrooks*.
Lodovjik's brother Philip is an opportunist who is ready to do
business with the godless Bolsheviks, since he believes that Russia,

with which his enterprise has dealt for half a century, has remained basically unchanged. He goes to the Soviet Union where his nephew Franz is trying to administer a huge timber concession granted to the van Rossums by the Soviet government. Things do not turn out as well as Philip expected, however, and Moscow cancels the concession—the Russians seem to have changed a great deal. Franz finds out about his wife's unfaithfulness and dies in an automobile accident, and Philip's only victory is his abduction of Claudia to Holland as his mistress.

This finale contains diverse implications: Claudia does give up her native land for Western wealth and comfort, but the real abduction is that of Europe; the Russians, a people who had never been considered technically minded, are rapidly acquiring European techniques. When the van Rossums lose their concession, Franz says: "The Russians have no need of us." Philip is wrong when he considers Soviet indifference toward the West a basic error: it derives simply from the fact that the Russians have already taken whatever they could from Europe—they have, in fact, abducted her thought and experience. The abduction of Europe has also another aspect: Russian ideals have not only seduced the masses in the West but have left their imprint on capitalism. Franz, who is a kind of technocrat, talks about planned economy, and Philip is ready to serve as a broker for the Soviets. Rogov points out in one of his articles that Europe is psychologically dominated by Russia; the Soviets prey on the minds of those who damn them as well as of those who bless them. "Since the Revolution not a day has passed without Europe's being reminded of the existence of the Soviets. Awareness of this fact is rewarding or awkward, but unfailingly present. Europe has been taken prisoner by Soviet ideas, Soviet problems, and the Soviet Revolution." Fedin must have been conscious of the dangers inherent in such an arrogant attitude. Claudia says to Rogov when they walk in the streets of Leningrad that Communist boastfulness assumes childish forms and becomes "the insanity of great numbers, the well known disease of Americanism; you have grown a Japanese radish somewhere of eighteen pounds and you rejoice. But why? What are you going to do with it, with your radish?" Years after the publication of *The Rape of Europe* Fedin conceded that his Rogov was too pale, and he recognized his own failure to oppose the well-painted members of the van Rossum family with equally live counterparts from the Communist world: the renegade Claudia, who goes to the highest bidder, is endowed with feminine charm and grace and provokes all sorts of emotions in the readers except indignation.

Another work with a European setting is the short novel *The Arctur Sanitarium* (1936). Like Thomas Mann in *The Magic Mountain*, Fedin depicts patients in a Swiss health resort, but the spirit of his work is quite different from that of the German novel. Despite the tragic end of Inga, the heroine of the tale, it hails the forces of life and symbolically opposes the illness of the West to the vitality of Russia.

During the Second World War Fedin served as correspondent on the front and also published his reminiscences of Gorky. Between 1940 and 1945 he concentrated on the first volume of a trilogy with a truly Communist hero whose roots were in the recent past. Thus the work assumed the character both of a contemporary and an historical novel. *The First Joys* (1945), *An Extraordinary Summer* (1948), each awarded a Stalin Prize, and *The Bonfire* (1961) form a chronicle of Russian life between 1910 and 1941.

The vast scope of the novels, the diversity of scenes and subplots fitting perfectly into a well-proportioned framework, the psychological portrayals of varied, often complex characters, and the masterful descriptions of different social environments make the trilogy Fedin's most ambitious and mature work. In style and composition it is also the most traditional, following the nineteenth-century models of Russian realistic narrative. *The First Joys* is probably the most successful of the three novels. Its backdrop is Saratov, a provincial Volga river town of "gingham, retired generals, and flour kings," and it re-creates the way of life and emotional atmosphere of pre-revolutionary Russia. Intellectuals, merchants, college boys and girls, Tsarist officials, and workmen are brought out in their personal relationships and social functions. The central figure is the young and poor Kirill Izvekov, a high school student, who works underground for the revolutionaries and is arrested together with his friend, Ragozin, a pro-

letarian. In *An Extraordinary Summer* Kirill and Ragozin return
in 1919 from Siberia to their native town, where they find confusion and changes stirred up by the Revolution. They also meet
the district attorney Oznobishin who had engineered their arrest
and exile, and their former friends and enemies: the playwright
Pastukhov who, like other members of the old intelligentsia, hesi-
tates a great deal before joining the Bolsheviks; the middle-class
hypocrite Meshkov whose pretty daughter Liza did not remain
faithful to Kirill, her young lover, and married a rich nonentity;
the actor Zvetukhin who tried to bring art to the people and
trains a company of enthusiastic youngsters, among them the
charming Annochka whose love idyll with Kirill is the most poetic
part of the novel. As a secretary of the local Soviet, Kirill plays
a leading role in the fateful events of the period and takes part
in the civil war on the banks of the Volga. In his picture of the
struggle between the Reds and the Whites Fedin, yielding to the
political pressures of the day, exaggerated the role of Stalin,
avoided mentioning Trotsky, and made many distortions of truth
in accordance with the demand for "rewriting history" imposed
by the Party on Soviet authors in the late 1930's and throughout
the 1940's. Such concessions seem surprising in a writer whose
novels otherwise are honest in their treatment of the past, earnest
in their approach to people and events, and faultless in technique.
Fedin's unexpected opportunism is doubly annoying because the
main theme of the first two novels is precisely the historical in-
evitability of the Revolution and its acceptance on that high
philosophical level. The conversion of Pastukhov, the activity of
Kirill, the opposition of Meshkov, the resignation of Oznobishin,
the ardor of the young generation during the civil war and reconstruction—all these episodes are linked together by a sense of
the epoch, by an acknowledgment of historical determinism. As
before, the relationship between the individual and his times is at
the center of the writer's attention. Next comes the problem of
the intellectual who is reluctant to accept the excesses of the
struggle; and finally the question of art and its role in life. In
The Bonfire, the last volume of the trilogy, all these issues come
again to the fore ominously illuminated by the flames of Hitler's
invasion. The catastrophe destroys Pastukhov's established and

comfortable place as a successful playwright, undermines Kirill's work and family happiness, and throws everybody into the bonfire of popular sacrifice. Intellectuals and peasants, engineers and workmen unite in the supreme effort to save the country. Even though Fedin still excels in psychological realism, and his heroes come out believable and colorful, the abundance of detail becomes tiresome, like small print in a book, and one wonders whether this "well made" novel is on the same level as the less perfect, less polished, but much more thrilling *Cities and Years*.

Between these two novels lies the ideological evolution of the author from the doubts and searchings of a fellow-traveler to the certainty of one who unconditionally accepts the existing regime. This, of course, assured Fedin the support of the Party, and in 1959 he was elected secretary general of the Union of Soviet writers. He joined the class of ruling bureaucrats and apparently enjoyed presiding at official ceremonies and academic celebrations and receiving awards, medals, and decorations. His desire for social status and power made him so subservient to the Kremlin's instructions that he was ready to denounce his former friends. His behavior was particularly unsavory during the campaign against Pasternak in 1958 and the trial of Siniavsky and Daniel in 1966. His hostile attitude toward Solzhenitsyn and the victims of police persecutions provoked surprise and indignation among the liberal intelligentsia and alienated him from the new post-Stalin generation. Young people refused to consider him the personification of a link between nineteenth-century tradition and Soviet prose. At best they saw him as a museum piece, and his public reputation went completely to pieces. In any case, by the 'sixties he had already stopped exerting any real influence on contemporary Soviet fiction.

15

Alexey Tolstoy

THE MASTER OF THE ANECDOTE

Alexey Tolstoy had already won a considerable following under the NEP, but only in the 1930's did he attain a nation-wide reputation. After Gorky's death in 1936 he was officially recognized as the dean of Soviet letters—although other writers were his seniors in age and not improbably his peers in artistic power. Deputy of the Supreme Soviet, member of the Academy, winner of a Stalin Prize, head of the Union of Soviet Writers, Ambassador to Bulgaria, entrusted with diplomatic and cultural missions to Europe, Tolstoy reached the zenith of fame and popularity.

This exceptional position was due not only to his indubitable talent but also to the almost symbolic significance of his work and life: he was the living example of the reconciliation between the Soviet regime and the intelligentsia. A writer whose style had been formed before 1917, who belonged by virtue of birth and literary manner to the traditions of nobility, and who had been for a time a White *émigré*, Alexey Tolstoy had finally accepted the revolutionary change in his country and had turned into a loyal supporter and servant of the Communist government. At a time when national revival was being encouraged and the Communists were acting as the heirs of and successors to Imperial Russia, Count Alexey Tolstoy had become "Comrade Tolstoy, the great writer of the land of the Soviets," as Molotov introduced him at an official gathering—a representative of the old and the new, a *trait d'union* between the two Russias.

He was probably the wealthiest of all Soviet writers; the circulation of his books equaled that of Sholokhov's, he earned huge royalties from his plays and films, and he lived in luxury, like a grandee of the old days. He had even kept his former valet, who, as the story went in Moscow, used to answer the telephone with "His Highness is at the Central Committee of the Communist Party." Tolstoy's death in 1945 was announced to the nation in a special message signed by the members of the government, the Party, the Red Army, the Academy, and other institutions; his funeral was an occasion for state mourning.

Alexey Tolstoy was born in 1882 (28 December, Old Style, or 9 January 1883, New Style) into a family of Volga gentry; he studied at the St. Petersburg Technological Institute, was deeply influenced by the symbolists, wrote imitative poems, and began publishing verse and prose in 1907. Three years later his stories won him wide recognition, and he devoted himself to literature. On the eve of the Revolution he had to his credit several volumes of novels and tales, and seven plays, most of them comedies. At the age of thirty he was considered one of the most talented and brilliant of the neo-realists.

The locale of his light and amusing stories was usually his native region, a sort of Russian Arkansas or South Dakota. In his childhood and youth he had had the opportunity of accumulating material on the mores of the squires whose estates were scattered beyond the Volga on the steppes of the southeast, and many of whom were related to his family. He himself said later that their world was for him "an artistic discovery." A chronicler of this wild provincial nobility and its decline, he enjoyed depicting absurd and colorful eccentrics, and presented a whole gallery of willful, ignorant, and fantastic people. All his tales have extremely foolish or grotesque plots. Stepanida Ivanovna, wife of a choleric general, embarks on a search for hidden treasure using black magic, bewitched cockerels, and with the help of a saintly countrywoman who proudly reports how successfully she has resisted the Devil disguised as a seductive cavalry officer. The walrus-like Mishka Alymov, who maintains a harem on his estate, provokes a riot at a wedding and, upon being tossed out, becomes nasty and takes to overturning benches and uprooting trees in the village square. Rabelaisian feasts are followed by Homeric fist fights, during which the athletic Rtishchev neighs like a colt while his crony Okoyemov, deep in his cups, chases the devils he spots in ventilators and windows. In addition to freaks, lechers, and firebrands there are other specimens of human folly such as Repiev, who invents an enormous flatiron drawn by four horses, to melt snowdrifts; and the landowner Chuvashov, whose complicated mousetraps "are based on purely psychological principles of taste."

These extravagant people are usually endowed with amazing physical strength and unlimited appetites of the flesh. They are brimming with energy, but they do not know what to do with themselves and consequently kill time in sloth or sprees. The only thing they are capable of is love (or what they call love): this ranges from wild sexual affairs, which make rich noblemen spend their entire fortunes on some perverse wench, to the almost platonic affection of a middle-aged squire for an adolescent, flaxen-haired schoolgirl (*Cranks, The Lame Squire*—probably the best of all this cycle—then *Adventures of Rasteghin, Cagliostro Defeated*, and other short novels and stories).

These anecdotal tales unite realistic observation with symbolic poetic allusions, and are written with a sweep, a brio, in a fluent, rich language, with concrete details and sensual images. As well as being extremely entertaining and full-blooded, they are enlivened by humor, cunning subplots, and erotic scenes. Tolstoy's drawings of eccentrics, bullies, superfluous men, and either passionate or ethereal girls could, in a way, be accepted as an exposé of a corrupt and declining class, particularly because of their strong satirical flavor. Soviet critics asserted that Tolstoy's gallery of drunken officials, dissipated noblemen, and superstitious ladies portrayed the disintegration of Russia's provincial aristocracy and that his stories were an additional indictment of the old regime that had bred and supported such a host of fools, drones, rakes, and scoundrels.

It is more than doubtful, however, whether Tolstoy ever had in mind any such lofty aim. His was an organic, spontaneous talent, a true, God-given gift. His power of observation, his mastery in telling an anecdote (either with tongue in cheek or with guffaws), his feeling for an intriguing plot, his art in choosing significant details and sharp contours, and his innate faculty of telling a yarn in a witty fashion were all unusually sparkling and authentic. But he was not interested in messages, ideas, or value judgments. "Tolstoy has plenty of blood, and fat, and lust, and a nobleman's snobbery," Blok wrote in his diary. "But everything is spoiled by his hooliganism, his immature approach to life."

This immaturity was responsible for his literary and political mutations, and he obeyed his impulses more than his reason. An ex-liberal with friends among the revolutionaries, he turned chauvinist during World War I and anti-Bolshevik in 1917. He joined the Whites, served in the propaganda section of General Denikin's staff, wrote thunderous pamphlets against Communism, and wound up in Paris as an *émigré*. He contributed to the exile press and published several volumes abroad: the delightful tale *Nikita's Childhood* (1919-20), in which the poetic image of the Russian personality and the Russian soil merges with a vision of the world seen through the eyes of a little boy; *Love, The Golden Book*, a romantic play; two collections of short stories, *Chinese Shadows* (1922) and *Moon Dampness* (1923), and the first part of *The Road to Calvary*, a trilogy, which, upon its completion and revision, was to become a Soviet classic. In its first version (1921) Tolstoy did not hide his anti-revolutionary feelings.

But life abroad was a trial to a man who was attached to his native country by a thousand ties of blood and flesh and language. He needed to have his feet on Russian earth and to be surrounded by familiar landscapes and people. Homesickness determined his change of views. He joined the "Changing the Landmarks" movement organized by *émigré* intellectuals who had come to believe that they ought to recognize the victory of Bolshevism and accept it on national grounds. In a letter addressed in 1922 to Nikolay Chaikovsky, a veteran Populist who was disturbed by rumors about "Tolstoy the turn-coat," the writer declared: "We must admit that there is no other government in Russia or outside of Russia except the Bolshevik government. And if we recognize this fact, we have to do everything to help the last phase of the Russian Revolution to take a direction that will make our nation stronger, enrich Russian life, obtain from the Revolution all its good and just elements." As usual with Tolstoy, he borrowed ideas from others, but he knew how to express them in a form accessible to hundreds of ordinary people. A year later,

after a series of articles in *On The Eve*, a pro-Communist Russian
paper in Berlin, he was allowed to return to Moscow as a "re-
pentant expatriate," and thenceforth his rise was steady; despite
all the attacks of the On Guardists he soon became one of the
most widely read authors and most influential figures of the
Kremlin.

A sensualist by nature, a great lover of comfortable living, good
food, and pretty women, always ready for a drink, a joke, or a
party, Tolstoy was a typical "mixer" but at the same time a
formidable worker endowed with inexhaustible energy. His output was great and varied, and it demanded a vast amount of time-
consuming effort: his collected works include ten novels, twenty-
five plays, ten volumes of short stories, a number of film scenarios,
numerous pamphlets, and hundreds of articles. He was intelligent
and crafty, and did not need to read Marx and Lenin to be able
to quote from them. Upon his return to Soviet Russia he hesitated
before adapting himself to the new situation and the new ideology, tried his hand at different things, made friends with members
of opposite groups, and finally, with his usual opportunistic flair,
chose the right Party protectors and the safest way to write what
he wanted. He was, naturally, classified as a fellow-traveler under
the NEP, but he did not commit himself to any faction.

He chose to produce entertaining novels with a sufficient
amount of social stuffing, and was one of the first to offer utopian
tales with strong adventure elements and what is now called
science-fiction—a genre highly appreciated by Soviet readers in
the 'twenties. His widely read *Aelita* (1924) deals with an expedition whose aim is to establish Communism on Mars; his
Hyperboloid of the Engineer Garin (1925, renamed *Garin the
Dictator* in 1927, and again retitled *The Death-Box* in an English version in 1935) is a super-thriller in which blond "vamps,"
sleuths, international crooks, financiers, and other criminals are
involved in a sensational discovery—a death-ray, quite as effective
as the atomic or hydrogen bomb—which enables Garin, its unscrupulous inventor, to impose his will upon shattered Europe and
to establish a fascist society. In other collections of tales (such as
Seven Days in Which the World Was Robbed), he continued to
exploit the sensational and the adventurous with just the right
tinge of the political. In "The Council of Five," a tale of 1926,

a clique of five Wall Streeters bombard and splinter the moon, seizing control of the world; but they are defeated when the general astonishment is succeeded by universal apathy and, at last, by world-wide revolt. Tolstoy also wrote potboilers, such as *Black Gold*, renamed *The Émigrés* in 1931, in which White Russians abroad and international intrigues over petroleum furnish the elements of a lurid melodrama in very bad taste. The plays he wrote in collaboration with Pyotr Shchegolev, the historian, are also melodramatic and were the delight of the provincial stage (*Rasputin, or The Conspiracy of the Empress*, 1924, and *Azef*, 1926). But even in all these entertainments of dubious quality, there was, alongside the vulgarity, brilliant inventiveness; the story was always told by a master plotter, and humor and talent were clearly in evidence. This is particularly true of *Ibicus, or the Adventures of Nevzorov* (1925), written in the manner of Tolstoy's tales about the Volga eccentrics and depicting in a picaresque style the misfortunes of a homunculus tossed about by the Revolution and the civil war. The realistic short stories of Soviet life—"The Viper" about a woman-fighter suffering from a middle-class environment, "Blue Cities" about a dreamer-architect who rebels against the inertia of ordinary Soviet citizens, and "Vassily Sushkov"—are well written without being remarkable.

In the 1930's, however, Tolstoy produced two major works that justified all the honors bestowed upon him: *The Road to Calvary*, a trilogy, and *Peter I*, an unfinished historical narrative. The trilogy he began in Paris, 1919, and it took him more than twenty years to complete it; he wrote the last word of the final version of the third volume on June 22, 1941, the day Hitler invaded Russia.

The Road to Calvary encompasses three periods in the life of the intelligentsia: that of the decadents, symbolists, religious thinkers, and aesthetes before 1917; that of the Revolution; and that of the civil war, with all its consequences. The chief characters—the clumsy, honest engineer Teleghin, who belongs in the "simple heart" tradition; Dasha, his fiancée and later his wife; her sister Katia, who is looking for a husband; Dr. Bulavin, their father, an old-fashioned liberal; and Roshchin, a young officer in love with Katia—all live gaily and carelessly under the old regime but are seized by the historical whirlwind and share in the tribula-

tions and sufferings of their country. The first panel of this tryp-
tich, *The Sisters,* written in exile, shows the intellectuals as a
leisurely, weak, and inconsistent group of people, completely
isolated from the rest of the nation and unaware of reality. The
two sisters think of nothing but their personal happiness and
dream of romantic love. All the personages of the novel affirm the
priority of personal destiny over history, and Roshchin says to
Katia: "Years will go by, wars will end, revolutions will be silenced, but one thing will remain—the imperishable, gentle, tender,
lovely heart of yours." When *The Sisters* was published in the
Soviet Union, Gorky showed some restraint in his praise of Tolstoy: "Very interesting, the psychology of a Russian girl ready
to love is nicely drawn. The background is the Russian intelligentsia before and during the war. Interesting characters and
scenes." But the two following panels—the second, *1918,* giving a
remarkable description of the general collapse and revolutionary
chaos, and the third, *Murky Dawn,* a panorama of the civil war—
show the changes provoked in all the characters by the dreadful
experiences of famine, destruction, and violence, and finally leave
Teleghin, Dasha, and Katia at the threshold of a new life among
ruins and confronted with new trials. This vast narrative now had
a main ideological thread—the evolution of men and women from
their closed worlds of personal feelings and aspirations to the
reconciliation of the individual and the collective through the
understanding of and participation in the historical and national
process. Teleghin, in particular, is the embodiment of this transformation. He is a simple ordinary Russian, healthy in body and
spirit, alien to the sophistications and sterile facade of the upper
classes; he is a well-rounded person and unlike most members of
the intelligentsia is not tormented by ambivalence and a split
personality. Teleghin understands that the vertical culture of the
intellectuals was an artificial superstructure; now he wants to live
and work close to the rest of his own people; the masses have
made the Revolution, and he wishes to be with them and help
them to find a better life. He loves his country and wants to share
its destiny, good and bad. Roshchin, an anti-Communist fighter,
comes to the same conclusion, identifies the service of the Revolution with patriotism, and decides to abandon the Whites.

In stressing the change of attitude toward the Revolution among intellectuals and even noblemen, a change often accompanied by tragic conflicts and bitter inward struggle, *The Road to Calvary* summed up the evolution which had taken place in the 1920's and the early 1930's and of which Tolstoy himself, as well as the whole "Changing the Landmarks" movement, was so representative. His heroes did not adhere to Communist doctrine and had no intention of joining the Party; they accepted the regime and supported its policy of reconstruction largely from patriotic and populistic motives—and this was true of many millions of Russians for whom Stalin eventually coined the label, Non-Partisan Bolsheviks. For most of them Russia and Revolution merged into one national image. Teleghin is not a Communist hero, he is a character with national traits, the representative of those who have maintained through centuries the Russian state and culture. People like him are the backbone of a country, and they cannot become strangers to their own folk. The fact that Tolstoy's trilogy expressed this feeling in emotional and instinctual terms, without any ideological pretensions, was the main reason for its immense success.

As an artistic whole, the trilogy has many flaws. Some of the characters, particularly the women, are magnificently drawn in the first part, but become pale and less convincing as the story goes on. In Parts II and III the historical material overwhelms and weakens the narrative. Although Tolstoy used authentic documents and dealt with well-known events, quite a few passages, such as those referring to Trotsky or Stalin, are obviously added because of political opportunism, and they distort the truth. Yet as a general vision of Russian life from 1914 to 1921 *The Road to Calvary* is equal, and in parts superior, to the works of Sholokhov and Fadeyev. Tolstoy the storyteller excels in vivid scenes and in secondary characters, such as Arnoldov the liberal journalist; Elizaveta the admirer of modernism; Makhno the rebel leader, and his assistants, two bearded and bespectacled anarchists; Sorokin the mad commander; and Kuzma the unfrocked priest. The novel portrays dozens of intellectuals, peasants, workmen, and military men in a colorful and realistic way, and they move in a lively procession; they may be pathetic, trivial, or comic, yet they all breathe the air of life.

Despite all the erroneous appraisals of Soviet critics, the trilogy can hardly be called an epic—its form is slighter and more episodic than the narrative of *Quiet Flows the Don*, it uses the technique of cinematographic shots, and has subplots and separate episodes that enhance the main plot but render the composition fragmentary and alien to the classical Russian pattern of psychological analysis. With a few modifications Tolstoy applied to his trilogy the method of neo-realism which marked his Volga tales—yet he toned it down and carefully avoided symbolistic devices. But to contend that the novel is an example of "socialist realism," as has been done time and again in Communist criticism, is completely arbitrary and ridiculous. It is highly debatable whether the trilogy is or is not a masterpiece; but it certainly belongs to a pre-revolutionary stylistic trend.

Tolstoy did attempt to bring out a novel to conform to what at the time was called socialist realism: entitled *Bread* (1938) it is a sort of chronological sequence to the trilogy. This contains a number of bright descriptive passages but they do not save the book from being marred by a crude political bias. It describes the defense of Czaritsyn (later Stalingrad, and then Volgograd) by the Reds in 1918, and "arranges" historical events *ad majorem Stalini gloriam*—apparently as part of an ideological core in fictional form. *Bread* and *Black Gold* are probably the worst and most irritating novels of Tolstoy.

However, he reached new heights in his historical masterpiece *Peter I*. Books I and II of this great novel appeared in 1929 and 1934 respectively, while Book III was published in 1944, and the last chapters of the final, unfinished part came out after the writer's death. It is to all intents a biography of the Tsar who changed Russia's destinies; his superb psychological and physical portrait from childhood until his battle with the Swedes at Narva in 1701 is painted in bold strokes against the background of the seventeenth century, with a tremendous cast of courtiers, princelings, dignitaries, priests, and representatives of all the social strata, including runaway serfs and highway robbers. Tolstoy portrays Peter as an implement of history, the hammer that mercifully smashed feudal Muscovy, and also as a man of passions and intense curiosity, ready to learn from anybody. Tolstoy supplies a brilliantly drawn gallery of Peter's supporters, such as Menshikov, the former pie-vendor, and of his innumerable enemies, including his own son, Alexis, whom the cruel Tsar tortured and killed. As is usual with Tolstoy, all the secondary characters are well executed (for example, Charles XII, the great Swedish warrior whom Peter finally defeated, to the surprise of all Europe). The succession of varied and dynamic events of the period when the new Russian Empire was being forged is unfolded in glimpses and scenes that offer, amid a wealth of visual details and anecdotes, a striking image of the permanent elements of Russian character. The Peter who attempted to europeanize Russia is at the same time interpreted as the true incarnation of her Scythian spirit, her pagan vitality, and her strength and frenzy in work, love, and revelry. Tolstoy adored this strength and he conveyed it fully in his novel.

This monumental work based on solid historical material has the precision and sharpness of old engravings; the flavor of a distant age is rendered by sparing use of seventeenth-century locutions, certain shrewdly inserted quotations from old documents, and references to extinct customs. Yet this reconstruction of a period has nothing of a chronicle about it: its freshness of presentation, its colorful characters, its dramatic dialogue, its swift pace of narration, and its rapid play of events make it as exciting as any novel dealing with contemporaneous events. Tolstoy denied that he had chosen Peter's epoch in order to project current problems into the past, to deliver a message or to teach a lesson. Like Pilnyak and other Soviet writers, he had always been attracted by the figure of the Great Tsar, and in 1917 had written a story called "Peter's Day" in which he depicted the Emperor as a despot. He changed his opinion, however, and in the novel showed other aspects of the builder of St. Petersburg; he now admired his intelligence, his genius, his devotion to the country, and his superhuman energy.

Of course, *Peter I* was bound to suggest certain analogies between the revolutionary changes brought about by Peter and those brought about by the Bolsheviks, and as long as both employed crass and brutal methods and did not spare lives, the conclusion seemed obvious: the justification of Peter was, indirectly, a justification of Lenin and Stalin. The novel was written mostly in the early 1930's, when the leaders of Russia, sensing the growth of patriotic feeling in the people, favored a blending of Communism and nationalism. Tolstoy felt keenly this transition from internationalism to national pride and the identification of the USSR as a direct successor to the Empire of the Tsars. On this point there was no discrepancy between the Party line and his own emotions: to Tolstoy, who was never a Communist and had rather vague notions on Marxism, dialectical materialism, and all the theoretical stuff he disliked so heartily, the patriotic urge and the epithet "Holy Motherland" did mean a great deal. He belonged to Russia, loved her, shared her destiny, and described her as an unbroken chain of generations. This explains the significance of *Peter I:* it linked the past and the present in a glorifying synthesis, interpreting the titanic figure of the Emperor as the ancestor of the Soviet man. Yet the greatest merit of the work lies in its power of creative evocation of the past. It is true that the novel lacks all unity of plot save a chronological one, that it is fragmentary and kaleidoscopic, and that some scenes are put together much after the fashion of a motion-picture film; but each sequence has such a dynamic rhythm, and glows with such descriptive brilliancy, each visual detail comes out so clearly, and the whole panorama of a century is so picturesque, that there can be no hesitation in ranking *Peter I* among the best historical works in twentieth-century Russian literature.

Many of Alexey Tolstoy's contemporaries were better equipped with ideas, refinement, intelligence, or wisdom. It was neither his intellectual nor moral qualities that won him his position. But he did possess such an infallible capacity for re-creating the very illusion of being that he triumphed by sheer richness of portraiture, by the concreteness of his images, by the lavishness of an organic generous talent. Whenever he attempted to convey a message and to be more than a storyteller—as in the case of his last play *Ivan The Terrible* (1943), in which he tried to whitewash the awesome tyrant in accordance with the Party line—he failed, producing an artificial and inferior work. But when he remained faithful to his basic, spontaneous gift and conveyed the flavor of his native country and of her true sons, he showed himself to be a master.

16

From the Five-Year Plan to Socialist Realism

The compromise of the NEP had come to an end in 1928, and the country was pushed into a new venture—the Five-Year Plan. This offensive, launched for the industrialization of the Soviet Union, had many traits common to military Communism, but this time everything was deliberate, planned, and controlled. Just as messianic ecstasy had turned young heads in 1918-19, enthusiasm for socialist construction now captured the nation's youth. The years 1928-32 saw not only harsh governmental measures but also the birth of a Five-Year-Plan mystique—the belief that socialism could be built in a single country. This was Stalin's formula, which, incidentally, he took from those very representatives of the rightwing opposition whom he "eliminated" as enemies of Communism a few years later. Instead of waiting for help from the World Revolution eagerly expected by Trotsky, the Party decided to concentrate all its energy on the creation of a mighty industrial base in Russia. This enormous task demanded great sacrifices and heroic efforts, because it had to be accomplished at an accelerated tempo. The Communists were eager to prove that a planned economy was capable of industrializing Russia and could therefore compete with capitalism. All the might of the nation was harnessed for the attainment of this end, and thousands upon thousands of non-Communists contributed to the success of the experiment, since they approved of it on patriotic and utilitarian grounds.

The industrial revolution in the West and in America in particular had been accomplished by capitalists. The fact that such a revolution was carried out in Russia by Communists endowed it with special features. Economic necessity and general poverty, which had compelled the state to build an independent national economy; the vastness of the latent resources of the Russian

Empire; the tremendous release of popular energy which followed the Revolution; the awakening of the masses; and at the
same time the specific theories, aims, techniques, and the methods
that stemmed from Communist doctrine—all these varied and
frequently contradictory forces produced a bizarre mixture. Genuine enthusiasm was coupled with brutal, often inhuman compulsion; high technical achievements were realized through primitive
means; human lives were sacrificed on a huge scale; idealism and
regimentation co-existed in a perverse *connubium*, and Marxian
slogans echoed feelings of national and racial pride. Trotsky had
said in his "Law of Combined Development" that a backward
economy had to take a leap forward, but this acceleration of progress was hindered by the lack or inadequacy of equipment.

There were many other contradictions in this industrial revolution which represented an inevitable development of the country
as well as a basic realization of the Communist program. On the
one hand, it evinced such familiar features of a typical capitalist
setup as administrative and technical hierarchies in mills and cor-
porations, sliding wage scales and bonuses that determined the
differences in living standards between manual and skilled labor
or between white-collar workers and executives. On the other
hand, the whole process was a collective one: private capital and
free enterprise had been eliminated together with the motive of
personal enrichment; the workmen were spurred on by civic
awards, by the vision of a common cause and a collective success;
the utilization of brawn and brain had long-range aims, it was
often bolstered by revolutionary romanticism, was rationalized
in terms of Communist ideology.

Marx believed that a high degree of industrial development
was a prerequisite for social revolution. The Russians practically
inverted his formula: social revolution was to lead toward aug-
mented production, to a great output of those very mills, machines, and manufactured goods which the capitalists were producing in other countries. This was the point that Communist
propaganda later utilized so successfully in the agricultural lands
of Eastern Europe, Asia, and Africa, where economic progress
was promised as the result of revolutionary changes.

Industrialization was to bring about a general reinforcement of military power and, consequently, an improvement in the international position of the Soviets; it was also to create a large proletariat, whose support of the regime seemed assured. Although the Five-Year Plan, carried through on a gigantic scale and at a rapid pace, was to draw considerable forces from the peasantry, the cultivation of the land was still the most important activity of the Russian people, and the collectivization of agriculture appeared as a tremendous task—even more difficult than the creation of heavy industry. Here the situation was extremely complex, and the results far inferior to those in industrial construction. The forced introduction of collective farms provoked a bitter class struggle in the village and the crushing of opposition through measures of terror: between 1929 and 1931 millions of *kulaks* (tight-fisted, well-to-do peasants) were imprisoned, dispossessed, transported, and even executed, and the dangerous label of "enemy" was given to hundreds of thousands of poor folk who had the misfortune to displease their rulers or their pro-Communist neighbors. Pressures exerted by over-zealous Party members in the transformation of the rural economy into a collectivistic one were such that Stalin felt compelled to issue a warning: "Success has turned many a head," declared the Secretary General of the Party and the *de facto* ruler of Russia, "but dizziness is quite a dangerous thing for any administration."

By 1932, toward the end of the first Five-Year Plan, the USSR had undergone a major change in comparison with the NEP period. The people had paid a tremendous price in lives and energy, but the objectives set by the planners had been attained—only partly in some fields, fully in others. The economic foundations of the Soviet Union had become collectivistic; the last remnants of capitalism as an economic system and of the bourgeoisie as a class had definitely been done away with; the enemies of the regime had been crushed; the Party and the state had spread and increased their controls more than ever; in general, the entire fabric of the Soviets had been rigidly strengthened.

To what extent all this was socialism or state capitalism of a new brand is a debatable question. In any case, the general standard of living had risen considerably, despite several dangerous crises in agriculture caused partly by the forced collectivization and partly by the drought and famine of 1932, all mention of which had been suppressed in the Communist newspapers, in the south and southeast of Russia. The standard of life in the USSR was certainly much lower than that in the leading industrial countries of the West, but the partial success of a planned economy gave hope and promise to millions in Russia proper and in all the peripheral republics. The wounds of the civil war had healed under the NEP, certain restrictions for non-proletarians were lifted, the consolidation of the regime proceeded amidst greater national unity, and an atmosphere of activity, optimism, and national pride prevailed during this era of practical achievements. The Soviet man of the early 'thirties was bursting with energy: he was a builder, explorer, traveler, inventor, and technician; with great confidence in himself and his country, his general mood was positive. But while this was true of the new generation, the older one and the intelligentsia felt differently and were often aware that the material progress was accompanied by a tightening of the grip which the Communist dictatorship and bureaucracy had upon the country. The supremacy of the proletariat and of the Party was turning into the rule of one master. Stalin was concentrating all power in his hands and was ready to consolidate it by despotism, intrigues, and violence. The edifice of the regime was being cemented by blood and fear. As the planned economy resulted in a tremendous centralization of power into the hands of state agencies, other functions and organs of the single-party government expanded considerably and tended toward rigidity: the army, navy, air force, and para-military organizations on the one hand, and, on the other, the police force with its own troops, secret service, counter-espionage, and a vast network of agents (including super-agents) who promoted denunciations, false accusations, and endless investigations. The well-oiled guillotine of suspicion, revenge, punishment, and ostracism worked incessantly to eliminate individuals and whole groups of people accused of opposition to the regime.

The Party itself had undergone important transformations. The doctrinaire Old Guard, which included many friends of Lenin, could hardly compete with the unscrupulous, purposeful scions of the new generation. The old Bolsheviks still had theoretical problems to solve and qualms to appease; the young ones acted like well-disciplined members of a Church Militant who believed in the infallibility of their doctrine and its high priests, and at the same time were conscious of all the privileges of power which they had no intention of relinquishing to anybody. They might well have repeated the words of Napoleon: "We are done with the Romance of the Revolution; it is time to make a start on history, to pay attention only to that which is real and possible in application of principles." The time for romantics and fire-brands, for utopians and self-sacrificing guerrillas was over; these were replaced by subservient functionaries and cold executives, who obeyed the Great Boss blindly.

Another important change was the spread of what was called "Soviet patriotism." Here again the tenets of dialectical materialism and Marxism became strangely mixed with national aspirations. The USSR was not only the guide and leader of revolutionary movements throughout the world, including the spectacular struggles of Asia and Africa against colonialism, but as the heir of and successor to the Russian Empire it was ready to resume its place in the concert of great powers. This blending of Communist ideology with national feelings and imperialistic traditions, which came as such as surprise to the West, replaced the old internationalism of Trotsky and became the determining factor in the Kremlin's foreign policy. This policy was shaped by Stalin, Lenin's vicar on earth. Marxism-Leninism-Stalinism now represented for the faithful the trinity of the Communist credo.

After the defeat of Trotsky and his followers in 1927-28, the star of Stalin had risen steadily. The true era of his immense power had, in fact, begun with the first Five-Year Plan and rural collectivization. He was not only the pope of international Communism, but also the builder of socialism in a single country and the leader who identified the Party with Russia's national aspirations.

The Communist onslaught on the economic and social front, or "the second phase of the revolution," had greatly heartened the partisans of proletarian culture and had given the signal for redoubled attacks against fellow-travelers and "NEP mentality in the arts." Various groups of Communist critics who had hitherto maintained only secondary positions, now made a stand for "the inclusion of art in the Five-Year Plan." They exploited the fact that the defeat of Trotsky had precipitated the downfall of all his literary friends and cast a shadow of suspicion on those who had shared his views on fellow-travelers and on the poor chances of proletarian literature. Backed by a few influential Party dignitaries who approved of the idea that art must support the Five-Year Plan, these groups rapidly seized control of editorial boards and literary organizations. One of their leaders, the critic Leopold Averbakh (b.1903) who was the brother-in-law of Yagoda, the head of the secret police, acted as if he were the virtual dictator of Russian literature. The members of RAPP (Russian Association of Proletarian Writers), as well as certain partisans of LEF, joined forces with Communist purists, and behaved very much like fighters in a civil war, transferring not only military methods but also martial terminology to their articles and speeches: they talked about *assault, siege, offensive, tactical errors* in poetry, of *strategy* and *artillery barrage* in literary criticism, and often called a novel they disliked "a *sortie* of the class enemy" or an "*attack in the rear*," and so on. The aim of all these extremists was not only to demand "100 per cent Communist ideology" in every printed word, but also to organize all creative activity along lines similar to industrial production: they wanted a captive literature, a sort of a gigantic art mill where poets and novelists would be attached to an assembly line from which useful books would issue in a unbroken stream. Sergei Tretyakov (1892-1939), author of *Iron Pause* and other poetry collections, became well known as a playwright. His *Roar China* (1926), a grotesque anti-colonial propaganda performance, obtained large success in Russia and abroad. An excellent journalist and polemist, he went further than any of his LEF friends—he was not satisfied with mere slogans of "factology" and suggested the creation of literary workshops presided over by "formulators" and supervised by experts whom he called "fixators." During Stalin's purges he was arrested and—being an Orientalist—executed as a Chinese spy.

"The depiction of the Five-Year Plan and of the class war within its framework is the one and only problem of Soviet literature," declared RAPP in 1930. The fundamental task of

Russian writers was the building of a literary Magnitogorsk *— a single work or a series of works that would sum up current events and be as effective in generating faith ånd correct convictions as the metallurgical giant of the Urals was in producing steel.

Authors were forced to give an immediate response to actuality: one publishing house turned down a novel because its action went back three years. Writers were encouraged (if not required) to fulfill useful functions, to make tours of factories and collective farms, or to take trips to the sites of new constructions, such as dams, power stations, saw-mills, and chemical concerns, and to collect material there for their stories and poems. Special writers' brigades were mobilized and given such assignments as describing conditions in Siberian manufacturing plants or in the Donbas coal mines. Special associations, such as LOKAF (Literary Union of the Red Army and Navy), were formed in the hope of furthering the development of military literature. One of the striking features of the period was the summoning into literature of tens of thousands of *udarniki* (shock-brigade workmen and farmers) who had shown some literary ability or inclination, in order to replenish the ranks of Soviet writers and to make their truly Bolshevik spirit triumph. The result of this undertaking was, not surprisingly, as poor as that of the early Proletcult.

As in industry, a spirit of competition was encouraged. Thus a poet might find himself challenged to execute a poem about the oil fields, while a novelist would be given two months to turn out a description of a Volga *kolkhoze*. Groups of authors also took public pledges to accomplish within a specified time certain "shock-commissions": of writing up, for example, the increasing output of bricks, or the progress of dairy products at some state farm. This was the period when "planned literature" was seriously discussed in literary magazines, when the proponents of "blueprints for prose and poetry" claimed that in this manner the gap between manual and creative or artistic labor could be closed.

The reign of the RAPP marked one of the gloomiest periods in Soviet letters. The extremist policy was applied with fanatical

---

* Magnitogorsk, the huge steel producing unit in the Urals, was built during the first Five-Year Plan.

ruthlessness for three years and provoked not only many painful incidents, but a slanderous campaign against fellow-travelers (attacks on Pilnyak and Zamyatin were parts of it). Literary works were evaluated purely in terms of ideology and political intent. Hasty, badly written, poorly composed, and occasionally illiterate novels and verse were brought out in large printings simply because the authors made their characters talk just as Averbakh and his followers did. In the best cases, works hailed for their "pure Communist spirit" were merely a reversion to the early years of naturalism or to the second-rate Populist writers of the 1870's. The standardization of "orthodox" themes created an atmosphere of insufferable monotony.

Such methods of regimentation, slander, and repression provoked a strong anti-RAPP movement in Moscow and Leningrad. It is significant that proletarian writers, such as Gladkov, Fadeyev, Libedinsky, and many other members of RAPP, strongly disapproved of the theory and practice of their own organization. At various literary meetings and conventions there were stormy protests against literary dictators, by fellow-travelers as well as by moderate proletarians, and the controversy assumed exceedingly meanacing forms.

By the end of 1931 it became perfectly clear that the attempt to impose a Five-Year Plan on literature was threatening to break up the ranks of Soviet writers, and perhaps condemn most of them to silence. The discontent of various literary groups, and the frustration of the readers, reached such proportions that the Soviet government felt obliged to intervene. An important role in this decision was played by Gorky, whose authority was high in the Kremlin: he rejected "military Communism in the Arts," as he called RAPP's antics.

Among other errors, the leaders of RAPP failed to perceive that Communist prose and verse were growing organically, without any need for coercive measures, that ideological hostility against the Soviets among the old intelligentsia was weakening, and that a considerable number of fellow-travelers were ready to give all their support to the regime. RAPP's negative attitude toward fellow-travelers seemed therefore outmoded and preposterous.

In April 1932, the Central Committee of the Communist Party promulgated an edict that proved to be even more eventful than the famous resolution of 1925. RAPP and other splinter organizations were dissolved, and their dreams of literary dictatorship brought to an abrupt end. The staffs of publishing houses, magazines, newspapers, boards of censorship, and educational institutions were changed or replaced. The leaders of RAPP, such as Averbakh, not only suffered an eclipse but were sent to remote districts into barely disguised exile. The uncompromising policy of the extremists was officially condemned, and all writers, regardless of their origin and present affiliations, were invited to join a general Union of Soviet Writers, within which the Communists were to form their own faction or cell. The majority of the Union was non-proletarian and non-Communistic, but the Party was acting upon the assumption that the majority sympathized with the efforts of socialist construction: it was therefore pointless to demand outward proofs of political loyalty. The underlying concept implied the "fundamental unity of Soviet literature," which could not be affected by the individual sallies of a few foes of the regime. This was the official doctrine of the period: the consolidation of the Soviet State was accompanied by the affirmation that all people of the country, including its intelligentsia, had accepted the regime and rallied around it. Only saboteurs, criminals, foreign agents, and reactionaries were attempting to undermine the new order.

The resolution of 1932 had a multiple impact: it put an end to the most stupid and irritating episode in the history of Soviet letters and brought about an improvement, even a liberalization of existing conditions. It held, however, the seeds of future evils, since its claim of unity actually entailed a demand for uniformity. The organizational setup was centralized: there was now but a single Union of Soviet Writers and a single board of censorship, while all literary affairs fell within the province of the Committee on Art, which performed the functions of a regular ministry. Herded under one roof, Soviet writers had to depend upon the same administration, the same governmental system of awards and penalties, and were subjected to the same strict surveillance by specially appointed functionaries. The result was the incorporation of literature into the fabric of the state, and this led to more thoroughgoing controls over all the arts.

It must be added that despite the suppression of RAPP and the defeat of the extremists, some of their allegations were retained in the new Communist aesthetics. First, literature was considered a social service and treated according to its usefulness to the cause. Secondly, whatever turned writers away from their educational duties was regarded as decadent, bourgeois, formalist, or whatever was the current label. And, finally, the writer was required to depict the contemporary Soviet scene and to "unite literature with life"—which meant that although the brigades and obligatory trips of the RAPP period were abolished, novelists and poets were expected to devote a great deal of their time to first-hand study of various economic, technological, or social processes under way in Russia.

The Union of Soviet Writers later became not only a professional organization but a powerful political body, ruled by officials who received their instructions from the Party, sometimes from Stalin himself. For twenty years the Union resembled a kind of a "literary Pentagon," as an American visitor called it. It directed literary affairs in the same way as any board of executives manages an industrial concern, and only after 1953 did a whiff of fresh air seem to pass briefly through the stuffy offices of this formidable institution. This respite was, however, of short duration and soon the Union reverted to its red tape practices and its dependence on ministries, security organs, governmental controls and censorship.

The most important consequence, however, of the 1932 change was the decision of the Kremlin to formulate its own literary doctrine, partly on the suggestion of Gorky, partly as developed by Stalin and other Communist leaders. This was the so-called "socialist realism" which derived from the concept that art is a reflection of reality and therefore has to be realistic, and that the only realism that should bloom in the land of the Soviets was that permeated by the spirit of Communism. Had the theoreticians of Communist aesthetics said that a "good" work of art is one that supports Communism, and a "bad" work one that either does not do it or does it half-heartedly, they would have avoided many further troubles. But instead of applying a purely political criterion (which at bottom was their sole preoccupation), they tried to disguise it in a pseudo-literary formula and hence created an impossible situation.

The official dogma was canonized in the following terms: "Socialist realism, being the basic method of Soviet literature and literary criticism, requires from the artist a truthful, historically concrete representation of reality in its revolutionary development. Moreover, truth and historical completeness of artistic representation must be combined with the task of ideological transformation and education of the working man in the spirit of Socialism." During twenty years of Stalin's rule, the formula "realism in form and socialism in content" was considered an official slogan on a par with "all proletarians unite."

Theoretically, the formula was vague and contradictory since it confused such different concepts as aesthetic method, artistic intention, and point of view, and also confounded such different elements as the requirements of a literary trend and the practical effects of a finished work on the readers (political education of the masses being the main object of the writer). To demand that a writer be "truthful" was not only naïve but even stupid. What is the standard of "truth" in a work of art? As long as this preliminary question was not asked, the term "truth" was devoid of any meaning. When at the convention of the Union of Soviet Writers in 1934, the delegates approved the formula of socialist realism presented by Andrey Zhdanov, the Party spokesman, they could hardly foresee all the implications and complications of this vote. The overwhelming majority in favor of the formula should not deceive the literary historian. It was a political and not a literary near-unanimity.

In their efforts to define and set up a literary school, Communist critics had but one premise: art is the reflection of reality, therefore realism is its essence. It is not necessary to see to what extent the first part of this statement is incomplete, and the second logically erroneous. The essential concern of the artist is not with the reality which is supposedly reflected or represented in his work, but with the way and manner it is to be represented—and this includes style, individuality, vision, form, means of expression, and all the specifics of each artistic idiom. The Communist theoreticians simply ignored the fact that art is in the first place the organization of material into a certain form, and continued to speak of the direct representation of life as if this were simple and feasible. They deliberately avoided the debate on problems of art and concentrated on the artistic purpose. The works of socialist realism have a Purpose with a capital P, as Abram Tertz, (the pen name of Andrey Siniavsky), wrote in his excellent essay on socialist realism (English version published in 1960). And the purpose is, of course, Communism. Poets, novelists, and artists have to help build Communism in the same way that workmen or engineers do. This explains why so many different works are put into the "socialist realism category"—the only link between them being the consciousness of "purpose." It also explains why the West does not understand Soviet critics when the latter discuss socialist realism and why the definitions of this elusive term have changed several times, provoking divergent opinions. Gorky, for instance, tried to speak of a *Socialist* realism as opposed to the *Critical* realism of the nineteenth century. The classical writers of Imperial Russia had criticized their society and opposed its evils and errors; Soviet writers, on the contrary, had to affirm positive aspects of Soviet society, and exalt man and his struggle for a new life—and this meant socialist content. It is easy to notice that the term "method" used in the official formula actually meant "requirement" and it is never defined in an aesthetic or literary sense.

In general, in all these discussions the distinction between form and content was always implied even though it was never explained; some critics endeavored to cover this duality by one sophistry or another. Gorky's interpretation found wide acceptance, but it raised another ticklish question: for almost a century and a half Russian literature had been "subversive"; it had been opposed to established regime and had fought the state and its representatives. Now the Communists wanted a literature that would support the regime, serve the state, and be submissive to the government. Breaking away from the long tradition of rebellion, writers had to turn into defenders of law and order. This meant more than a mere change of psychology and political attitudes: it involved the basic issue of whether literature can exist without conflicts, discontent, tragedies, and a refusal to accept reality; and whether the compulsion to conform and to act as permanent agents of optimism and utilitarian rationalism would not have disastrous effects on the creative artist. Communist theoreticians could argue that the struggle against the relics of the past in Russia and the inimical capitalist world outside would furnish many themes of conflict and even tragedy; yet, according to the basic tenets of socialist realism, these conflicts were bound to terminate with an assertion of hope and faith—just as any conventional Hollywood production is bound to have a happy ending.

Gorky and some of his friends tried to avoid the pitfalls of their position. They insisted on identifying socialist realism with revolutionary romanticism, and advised young writers to extol enthusiasm, sacrifice, heroism, and to choose topics of struggle and conflict—even if their stories involved failures and the death of the hero. This did not make things clearer; here again the terms "realism" and "romanticism" were used in a most arbitrary manner, and their identification simply canceled any distinction between literary schools and currents. Moreover, it did not eliminate the fact that Soviet literature could never be tragic, since in tragedy man is vanquished by fate and the gods, whereas it was the very essence of socialist realism to proclaim man's invincibility, his inexhaustible capacity for overcoming all obstacles, including nature, and defeating all enemies. Basically, socialist realism negated human limitations and avoided the problem of death and the human condition in the universe.

In further discussions socialist realism was treated as a general outlook on the world (a sort of *Weltanschauung*), as the application of "the Party line in literature" proclaimed by Lenin, as a literary school, as a "weapon which dialectical materalism handed over to us in order to create Communist culture," and as "the most advanced progressive and fruitful literary method." In the discussions that flared up in the era of revisionism, after Stalin's death, the main question concerned the criteria by which a work of art can and should be labeled socialist realism. In the early 'thirties when the formula was still brand new, the problem was solved in a most elementary manner: all works inspired by Communist ideology were proclaimed representative of socialist realism. Thus novels by Gladkov, Fadeyev, Sholokhov, and other Party members, even though they had been written before 1932, were all lumped together, regardless of their manifest diversity of style and method. *Cement* by Gladkov, *The Rout* (*The Nineteen*) by Fadeyev, *Quiet Flows the Don* by Sholokhov, *Tempering of Steel* by Ostrovsky, *The Pedagogical Poem* by Makarenko, and quite a few other novels belonged to this motley category. It would have been much safer to say that these Communist writers expressed their faith and support of the regime in different literary forms which did not represent anything new but continued various established literary traditions.

17

Literature of Communist Persuasion

FROM FURMANOV TO OSTROVSKY

The theory of socialist realism was formulated in 1932 but the works classified as the "gold fund of Soviet Letters" were published earlier. Although completely different in style and manner, they all had common traits: written by supporters of realism, by convinced Communists, they all presented specimens of purposeful art and were recognized by the Party as powerful vehicles of mass education.

Symbolism, acmeism, futurism, and various groups of the literary avant-garde had functioned successfully in the 1920's because they were carried over from the past, and because their leaders sincerely believed in the intimate link between new literary forms and social revolution. But the pressure of a changed environment, the transformation of the audiences, the assertion of Communist aesthetics, and the stabilization of the Soviet regime curtailed and then interrupted their development.

The pre-revolutionary currents did not run dry because of any organic deficiency: their natural course was stopped by the conscious efforts of the Party and of competing literary groups. The fact that the leading poets and novelists of the 'twenties and early 'thirties, such as Mayakovsky, Essenin, Pasternak, Babel, Pilnyak, Zamyatin, Leonov, and others, belonged to the camp of innovators, did not prevent the resurgence of the realistic tradition. Of course it had existed before 1917 along with symbolism and experimentation, but now it received a vigorous impulse from the new order. Young Communists, often of proletarian origin, and some of the old writers, mainly followers of Gorky, formed the core of the realistic group. Lenin and most of the Party leaders favored realism because of ideological premises and personal taste, but they also believed that the masses instinctively shied away from sophisticated modernists. New audiences coming from the lower strata of Soviet society undoubtedly preferred works of representational art. Future historians will probably find a curious analogy between Russian and Western art: in both, during the third and fourth decades of our century, we discover an interest in the social novel, decline in formal experimentation; traditional trends in neo-classicism and realism co-exist with surrealism and abstractionism. In some fields—such as music—this parallelism is even more striking. The problem of two cultures—one for the limited and refined elite, and another for the huge and aesthetically uneducated masses—existed not only in Russia but in all the countries of the world.

Communist ideology and particular social pressures naturally caused the realistic revival in the Soviet Union to assume a special character. At first, in the early 1920's, when most of the fellow-travelers had been spellbound by experimentation, many proletarian and Communist writers made their debuts as strict naturalists; they had paid little or no attention to form and to the subtleties of art but had simply aimed at what they called the "faithful reproduction of reality." Some critics favored this attitude by stating that the era of the Great Upheaval demanded chroniclers and reporters. In this writer's opinion Soviet literature has never been able to get rid of this idea completely. It gave rise to a factual narrative which flourished in all Russian periodicals under the title of *ocherk* (a genre between a journalist's report and an essay). The purpose of the *ocherk* was defined as "accurate and faithful reproduction of people and conditions of labor with an emphasis on industrial, agricultural, military, and other achievements of the country's economic and social life." This descriptive prose occupied and still occupies a large and honored place in Soviet letters: each issue of a Moscow magazine carries several *ocherki*—about a factory, a *kolkhoz*, a school, or about professional workers from wood-cutters to mechanics. The techniques and methods of the *ocherk* were applied to all fields of art: thousands of stories, tales, and even novels in the USSR are nothing but fictionalized sketches. This camera-eye genre, is however, very far from being objective; it was largely used for propaganda and educational purposes, particularly between the first five-year plan and the death of Stalin. In the middle of the 'fifties some young writers, such as Valentin Ovechkin and Vladimir Soloukhin, tried to revive the *ocherk* by liberating it from false rhetoric and outright mendacity, but single successes in the field could not change the whole tone and style of Soviet journalism.

An early factual narrative, based on firsthand experience, was offered by Dimitry Furmanov, whom Communist literary historians rate as a classic writer. Furmanov (1891-1926), the son of a bartender, was close to the socialists during his university years and joined the Communists in 1918. As a political commissar, he was active in various fighting units—among them the 25th Division led by Chapayev, a picturesque guerrilla leader. *Chapayev* (1923), Furmanov's main opus which was made into a famous film, presents a lengthy and, at times, strikingly impressive description of the colorful commander, a former private in the Tsarist army and later a legendary hero of the southeastern steppes beyond the Volga. Undisciplined, boastful, and brave, Chapayev personified the elemental force of a people in revolt, but he had rather hazy notions of political programs and party ideologies. He used to say, according to Furmanov, that he disliked the Communists because they were internationalists, but that he loved the Bolsheviks since they were friends of the common man. Furmanov, a gifted and observant writer, succeeded in catching the national traits of Chapayev who grows into a symbol of the Russian mentality. It is evident, however, that the author did not have a very high purpose: his goal was simply to report facts with the utmost accuracy, to cite orders of the day issued by the Reds and the Whites in the civil war, to quote documents *in extenso,* and, in general, to sacrifice story, construction, and artistry to factual authenticity. Furmanov, abandoning all fictional adornment, wrote in a direct, unassuming, expository manner. This makes him quite different from other Soviet authors, such as Pilnyak, Babel, Vsevolod Ivanov, and even the realist Alexey Tolstoy, who also depicted primitive fighters projected by the revolutionary explosion. Another trait made Furmanov quite alien to the fellow-travelers: he looked at his heroes and the events they helped to shape from a Communist point of view and glorified them as the prototypes of men to come. Both *Chapayev* and *Revolt* (1925), Furmanov's second large chronicle, are interesting documents of the civil war in a forlorn region of Russia. They also remain as typical examples of "factography" in literature—a trend that found defenders in the late 'twenties among the members of the LEF and the formalists. In 1929 *The Literature of the Fact*, a collection including essays by Victor Shklovsky, Ossip Brik, Sergei Tretyakov, and other highly sophisticated writers, proclaimed "the death of fiction" and the advent of a strictly empirical form of writing destined to become a true expression of the materialistic, Marxist-Leninist epoch. They failed to promote any new movement in the novel or the short story but contributed to raising the level of craftsmanship in the *ocherk*.

The naturalists of the 1920's either showed a tendency toward the slice-of-life manner or reverted to the old Populist vein. Sergei Semenov (1893-1942), the son of a metal worker, and a member of the Party, was the author of *Hunger* and *Typhus*, which resembled hospital bed-charts of clinical cases. They showed how family life disintegrated during the years of famine when husbands hid bread from their wives, and children stole potatoes from their parents. He also wrote *Natalia Tarpova* (1927-29), a novel on the life of workmen and Party members in a factory. Alexander Neverov (1886-1923) dealt with the famine also but this pre-revolutionary writer of peasant origin combined "factography" with humor and folklore. His best tale *Tashkent City of Bread* (1921) has for its hero the teenager Mishka, who sets out on a long and perilous journey from his native village on the Volga in search of food for his ailing mother. Caught by the chaos of revolution and civil war, confronted with death and tragic adventures intermingled with comic situations and childish escapades, Mishka succeeds in fulfilling his mission. Neverov wanted to present a straight report of facts but he could not help being pathetic, sentimental, and ironic, and this saved his story, making it moving and alive.

Lydia Seifullina (1889-1961), a Siberian schoolteacher, also began as a naturalistic writer: her popular story *The Lawbreakers* (1921), which deals with the waifs and strays of the early revolutionary period and their painful moral regeneration, is written in a style reminiscent of the Populist writers of the 1860-70 period. *Humus* (1923), a novel of the civil war depicting the atrocities of the class struggle in a village on the border of Asiatic and European Russia, was purely naturalistic narrative. Seifullina attained popularity with her *Virineya* (1924), a drama with a new heroine—the emancipated peasant woman. After the 'twenties, however, Seifullina found herself relegated to the rear-guard of Soviet literature. Her works were hasty, untidy, and coarse. She was aware of these defects and tried to counter criticism by statements that sounded like the apology of a whole school: "Life is enormous, one ought to write volumes. But everything around one is seething. There is no time for writing and narrating at length; it is better to give excerpts" (preamble to *Four Chapters*, 1922).

In the first decade of the Revolution naturalism had a certain success because the readers liked literary snapshots of their own life. This explains the vogue of amusing naturalistic anecdotes by Panteleimon Romanov (1884-1940), a fellow-traveler whose works became best-sellers under the NEP. His stories often were verbatim transcripts of talk in factories, villages, and public meetings, or flat descriptions of daily life. He had humor and knew how to tell a story, but most of his tales as well as his novels on the new generation and on sex and love (*Comrade Kisliakov* or *Three Pairs of Silken Stockings*, 1930, *The New Tablet*, 1927, *Without Cherry Blossoms*, 1925), were mere colored photographs or tintypes.

While Romanov with his "bourgeois mentality" was a fellow-traveler, most of the naturalists were Communists. They were in search of "literary ancestors," and imitated Reshetnikov, Pomialovsky, Sleptsov, Uspensky, and other minor writers of 1860-70 whom they hailed as representatives of "democratic art." The parallel between these naturalists and their Communist followers was truly striking. Despite the attacks by a few perceptive critics and the occasional anti-naturalistic statements by Party officials, naturalism continued to be a strong element in Soviet letters, even though it was often disguised as socialist realism. One easily discovers it in the numerous hasty, slovenly, verbose compositions on topical subjects that have flooded (and continue to do so) Soviet periodicals since 1923. The Party accepted them as a "healthy reaction against patrician aestheticism," a reaction inspired by Communist ideology. In other words, they were poorly written but politically safe. Not a single work of merit emerged from this morass of primitive and tendentious narrative.

In the 'thirties when socialist realism rose to power, naturalism was dubbed "outdated" and unsuited to Party requirements. The cause of its poor rating was the insistence with which the naturalists represented the negative aspects of life—ignorance, poverty, cruelty, sloppiness. Many naturalists were reluctant to "varnish reality"—a term widely used in post-Stalinist criticism.

It is true that the works the Communists recognized as their highest achievements, although they often contained many naturalistic elements, did not belong to the naturalist school. Such was the case of *The Iron Torrent* (1924), by Alexander Serafimovich-Popov (1863-1949), which depicted the civil war in a series of pseudo-impressionistic flashes. The Soviet critics acclaimed it as a masterpiece because the retreat of the Red Cossacks and their families through the defiles of the Northern Caucasus, under the pressure of the Whites, was treated in a panoramic manner which they confused with heroic epic. The real hero of this crude novel (Gorky complained in his letters of its artistic defects) is the thousand-faced rabble gradually becoming disciplined by class-conscious leaders; speech and actions are reproduced with dull but naturalistic fidelity. On the other hand, much of the book is rhetorical and declamatory; to re-read it today is a boring experience, and one wonders how much longer it will be allowed to stand among the classics of socialist realism. The reason for the exaggerated evaluation of a work which is patently on a low artistic level is that it belongs to so-called "books of faith." It does express a firm belief in Communism and makes an attempt to glorify the effort of the masses. But it does not match other works of the same persuasion. The most successful ones in this category, such as Gladkov's *Cement* or Fadeyev's *The Rout* (in the English version *The Nineteen*), have more right to be classified as "realistic" than the loose and inflated *The Iron Torrent*. The fact that it had imitators and is studied in literary institutions for the indoctrination of naïve students does not make it better.

The writings of Gladkov, Fadeyev, Ostrovsky, Gaidar, Makarenko, and the epic narratives of Sholokhov form, however, the core of distinctly realistic Communistic literature. Each of these authors has his own individual features, and it would be wrong to put them all into the same literary school: the one thing they have in common is that their works, which are of considerable artistic variety, express identical beliefs.

Fyodor Gladkov (1883-1958) the son of a Volga peasant, who had been compelled to become a proletarian, spent his childhood in squalid poverty. His parents worked in the fisheries of the Caspian Sea, and in the mills of the Caucasus. He himself tried many trades and callings, until he finally became an elementary schoolteacher. Later he joined the socialist movement, was arrested, and exiled to Siberia. He started publishing in 1900 and turned to journalism and fiction. His early stories, strongly influenced by Gorky, and, to a lesser extent, by Korolenko, are impressionistic and weak. Later he wavered between the decadents and the naturalists. In 1922, two years after he had joined the Party, Gladkov published *The Steed of Fire*, depicting the revolution in the Kuban Cossack region: its style was flowery and anti-realistic. His next novel, *Cement* (1925), was hailed in the USSR as a successful affirmation of Communist ideology. It is written in the emotional and highly ornamental language of the period; in fact one can easily find in this proletarian novel what Communist critics dubbed "Decadent stylization"—mostly of dubious taste ("the sea was boiling like hot milk and bits of sun, in a fiery glow"). Three decades after the publication of *Cement* Gladkov revised his work according to the requirements of socialist realism, but only made it flat and pedestrian.

The arty style of his original was only a contrivance for evoking the hard facts of life. The heroes of this "first Soviet novel of the working class" are true proletarians. After three years of fighting in the Red Army, Gleb Chumalov, a former mechanical worker, returns to his home town, a Black Sea port (apparently Novorossiisk), only to find his living quarters as well as his plant destroyed. Famine and desperation have scattered his fellow workmen; epidemics have carried off their children. His wife Dasha has gone through the horrors and ordeals of the civil war but has become a New Woman, conscious of her rights. She affirms her freedom in all things, including sex, and no longer accepts Gleb's attitude of the conquering and brutal male. Despite fits of jealousy Gleb has to adapt himself to changed conditions and to rebuild his marital relationship on the basis of the "new morality." Everything in general has to be rebuilt; life demands complete reconstruction—of mills, houses, cities, and habits.

The most urgent thing, however, is to resume work in the half-demolished and abandoned plant—the chief enterprise of the town. Gleb devotes himself wholeheartedly to this tremendous task. He has to overcome the apathy of workers exhausted by privations and bloodshed, the lack of building materials, and the threat of counter-revolutionaries whose raids create havoc and panic. His enthusiasm and unyielding will power win over the old engineer Kleist, an enemy of the Soviets, and harness the energy of Bad'in, a debauched bureaucrat. Despite many blunders and reverses, despite personal anxieties and family difficulties, Gleb finally triumphs—and the reopening of the plant symbolizes a new era: "we relied on blood and our blood made the whole world flare; now, tempered by fire, we rely on work," proclaims Gleb in his speech applauded by hundreds of workmen.

The defects of *Cement* are quite obvious. Its impressionism is cheap and incongruous; there are scenes of torture and various episodes of violence and death that remind one of Andreyev—or, even worse, of Artzybashev; Gleb and Dasha, the pivotal characters, are stilted and two-dimensional, and the secondary ones, such as Ivolghin the intellectual, are weak and stereotyped. Nevertheless, all those literary shortcomings did not prevent *Cement* from scoring a tremendous success in Russia as well as abroad. Translated in all the languages of the Soviet Union, it had sold 2 million copies by 1937 and still continues to be widely read.

There are several reasons for its popularity. This truly "proletarian" novel emphasizes the main theme of Communist literature —the victory of confidence over skepticism, of effort over indolence, of labor over inactivity. And it established a pattern that had nothing to do with literary perfection: the most important thing for fiction of Communist persuasion was to express faith and to show the triumph of hope. Moreover Gladkov pointed at constructive work as a vehicle for the resumption of normal life, and this was on everybody's mind in the 1920's. The fellow-travelers talked too much about the holocaust of the Revolution and civil war: and here was a novel about material reconstruction and new ethics. Gladkov also attempted to introduce a new hero—his greatly romanticized Gleb begins a long series of strong-willed, purposeful Communists—and a new heroine, the woman who rejects the old code of morality and does not want to be "just a housekeeper and a wife." *Cement* dealt with all these themes in a rather primitive way—a way that proved to be accessible to the masses, who were interested in direct representation.

The mechanics of making a best-seller in Russia are much the same as in capitalist countries, the difference being that social content and an affirmation of incorruptible conviction, rather than an adventurous or salacious story, form the basis of mass appeal. In the U. S. (and in the West, in general) large sections of the public seek in books primarily entertainment, excitement, or escape, but the Russians have been so conditioned by tradition and by the Revolution as to expect in their reading an echo of their own thoughts and an answer to their perplexities and anxieties—or at least an indication of what is good or evil. New audiences in the Soviet Union, less sophisticated than those of the pre-revolutionary epoch, yet much more numerous, demand moral and social inspiration from works of fiction—hence the fact, that while second- or third-rate Western literature offers simple trash, poor Soviet literature produces tendentious and didactic trash.

Whatever Gladkov wrote after *Cement* never equaled the popularity of this novel of reconstruction. His *Energy* (1933), a naturalistic description of the building of a gigantic power station on the river Dnieper, had a dull plot and sentimental portraits of Communist engineers; the central figure of Miron Vataghin, a Party organizer who arranges everything and overcomes all the obstacles, is particularly pale and artificial.

During the Second World War, Gladkov supplemented his sketches of factory life in the Urals with *The Oath*, a short novel written in affected language about heroic labor spurred by patriotic feelings. Much better are his autobiographical novels, *The Tale of Childhood* (1949), *The Free Gang* (1950), and *The*

Wicked Year (1951), which depict life in a pre-revolutionary village and in Caspian Sea fisheries in a crude but colorful manner, strongly imitative of Gorky. None of these mediocre works made any significant contribution to Soviet letters.

It was not until 1927 that Communist literature had another glamorous success—this time with a novel of definite aesthetic merit. *The Rout*, which met with enthusiasm from readers and critics alike, was superior to *Cement* in every sense. Its author Alexander Fadeyev (Bulyga) was born in Central Russia in 1901, but his father, a medical assistant, moved to the Far East; Alexander was graduated from a commercial high school in Vladivostok, then attended the Mining Technical Institute. He took part in the civil war, was wounded twice, joined the Communists in 1918, and was active in Siberia and the Ukraine as a Party organizer. The works he published in 1923 (*The Overflow* and *Against the Current*) were of little interest, but *The Rout*, which appeared four years later, brought him to prominence. This novel, based on personal experience, was realistic and at the same time highly polemical. It told the story of Siberian Red guerrillas whose small detachment was encircled by the Whites and the Japanese. The guerrillas are fighting their way out against terrible odds, and only eighteen men and their leader succeed in breaking through. Unlike Serafimovich, who depicted an anonymous multitude and its elemental urges, Fadeyev broke his work down into psychological portraits of individuals. Each character is presented with his own thoughts, emotions, and unique destiny: the simpleminded shepherd Metelitsa, who is taken prisoner and put to death by the Whites; the adventurous, bold, and anarchical miner Morozko; his warm-hearted, warm-blooded, none too virtuous wife, Darya; Mechik, a young student, who, like so many intellectuals, is attracted by the romantic appeal of the Revolution but cannot take its hardships and finally deserts the detachment; Goncharenko, the benevolent giant; the old workman, Pika; and the ignorant, inarticulate peasants who joined the Reds because of the infallible instinct of the poor and the oppressed.

The physical characteristics, mannerisms, and reactions of all these people, as well as the mechanism of their inner lives, were carefully analyzed by Fadeyev. One of his best portraits is that of

Levinson, a Jew who leads the detachment and is the only true Communist amid this riffraff. He understands the difference in motivation that had forced such diverse people as Morozko and Pika to take up arms, and he knows that to be able to command others, "one must show them their weaknesses and overcome one's own." He also thinks that a leader should say nothing but "Yes" or "No," never evince doubt or hesitation, and act as if he were perfectly sure of himself and his decisions. The guerrillas are firmly convinced that Levinson has a carefully prepared plan that will save them, that he knows how to get out of their awful predicament; actually he has no plan and has not the slightest idea what to do. But he acts as if he did, and this generates a confidence that keeps everyone going. The theme of trust is here linked with the problem of authority, for the philosophy of Bolshevik government is formulated by Levinson. Manhood and courage are other themes, and Fadeyev deals with them much as Tikhonov does: to live and to win one must be hardy, strong, and devoid of sentimentality. Sentimentality and false romanticism seem to him the sins of soft, irresolute intellectuals, such as Mechik, and he exclaims "Down with Schiller," condemning a whole tradition of eloquent but passive rhetoric.

As the guerrillas are retreating through Far Eastern forests, they are compelled to shoot one of their own band, the badly wounded Frolov, for they can neither drag him along nor leave him helpless in the wilderness. And when the nineteen at last break out of their trap, the epic concludes with: "now they would have to live and fulfill their duties." This was the code of morality accepted by the Party, and a parallel theme that runs through the novel is Levinson's transformation of anarchical guerrillas into a disciplined body. His efforts show what the Communists intended to do with the people of Russia.

Later in *The Last of the Udegs* (1936), a lengthy epic of the civil war and of Japanese intervention in the Far East, Fadeyev, following the Party doctrine, tried to combine psychological portraiture in Tolstoy's style with the "synthetic monumental realism of Goethe or Pushkin." He attempted a vast panorama encompassing Siberian capitalists such as Gimmer and ideal revolutionaries such as Langovoy, the main "positive hero," and offering a

whole procession of diverse characters from the charming Lena
and her young suitors, to Kazanok, a native, the last of his tribe,
conceived partly as a Fenimore Cooper type, partly as one of
Rousseau's "noble savages." Despite excellent chapters of realistic
description, this ambitious project was unfortunately bogged
down beneath overbearing details. The author himself recognized
his failure—and this at a time when critics saw in his voluminous
novel a triumph of socialist realism.

A man with a good critical mind and a hard worker, Fadeyev
was interested in various literary and moral problems, as proved
by his lively diaries and letters, but sacrificed his innermost aspirations to Party activities. Bearer of the Order of Lenin, secretary
general of the Union of Soviet Writers, member of the Party Central Committee, he turned into a functionary and a dignitary and
did not publish any more fiction until 1945 when his *The Young
Guard* was received with great praise. This war novel, with its
mixture of psychological realism with romantic pathos, tells the
story of the resistance movement organized in 1942-43 under the
German occupation by the teenagers of Krasnodon. Based on true
facts, it depicts the boys and girls who fought and perished "chin
up." The martyrdom of Oleg Koshevoy and other young conspirators who were actually tortured and executed plays but a
small part in the narrative. The attention is primarily directed to
their moral rectitude and utter devotion to Russia. After its initial
success, *The Young Guard* was denounced in 1947, during the
years of political and literary reaction; Fadeyev was accused of
"deviation," despite, or perhaps because of, his high Party position.
"The serious ideological and artistic errors of the writer," the
critic Lev Subotsky wrote in 1948, "lie in his not having created
in the novel a complete image of the Bolsheviks who are guiding
and educating our youth, in his failure to show the activity of the
Party organization in the underground." Obediently Fadeyev revised *The Young Guard* and published in 1951 a new edition of
the novel in which Lutikov, the Party organizer, as well as other
excellent Party members, were introduced as central figures. This
mutilation of his work must have cost Fadeyev a great deal but it
was not the only compromise he made with his conscience. After
Stalin's death there were rumors in Moscow that he had played an

ambiguous if not downright shameful part in political purges and had caused the tragic end of several former friends and colleagues. He began to go to seed, drank heavily, and committed suicide in 1956. The official version attributed his death to alcoholism, but some of his intimates believed that the real cause of Fadeyev's untimely voluntary demise were pangs of conscience and the feeling that all his activities under Stalin, and perhaps his whole life, constituted a tragic, useless error.

It is quite obvious that in the history of Soviet literature Fadeyev stands out principally as the author of *The Rout*. What made this work virtually a landmark in Soviet letters was its contrast with the abstract schemes of most proletarian writers. It was a well constructed and carefully written novel; its main virtue lay in the psychological portraits of the characters. In this Fadeyev followed the Tolstoyan tradition, thus initiating a trend that became predominant in the 1930's. It is common knowledge that Leo Tolstoy depicted a total man, or what was later called a "rounded" character, analyzing the evolutionary flux of inner changes and sharply distinguishing between the appearance and essence of emotions and thoughts. This artistic method could be called "psychological realism." Soviet critics disliked this term, and some of them insinuated that it was invented by the writer of this book with the special purpose of disparaging socialist realism. The truth is that the expression "psychological realism" has been used for decades, and that a whole group of Communist novelists, including in the first place Fadeyev and Sholokhov, followed the Tolstoyan method long before socialist realism was launched. Of course, the polemical ardor concerning various terms can be explained by the desire of Soviet historians to apply—quite gratuitously—the label of socialist realism to all works of merit published by quite diverse writers, regardless of the fact that each of them belonged to a different literary tradition.

The problem of Tolstoyan influence, however, is not simply a matter of academic controversy. It can be safely assumed that Tolstoy's impact on Soviet authors went beyond their mere acceptance of his artistic manner and analytical method. He was not only the patron of the resurgent realistic school, mainly promoted by the Communists, but also the precursor of their aesthetics. Tolstoy demanded a direct projection of reality though he also insisted on the writer's "moral point of view," for which the Communists substituted a socio-political one. His condemnation of contemporary works of fiction as mere playthings for the upper classes, his rejection of decadents and symbolists as "rich and brainless snobs," his emphasis on the "message" and the universal significance of great works of art, his desire to transform literature into a vehicle for moral mass education, were fully accepted and utilized by the Communists. The latter were also attracted by his contempt for stylistic "embroidery," by his love of simplicity in art, and his puritanical attitude toward sex and entertainment. In short, Tolstoy's treatise *What Is Art?* is more enlightening for the understanding of Soviet literary criticism than the few pages of Marx, Engels, and Lenin which are always quoted in Moscow as the sources of Communist aesthetics. Such diverse essayists as Bukharin, Lelevich, Kogan, Frietsche, and Gorbov, among others, used Tolstoy's definition of art as the communication of emotions (and ideas); as a logical corollary, they contended that the aim of literature was "to infect readers with class ideology."

In 1927-32, when the great debate centered on the question of how the new hero should be portrayed, the artistic method of Tolstoy was invariably dragged into the discussion. The anti-psychological school claimed that introspection was the typical feature of bourgeois individualism, and therefore ought to be relegated to the past; present-day authors ought to show man in action and, specifically, depict him as a social being. Tell us what your heroes do, demanded those Soviet behaviorists, and not what they intend to do, think, or dream; we are interested in facts and acts, not in the analysis of feelings and words. They bitterly attacked Leonov and other fellow-travelers for "splitting hairs, piling up complications," and imitating either Dostoevsky, the avowed enemy of socialism, or Tolstoy, the religious apostle of non-violence and humility. Their ideal image of literature was that of a broad canvas of social occurrences, on which individuals figured as mere parts of the whole, as illustrations of the dialectical laws of economic development—and therefore were to be shown in their relationship to groups and society. This approach hailed the ideological awareness of the writer and banished all mention of the instinctual or subconscious life of man, both of which were dubbed "relics of suspect biologism or metaphysical and religious idealism." This doctrine, which in a disguised or barely mitigated fashion still dominates Soviet letters, was challenged in the late 1920's by a group of RAPP members led by Fadeyev, Libedinsky, Gladkov, Vishnevsky, and a few others, who won strong backing inside and outside their own organization, mainly among such critics as Voronsky, Polonsky, Lezhnyov, Gorbov, and others.

The rift became apparent and the discussion particularly bitter after the publication of *The Rout*, and later, in 1930, of Yury Libedinsky's novel *The Birth of a Hero*. Son of a physician, Libedinsky, born in the Urals in 1898, joined the Party in 1920. A member of the October and the On Guard groups, and a militant Communist, he attempted to depict his comrades favorably in fairly popular novels: *A Week, Tomorrow, The Commissars* (1923), and *The Turning Point* (1924). *A Week*, describing revolutionary events in a provincial town and their international implications, was welcomed as a transition from romantic abstractions to realistic concreteness. In *The Birth of a Hero* the author analyzed the "mute and blind" sensations of Shorokhov, a Communist functionary, and paid as much attention to his unsuccessful love affair as to his important Party activities—thus putting them on a par. The novel as a work of fiction is insignificant, but it did serve as a weapon in the war that the Tolstoyans waged against factography, tendentious naturalism, and social behaviorism.

According to Fadeyev's momentous manifesto, *The Road of Soviet Literature* (1928), proletarian writers were striving to explain the attitudes of the new Communist heroes by disclosing their motivations and by drawing detailed psychological portraits in general, by dealing with them as human beings. The purpose was "to depict live men and to give a truthful rendering of Soviet reality." Truth-in-art, as Tolstoy understood it, became the slogan of a vast literary group. Many fellow-travelers were ready to rally to it, together with the proletarians. By the time the Central Committee had published its literary edict of 1932, the partisans of psychological realism seemed to have won on all fronts. This meant the strengthening of realism in Soviet letters, and the victory was strongly felt in the pre-war decade. Unfortunately, the doctrine of socialist realism distorted the development of Russian prose and poetry, imposing upon them artificial norms and mendacious habits. It is true that the peak of psychological realism was reached by Sholokhov, and his success brought many followers. But the victory of the movement raised one of the pivotal problems of Soviet literature.

The main aim placed before Soviet writers was the search for the New Hero. It was approached from two points of departure which in turn diverged or merged. One was the realistic portrayal of psychological changes that had occurred in Soviet men and women as the result of social and economic conditions. In a collectivistic society attitudes toward property, money, and work were inevitably at variance with those of a capitalist regime, and fiction explored these new patterns. As long as the readers identified themselves with the literary characters and found in fiction a mirror of topical problems, they felt that well-known pleasure of recognition which accounts for the success of so many second-rate "representative" novels. The readers wanted, however, more than their mere self-reflections—they also longed for an idealized image, in keeping with the accepted moral code and with the high principles honored by their society. This second aspect of the New Hero— that mythical vision which each community or each culture is pleased to shape—depended entirely on Communist ideology. Theoretically, the officially accepted image was that of the Man of the Future, the 100 per cent Communist citizen; and literature was made to create such an image and to give it flesh and blood.

What made this task so difficult among other things was the critical and negative tradition of the nineteenth century. Russian classics had made impressive exposés of social and moral evils and excelled in portraying sinners and weaklings and dealing with foibles and vices; but they had never been too successful in depicting saints or just plain affirmative characters, except the "simple heart" types. How can one compare the pallid and impossibly good Murazov with the colorful scoundrel Chichikov in Gogol's *Dead Souls?* Goncharov's man of action, the worthy Stolz, is, as an artistic achievement, infinitely inferior to the unforgettable and superfluous Oblomov, the laziest man in the world; Turgenev made only a few of his women seem "positive," while his men, with the exception of Bazarov in *Fathers and Sons*, were presented as failures or ineffective dreamers, and the strong hero of *On The Eve* was not Russian but Bulgarian. Dostoevsky's prince Myshkin, the hero of *The Idiot*, and Alyosha, one of *The Brothers Karamazov*, were embodiments of passive and active Christian virtues, and Leskov's "righteous men" were also conceived in a highly religious spirit. Tolstoy was one of the few Russian writers whose characters were positive, although some, such as Platon Karatayev in *War and Peace*, were only a Populist version of the "simple heart" theme, while others, such as Levin in *Anna Karenina*, or the revolutionaries in *Resurrection*, were realistic pictures of "whole men" rather than models to be followed.

Communist theoreticians claimed that the New Hero had already been born within Soviet society or, at least, was in the process of emerging from its womb. But at the same time they were eagerly discussing the problem of what his basic characteristics were and what he ought to be. Was he to be like Rakhmetov, the perfectly rational hero of Chernyshevsky's *What To Be Done?* (a novel of the 1860's) who renounced all human pleasures and emotions for the sake of the cause? Hundreds of Soviet works attempted to produce up-to-date copies of Rakhmetov, but these appeared as bloodless as their cerebral prototype. Others, however, dismissed Rakhmetov as a clumsy lifeless manikin; they insisted that the main problem was not so much that of a strict application of political principles as one of faith. The New Hero had unwavering faith in Communism and this forged his mentality, ruled his actions, and dictated his attitudes. Communist critics hailed works that expressed this faith without taking any real interest in their literary efficacy: hence the success of certain books that seem so inferior to the Western reader. One such case is *The Tempering of Steel* by Nikolay Ostrovsky, serialized in 1932 and 1934 and issued in book form the following year. It remained a best-seller for a decade (with a total circulation of five million copies) and has often been declared the top favorite among Soviet youth.

Nikolay Ostrovsky (1904-36), born into a poor family in the Ukraine, joined the Red Army at the age of fifteen; a year later he was badly wounded and gradually became half blind. A member of the Party from 1924, he was forced into inactivity by his declining health. Suffering from polyarthritis, bedridden, paralyzed, he led the existence of an invalid and a martyr, knowing perfectly well that he was doomed but never despairing and showing an extraordinary love of life and a zest for work. By 1929 he was blind and could hardly move his hands and arms, yet he composed his novel, half-writing, half-dictating: literary creativeness was for him a means of serving his fellow men. He praised heroic efforts as the highest accomplishment on earth—and his writing was in itself an act of supreme will power and courage. His autobiographical work and the life story of its gallant author merged into a single image of moral beauty creating a kind of collective myth with "a realistic surface but with a kind of internal burning," to use the definition coined by the British writer Elizabeth Bowen. There was definitely a pure flame in *Tempering of Steel*, and this explains its hold over millions of readers. Otherwise it is a poorly constructed novel, devoid of any artistic originality and written in a frankly mediocre, semi-naturalistic, semi-romantic prose, greatly influenced by Gorky's *Mother*. It tells the life story of Pavel Korchaghin, a poor Ukrainian lad who has to work as a busboy and a railroad apprentice to earn a few rubles. During the Revolution his native town is successively occupied by the Germans, the Whites, and the Ukrainian nationalists. Pavel helps the Reds in the underground, learns about the class struggle and Communism from everyday practice, goes through many adventures and perils, witnesses the death of the sailor Zhuray, his friend and teacher, and emerges as the leader of a reconstruction brigade when the turmoil is over. Crippled by wounds and disease, he overcomes all his handicaps by will power and relentless effort to become a fully and socially responsible person. The account of this growth, which goes on under such strained conditions, is the backbone of the novel; it is the eternally exciting, ever marvelous story of man's struggle, progress, and victory. Most of readers who came from the peasant and working classes had a similar past, and Ostrovsky spoke for them.

Pavel Korchaghin represented, moreover, what the new generation of the 'thirties dreamed of becoming. Western critics dubbed him a Soviet version of Horatio Alger; but the basic differences are that Pavel's aim is social service, that he works for "common betterment" and not for personal success, and that the term "self-made" can scarcely be applied to an individual whose life is histor-ically and politically determined and whose ideals are outlined with a religious fervor by the Party. The popularity of Pavel Korchaghin before, during, and even a few years after World War II took on the proportions of a cult. Identification of self with literary creations, the wish for sublimation, and the strong drive for myth-making, all deeply rooted in the Russian character, have contributed to the tremendous and lasting fame of Ostrov-sky's book. Here again, however, the heroic individual, the posi-tive type, is portrayed with inadequate artistic means, and the novel never attained in aesthetic terms what it achieved in psycho-logical and social ones. Ostrovsky had high moral stamina but his literary abilities were poor and limited (his second unfinished novel on Poland's upper classes, filled with all sorts of villains, spies, traitors, and lechers, has all the stigmata of a potboiler).

Ostrovsky played an important role in the literature devoted to Soviet youth, a literature which pictured the New Hero in terms of arty idealization and Communist stoicism. We find the same intonations, the same exaltation of stern single-mindedness and purity (including sexual purity), in dozens of heroic-romantic works of faith (for example Simonov's play *The Lad from Our Town*, Fadeyev's *The Young Guard*, the image of Travkin in Kazakevich's *The Star*, and the heroes of Polevoy).

The theme of the new hero in Ostrovsky's sense of the term was taken up by a number of Communist writers—from Arkady Gaidar (1904-41) in his tales of *Timur*, a favorite among Soviet children, to Anton Makarenko's (1889-1939) *Pedagogical Poem* (1934), which enchanted thousands of readers because it proved that man is perfectible and can be regenerated. Makarenko recounted his own experience in a reform school for juvenile delinquents: his patient efforts refashioned the lives of most of his pupils who grad-ually developed into conscientious citizens within a collectivistic community. Makarenko's faith was sincere, deep, and infectious, hence millions of readers enjoyed his healthy optimism. But when in a sequel to the *Poem* he tried to picture an ideal Soviet society, it was a failure.

18

Mikhail Sholokhov

THE EPIC NARRATOR

For almost half a century Mikhail Sholokhov, winner of the Nobel Prize in 1965, has been recognized at home and abroad as the leading writer of the Soviet Union. But he was not only a favorite novelist whose works had attained by 1965 a circulation of forty-two million copies in thirty-two languages of the Republic—he also occupied an extraordinary social and political position—deputy to the Supreme Soviet, recipient of numerous prizes, awards, and decorations, participant in Party councils, a welcome guest at the Kremlin, and a member of the Academy. Sholokhov's place in the higher echelons of the ruling class can only be compared to that of Gorky after his return from Italy. It took Sholokhov twelve years to complete *The Quiet Don*, the lengthy epic published in four parts between 1928 and 1940, and when the last volume was finally issued in 1940, crowds of people stood in line in Moscow streets waiting for the bookshops to open.

Sholokhov's way of life and temperament have also contributed to his fame. Born into a lower middle-class family in 1905, brought up in the Don Cossack region, he took part in the civil war, joined the Communists in 1920, went to Moscow where he had to earn his living as a manual laborer, and returned to his *stanitsa* (village) of Veshenskaya to settle there and devote himself to writing. Fishing, hunting, and cattle breeding are his hobbies, which attract him more than the big city lights: he makes only brief appearances in the capital. He belongs to the soil, particularly to the land of the Cossacks, those half-warriors, half-peasants, who continue to maintain old traditions within the structure of Communist society. The legend being built around Sholokhov's name in Russia portrays him as a man of character and independence, a staunch Soviet patriot, much more interested in national life than in world affairs. Even though he had to yield to Party pressures and revised his novels, he is often very outspoken and does not mince words in attacking literary bureaucrats, fat-headed censors, or overcomplicated authors. Some of his speeches at congresses and reunions of Soviet writers caused dismay in the special agencies entrusted with controls over Russian prose and poetry. But Sholokhov's position is so high that he can afford to say almost anything. He is the greatest and the most successful artist of Communist persuasion. But his works are not simple acts of faith; they are indeed good literature.

His first efforts as a local journalist and as the author of crude naturalistic sketches of the civil war, collected as *Tales of the Don*, were rather mediocre. It is true that they revealed a certain gift in the eighteen-year-old author, but his future growth could hardly have been foretold. Apparently Sholokhov had dreamed of writing a monumental narrative ever since his youth. We know very little of his literary apprenticeship and hardly anything about all the sources he used when he began to compose *The Quiet Don* at the age of twenty-one. The first part of the novel appeared two years later in 1928—first serialized in a monthly magazine, and then in book form. His great work is obviously conceived and executed under the influence of Tolstoy. It is not only the wide scope of Sholokhov's work that reminds one of *War and Peace;* there is the structure, the artistic manner, and the psychological portrayal of the protagonists. This does not mean, of course, that *The Quiet Don* is nearly as magnificent as its model, but Sholokhov, following in the wake of the master, interwove biography with history, scenes of battles with domestic incidents, movements of masses with the throb of individual emotions; he showed how social upheavals changed personal destinies, how political struggle determined the happiness or ruin of different individuals. Thus the love affair of Grigory Melekhov, the hero of the novel, and Axinia, a married woman (who was dubbed the Cossack Anna Karenina), forms the core of the narrative, the erotic and dramatic episodes setting and keeping the plot in motion. *The Quiet Don* encompasses the life of the Cossacks, the traditions and customs of their military-agricultural communities on the banks of the river Don;

it also describes Russia under the Tsar at the beginning of this century and the First World War, and then gives a striking picture of the Revolution and the fighting between the Reds and the Whites during the years 1918-21. The latter part includes newspaper accounts, official pronouncements, and other factual material—particularly in the third volume, where they weigh far too heavily on the narrative. One could easily utilize *The Quiet Don* as a fictionalized history of the most fateful decade in the life of the Don Cossacks but it would be unfair to take the novel as a mere socio-political document (an error often committed by Communist critics). It is, fortunately, a true work of imagination, it conveys the feeling of reality, it creates vivid images of people, and it has its own vision of nature and humanity which are presented in an aesthetically valid fashion.

Grigory Melekhov, the central figure in this epic, is a native Don Cossack who had been promoted to the rank of non-commissioned officer on the Russian-German front during World War I. When the Revolution breaks out, he sympathizes with the abolition of Tsarism but cannot stomach the Bolsheviks, and leads an armed band against them. He hates the Reds, yet does not feel too comfortable among the Whites, who look down upon him as an uneducated upstart. The White generals do not realize what Grigory comprehends instinctively: that the old Russia is over and done with and that new times have begun. He has lost faith in Denikin and Wrangel and after the nightmare retreat in the Kuban region, amid pestilence and beastly internecine strife, he realizes that the White cause is lost. In Novorossiisk the remnants of the counter-revolutionary armies embark for Constantinople and exile. Grigory with a few friends chooses to remain and await the Communists. This is a turning point; a great change comes over him. He joins Budenny's Red Cavalry and takes part in the campaign in Poland. His situation, however, is not enviable: his past as the commander of anti-Soviet rebels makes him suspect, so he is promptly demobilized.

His native village is now administered by the Communists. Grigory's return provokes distrust and hostility, particularly from his former friend and brother-in-law, Mishka Koshevoy, the chairman of the local Soviet. Grigory is made the butt of bureaucratic drudgery, and this is followed by threats and persecution. He finally escapes, hides, and resumes his anti-Red activity: in hate and despair he joins the Cossacks who are harrying the Red detachments sent out to requisition foodstuffs. The band's slogan, "For Soviet Power but against the Communists," strikes a responsive chord among the peasants, but they cannot contend against the regular Red Army units and are defeated. Grigory is again alone and a loser. For almost seven years he has ridden the war path, killing Germans and then his fellow Russians; he has been wounded fourteen times—yet it seems that his sacrifices, his bravery, his fierce expenditure of energy have all gone for nothing. He feels confused and disappointed, he can no longer distinguish right from wrong, and has no more physical or moral strength; the only dream left is that of tranquillity and peaceful labor. His wife and his parents are dead; Axinia, his mistress, has been killed; his house is half in ruins, and Grigory stands on its threshold as if on the rim of a desert. The little son he is holding in his arms is the only link between him and the earth, "that enormous world resplendent under the chill sun."

These words conclude the story—and a new life begins for Grigory, his son, and all the children of the Don. Sholokhov's hero is the embodiment of millions who had likewise wavered between the Reds and the Whites, he belongs to a generation whose lives and homes were reduced to ashes during the civil war and whose task it was in the 1920's to resume work and rebuild everything. No wonder, then, that Russian readers recognized themselves and their recent past in Grigory's trials and errors.

What made this recognition so easy and so suggestive was the fact that initially the author did not try to exert "ideological coercion." Himself a member of the Communist Party since 1932, he never concealed his political allegiance and made his convictions quite obvious. Moreover his portrayal of Communists as positive, attractive, heroic characters often seemed biased and artificial. Under the pressure of the Party critics he made several revisions of *The Quiet Don* in which his full acceptance of the official requirements was heavily marked. In the 1953 revision Sholokhov stressed the role of his Communist protagonists and toned down the stylistic exuberance of his epic. All this greatly marred the novel and mutilated many of its chapters.

The establishment of Soviet power in the Don region was a protracted and painful process; the Cossacks fought the new regime and were divided about it, then after bloodshed and fratricidal battle they grew resigned and accepted Communist leadership. This evolution had its parallel in all parts of Russia; *The Quiet Don* thus tells a story of nation-wide significance. What is more, it describes the conflict between faith and disbelief, between doubt and apprehension, between tradition and change, in terms of real human beings, through their lives, and the reflection of their thoughts and feelings. Sholokhov never subordinated these stories to his political ideas, never used his plot to drive a point home forcibly. He delivered no message; he simply unrolled a panorama of events and represented the flow of life in all its meanderings. An excellent portrait-painter with a mischievous sense of humor and a keenly observant eye, he drew each of his numerous protagonists wih distinct psychological and physical traits. Not only the main characters—treated in detail—but all the incidental ones possess individual ways of speech and behavior; modeled by a sure hand, they exude a solid, earthy quality. The well-rounded characters of the men and women are definitely one of the novel's principal attractions.

This *roman fleuve,* with its unhurried pace, strong feeling for nature, and vast range of space and time, is entirely in the nineteenth-century tradition of the long realistic novel. Whatever Sholokhov chooses to depict—the death of a horse, a sultry afternoon on the banks of the river, Axinia's sexual frenzy, or a crone who takes pity on a prisoner—he makes as vivid and convincing as a painting by an old master. He is at his best in evoking sensory details, in conveying the illusion of a palpable world. His psychological analysis is less satisfactory, although he does devote to it a great deal of his attention. There is often something naïve in his reading of the human mind and heart.

It may be objected that since his characters are simple and primitive, he could not avoid depicting their intellectual and emotional processes as such too; but it is doubtful whether Sholokhov is as successful in rendering psychological complexities as he is in dealing with instinctual drives. In any case, the fact that passions and irrational impulses determine the behavior of his characters give him a good reason for ignoring the demands of the "Ideologists."

Faithful to the tenets of the Tolstoyan school that he represents so brilliantly, Sholokhov aims at a description of the "organic man," his unconscious as well as his conscious self. Certain Communist critics consoled themselves for the writer's refusal to draw appropriate "rational and ideological conclusions" by asserting that the very concreteness of Sholokhov's images and character studies was in perfect keeping with the Marxian philosophy of dialectical materialism, which (in opposition to metaphysics and idealism) accepts the reality of the visible world and of sensory experience.

Other features enhanced the appeal of *The Quiet Don* for Soviet readers. They found in its descriptions of the southern steppes, rivers, and forests, and of the rhythm of the seasons, a strong feeling for the Russian soil, an all-pervading national spirit. This novel is a true epic of an agricultural people, it emphasizes the link between man and his physical surroundings; its action takes place not in Moscow or in the large towns but in the hamlets and villages of the countryside, and Grigory (with his kin and friends) is for the most part a spokesman for the peasantry; his dreams of peaceful meadows, of labor in the fields, of vespertine tranquillity are those of a farmer. It is highly relevant that Sholokhov, the contemporary of various five- and seven-year plans, never attempted to write about factory workers and never dealt with the theme of industrialization. And since the remnants of a rustic mentality and nostalgia for the native earth are still strong in every Russian city-dweller, Sholokhov is hailed, even unconsciously, as the poet of a disappearing agricultural world.

The flavor of the earth was accompanied, in the case of Grigory, by another national trait: his search for truth, for a "righteous life," for justice and a decent social order, symbolized the moral quest of the Russian people that lay behind all the cruelty and harshness of the ordeal they had undergone.

The magnitude of *The Quiet Don* was also meaningful. Its vastness, the multitude of its personages, the diversity of its episodes, the variety of its scenes corresponded to the greatness of a country which forms a whole continent. The novel radiates strength. Whatever it represents—passions, battles, labor, love—has intensity and vigor. The tumultuous life of the Cossacks, the adventures of Grigory, his passion for Axinia, the thunder of revolutionary eruptions, the outbursts of violence during the civil war, all the extremes of action and emotions are rendered with fullness and dynamic power. In general Sholokhov displays that exuberant vitality mitigated by human warmth which is so typical of Russian classics.

It could be argued that *The Quiet Don*, a panorama that conforms to the laws of perspective and life-size figure drawing, is lacking in literary originality. Except for some lyrical treatment of landscape, the author's occasional impressionistic remarks and certain passages in a strong patriotic vein, it follows the pattern of nineteenth-century representational art. It is true, however, that its racy, uninhibited (particularly in the erotic scenes of the first version) idiom has a freshness of its own. Sholokhov portrays people through their way of speaking, he uses slang for social characterization, his dialogues are built on various linguistic levels which correspond to differences in temperament and political leanings. The language of *The Quite Don* is rich and varied, at times crude but always expressive and colorful. It is a pity that in his other works Sholokhov used this exceptional verbal gift for exaggerated comic effects. This is especially true of the second part of *The Virgin Soil Upturned* and the first part of *They Fought for Their Country*.

The Virgin Soil Upturned (in English, called *Harvest on the Don*), Sholokhov's second large novel, is devoted to the upheaval caused by Stalin's militant drive to socialize agriculture. In the early 'thirties the forced collectivization of the farmlands and the extermination of the well-to-do farmers were a burning issue, and Sholokhov interrupted his work on *The Quiet Don* in order to write a novel on this subject. The first volume (1932), a tremendous success, was essentially a social profile, and the government, accepting it as such, made it required reading for all collectivization inspectors. But the ordinary readers, who bought two million copies in fifteen months, were attracted not only by its topical actuality but also by the human drama of victors and victims, told in a naturalistic manner, often close to the melodramatic and less effective than that of *The Quiet Don*. It was however superior to numerous novels on the same theme, among them the much publicized (despite Gorky's criticism) four-volume *Bruski* (1928-

37) by Fyodor Panfyorov. The main character in Sholokhov's novel is Davydov, a former sailor and worker, òne of the 25,000 picked Party members sent to the villages in 1930 to impose collectivization by persuasion and repression. Davydov plunges into the political fight in Gremyachy Log, a village on the banks of Don, leads the battle against the *kulaks*, and shares its cruelty and violence; he also becomes involved in a tortuous love affair with the enticing and treacherous Lushka, a Cossack Carmen. The first part ends with Davydov becoming the chairman of the collective farm. The readers had to wait twenty-seven years before the second part came out in 1960 (previously serialized in 1958-59). The plot revolved around the conspiracy of a group of White officers who hide in the village. Their plans are exposed but Davydov and Nagulnov, the former husband of his mistress, are killed trying to arrest the counter-revolutionaries. Davydov's death, however, does not detract from the optimistic spirit of the narrative. Though it is a fictional record of a recent past, its principal merit lies not in the evocation of a period but in the character portrayals of peasants, Communist officials, White conspirators, country wenches, and village eccentrics. It has a few tragic scenes, such as the sufferings of an old Cossack mother starved to death by her own son, or the tale of a vendetta by the coachman Arzhanov whose father was beaten to death. Yet, the novel is basically humorous, particularly in the second part. Secondary characters, such as the huge woman of the farmer's camp who has driven three husbands to the grave, or the loquacious daddy Shchukar, are truly facetious, and their antics, salty jokes, and malapropisms are a constant source of laughter—and the despair of translators who attempt to find an equivalent in any language for the idiomatic speech of the Cossacks.

In *The Virgin Soil Upturned* Sholokhov slips into verbosity, overloads the narrative with tales within a tale, and loses his sense of proportion as he piles up anecdotes and funny gossip. This defect is even more irritating in his third novel about the war *They Fought for Their Country*, of which only separate chapters were serialized between 1943 and 1960. Most of them are marred by ludicrous episodes and repetitive comic talk. In opposition to their drollery stands the glowing short story "Man's Fate" (1957) about an average Soviet citizen whose peaceful existence has been ruined by war. All the horrors the hero has gone through, however, have not destroyed his innate stamina and kindness. In another story, "The Russian Character," Sholokhov extolled the same national traits.

In general, this novelist, who in his major works has depicted men and women of the Don, belongs to provincial Russia. He shares with her a certain mistrust of the West, a profound interest in local affairs, and a strong nationalism that is lacking in philosophical depth and is largely instinctive and emotional. He has traveled a great deal and even accompanied Khrushchev, with whom he has something in common, to the U.S.A., but neither America nor Europe attracted or influenced him. To all their wonders he prefers the quiet of his native village and the society of simple laborers. His total acceptance of Communism came like almost everything with him, more from the heart than from the head. He remains aloof from theoretical discussions, and finds debates on socialist realism and artistic currents a mere waste of time. At writers' councils he often made unconventional speeches against "stuff and nonsense," mingling common sense with ironical scoffing and advising novelists and poets to leave Moscow and settle down in the country among "real, ordinary people." Far from being an intellectual, this rough and actually conservative man (who called himself a hick), often seemed brutal and unjust at literary gatherings. Moreover, his attacks against Pasternak, and later against Solzhenitsyn, as well as his unfair and rude hostility toward dissident writers and other victims of repression greatly shocked the liberal intelligentsia in the 'sixties and 'seventies. In the spring of 1966, in his address to the Twenty-third Party Congress, Sholokhov vituperated the writers Siniavsky and Daniel condemned to hard labor, called them "traitors," qualified the court's verdict as "too mild," and intimated that in the 1920's they would have been executed. The indignation provoked by these harsh words found its expression in an open letter by the writer Lydia Chukovskaya, daughter of Korney Chukovsky (1882-1969), a critic and popular author of children's books. She accused Sholokhov of betraying the best traditions of Russian literature and of assuming the role of a ruthless prosecutor who distorts the truth and replaces justice by demagogy. In any case all these incidents greatly undermined Sholokhov's national and international reputation. Another blow came from a booklet printed in Paris and containing Solzhenitsyn's preface and postscript. It challenged Sholokhov's sole authorship of *The Quiet Don* and intimated that he had appropriated and largely usurped other people's manuscripts, principally that of Fyodor Kriukov, a Don writer who died in 1920. Rumors casting doubt on Sholokhov's part in his main work have circulated in different forms in Moscow since 1928. The following year *Pravda* published an article accusing "the enemies of proletarian dictatorship who dare to spread such infamous calumnies." This sharp rebuttal, however, could not stop the gossip in literary circles about the writer's real or imaginary plagiarism. The fact that his archives were destroyed in 1943 seemed to revive and strengthen all these unsavory speculations and to bring forth numerous arguments *pro* and *contra*.

19

Leonid Leonov

THE PSYCHOLOGICAL NOVELIST

In introducing Leonov to the Soviet readers of the 'twenties Gorky called him a disciple of Dostoevsky. What made him say this was not any similarity of ideas—Leonov did not share the political and religious opinions of the master—but a similarity of approach to character and to plot structure. Like Dostoevsky, the young Soviet writer possessed an almost morbid curiosity about the complexities of mind and flesh, a bent for exploration of the unconscious, and an unfailing interest in hidden motivation and subterranean drives. When critics blamed Leonov for not showing his heroes at work, he answered that he preferred to take them out of their daily environment and to leave them alone, facing their own thoughts and conscience. "It is difficult to remain in solitude and have oneself as the interlocutor, in such a situation we discover what a man is worth." If Leonov were left alone, in creative solitude, he would have undoubtedly followed the "Dostoevskian" line. Yet this genuine and natural psychological bent was curbed and at times distorted by external pressures. Too often he was compelled to yield to the social demands of his times, and many of his artistic failures or lengthy periods of silence were due to his incapacity to solve a conflict within himself or to rise above historical contingencies. Whenever he dealt with tragic characters in crisis, describing twisted minds and depraved passions in a highly romantic, ornamental, and symbolic prose, he attained literary fulfillment; but as soon as he attempted to pursue the weary road of didactic realism and to produce stereotyped happy endings and socially useful "new heroes," he became redundant and unconvincing. This rift undermined his work and prevented him from realizing fully the possibilities of his unusual literary talent.

In fact, he remains, even with all his defects, one of the most original Soviet writers. Fortunately, the Moscow critics do not try to pretend that he is a true socialist realist: his work is outside the official literary encampment.

Leonid Leonov, born in Moscow in 1899, the son of a journalist who was of peasant stock, graduated from a *gymnasium*, and then served in the Red Army. In 1922 he settled in the capital and published his first tales: "The Wooden Queen," obviously suggested by the Serapion Brethren with whom Leonov had a great deal in common; "Tuatamur," written in a rhythmic poetic prose, the story of a Tartar khan who suffers from unrequited love for the beautiful Ytmar; and "Kovyakin's Diary," the description of a sleepy provincial town, where the Revolution has degenerated into a caricature of itself because it has to deal with "smug citizens" and "dead souls." The striking stylistic qualities of these tales attracted general attention. They certainly indicated that their young author owed a great deal to Leskov, Remizov, Bely, and Zamyatin, but they showed too, that he had his own approach to literary material. The opulence of his language, which was studded with flowery epithets and involved metaphors, was matched by the emotional complexity of his chief characters.

An opponent of naturalism and of the novels of manners or environment, Leonov was mainly interested in man's doubts and sufferings. He was attracted by problems which he regarded as the natural outgrowth of the individual's intricate relationship with the universe and society. In "The End of the Little Man" (1925), Leonov's first important short novel, he raised the same problem that Zamyatin had dealt with in "The Cave." His scholarly hero, Likharev, who is about to complete a study on Mesozoic fossils, is so disturbed by the bloodshed and horrors of the revolutionary upheaval that life loses all its meaning for him. A catastrophe has smashed his old world to smithereens and nobody needs books or scientific research any longer: all that people actually care for is food and fuel. A morsel of bread and a stick of wood are of far greater importance than culture; a holocaust leaves little room for illusions. People of Likharev's own class are no better than the "new barbarians," and all this had become clear "from that very day when the steel wing of a tremendous earth-

quake had swept over Russia, and somebody armed with a whip
had hustled her out of darkness into a new, flame-breathing space
where hundreds of thunderous tubas were bellowing like steers—
whereupon the earth had begun to spin around the sun twelve
times faster than before." Likharev knows that "the soul is frozen
just like the water in the pipes," there is no salvation for a little
man, crushed by the Revolution, and he burns his manuscript.
This short novel belongs to a whole series of stories devoted to
the collapse of the old intelligentsia and its culture.

The cruelty and insensibility of peasants who beat a horse thief
to death is the theme of another, earlier work by Leonov, "The
Breakthrough of Petushikhino" (1923), written in a lyrical mood;
here, however, the grim picture of evil in man is counterbalanced
by the image of Alyosha, a sickly lad who feels the spell of spring
as a revelation of God and who longs for justice and kindliness.

From this preparatory stage in his career, Leonov turned to
what was his true literary vocation—long, epic-like narratives
built on several levels and including various social strata. Gorky
believed that Leonov proceeded "by jumps" and that he leaped
from the tale to the novel, but such a statement seems very debatable: Leonov's development as a writer was organic, and from
the beginning he was much more of a novelist than a short-story-
teller.

Leonov's *The Badgers* (1925) was as typical of the revival of
the traditional novel form as Fedin's *Cities and Years* which came
just before it. In this lengthy book Leonov deals with two Russias: the pre-revolutionary Russia of bearded Moscow merchants
who rule with an iron hand over their families and employees,
and the new Russia of young rebels growing up unsuspected in
the merchants' very homes and warehouses. The beautiful and
willful Nastya is in revolt against her rich family, and the brothers
Senya and Pasha, two peasant lads painfully making their living
in Nastya's father's firm are ready to blow up the entire old order.
Pasha joins the revolutionaries, and Senya, desperately in love
with the unattainable Nastya, goes through many adventures during the war and the Revolution before winning her. Deeply rooted
in his rural background, he finally becomes the leader of rebellious
peasants who refuse to yield to Communist rule. They hide in the

forests like badgers, and it is Pasha who commands the troops
sent by Lenin's government to quell the uprising. The village represents the anarchical, instinctual element, and is contrasted with
the city, which is hated by the peasants and is symbolized by the
Communist Party. "We are millions," says Senya, "we give bread
and blood and strength ... we are the soil, and we are going to
destroy the city." Thus the conflict of the two Russias shown in
the first part of the novel acquires an entirely different meaning
in the second part in which the peasants are shown as enemies of
urban and rational Communism. Although Leonov's interpretation of the Revolution seems close to that of Pilnyak, it is offered
more as a hypothesis than as an affirmation, and the author of
The Badgers apparently wonders about the philosophical implications of the issue he has raised.

"Legend of Kalafaat," a story-within-a-story in *The Badgers*,
caused a good deal of distress to Soviet censors and was eliminated
from further editions of the novel. In it Leonov describes a Tsar
of peasant folklore who wants to have all the stars filed away, to
issue passports to all the beasts of the forest, and to register every
herb. When he finally carries out his project, "everything became
sad. The groves turned silent, clearings became overgrown with
underbrush ... All nature was completely messed up. Even the
bear became sickly: what with the passport and all, he did not
know any more whether he was a beast or a man." Next Kalafaat
decides to build a tower as high as the skies, and it takes him
twenty years to do it: "twenty years to him, twenty centuries
to us." When the tower is completed Kalafaat begins climbing
to its top. He climbs for five years, but when he finally reaches
the flat roof and looks around him, he lets out a howl worse than
any beast's. While he has been ascending the inner stairs, the
tower, under his enormous weight, has been gradually sinking
into the ground: for every step he has been taking upward, the
tower has been sinking the same distance underground; despite
all his trouble he has not gotten an inch above the earth's level.
Moreover, during his futile ascent nature has done away with all
his seals and passports—and the birds and beasts are enjoying themselves again in the free forests and blooming fields.

The "Legend of Kalafaat" has often been cited as a symbolic

interpretation of the peasant's attitude toward the building of Communism. It has, however, a wider significance: Kalafaat personifies the principle of blind bureaucracy, of a mechanical order that challenges nature and kills life and joy. Like Leo Tolstoy, the author of *The Badgers* hailed simplicity, naturalness, and conformity to organic laws as the highest moral virtues—without, however, sharing either Tolstoy's religious beliefs or his moral dogmatism. In any case, *The Badgers* did not try to formulate a message and its value, which is unquestionable despite its shaky structure and the strange coincidences in the plot development, lay in the author's gift for presenting in an impressive, dynamic, and yet poetic manner the conflict of generations, classes, mentalities, and temperaments. The psychological characterization of its heroes lacked, perhaps, the depth we will find in Leonov's later novels, but he did succeed in populating his vast narrative with many different kinds of human beings and in giving a broad picture of Russia and its basic problems.

Leonov's next and perhaps his best novel, *The Thief* (1927), was a great step forward from *The Badgers*. It deals with modern Moscow and with a very special section of life there, and its tone and structure are obviously inspired by Dostoevsky. Here the characters and events are depicted under a double aspect: through the author's exposition and through the eyes of Firsov, a writer, whose diary carries notes for a novel about the same characters and the same environment. This device of a "mirror gallery" (which André Gide used so successfully in *The Counterfeiters*) makes the structure of *The Thief* somewhat sophisticated. No less intricate is its plot, which unfolds a startling panorama of the Moscow underworld under the NEP.* Mitya Vekshin, the central figure of the novel, a former commissar in the Red Army and a Party member, is a kind of Soviet Raskolnikov. A romantic rebel, disappointed with the "retreat" of the NEP, he becomes a thief and the leader of a gang of criminals. He challenges law and society but is tormented by remorse and persecuted by the

---

* The theme of the criminal underworld appears very seldom in Soviet literature; between 1930 and 1955 it was banned from fiction, and the reader of Soviet novels had the impression that crooks, thieves, and murderers simply did not exist in Soviet society.

furies: once he had killed in cold blood a captive White officer, and a sense of guilt gnaws him still. The "anti-heroic" NEP adds to his anxiety and feeling of frustration. Temperamentally he is an individualist, politically an idealist disgusted with surrounding reality. His pals are the grim, taciturn bandit Ageika, haunted by his own isolation; Manyukhin, a former landowner who earns his living by telling off-color stories in dives and taverns and behaves like Marmeladov, his literary predecessor; and the heartless Chikilyov, a cynical nihilist who distrusts and loathes his fellow men, striking the pose of the hero of Dostoevsky's "Notes from the Underground." Chikilyov says that "thought is the source of suffering, and whoever will destroy it will be eternally honored by mankind." Mitya is also surrounded by "infernal" women, such as the proud Masha Dolomanova, whose love is a torture and a delight, and by prostitutes and gangsters. They all move in a feverish twilight of danger and passion; they spend hours in morbid introspection while drinking in clandestine night clubs; they humiliate, hurt, and offend one another. Masha, who both adores and fights Mitya, makes him alternatively miserable and ecstatic, without ever arriving at the fulfillment of her love. "The best fictions of old mankind are God and Love," says Leonov, and all his protagonists search for truth and warmth as a possible escape from their impasse. They are all plagued by pain, anguish, and struggle, and they know that such is their human lot. The Communist Matvey tells his sister Zina, who is also in love with Mitya, that some day man will know and measure everything, and that great happiness will result from such rational awareness. But the voluptuous Zina laughs at him: "Happiness without torment? Made on an assembly line? Impossible!" The writer Firsov does not wish to depict socially useful types and exclaims: "But what if I am interested in the hidden roots of man? . . . There is no other task as poignant as to scrutinize man face to face."

The pathologically warped characters and the dramatic plot of *The Thief*, which depends on murder, suicidal drives, and the clash of passions, remind us quite obviously of Dostoevsky. The moral denouement of the novel is, however, not a religious one. Mitya is purged by suffering, "the fire of his soul burns him clean," but his recovery and his awakening to new life are due to social causes: the rebel promises to become a citizen and accepts the pattern of the Soviet community. The Communist critics felt that this ending was not strong enough, and that the individualist Mitya had not passed through an "ideological conversion." They also reproached Leonov for the morbid atmosphere of his novel and the "decadent psychological introspection." They missed the fact that *The Thief*, despite all its melodramatic devices, has a variety of excellently drawn characters, and is striking in its use of different levels of the Russian language, including the slang and vernacular of various social groups.*

It was obvious from whatever Leonov wrote in the 'twenties that his fiction was rooted in moral and psychological problems, and in the late 'twenties, when the first Five-Year Plan demanded new sacrifices, he began wondering whether the requirements of the collective state could be reconciled with the aspirations of the individual. In his remarkable *Stories About Unusual Muzhiks* (1930) the basic conflict is impressively illustrated. Ivan, a deaf-mute carpenter who has never known success or love, attends a village meeting that is to decide the fate of a blacksmith, who has been caught stealing horses. There is but one blacksmith in the village, whereas there are several carpenters. The peasants stare at Ivan: everybody knows that he is innocent. Yet crime calls for punishment—the equilibrium between the law and transgression must be restored, and someone has to pay. Ivan is chosen as an expiatory victim, and the villagers embrace him and promise him a good burial as he is led off to his death. The community has demanded and obtained human blood to furnish a deterrent and to maintain justice.

The same contradiction between the blind rules of society and the personal life of an individual is brought out in other works by Leonov, but he gradually began to accept Communism as the supreme judge and settler of such conflicts. Like many fellow-travelers of the period he suppressed his own doubts and hesitations. The industrialization of the country supplied him with a

---

* Leonov, unfortunately, took these criticisms quite seriously, and began to rewrite *The Thief*. He published in 1959 a new, expurgated version of the novel in which the pernicious effects of individualism are clearly condemned.

new argument in favor of the rulers who, regardless of the cost in lives and energy, were accomplishing an historic mission in a backward nation. It was not the social command but a sincere feeling for the revolutionary transformation of the country and his desire "to bring literature closer to life" that determined the subject matter of Leonov's next novel.

Sot' or *Soviet River* (1930), published with a foreword by Gorky that placed Leonov very high among contemporary writers and declared that his words "shine," was inspired by the Five-Year Plan. The action takes place in millennial forests, in forlorn hamlets, in the chapels of the Old Believers (Schismatics), in medieval monasteries, and on the shores of rivers in a remote Northern province. Ignorant *muzhiks* and superstitious monks still talk of the advent of the Antichrist and listen to seventeenth-century chants, but new men and machines invade the peace of this wilderness. Moscow needs cellulose and paper; the plan calls for an erection of paper mills on the banks of Sot'. Thousands of workmen and technicians shatter the stillness of the forests; a dam is built to harness the turbulent waters of the river. A deadly struggle ensues between the pioneers led by the chief engineer, the Communist Uvadiev, and the monks and peasants, stirred up by Vissarion, a former Imperial army officer. Like Senya of *The Badgers*, Vissarion hates the city. Man has no need of this crazy realm of machines, huge towns, and artificiality, he declares. Only people who are living in the simplicity of a communion with nature are obeying the Divine Law. To save mankind from the iron age of impiety, corruption, and technology, a new invasion of barbarians is needed: Vissarion has fantastic dreams of Mongolian hordes that will sweep over Europe and Russia in a purifying torrent of blood and fire; Communism will perish along with the old and false civilization, and luxuriant crops of grain will grow freely upon its ruins. But Vissarion's phantasmagoria amounts to no more than impotent raving, and he dies an ignominious death.

The anti-Soviet conspiracy proves less dangerous than the enmity of the elements. Symbolically, they both stem from the same source—from the blind irrational forces man must control within and outside himself. The builders have to conquer land

and river inch by inch, and only through perseverance do they finally overcome the fury of the river and the insidiousness of the people's ignorance and reaction. The theme of the "conquest of nature" is parallel to that of the conquest of man; and the opposition of the past to the present takes more dramatic form than the same confrontation in *The Badgers*. It is curious that in all these conflicts the writer seems ambivalent: he is nostalgic toward the past and has a great love of nature; his sympathy, however, goes finally to the rational man who imposes his will over storms and floods and destructive passions. In *The Thief* the elemental rages throughout the novel. In *Soviet River* it explodes but is curbed, despite almost insuperable difficulties. Uvadiev, the leader of the workmen, the puritanical, almost inhuman hero, becomes an abstract symbol: if Leonov wanted to embody the ideal Communist in this "iron-like" character, he most certainly created a misfit.

Stylistically, *Soviet River* is an accomplishment: the combination of archaisms, of regional idiom, of neologisms originated under the Soviets, and literary stylization forms an attractively bright verbal pattern. Some secondary characters, such as the engineer Burago, an intellectual planner, or Renne, Suzanna's old-fashioned father, or Uvadiev's powerful mother, who is reminiscent of Gorky's creations, are extremely vivid and aesthetically successful. *Soviet River*, one of the best books about the Five-Year Plan, fortunately lacked the blaring rhetoric which spoiled most of the works devoted to the same subject in the 'thirties; it represented, however, Leonov's official salute to Communism. Like most of the intellectuals of the same decade, he interpreted Communism idealistically, not in terms of a doctrine derived from Marx and Lenin but as one of the variations of radical humanism. He also insisted that the chief motivation of the intellectuals who were giving their support to the regime was their desire to "serve the people," that dream of the Populists, which has always been one of the most powerful determinants in the development of the Russian intelligentsia.

Leonov's effort to make a complete adjustment to the new order is clearest in *Skutarevsky* (1932), a novel about an old scientist whose cautious, almost hostile, attitude toward the Communists gradually changes into a friendly acceptance of their aims and methods. His son Arseny, however, calls the Five-Year Plan "enthusiastic hysterics," gets involved in a counter-revolutionary conspiracy, and kills himself. The clash between father and son symbolizes, in an inverted fashion, the opposition of two eras and two mentalities. Their strange relationship, Skutarevsky's domestic complications, his love for a young girl whose embrace he refuses, leaving her to a younger rival, and the suggestions of sabotage and imperialistic intrigue make the plot involved and fairly melo-dramatic, as is often the case with Leonov. It is obvious that the campaign against non-Party technicians and the trials of 1930-31 were to a certain extent reflected in the novel, but Leonov came to the defense of the intelligentsia and affirmed its loyalty; he could not, however, refrain from depicting imaginary or real conspiracies, and accepting the sensational revelations of enemy activities which, according to the claims of the Security Police, were taking place all over the country. But the character of Skutarevsky and the painful process which led him to a political conversion were treated with intelligence and subtlety. As for the new Communist man (this time called Cherimov), Leonov again failed to make him come alive.

More complex but less convincing is *Way to the Ocean* (1935), a novel with excellent passages that fails to become an artistic whole. It was certainly Leonov's most ambitious attempt to create a truly Communist work, but he succeeded only in the parts devoted to the pre-revolutionary past and in the portrayals of negative characters; the sketches of virtuous heroes and the pano-rama of beautiful times to come seem strained and pompous. The composition of *Way to the Ocean* is very intricate: it is built on several levels, with the chronological sequence of the narrative being constantly interrupted by flashbacks or predictions of the future. It is quite possible that Leonov, conscious of the prominent place occupied by the problem of time in modern European literature (especially in works by Proust, Joyce, Mann, Virginia Woolf, Faulkner, and others) wished to introduce it into Soviet literature. Unfortunately, he lacked a firm point of view, and his treatment of time often becomes obscure and blurred.

The plot of the novel centers around Kurilov, an old Communist and director of a local Siberian railroad, who is very ill; the approach of death makes him think of the years gone by and of the people he has known—of Liza, whom he loves and who torments and illuminates his last days; of her husband, the surgeon Ilya Protoklitov, whose father, a Tsarist official, had sentenced Kurilov to prison and exile; of Ilya's brother Gleb, a former White officer who had wormed his way into the Party. The unmasking of Gleb and of a conspiracy against the regime and the intricate relationships of Kurilov, Liza, and the surgeon form the core of the story and are described in the present tense. The reminiscences of all the protagonists make up the second level of narrative, and the third level gives a vision of the future (in three separate chapters) along with predictions of war (apparently with Japan), of a revolution in China, of new formidable weapons of destruction, of a Communist army led by a Negro commander. There is a description of Ocean, the world capital somewhere near Shanghai, and a resplendent picture of Communism, toward which all the hopes and achievements of mankind will converge, even as all the streams and rivers find their way into the mighty ocean. Above all individual destinies will shine the bright star of collective action and "service for the people."

Despite all his utopian excursions into the future, which merge with Kurilov's dreams, Leonov failed to make Kurilov a new hero: he portrayed him as a nice ordinary fellow, a romantic, who looked no different than other, non-Communist personages. The grandiloquence of style and the overdramatization of plot added to the heaviness of this artificial work. Critics, writers, and readers received it without enthusiasm, and this lack of success affected Leonov so deeply that he decided to stop writing novels and, in fact, his next one did not appear until eighteen years later, in 1953. Between 1936 and 1946 he turned to the stage and wrote twelve plays. Eleven of them were produced by leading Moscow theaters but the twelfth, The Blizzard, was killed by the censors and not released for publication until 1963.

Leonov's ideological and psychological complexity made his plays stand out among Soviet productions, but he often was too eager to fulfill the political·requirements of his times. His best play was Untilovsk, an exposé of provincial evil and boredom, staged in 1928 by the Moscow Art Theater; one of its main characters Chervakov, reminiscent of Chikilyov of *The Thief*, is a cynical philosopher who laughs at idealists and liberals, and who maintains that "everything on earth has the hole in which it is destined to disappear, just as man is gulped up by his grave." Critics reproached Leonov for having made Chervakov more interesting than his life-affirming opponents.

A characteristic dramatic work of Leonov is *The Orchards of Polovchansk* (1936). In its first version the playwright opposed Makkaveyev, head of a large family, the creator of gardens, and a man of purposeful and fruitful life, with Pylyayev, a superfluous man. With its lyrical and symbolic scenes, the drama had a consistency of mood and tone. But after the purges and trials Leonov wrote a second version in which he made Pylyayev a secret foreign agent, and the whole play became a melodrama centered around the discovery of subversion. *The Wolf* (1938) was simply a potboiler about saboteurs, cunning villains, and noble police investigators. *An Ordinary Fellow* (1940), a comedy, is slightly better and does not show that eagerness to please the masters of the day which Leonov had displayed in other dramatic works. During the war he overcame his political servility in two outstanding plays, *Invasion* (1942) and *Lyonushka* (1943). The first is a study of an embittered character who changes under the pressure of circumstances; Fyodor Talanov had attempted to kill his wife and was sentenced to hard labor. He is released and returns home just when the Germans overrun his native town. The disappointed and lonely outcast, an enemy of the Soviet regime, emerges reluctantly from his shell and avoids contact with other people. Their sufferings, however, lead him finally to forget his own troubles; he helps the victims of the Nazis and becomes active in the underground resistance. When caught he pretends to be Kolesnikov, the leader of Red guerrillas whom the Germans are vainly trying to arrest. In order to protect Kolesnikov and his men, Talanov is ready to die. His mother understands what he is attempting to do and identifies him as Kolesnikov, thus accepting and blessing his sacrifice. He is hanged by the invaders, and dies at peace with his conscience. This is his redemption: the "lonely wolf," as he called himself, has given his life for the people to whom he belongs, for the country he cannot help loving. The gradual "conversion" of Talanov and the dramatic incidents of *Invasion* make it one of the most breathtaking of war plays. Some theaters, however, tried to "correct" Leonov and gave undue prominence to Kolesnikov, in order to stress the role of the Party in the ultimate victory over the Germans.

In *Invasion* the hero's parents, the kind and rather Chekhovian doctor Talanov and his forthright wife Ann, are presented as "average Russians." The interest in national traits is even more distinct in *Lyonushka*, a symbolic drama, "a popular tragedy," as the author calls it. Lyonushka, a peasant girl, is in love with a badly burnt flier whom the guerrillas are hiding in their forest camp. Lyonushka wants to bring hope and joy to the dying man, and stages songs and dances for him. The strange scenes of Russian revelry serve as a symbolic background to the flier's agony. The play has an intricate psychological design and a remarkable merging of tragic elements, folklore motifs, patriotic emotions, and allegorical allusions. Theatrical directors were afraid of it: it was obviously not a realistic drama, and it contained dangerous formalistic devices and ideological deviations. From the literary standpoint it is a very interesting work even though it can be accused of rhetoric and intellectualism. Less intellectual, but also intricate and definitely symbolic is Leonov's short war novel, *The Taking of Velikoshumsk* (1944), in which the themes of war and defense of the motherland are treated in elaborate prose. It tells the story of an old battered tank and its crew, whose members, despite individual differences, represent the basic unity of Russia. Realistic details of combat mingle with the image of the tank as a living person; characterizations of generals and soldiers are as valid psychologically as they are symbolically, and the whole plot, although perfectly believable in terms of military operations, has a hidden philosophical meaning—again dealing with the essence and fate of Russia, its traditions and its aspirations. The extent to which this problem preoccupied Leonov is shown by *The Russian Forest*, a huge novel published in 1953. Here again Leonov resorts to multi-level composition. The story deals with the deforestation of Russia and the struggle between Vikhrov, an honest and patriotic scientist for whom the forest is the source of life, and his enemy and rival, Gratsiansky, an embodiment of deception and the death instinct. The exploration in depth of this villain is accompanied by the confrontation of past and present in the light of Russia's historical heritage, by the opposition of the rational and the elemental, of self-centered egotism and creative collectivism—in short by all Leonov's favorite themes. The treatment of time is much more skilled than it was in the *Way to the Ocean* and Leonov deals now only with the past and the present, making but vague hints about the future.

The beginning of the novel is perhaps its best part: it depicts the arrival in Moscow of Polya, Vikhrov's daughter, her wanderings through the streets, and her youthful intoxication with whatever she sees. She is so thrilled and elated that she sends a telegram of welcome to herself. The charm and freshness of Polya and her wondrous impressions are rendered with a poetic sweep reminiscent of early Leonov. It is not, however, completely devoid of the author's customary ambivalence. Polya makes a pledge to Lenin in the Mausoleum to be a good girl and a good Communist; the scene resembles the taking of a religious vow by a novice in front of the holy relics of a Christian saint. Later Polya is swept into the whirlwind of war and behaves like a heroine when imprisoned by the Germans behind their lines. But neither the description of war nor the treatise on forest preservation, including a thirty-two-page lecture by Vikhrov on the subject, hold the attention of the reader. Dramatic episodes from Gratsiansky's shady past or from Vikhrov's virtuous youth hardly relieve the monotony of an overwritten work in which villains are more interesting than the characters in whom the author wishes to incarnate the high qualities of the new Communist man. Here again, Leonov, eager to march in step with the "army of Communism," tries to be what he is not. It does not suit him to make sermons and glorify dogmas. This is confirmed again by his short novel *Evgenya Ivanovna* (1965), a moralizing and pseudo-patriotic tale about the fate of a Russian *émigré* woman.

Leonov's work is long-winded and heavy; verbal twists, bizarre metaphors, poetic embellishments render his style baroque, at times obscure and often artificial. There is an overabundance in his multi-level compositions. His novels resemble old mansions with dark passages, recesses, winding staircases, corridors, wings, and annexes. What saves these voluminous productions from being overwhelmed by their own weight is Leonov's dramatic sense and his psychological insight. He develops his themes like musical motifs, and he is deeply interested in moral and philosophical problems. Above everything else, he is attracted by man's complexity, which is paralleled in his work by linguistic complexity. He likes a rich, inflated, rhetorical, literary idiom just as he likes to portray human beings with emotional deviations, ranging from fads to neuroses and psychoses. Leonov is preoccupied with the ambivalence of human nature, by the drawing power of evil and the need for supreme justice, by our desire for sublimation and the urge for self-abasement. His work is perhaps the only significant counterpart in Soviet literature to the Western psychological fiction of the 1930's. The question remains, however, whether Leonov did use his talent to full capacity; it is probable that his deliberate endeavors to conform limited his freedom of self-expression and curbed his natural development.

20

Ilya Ehrenburg

THE MASTER JOURNALIST

Ilya Ehrenburg is one of the most popular and widely read Soviet authors. Whatever criticisms may be made about his books—and there are many—his readers always find him brisk and witty, full of amusing facts and interesting stories. He is never dull, and he is very clever, at times to such an extent as to provoke mistrust. But unlike other popular writers he is not a born novelist: he is a born journalist, and at its best his writing is fictionalized reportage. The twentieth century has produced a vast numbers of similar works by well-known authors. Arthur Koestler, for instance, is a sort of anti-Communist Ehrenburg, although, of course, their literary manners differ greatly.

As a craftsman, Ehrenburg possesses brilliant qualities of intelligence and verbal expression. He has his own easily recognizable style, a combination of irony and sentimentality, couched in taut sentences and explosive aphoristic similes. There is a strong lyrical streak in Ehrenburg, but the poet in him is curbed by a keen, analytical intellect. All his travelogues, memoirs, stories, satires, collections of articles, novels, and other books (for he was tremendously prolific) are vivid and mordant—even though few of them are free from a slightly irritating egocentrism and literary or political twists. Whenever he sings the praises of Communism and of the new revolutionary hero, he seems to be playing a part. But the reader's confidence in the sincerity of Ehrenburg's ideas and feelings is restored as soon as the writer throws the full weight of his castigation, contempt, and anger against a given social and human target. His work is thus characterized by a profound and incurable ambivalence.

Ilya Ehrenburg was born in 1891 into a middle-class Jewish

family living in Kiev and then moved to Moscow. He never finished school because at 16 he got involved in revolutionary activities, was arrested, and escaped trial by emigrating to France. Paris, where he stayed from 1909 till 1917, shaped him as a man and as a writer. Fascinated by all the latest artistic and literary vogues, he belonged to the motley crowd of bohemians who congregated in the cafés and studios of Montparnasse and Montmartre. At one time he was attracted by Catholicism and dreamed of withdrawing into a Benedictine monastery. But he was also familiar with socialistic circles and with political *émigrés*, and he got to know some of the future leaders of Russian Communism. In 1911 he began publishing poems inspired by the Middle Ages, symbolism, and decadent aesthetics. During World War I he served as a correspondent at the front for several Moscow newspapers, and he returned home in 1917 after the fall of the monarchy. At that moment he was an anti-Communist and, when Lenin seized power, wrote "A Prayer for Russia" (in verse), a virulent attack against the Bolshevik rulers. He went through the harrowing experiences of the civil war in the Ukraine, came back to Moscow, led the hazardous existence of a half-starved intellectual, became associated with the constructivists and the futurists, wavered between joining the Revolution and rejecting it, expressed his doubts in poems entitled *Meditations* (1921), and finally decided to return to Europe. After being expelled by the police from Paris in 1921, he lived in Belgium and Berlin, joined the "Changing the Landmarks" movement, and then officially rallied to the new government. But the shifts in his political or literary allegiances were of minor importance: they appeared much more as concessions to prevailing trends than as expressions of belief. In 1924 Ehrenburg returned to Russia. As a fellow-traveler, he took part in the hectic literary life of the capital, but he was shortly sent to Europe as a foreign editor of the Soviet dailies and spent many years in the West. In 1936-37 he covered the Spanish war together with Mikhail Koltsov, one of the most talented Communist journalists, who was liquidated later in the purges. In 1941 Ehrenburg came home from Paris, which was then occupied by the Germans, and officially settled in the Soviet

Union, visiting Europe and America only on official cultural or diplomatic missions.

Ehrenburg's best work of fiction, *The Extraordinary Adventures of Julio Jurenito* (the whole whimsical title takes up half a page), written in Belgium in 1921, is a philosophical novel, inspired by the masters of French satire from Voltaire to Anatole France and, in part, by Chesterton. Jurenito is a modern Zarathustra, of sorts, but he is a false prophet and his anarchical convictions are highly ambiguous. He discusses man's hypocrisy, he talks about war, love, money, marriage, and art, and he derides his seven disciples, each of whom bears all the stigmata of the race and nation to which he belongs. All of them travel to different countries, including Communist Russia, and find under various skies the same human stupidity and illusions. Ehrenburg, at that time, a bohemian nihilist who did not believe in anything save amusing games of intellect and sensuality, occasionally interrupted by sentimental dreams, put into *Jurenito* not only the poison of his own skepticism, but also his humor and wit: the devil of mockery who sat at Ehrenburg's elbow while he was writing made him compose both a satire on modern civilization and a parody of traditional models at the same time. The spirit of negation is so strong in this work, which is not, properly speaking, a novel, that Communist critics preferred to dismiss it in a few sentences; after a few reprints in the 'twenties, *Jurenito* disappeared from Soviet bookshops for a quarter of a century. Still in no other work of fiction was Ehrenburg as explicit and frank as in *Jurenito*: he truly discloses himself in these highly autobiographical dialogues.

As a fellow-traveler and a participant in the LEF, Ehrenburg began writing prose in the experimental and daring style of the 1920's. The brittle stories of the *Thirteen Pipes* collection (1923) bear a resemblance to the tales of the Serapion Brethren. When his LEF friends opened fire on the traditional novel and advocated replacing it with political pamphlets, Ehrenburg defended their new aesthetics in a theoretical essay *And Still It Is Turning*, and brought out a series of half-sociological, half-fictional narratives: *Trust DE*, which forecast the conquest of Europe by American capitalists not later than 1940; *The Factory of Dreams*, a diatribe against Hollywood moguls which today, after all the

American works on the subject, seems mild and naïve; *10 HP*,
an exposé of the European automobile industry, and so on. These
books, published between 1923 and 1926, were larded with ironical and insolent remarks about Europe's and America's political
and social shortcomings. They belong to the vast literature against
the capitalist world that was being promoted in Russia, and their
sharp wit delighted their readers. Yet when the movement for
the revival of the old novel form began in the Soviet Union,
Ehrenburg registered this change of weather on his highly sensitive literary barometer and wrote more conventional narratives
in the NEP and post-NEP periods. He allowed himself greater
freedom of expression in *The Racketeer* (1925), *Summer, 1925*
(1926), and *In Protochny Lane* (1927), all of which were criticized by conservative Communists for their pessimistic and negative descriptions of contemporary Russian reality. The resurgence
of the historical tale made him publish *A Conspiracy of Equals*
(1928), devoted to Baboeuf. During the decline of the RAPP
dictatorship, Ehrenburg produced romantic or semi-realistic stories and European travelogues, which the Soviet public thoroughly
enjoyed.

He had by then become a specialist in the "twilight" of the
West and depicted with sardonic pleasure the disintegration of the
European upper classes, without sparing scatological details or
omitting sexual perversions. Most of his novels on Europe, such as
The United Front (the life story of Ivar Kreuger, the match
king), were sarcastic, and they displayed the author's love of the
paradoxical and the grotesque. His criticism of bourgeois society
and of capitalist mores, his exposé of greed, of the mercantile civilization based upon success, money, and egotism suited his temperament and his bent for negation. The refinement of a Parisian
cynic, the social revolt of a Russian intellectual, and the curiosity
of a talented journalist with a nose for news and sensations formed
an amazing amalgam in all Ehrenburg's works of that period. His
literary devices were often crude and exaggerated: he used only
the basic elementary colors and the bold strokes of a poster, and
he emphasized all the symptoms of European moral corruption
and even physical decay; but his picture, both coarse and morbid,
had the immediacy sometimes achieved by the mass media. His

ironic tone, however, did not exempt him from a thin layer of vulgarity, and Ehrenburg's effort to integrate the slogans of Soviet anti-capitalist propaganda into his novels certainly did not make them more artistic.

The novels' main defect, however, came from Ehrenburg's inability to create living characters. Human beings are presented in his books either as standard-bearers of concepts and catchwords, or as scions of social groups and ways of thinking. They are all done in black and white, as either villains or saints. Capitalists are soulless, empty-hearted, aloof to human suffering, while the Communists are weighed down by their own virtues. For example, Kurbov, the hero of the cheap and melodramatic *The Life and Death of Nikolay Kurbov*, falls victim to his puritanism in an encounter with love. Ehrenburg's "nice" girls, such as the blind Jeanne Ney who gives her heart to the Russian Communist (*The Love of Jeanne Ney*, 1924), are carbon copies of the heroines in grade "B" Westerns. The extent to which such a cunning writer endowed with so observant an eye loses his critical sense when he comes to grips with human beings is almost incredible; most of his protagonists are schematic, artificial, stilted, and even in the best of cases imitative of well-known literary models. For example, the hero of his *Turbulent Life of Lazik Roitschwanz* is a twin brother of Hashek's good soldier Schweik; the story of all the mishaps that fall on the head of this poor little Jew, told with the bitter-sweet humor of Yiddish literature, is credible because it is clearly a parody. Even today, incidentally, Communist critics consider this work (although written in the late 'twenties) "subversive and cynical in its ambiguous attitude toward the Soviet regime."

Summing up the main characteristics of Ehrenburg's work, we discover that he is not a creator of fictional characters, not a refined artist, not a profound psychologist: he is a polemicist, an excellent foreign correspondent, and a gifted writer who reflects in his hybrid work the literary, political, and sometimes intellectual stimuli and fashions of his times. His very facility turns against him: he wrote one book after another with astonishing speed, in a sort of literary stenography, and although he often touches upon deep problems and important issues, he is always

superficial and, despite his darts and *bons mots,* rather trivial. This
defect derives from his fundamental opportunism. He is opportunistic because he could never conquer his inner ambivalence:
he accepted the Revolution and he tried to serve it with his pen;
he even pretended fiery enthusiasm for it, but actually he remained cold and critical and skeptical. He made biting exposés
of the West, but he has always been the most Western of Russian
contemporary writers, with many ties in European culture,
including friendships with its prominent representatives. In
the late 'twenties and early 'thirties his expressive, brittle style,
his streamlined linear composition, his dry irony, his intellectual
clarity, and his knack of spicing the leftovers of formalism and
avant-garde eccentricities with pseudo-Marxism and even Stalinism found many followers (Lev Slavin, Mikhail Kozakov, Pyotr
Pavlenko, Ovadi Savich, although Savich's only novel *Imaginary
Interlocutor* (1928) is much more than mere imitation).

In 1932 Ehrenburg, pretending to join the school of socialist
realism, discarded his own experiments and innovations and took
to writing novels of Communist persuasion. In the 1920's he had
probably considered Communism a new intellectual plaything. He
quickly learned, however, that it was a very serious matter and
attempted to adapt himself to the state religion, although, as an
inveterate miscreant, he knew perfectly well what was wrong
with the doctrine and its supporters. Moreover, he could not have
been so blinded by political ideology as to believe, for example, in
representational art under the guise of socialist realism. Of course,
he preferred the paintings by Picasso, Braque, and Leger which
adorned his Moscow apartment to the third-rate illustrations by
Gerasimov and Serov, the official painters of the regime; of course
he knew well the scant artistic value of a Nikolay Ostrovsky or
Gladkov, as compared with that of Gide, Giraudoux, Cocteau, or
his former surrealist friends, such as Breton and Aragon. But he
wanted to survive—as a man and as a writer—and he succeeded in
remaining unscathed through all the Stalinist purges and deportations.

His novels of socialist realism were, of course, highly topical:
The Second Day (1933), about the Five-Year Plan, depicted the
building of plants in the coal region of Siberia and portrayed a

good boy, Rjanov, and a bad one, Safonov, who is a decadent and
finally commits suicide. *Without a Breathing Spell* (1936) attempted to deal with the problems of family and youth and
Genka, its protagonist, was supposed to be a New Hero. *Moscow
Does Not Believe in Tears* (1937) reflected the current patriotic
wave and stressed the difference between Russia and the West—a
theme which always haunted Ehrenburg (in 1932, with O. Savich,
he had compiled *We and the West*, an interesting anthology). In
all these custom-made novels, the acceptance of Communism was
total. It might have sounded unconvincing to a discriminating
reader who knew that Ehrenburg was at his best when demolish-
ing beliefs and attacking established institutions, but the mass con-
sumers for whom all this literature was produced in industrial
quantity were satisfied. After all, Ehrenburg did not lose his gift
of entertaining even though he had to perform literary acrobatics
in order to follow, without being a Party member, the fluctuations
of the Party line.

In 1942 (after some scraps with the censors), he published his
most important narrative *The Fall of Paris*, for which he was
awarded the Stalin Prize. This social chronicle of French society
between 1935 and 1940 was patterned after the series of novels by
Jules Romains (*Men of Good Will*) and, in particular, after Louis
Aragon's *The Bells of Basel*. But Ehrenburg's book had a style all
its own, compounded of sarcastic aggressiveness, cinematographic
sequence of rapid scenes, and short mordant sentences. The work
contains good descriptions of Paris, interesting observations, colorful adventures, and a host of figures from different social strata—
but all this served only to enhance or relieve a narrative of political intrigues and class struggle in a country fatally running toward
its own doom. It is a novel of events, not of men, and its characters are composite portraits in which one can easily recognize the
prominent statesmen and politicians of the Third Republic. Some
of these portraits are sharp caricatures or grotesque images, but
they are clever. The aim of *The Fall of Paris* was to show the
perfidy, corruption, and stupidity of the French bourgeoisie who
led their country into military disaster and brought it under the
heel of the Germans. The protagonists in this vast canvas, as is
always the case with Ehrenburg, hardly come to life, particularly

the positive ones, such as the young woman Mado, who drifts toward the left, the Communists, and the anarchically-minded artists. The only warm note in this cutting, highly patterned work is the author's attachment to the city: when speaking of Paris he cannot restrain his genuine emotion.

During the German invasion of Russia, Ehrenburg reached the peak of his journalistic career and his influence. He wrote articles against the Germans that were read and remembered by hundreds of thousands, especially those at the battlefronts. His hatred of the enemy, his patriotic indignation, the vigor of his attacks, and the fervor of his exhortations merged into a rhetorical flow which bolstered the morale of both combatants and civilians. By describing Nazi atrocities, by reminding all of the crimes of the invaders, Ehrenburg efficiently countered Goebbel's propaganda and called the fighters to wrath and revenge. Again, though one may say that this was merely an expression of the writer's natural talent for aggressiveness, polemics, and intellectual offensive, there is no doubt that his articles aroused a strong emotional response and were a potent weapon of psychological warfare.

When the need for this kind of literature was over, Party watchmen asked Ehrenburg to tone.down his anti-German forays, whereupon he went back to writing novels. In 1947 he brought out another long narrative, *The Storm* (partly a sequel to *The Fall of Paris*), which won another Stalin Prize, and in 1951 he publishd *The Last Wave* (Originally *The Ninth Wave* or *The Stormy One*). The action of both novels takes place in France, in the USSR, and in the USA, and deals with the collapse of the French Republic, the resistance movement under the leadership of the Communists, the fighting between the Germans and the Red Army, and the post-war international tension leading to the cold war between America and Russia. *The Storm* contains many cliché-ridden portraits of Russian soldiers and intellectuals, while *The Last Wave* has the cast of a bad thriller, including a money-grubbing American senator, spies, unscrupulous journalists, evil imperialists, and scheming foes of the Soviet regime. Here, too, Ehrenburg did not miss the train; his novel coincided with the sharpening of the Stalin's postwar anti-Western policy. It must be pointed out, however, that despite all the mendaciousness in his novels, Ehrenburg is hardly responsible for the exaggerations and lies of this anti-European and anti-American campaign of 1948-52. He had enough common sense to draw the line between an indictment of capitalism and the outright condemnation of Western culture; he had, on several occasions, defended its high achievements and warned against chauvinistic smugness. He was even criticized by the intransigents for his "complacency." But shrewd and cautious as he was, he never disregarded danger signals and he navigated warily in stormy waters. For instance, when some of his friends who were Jewish writers and artists, were dragged before the firing squad in the 'fifties, he preferred not to open his mouth and carefully remained in the background.

But as soon as Stalin died, Ehrenburg was one of the first to announce the change of season. In 1954 he published *The Thaw* (followed by *The Spring*, its sequel in 1956), and the title of this novel served as the slogan for the whole period. The time had come for a revision of Stalinist precepts and aesthetics, and Ehrenburg did the job. Instead of depicting heroes of industrial and agricultural progress as he had done in the late 'thirties, he unfolded in *The Thaw* the destinies of average but typical Soviet men and women in an equally average and typical provincial town. They are all bound by social conventions, moral prohibitions, and Party taboos, and it is not until they begin an inner revision of all that prevents them from being happy that the ice melts around them and their problems begin to be solved satisfactorily. This is particularly true in *The Spring*, which is, unfortunately, inferior to *The Thaw*. The central character in both novels is Volodya Pukhov, a painter who had followed the rules of the game and painted heroic images of workers and peasants exuding official optimism. He understands, however, the falseness of his art, especially when he meets Saburov, a true artist who refuses to compromise and who preserves his integrity despite poverty and loneliness.

After the publication of *The Thaw* Ehrenburg did commit himself to the cause of revisionism in literature and art. He returned to the loves of his youth. In various articles and public statements he avoided talking about socialist realism and hailed innovations in painting and writing; to young men and women eager for fresh air and new forms of art, he personified all the forbidden currents of experimentation coming from the West. This impression was enhanced by Ehrenburg's activity in 1954-62 when he promoted the publication of works written by condemned and later "rehabilitated" authors, and also by his long autobiography, *Years, People, Life,* in which he described in detail his friendship with the French surrealists and wrote portraits of writers who perished under Stalin (Babel, Mandelstam, Tsvetayeva, Koltsov, and others). For the Soviet reader surrounded by the barbed wire of censorship, the pages of Ehrenburg's memoirs seemed not only exciting but daring. A more attentive perusal of this vast and often highly interesting testimony, however, reveals a conscious avoidance of certain dangerous subjects (such as his own position under Stalin and his silence during the executions of the 'fifties) and a very cautious treatment of others. It is obvious that Ehrenburg was trying to express his intimate thoughts and that he made an attempt to be candid, at least in his old age; but the self-defense reflex was too strongly rooted in him, and he still could not overcome his ambivalence and opportunism. In any case, even his discreet support of creative freedom and experimental art had brought official wrath upon him in 1963 when the thaw was replaced by a new cold wave. Of course, Ehrenburg, inured as he was to the fickleness of the Moscow climate, knew how to keep silent in times of trouble. He concluded his *Memoirs* with the question: "What will come tomorrow?" Did he intend to foretell the future in the last, unachieved part of his *Autobiography?* He died in 1967, and two years later the Samizdat circulated excerpts from his unpublished manuscript which, among other things, described the 1954 Second Congress of Soviet writers and the meeting of the delegates with Khrushchev and Party dignitaries.

In the 'seventies Ehrenburg's popularity declined considerably.

21

Boris Pasternak

Some thirty years before *Doctor Zhivago* made him world famous, Boris Pasternak was acclaimed as the greatest Russian poet of the post-revolutionary era. His audience, however, was limited to young poets and discerning readers, and he never achieved the wide popularity of a Mayakovsky or a Essenin. A difficult poet, he cut the figure of a heretic who had a "litigation with his century" and opposed his individual convictions to the collective myth. Sholokhov called him a "hermit crab." Despite its disparaging intent, this remark simply stated a fact. Pasternak remained lonely and isolated, lost in the turmoil of his age. While opportunists celebrated five-year plans, Stalin's wisdom, and official enlightenment, Pasternak refused to see literature as a means of mass education and to compose topical and functional verse. He continued to write about whatever he pleased—about nature, and love, and loneliness, and the "high malady, the sublime old malady which still calls itself a song"—and in the form he had freely chosen. This made him unique among his more pliable contemporaries and determined his fate. Even Pasternak's Communist enemies had to acknowledge his genius and superior craftsmanship—but they made him the target for constant attacks and never missed the opportunity to denounce him as a "decadent formalist not attuned to our epoch and alienated from the people." His voice might have sounded strange and was often drowned by military marches and choral cantatas, but now it is quite clear that in his own way he expressed the laments and appeals of those whom the struggles of the Revolution and the oppression of the dictatorship condemned to enforced silence.

His whole philosophy, which blended the pagan exultation·of

life and pantheistic love of nature with the Christian concept of spirituality and brotherhood, ran counter to the Communist dogma. Although he rejected the theory of art for art's sake, his aesthetics contrasted the compulsory and primitive canons of Leninism-Stalinism-Krushchevism. And he had a moral stamina which made him in days of conformity and recantation a very symbol of courage and artistic integrity. All this determined his precarious position in the Soviet Union where he was barely tolerated by the authorities and periodically exposed to campaigns of slander and vituperation.

Boris Pasternak was born in 1890 in Moscow into a highly cultured family. His father Leonid, a noted portrait painter and illustrator of Tolstoy's works, particularly *Resurrection*, held, despite his Jewish extraction, the post of professor in the School of Painting, Sculpture and Architecture. His mother, pupil of Anton Rubinstein, was a gifted and well-known pianist.

The presence of Tolstoy hovered over Boris's childhood (he saw the great man for the first time when he was four). In his recollections Pasternak describes in moving terms how at the age of twenty he paid the last homage to Tolstoy laid out in the mortuary chamber of a forlorn railroad station. One wonders how much the creator of *War and Peace* influenced the moral development of Pasternak, particularly his attitudes toward history and civilization. Parallel to Tolstoy's influence there was that of Boris's nanny, who introduced the child to the rites of the Greek Orthodox Church (in a letter to Jacqueline de Proyart he speaks even of a secret baptism). As an adolescent he has been simultaneously attracted by the Gospel, the study of philosophy which he pursued at the University of Moscow and for a short time in Marburg, Germany, and by music. Scriabin, the famous Russian composer, impressed the 15-year-old Boris so much that he decided to become a musician and for six years studied theory and composition under professors of Moscow conservatory. His achievements, however, did not satisfy him, and he renounced music. This decided his final and total dedication to literature. On the eve of the World War I he became associated with the futurists. His first collection of poems, *A Twin in Clouds* (1914), appeared with a preface by Aseyev, Mayakovsky's friend, and the second, a more important one, *Above the Barriers* (1917), reprinted in 1931, bore the imprint of "Centrifuga," a futurist group directed by S. Bobrov. It was between 1922 and 1933 that the main works were published which established Pasternak's reputation and provoked a stir among readers and critics; the collections *Life, My Sister* (1922), *Themes and Variations* (1923), *The Second Birth* (1932), the long poems *The Year 1905, Lieutenant Schmidt* (1927), and *Spektorsky* (1931), as well as his prose writings such as *Tales* (The Childhood of Luvers, Tratto d'Appelle, Letters from Tula, Aerial Ways, 1925), the autobiographical *Safe Conduct* (1931), and *The Tale* (1933). With the exception of the "omnibus" selections of 1933 and 1945, all these books were issued in small printings. Between 1933 and 1943 no original works by the poet were passed for publication in the USSR, and Pasternak earned his living by translations. Those he made of Shakespeare's tragedies and Goethe's *Faust* were truly magnificent. His versions of poets from Soviet Georgia won Stalin's approval and probably saved him from being "repressed" during the era of purges. It was not until 1943 that he was permitted to publish *On Early Trains* (fifty-two pages); *Terrestrial Expanse* (forty-seven pages) followed in 1945, with *Selected Poems* in 1948. Some of his new verse appeared in periodicals, but the poems written in the last ten years of his life, as well as *Doctor Zhivago* and the autobiographical sketch of 1957, have never appeared in the USSR and are available in Russian only in editions published outside of Pasternak's native land.

Pasternak's literary career can be easily divided into several periods. The first, from his debut to 1932, includes works so remarkable in their linguistic innovations that they exerted a strong influence on a whole generation of Soviet and *émigré* poets. Composed in the revolutionary 'twenties, when the search for new style was in full swing, they bestowed upon Pasternak the title of master and leader of the poetic avant-garde and fixed forever his place in post-revolutionary poetry. In the following decade and the war years he strove for greater simplicity. During this second period his poems were often of great excellence but hardly superior to his earlier works. Between 1945 and 1955 he entered a new phase and turned to prose and to the composition of *Doctor Zhivago*. In these years and until his death in 1960 his poetry became more concrete and direct. Was it the result of an inner change or crisis which compelled him to condemn the virtuosity and verbal brilliance he had displayed in his youth? Some *émigré* critics are inclined to think so and to accept fully the poet's disapproval of his earlier "mannerisms." Apparently, even at the age of forty-five Pasternak had turned his back on those very characteristics of his poetry which made him so influential in the 1920's and 1930's. His denial of of own past, however, should not be taken too literally: Pasternak belongs to those artists for whom the days gone by are always less important than the reality of today. And although Pasternak did travel a complex, most difficult road, its direction has been the same from the beginning to the end, and his writings preserved an inner unity throughout their evolution. In general what strikes one in Pasternak's work is its stability and consistency.

His poetry may be regarded as a synthesis of the classical tradition, a symbolist musicality, and of the colloquial bent of the futurist, combined with surrealistic imagery. He rarely resorts to neologisms, his meters are for the most part regular iambs and dactyls, and he is neither esoteric nor obscure. Yet his poetic delivery is so unusual, his choice of words so surprising, the range of his vocabulary so wide that only by a sustained effort can the average reader gain access to the exclusive and self-contained world of the poet. The first shock comes from his metaphor. He will say: "The surf bakes waves like waffles"; "The Caucasian range lay like a rumpled bed"; "The glaciers uncovered their faces like the resurrected souls of the dead"; "my kisses across your breast like water from a jug." This manner is equally remote from the hyperbolism of Mayakovsky and the whimsical challenge of the imagists; the most paradoxical of his similes and metaphors preserve a curious mixture of logic and fantasy:

> Spring! I have come from the street, where the poplar stands
>   amazed,
> Where the distance takes fright, where the house fears to
>   fall,
> Where the air is all blue, like the bundle of linen
> Of a patient just discharged from a hospital.

It is true that Pasternak usually gets an approximation of concepts deriving from phonetic kinship of words and sounds ("you spread your bedding on slander and you slept") and that he omits the links between the components of a metaphor. In this he is both following the formalist theory of "rendering strange" as a basic poetic device and the use of unexpected associations and contexts practiced by the futurists and surrealists. No less striking is his constant use of colloquialisms and a deliberate mixture of poetic and idiomatic levels of speech. It would be wrong, however, to see in all these oddities a cold application of theoretical principles. Pasternak's poetry is as natural and spontaneous as Blok's: it is like heavy but perfectly normal breathing, and all its alliterations, involved tropes, autonomous images—all the prodigious verbal wealth and inventiveness, are what may be called a perfect poetic pitch. There is no pose or pretense in the impetuous stride of his muse. His verbal virtuosity often created incorrectly the impression of linguistic acrobatics. But all his phonetic discoveries and sophistications are not formalistic tricks. They reflect the innate originality of the man and the poet for whom the sonority of sound was but an expression of meaning, and who believed in the indissoluble union of essence and ways of expression. One of the reasons he condemned in later years the ebullience and intricacies of his own early diction, was the fear that they hid the substance of what he wanted to communicate.

In his wonderful autobiographical narrative *Safe Conduct* Pasternak wrote: "Focused on a reality which feeling had displaced, art is a record of this displacement." The intensity and the direction of emotion determine the degree and the character of this displacement. Therefore, in his own words, "art is concerned not with man but with the image of man ... the image of man as it becomes apparent, is greater than man ... the direct speech of feeling is allegorical and cannot be replaced by anything." The enchantment of Pasternak's poetry consists precisely of his capacity to displace shapes, objects, events, and concepts, and to create a poetic reality in which the phenomena of this world are simply a pliable material for transformation and transposition. In the same way physical and spiritual levels, nature and history, every-day occurrences and imaginative flights are considered as mere

aspects of one and the same unity. Whatever Pasternak chooses
to draw into the field of his vision is suddenly illuminated by a
powerful beam of emotion—which reveals, as he believed, the true
reality, the substratum of things. Marina Tsvetayeva, whom he
considered one of the greatest Russian poets of the twentieth
century, defined his poetry as "a downpour of light." Pasternak
often called his own work "realistic" and dismissed fantasies in
Hoffmann's manner or pseudo-mystical nebulosity. For him the
visible world did exist, and the truth was revealed through the
observation of natural phenomena, the experience of the senses,
the activity of men within their physical environment. The philosophical contemplation which lies underneath all his poetic exploration, is rather pantheistic. He constantly shifted his frames
of reference—passing from objects to feelings, comparing things
with ideas, playing with concepts of time, space, and movement.
His allusions and parallels are often oblique and bizarre but they
are never abstruse. He filled his poems with a whole galaxy
of concrete details, of sounds, colors, and shapes—but he did not
employ them as Eliot's "objective correlatives," as mnemonic pegs
for association of ideas, but as self-contained living signs of a
beautiful, real, and mysterious universe. This resulted in a unique
combination of intellectual and sensuous fervor, of sophistication
and naïve candor, of earthy attachment to the corporeal and
Christian love and idealism.

In a letter written to Eugene Kayden, his American translator
in 1958, Pasternak says that "art is not simply a description of life
but a setting forth of the uniqueness of being . . . the significant
writer of his epoch . . . is a revelation, a representation of the
unknown, unrepeatable uniqueness of living reality." In one of
his late poems he wrote: "be alive, this only matters, alive to the
end of ends." The oneness of being, the link between man and
the cosmos, and the interpretation of human destiny as a world-
wide pattern form the main themes of his work. Next to these
is the theme of the poet as the spokesman and of man as the bearer
of the creative spirit of the universe. Here lies the source of the
basic conflict between Pasternak and the official Communist philosophy which reached its peak with the publication of *Doctor
Zhivago*.

Pasternak's poetry and his *Weltanschauung* matured amidst the revolutionary upheaval. Apparently he did not suffer from the "draught of history" to which his whole generation was brutally exposed. He continued his variations on the themes of intimate thoughts and emotions, communion with nature and philosophical meditation in an era when the clatter of political fight seemed to deafen all songs. Stalinist critics reproached him for his aloofness and quoted his famous lines of the 1920's: "with a muffler around my throat, shielding myself with the palm of my hand, I call out in the courtyard: 'What millenium are we celebrating there?'" Yet he realized, in his own way, the dynamism and the aspirations of the Revolution. He welcomed the "mighty storm" and the political and social changes that swept over the country. He wrote epic poems about 1905, the "dress rehearsal of the Revolution," and about its martyr Lieutenant Schmidt, the idealistic hero of the Sebastopol mutiny. His semibiographical *Spektorsky* will remain, together with Blok's *Retaliation*, among the most striking poetic homages to the pre-revolutionary generation of anti-Tsarist rebels; and he spoke highly of Lenin. In political terms he has always been a fairly consistent fellow-traveler and a member of Russian intelligentsia from which he inherited his radical leanings. But precisely because he believed that poetry is "the expression of the new in birth pangs," he demanded freedom for the artist who "listens to the world through his soul," as he himself put it. Not unlike Zamyatin, Pasternak was much more revolutionary in spirit than were many of his contemporaries who turned out incandescent poems spluttering with exclamation points. But since his enemies were examples of inertia, the obduracy of stupidity and all the chains of violence and oppression which prevent the unfolding of personality, he was surprised and hurt by the turn of events in the 'thirties. It was not only the hypocrisy, the lies, and the terror of the period, but also its intellectual poverty and aesthetic obtuseness that affected him and he felt that he was addressing the deaf or talking a foreign language when he declared: "I feel the universe like a cathedral infinite with calm."

"What can I do with my thoracic cavity?" he asks in one of his poems which sums up his quarrel with his times. Prodded in the 1930's to make comments on economic reconstruction and the

anti-Soviet intrigues of the capitalist West, he answered that
although both topics were of utmost importance, he, as a poet,
preferred to do what he knew best and what had always been
essential for an artist: he wanted to explore the conflicts within
the human breast, the constant flux of emotions in human hearts
and the hopes in human minds. The hustlers objected that the age
called for an immediate reaction to events—and he replied in 1934:
"in an epoch of rapid tempos it behooves one to write slowly
as well."

In a society in which action was hailed as a supreme virtue,
Pasternak turned to contemplation. He understood that this
alienated him from his social environment and exclaimed not without a certain bitterness: "during the days of the Great Soviet
when seats are assigned to Supreme Authority, in vain the poet's
place is reserved; it is dangerous or it is vacant." He also compared his own destiny to that of a man in a rowboat who is being
outdistanced by a big fleet heading down the river of history
"toward the sea, into the light—into the socialism looming ahead."
Had he the right to row alone toward that bright expanse? He
also wrote that he was not a jester or a idle singer, but "a rider
on a speeding steed" who looks at the contemporary world "from
the heights of fate and imagination." Each of his poems claimed
directly or allusively the right of the individual to dream, or to
experience "this fit of madness which rattles and rises like the
quicksilver in Toricelli's tube."

In Soviet surveys of poetry, Pasternak's individualism is always
labeled "bourgeois, morbid, and pessimistic." These derogatory
judgments are completely wrong and gratuitous. Pasternak's
poetry is not only terse, muscular, and vigorous like that of Lermontov, but it possesses an extraordinary vitality, a dynamic affirmation of life, for its spirit is that of optimistic strength. The
same can be said about his prose, and particularly of *Doctor
Zhivago*.

This monumental novel sums up and develops the main themes
of Pasternak's poetry and brings forth various concepts and attitudes he could not fully express in his previous works. He felt
that this was possible only in an epic form. "I always dreamt of
a novel," he said, "in which, as in an explosion, I would erupt

with all the wonderful things I saw and understood in this world."
For five years he worked on *Doctor Zhivago* in the solitude of
his cottage in Peredelkino, in the neighborhood of Moscow. "It
seemed to me," he declared to the German journalist Gerd Ruge,
"that I had to earn the name I won not by poetry but by prose,
by something that might well cost more labor, more effort, more
time and whatever else. I have borne witness as an artist, I have
written about times I lived through." During the thaw of 1955
there were hopes for the novel's publication in Russia, but after
a close examination of the manuscript and instructions from the
higher echelons, the work was barred. Its appearance abroad, first
in translations and then in the Russian original, and the awarding
of the Nobel Prize to the poet provoked violent attacks in the
USSR and poisoned the last years of his life. A victim of ostracism,
he remained, however, till his demise in 1960 the central figure of
Russian post-Stalin literature.

Doctor Zhivago, a best-seller in most European countries, is
a highly controversial work. Its central figure is Yuri Zhivago,
son of a rich Siberian industrialist and an orphan at the age of ten.
He is brought up in the house of Moscow intellectuals and patrons
of the arts and becomes a typical product of upper class, pre-
revolutionary Russian culture. Yet as an individual, Zhivago cannot be so easily classified. An excellent physician, he studies philosophy and literature and has decidedly personal views on many
matters. He writes poems, twenty-four of which form the ending
of the novel and offer a key to its right interpretation. It is a
pity that their unsatisfactory translations in English and other
languages prevented the Western reader from understanding their
high importance which transcends the boundaries of the novel:
they are extremely revealing of Pasternak's mentality in the 1950's.

Zhivago's main aim is to preserve his spiritual independence.
Although involved indirectly in war and Revolution he acts as
an outsider and refuses to become "engaged." His reluctance to
make a commitment, is of an entirely different nature from the
aloofness of a Camus "stranger": Zhivago loves life and lives intensely, he does not feel alienated from nature but he does not
want to be limited in his freedom. He welcomes the Revolution,
and at its beginnings enjoys its sweep, its dream of universal

justice, and its tragic beauty. Yet when the Communists start to tell him how to live and how to think, he rebels, leaves Moscow with his family, and takes refuge in a forlorn hamlet beyond the Urals. To reach this haven he crosses the whole of Russia, going through burning cities and villages in uproar, through districts hit by famine and regions ravaged by civil war.

In the Urals he enjoys calm but only for a short time. Soon his life is upset first by his passion for Lara, a young woman he met earlier and has found in a neighboring town, and by his wanderings in Siberia with the Red guerrillas to whom he is forcibly attached as a physician. By the end of the fratricidal strife he finds himself all alone: his family has been banned from Russia by the Soviet government, his mistress has to flee to Manchuria, Zhivago returns to Moscow, a broken man, to die in the street from a heart attack.

This vast epic has varied layers of narrative, besides combining two styles—the lyrical-poetic and the epic-descriptive. It is obviously autobiographical and is based on Pasternak's own experiences, including the sojourn in the Urals and the love for a woman who was not his wife. Chronologically it encompasses three generations and gives a picture of Russian life during the first quarter of our century, between 1903 and 1929 (its epilogue is placed at the end of World War II). It is primarily a chronicle of the intelligentsia but it contains some sixty characters from all walks of society. All form part of a complex and often symbolic plot, and the interdependence of individual destinies constitutes one of the main themes of the novel. Pasternak's heroes and heroines are presented not as actors in a historical show, but as human beings obeying the laws of attraction and repulsion, in an open universe of change and coincidence. Some naïve critics saw in these coincidences examples of the author's artistic failure, without understanding that they are treated not as exceptions in a logical, linear order but as normal features of an irrational, multiplane cosmic reality. This is particularly true of the love affair between Zhivago and Lara, a highly romantic and beautifully written story of chance, choice, joy, adventure and death. Lara herself is one of the most poetic feminine images in modern Russian literature.

Structured as a succession of scenes, dialogues, descriptions, and reflections and divided into seventeen parts, *Doctor Zhivago* deliberately avoided psychological dissection and in a way marks a reaction against the modern analytical trend. It also breaks away from the tradition of well-made "flowing narrative." Critics who pretend to know how good fiction should be written, were puzzled and distressed by this suggestive and realistic, symbolic and impressionistic, fragmentary yet highly unified novel. They wanted to put on it some stereotyped label, and failed because *Doctor Zhivago* creates its own form, a unique mixture of drama and lyricism, of verbal simplicity and emotional complexity, of poetic fancy and philosophical depth. It is a tale of social history seen through individual destinies, and it has the same radiance, the same art of "displacement of reality through emotion" that illuminates Pasternak's poetry. This explains the alternative of descriptive precision with romantic passion, and the shifting of the story from the phenomenal to the ideational level. Like all great books it does not resemble other novels and remains a novel *sui generis*. Therefore the term "epic" used to define its range and diversity is hardly fitting for this poetic prose, this tale with numerous discursive asides and episodes which often sound like parables. In any case it stands in splendid isolation in Soviet literature. One wonders how it was possible for Pasternak who spent all his life in the USSR, to resist all the external pressure and strictures and to conceive and execute a work of such artistic and conceptual boldness and of such unusual imaginative power. Its emergence among the sands of socialist realism amounts almost to a miracle.

Doctor Zhivago, because of its incredible originality, was often mistaken for a work with a hidden political message. It may sound paradoxical but the main political impact of *Doctor Zhivago* is precisely the fact that it was written as a nonpolitical book. Communist fiction always depicts man as a "political animal" whose acts and feelings should be determined by social and economic conditions. In *Doctor Zhivago* man is projected in his individual singleness, and his life is interpreted not as an illustration of historical events, but as a unique, wonderful adventure in its reality of sensations, instincts, thoughts, and spiritual strivings. Pasternak treats politics as fleeting externals, and concentrates on the un-

changeable fundamentals of the human mind, emotions, and creativity. The latter is for him one of the rungs in the ladder by
which the living attempt to ascend to divinity. Zhivago and Lara
are bent on protecting their human essence, their personal privacy
and dignity, and they are defending those values against the intru-
sion of distorting and destructive political forces. What makes
them so distinct from their officious contemporaries is that they
are victims and not agents of history. This does not mean that
they are reactionaries. Zhivago does not want to turn the clock
back, and he accepts social and economic changes brought about
by the Revolution. His dispute with the epoch is not political but
primarily philosophical and moral. First of all he does not share
the illusion of revolutionary leaders that their decrees and executions can really transform human beings. And, secondly, he rejects
violence, especially when justified by sectarian rhetoric and
abstract formulas. Only through goodness do we reach supreme
good, says Zhivago: if the beast in man could be overcome
through fear and brute force our ideal would be a circus tamer
with a whip and not Jesus Christ. He believes in human virtues
glorified in the Christian ethic, and he asserts the supremacy of
nature, love, and beauty. His main objection to the accepted Communist dogma is its ignorance of the link between man and the
universe. If religion can be defined as an outlook which establishes
the connection between man and the mysterious, transcendent
essence of the world, then *Doctor Zhivago* is a basically religious
book—in a very general, theistic sense of the term but with strong
Christian overtones. Zhivago laughs at the guerrilla chief Liberius
for whom "the interest of the revolution and the existence of the
solar system are of the same importance." His broad vision makes
him call Marxism "a self-centered movement which remains far
away from facts and is uncertain of its grounds." And men in
power are so anxious to assert "the myth of their own infallibility
that they do the utmost to ignore the truth."

Of course, it would be wrong to attribute to Pasternak all the
statements made by his protagonists and to identify the author
completely with Yuri Zhivago. It would also be futile to read
into the novel a hidden symbolic meaning to each episode, and
even to each street name or characters. But there is no doubt that

the opinions of Pasternak's hero do reflect the poet's intimate convictions, and that *Doctor Zhivago*, as a work of art, is of allegorical significance. It seems that the latter is primarily contained in the themes of man's relation to nature and to history. Pasternak's beautiful descriptions of landscapes and seasons put nature at the focal center of *Doctor Zhivago* in the same way as time and space are the main protagonists of Tolstoy's *War and Peace*. And the concept of history derives from that of nature. Before his death Zhivago "reflected again that he conceived of history . . . not in the accepted way but by analogy with the vegetable kingdom." Leaves and trees change during the cycle of seasons in a forest, but the forest itself remains the same— and so does history with its fundamental immobility beneath all temporary mutations. And so does life which can be understood and felt and lived only within the framework of nature.

This organic, one would say cosmic, feeling gives a special dimension to Pasternak's poetry and prose. Even if we admit that Communism represents a large and important part of Russian life, mentality, and history, it does not encompass all the Russian people and all the country's traditions and aspirations. A whole world of passion, yearnings, ideals, and creativity exists next to or underneath the Communist Establishment. They are expressed by Pasternak, a great writer, whose destiny it was to become the voice of the "other Russia."

22

The Era of Stabilization and Dictatorship

It was during the 1930's that a distinctively Soviet society, with its numerous contrasts and achievements, stigmas and hopes, crimes and aspirations began to take shape. The overflowing of a great social and political revolution was now contained; out of the storm emerged a collectivistic economy in a totalitarian state dominated by a single party, itself under the autocratic rule of one man. World War II upset and temporarily halted this process of general stabilization and personal dictatorship (even though it did intensify some of their tendencies), but after 1945 the USSR picked up where it had left off before Hitler's invasion of 1941, with only such changes as were called for by international events and post-war reconstruction.

Stabilization embraced all fields, from the legal structure crowned by Stalin's Constitution in 1936 to a more academic and rigid school system; from an emphasis on family life to the promotion of sports; from the hardening of ideological controls to the resuming of white collars by clean-shaven state functionaries and army officers.

The return to normalcy was achieved mainly by economic recovery. The first two five-year plans, despite their high cost in lives and money, had paid a dividend in improved living standards. The third Five-Year Plan began in 1938 in an atmosphere of hope for a brighter future. Even the menacing clouds of international tension could not dampen the growing optimism of the people. When Stalin declared, "Life has become better and more joyful, comrades," he was simply stating the fact that food, clothing, and housing were available—in limited quantities—to more and more people. This marked a considerable advance over the wretchedness of the 1920's. Industry, trade, and communication developed rapidly along prescribed lines; agricultural production also increased considerably.

Despite the propaganda bogeys of counter-revolutionary plots and mysterious saboteurs, everything, from the petrification of red tape to the resumption of rank and status in the government hierarchy, from the white-gloved policemen on the streets of Moscow to law enforcement in public squares, indicated the self-reliance and assurance of an enduring, solid order. Communism was obviously here to stay. The jurisdiction of the supreme organs of the Soviets, the make-believe of one-ticket elections, the insertion of a single-party authority into the basic laws of the country—and even the cult of Stalin as an organic part and symbol of the regime—were all defined and established with utmost precision.

Soviet society acquired a certain stability in its customs and in patterns; abandoning the anarchical, centrifugal proclivities of the upheaval period, average citizens showed a strong inclination toward a code of secular morality along the lines of civic and domestic virtues, patriotic duty, and devotion to the collective cause. And whatever socialistic elements there may have been in this new code, in its application it was often strikingly bourgeois, placing great emphasis on social approval, respectable standing, and external signs of success—decorations, honors, uniforms, awards, and publicity.

The very diversification of social strata became more pronounced: Party officials, army commanders, *spets* (specialists), Heroes of Labor in industry and agriculture, all formed a new upper crust, the "noteworthy people of the Soviet land," as they were called in the press, while a large middle class, of sorts, was thriving in both town and village. The relationship between these groups, especially between political and economic "bosses" and their subordinates, followed a pattern that had nothing to do with the flashy slogans of Communist equality. And the new middle class had definite traits of conservatism which became even more pronounced (particularly in its artistic taste and its way of life) during the late 'thirties.

The methods of government lost their erratic character and followed a well-organized routine. Even the contradictions had stiffened into legal practice: the centralization of administrative and economic power in Moscow stood side by side with the multinational structure of the Soviet Federation and the relative cultural autonomy of tribes and nationalities; official pronouncements of humanism and progressiveness of "true Soviet democracy" and of "Communist moral superiority" co-existed with concentration camps, slave labor, daily arrests, executions, absence of individual freedom, and ruthless suppression of political opponents.

There was a considerable difference between the high principles of Communist doctrine and the reality of a bureaucratic state, as the Party was transformed into a weapon of Stalin's dictatorship. What he promoted was not a Russian Thermidor, as so many foreign observers were then tempted to believe, but simply a consolidation of personal power through the elimination of competitors. Communist idealists, intellectuals, companions of Lenin, civil war heroes, and a large number of young Party members were potential trouble-makers, and Stalin sent them to jail or the scaffold. Of the twenty-four members of the Party's Central Committee under Lenin, eleven were executed by Stalin. Out of 1966 delegates to the Seventeenth Party Congress in 1934 (which ended with a huge standing ovation to Stalin), 1108 perished in torture chambers and concentration camps. The same fate befell 98 of the 139 former members of the 1934 Central Committee. During the purges of 1935-37 and the notorious Moscow trials at which the defendants under duress made full confessions of the most fantastic crimes, former leaders—Rykov, Kamenev, Bukharin, Zinoviev—and Red Army marshals and generals—Tukhachevsky, Blucher, Yakir—and hundreds of other prominent men, including Stalin's friends, were sentenced to death. Thousands took the way of exile or languished in prison. Under the direction of Yezhov, Beria, and a specially trained corps of investigators, prosecutors, and secret service men, the mechanism of terror worked with blind efficiency; the liquidation of opponents, dissenters, and non-conformists became a daily routine, spreading fear among all strata of the population and hurting most of all the intelligentsia, professional workers, and Party officials.

From 1935 until 1953 Stalin's leadership, cemented by blood and intimidation, remained unchallenged and the official religion of the omnipotent Communist State and its prophet, later designated as "the cult of personality," triumphed on all fronts.

In international relations Moscow adopted the line of *Realpolitik*, with an emphasis on the permanent interests of Russia and the perennial game of the balance of power: for this purpose it used indiscriminately the underground activities of foreign Communist parties and the Byzantine diplomacy of foreign office functionaries in their gold-braided uniforms. The practical opportunism of Stalin passed easily from anti-Fascist intervention in the Spanish civil war in 1936 to the pact with Hitler in 1939. The ultimate aims—world revolution, the overthrow of capitalism, the victory of the New Trinity (Marxism, Leninism, Stalinism) —remained the same; the tactics became, however, as supple as those of any bourgeois government. The Party line changed often, but with each change became more intransigent than ever.

The increasing significance of the USSR in world affairs was accompanied by the undisguised return to Russian national traditions in culture, customs, and administration. The Kremlin was publicly accepting and endorsing the legacy of the Empire; it was resuming the ways Russian autocracy had adopted centuries before—in its foreign policy, its building up of military might, and in its program of territorial and political claims. The Communist State was now promoting national feeling at every social level. The younger generation was urged to be proud of the USSR, and a new term "Soviet patriotism" was coined to disguise the return to nationalism and chauvinism. Popular songs hailed the might of the Communist State and its superiority over the capitalist West. And since relations with the outside world were limited to state affairs and travel permitted only to government officials and a few elect, the very isolation of Russia was presented as an asset: smugness, self-complacency, and hostility toward Europe and America became dominant psychological attitudes under Stalin.

Notwithstanding all the discontent that certainly existed not only among intellectuals but also among the peasants and workmen, and despite the heavy load of work, the annoying pressure of governmental controls, and all the material difficulties, the cohesiveness of Soviet society increased greatly. At the same time the struggle going on beneath the surface unity of the Party often exploded in dramatic events. Not only individuals but entire groups were made the scapegoats for inter-Communist feuds.

During the same period, a cultural expansion took place all over the USSR. In education the number of schools and students trebled in comparison with the last years of the Tsarist Empire; despite all the Party rigidities, there was definite progress in scholarship and science, and the cultural level of the masses rose steadily. The breadth and scope of this educational movement were certainly superior to its depth and refinement, and it was often corrupted and distorted by doctrinary blindness and Party strictures. Yet the eagerness for learning among the younger generation, the avidity of the new readers, the prominent place art, music, theater, and dance took in the daily lives of millions attested to a tremendous cultural uplift, which extended to the remotest and most backward regions of the USSR. Communist policy and the undeveloped taste of the new audiences, however, deprived the movement of its initial revolutionary impetus. The artistic avant-garde was rejected and its exponents were often exiled or liquidated; the official direction pointed inexorably toward a conformist socialist realism.

Stalin's era created its own official style. It was pompous, monumental, mendacious, loud, and vulgar. It adopted clichés in all means of communication, in poetry and prose, in architecture, and in painting. A foul language of triteness and bureaucratic jargon contaminated press and Party declarations. Decisions of the Central Committee were always "wise" or "great," Stalin's words were those "of a genius," and he himself was "the leader of mankind, the chieftain of the people." The familiar epithets took on the character of a liturgy: "disintegrating capitalism, declining West, everlasting Party unity, indestructible Communist faith," and so on. The whole picture resembled that of a hundred years before, when a similar official optimism, mixed with hypocrisy and crudeness, was imposed on Russia by Tsar Nikolay I. But the Tsar's regime was just despotic while Stalin's was despotic and totalitarian. For the most part the writers and artists of 1830 were simply prevented from saying what they thought; Stalin's subjects were told both what to think and what to say. Socialist realism meant not only adherence to Communist ideology but it also represented reality in bright colors (leading to a "varnishing of reality") with deliberate elimination from fiction of any unpleasant facts, such as poverty, suicide, unhappy love, illegitimate children, accidents, theft, or crimes (except those committed by counter-revolutionaries and spies). A special theory was concocted to sustain this spurious literature: it declared that Soviet writers do not need to dwell on vice and conflicts because the latter are disappearing from Communist society; fiction should, therefore, show only the positive sides of life, the fruitful labor of Soviet citizens, and should portray the New Hero of our times as a rational, active, and energetic member of the collective.

Unquestionably a new intelligentsia, for the most part of peasant or proletarian origin, was being formed between 1932 and 1941; its ranks were filled either by self-made men and women who had come by their education the hard way, in combat detachments and labor brigades, or by people who had received formal training in Soviet schools. By comparison with their predecessors, the old intellectuals, they lacked finesse and displayed an earthy matter-of-factness; their mentality was directly or indirectly influenced or inspired by Communist ideology; they usually belonged to the Party or remained within its orbit. In contemporary literature, they sought a reflection or their own lives and preoccupations. What they were offered in most cases were images of blameless heroes and verbose hymns of constructive deeds. "Our literature of Stalin's era," said an anonymous Soviet critic, "was so padded with the fluffy cotton of optimism, heroism, lack of conflict, official slogans, and bombastic patriotism, that its protagonists looked twice their natural size and resembled Mme. Tussaud's wax figures."

This does not mean that the new readers were not genuinely interested in the themes of reconstruction, industrialization, and socialistic effort, strongly colored by nationalistic overtones. But most of the novels and plays on these subjects were literary misfits; the amazing fact is that members of the Party and the proletarian writers usually failed to depict the contemporary scene, while former fellow-travelers produced the best specimens of topical prose. Works such as Alexander Avdeyenko's (b. 1908) *I Love* (1933), the story of a waif educated in a working collective, and *Fate* (1936) about a peasant who participates in the building of the Magnitogorsk, or Yakov Ilyin's *The Big Assembly Line* (1934) written when the completion of each mill was celebrated as a great victory, are of inferior caliber. Only novels by Leonov (*Soviet River*), Paustovsky (*Kolchida*), Marietta Shagynian (*Hydrocentral*), and Valentin Katayev (*Time Forward, 1933*) are valid as fictional documents of the times. All of these were written by non-Communists.

The most significant is *Time Forward*, which not only depicts the efforts of undernourished, badly equipped, and poorly housed workers to build a gigantic steel plant in the wilderness of the Ural mountains, but also deals with the problem of socialist emulation.* Without losing any of his humor or capacity for deft characterization, Katayev, who was also the author of *The Embezzlers*, tackled here various aspects of the "Five-Year Plan enthusiasm." His protagonists, men from all parts of Russia have different temperaments and motivations. They are mixing concrete under the supervision of Margulies, an engineer from Moscow who wants to speed up the process despite the discouraging warnings of old scholars. Margulies understands, and his men feel, that there is no time to lose: in fact Russia has remained poor and backward because she has wasted so much time in the past. Now she must catch up with other, more fortunate nations or she will be crushed by powerful enemies. It is a race, a race against time in all spheres, including concrete-mixing. This explains the title of the novel and its symbolic meaning.

The way the brigade goes about its task in the twenty-four hours allotted to it to beat the record established by a Ukrainian team in Kharkov has the thrill and excitement of a sporting event. Men forget to eat and sleep in their relentless effort to win. An

---

* The whole movement of contests, competitions, prizes, and honors was called after its initiator, Alexey Stakhanov, a young coal miner from the Don basin. The best literary treatment of the theme is to be found in *The Tanker Derbent* by Yury Krymov (1908-41, pen name of Beklemishev) and *Don Basin* (1951) by Boris Gorbatov (1908-54).

American businessman who regards Magnitogorsk with astonishment because it resembles a nomad camp more than an industrial center, cannot understand this wild passion and enthusiasm of the Russians; he has no use for a mechanical civilization, which has dried up his emotions and drained his soul. Why do the Russians make such a fuss about concrete or bulldozers or towering smokestacks? Katayev intimates that this fervent attitude of Soviet man springs from deep sources: industrialization has become a religious myth, it will pave the way to progress and prosperity, it will bring socialism and national independence, and consciously or intuitively all the people of the USSR know this.

What made *Time Forward* so typical of the period was its integration of technology into fiction. Since 1930 Soviet authors, more than any others in the world, have shown themselves to be men of the machine age and have written on all sorts of industrial matters, from the extraction of petroleum to the functioning of precision instruments, from the production of pig iron to the construction of dynamos—all themes requiring expert scientific knowledge. Soviet literature became extremely technique-conscious; it constantly dealt with all aspects of modern technology. Novels on coal mining, steel plants, power stations, dams, tractors, agronomical devices, and agricultural equipment are legion.

The old contention of Western statesmen that the Russians are not technically minded always provoked peals of laughter in Moscow. One can easily see the link between the attention paid by Soviet writers to how things are made and Marxian philosophy that stresses productive and manufacturing processes. The objections this writer makes to the Soviet technological novel do not arise from any theoretical considerations. There is no reason why material activity to which millions devote all their time should not be encompassed by art. The problem is not the theme but the way it is treated in Soviet fiction. When an author goes into the details of autogenous welding or the use of fertilizers for technical plants, he can become boring. But the dullness does not derive from the perfectly legitimate themes of man's working activities, but rather from the uniform and dated fashion in which they are explored. Just as we possess a pattern for "boy-gets-girl" tales or for detective stories, so Soviet authors established an archetypal pattern in their industrial novels. The majority of the latter were (and still are) composed in a style which brings us back to Russian naturalistic-minded writers of 1860-80. They are burdened with long dialogues, stock characters, and a diction that is either trivially colloquial or artificially rhetorical. Technological fiction in Russia has failed to produce convincing literature, it has remained heavy, abstruse, and has formed an inferior genre. Very seldom are technological descriptions wedded to the plot, as was the case in *Time Forward*. Katayev's novel has, perhaps, more line than color; its cinematographic style of flashbacks, rapidly shifting scenes, terse dialogue, and black-and-white character portrayal projected against roughly sketched backgrounds is definitely a departure from psychological realism and is somewhat reminiscent of American expressionists, particularly of the early Dos Passos (who, in the 1930's had many admirers as well as excellent translators in the Soviet Union). But, of course, there was a fundamental difference between the Russian and the American: Katayev was aggressive, gay, and optimistic; his was a glorification of labor and of man's physical and moral effort. Man was about to change the face of the earth, and he was making a good start at it by transforming Russia: this main theme is as obvious in Katayev's novel as it is in the works of scores of other writers who differed from him in literary manner and merit. Here again a demarcation line must be drawn between the official optimism imposed from above, and the general mood and tone of a country entering a new phase of its existence with high hopes and undaunted energy. From a religious and philosophical point of view, the faith in man's infinite possibilities affirmed as a principle of Communist ideology may seem naïve, but it pervades all the activity of the Russians, from industrialization to the conquest of space, and its reflected in the works of many non-Communist writers (for instance, *Year 1930* by Evgeny Gabrilovich, or *Prologue*, 1931, by Venyamin Kaverin).

That the romanticism of creative labor and of positive endeavor has become one of the principal themes of Soviet fiction should not surprise anyone who knows nineteenth-century Russian literature. Were not the indictments of the "Superfluous man," the longing for a man of action, the exposé of slothfulness, the glorification of productive effort (including Leo Tolstoy's hymning of manual labor and the hailing of the moral value of work by Chekhov's heroes)—were not all these a significant trend in the past, and a forecast of what was to come?

The theme of labor was connected with that of man's effort to overcome the hostile forces of nature. It is significant that Victor Hugo's *Toilers of the Sea*, a long-winded tale of how simple men battle and curb the elements, which has never been very popular in France or anywhere else, was highly regarded in Russia. Here again the spirit of the pioneers was enhanced by doctrinary tenets. Man can change nature, his activities transform his environment— the whole environment, physical and social—and this is the meaning of history and the essence of culture; this is likewise the premise of what Communist theoreticians call their New Humanism. The idolizing of the human being in his most dynamic manifestations (which, by the way, is a typically Western concept) became one of the main literary themes between 1930 and 1950. This may explain partly why scores of badly written novels and tales, tales which seem juvenile to a sophisticated Western reader, touched such a responsive chord in the USSR. Industrialization was closely bound in with and partly depended upon an inventory of the country's resources. It led to discoveries in geology, to the exploration of remote regions, and to the colonization of backward, wild areas. The government backed this movement for economic and military reasons; the *mystique* of the Five-Year Plan was thus bolstered by the excitement of pioneering and adventure. And it had deep roots in the national character: a gigantic empire was being built by Russian pioneers, and colonization was the backbone of its territorial expansion.

All the works on the Arctic regions, on Siberia, and Central Asia depicted the three-pronged drive of explorers, builders, and settlers. Many books were devoted to the story of the *Chelyuskin*, the experimental ice-breaker that, in 1933, inaugurated the northern route through the Arctic Sea, from the Baltic to the Pacific, and to the extraordinary adventure of its men, who, after being shipwrecked, lived on a drifting floe and were saved by an air lift.

Arctic expeditions, past and present, furnished the material for Ivan Kratt, Vadim Kozhevnikov, Yury Gherman, and Venyamin

Kaverin, whose thrilling *The Two Captains* (first volume published in 1939, the second in 1945) became a best-seller. Some of these stories vaguely echoed Jack London and Bret Harte, yet their heroes, mushing through hundreds of miles on dog sled merely for a look at a young woman, or dreaming of future towns and flower beds on the banks of the lower Yenissei River, were certainly very different from the gold-seekers of the American storytellers; they were serving a common cause, and endured privations not for personal enrichment but to further the triumph of science and insure the future of their country.

The Siberian locale attracted many writers, both native and from other regions. To the Russians of the two decades from 1930-50, Siberia symbolized what the Wild West meant to the Americans; Greely's advice could be paraphrased "Go East, young Russian." The building of the steel industry in the Urals, connected with the development of coal mines in Kuznetsk at the foot of the Altai range, the transformation of many Siberian towns into great machine-building centers (Novosibirsk, Tomsk, Irkutsk), and the general shifting of industrial production beyond the Urals (Chelyabinsk, Sverdlovsk) that took place in the 'thirties, were immediately depicted in literature. A good example is *Red Planes Fly East* (1937) by Pyotr Pavlenko (1899-1950) which depicted the building of Komsomolsk, in southeastern Siberia (it numbered a hundred inhabitants in 1932 and 80,000 five years later), and the tension on the Far East border. Pavlenko prophesied a war between the USSR and Japan; the last part of the novel draws a staggering picture of the Russian air force bombarding the Japanese islands and of the revolution that breaks out in Tokyo, Kobe, and Nagasaki as a result of Japan's military defeat.

In this pioneer literature the struggle for the control of nature is usually opposed to decadent Western mysticism or to a pessimistic surrendering to animal brutality. But ideological tendencies do not deprive it of a strong exotic flavor, which is particularly felt in stories of the primitive and colorful world of Central Asia. Tractors drawn by camels, planes flown over the desert of Black Death, ancient cities dug out of millenary sands, veiled women promoting the struggle for collectivization of Uzbek villages, whole tribes of nomads helping to irrigate the parched earth—all the contrasts between the medieval Orient and the onrush of modern technological civilization inspired numerous books, from *The Locusts* (1934), a remarkable tale by Leonov, to *Mountain and Night* (1945), Alexander Kozin's stories of Kirghiz shepherds, and Ivan Efremov's half fantastic narratives about geologists and mountain climbers. These works, translated into many oriental languages, certainly had an impact on China, India, and the Near East; one should not underestimate the influence of Kazakstan, Uzbekistan, Turkmenistan, and other Soviet Republics beyond the Urals on the nationalistic and revolutionary movements in Asia.

There was something frantic and yet monotonous in what fiction reported about the enthusiasm of the builders of roads and dams, the explorers of the earth's bowels, the planners of new towns and mills. The mirroring of these ventures in prose and poetry either shocks or bores the Western reader. It does, however, hold enchantment for the Russians. "In his sleep he had dreams and visions of oil and gas," Arseny Rutko tells us about the hero of his *Immortal Earth* (1950). "He worked with a frantic heart," Vassily Azhayev says about the main protagonist of his widely popular novel *Far from Moscow* (1948); and such expressions sound perfectly natural to the average Soviet reader. Western critics often make the mistake of attributing these and similar attitudes entirely to propaganda. Many Communist slogans and doctrinal principles, however, do correspond to the drives and aspirations of the masses. This explains the success of various topical works of fiction devoid of true artistic value.

23

The Fate of Poets

MANDELSTAM, AKHMATOVA, TSVETAYEVA

Mayakovsky, Essenin, and Pasternak are usually considered the leading poets of the Soviet era, but three other names should be added to theirs—those of Mandelstam, Akhmatova, and Tsvetayeva. They became well known before 1917 and, therefore, might be regarded as kind of a link between pre-revolutionary poetry and the poetry of today—even though their creative personalities and poetic contributions are completely different. Yet there is something common in their destinies, in the fate of their writings and the vicissitudes of their fame. Despite their steadily growing popularity and the secret circulation of their works among hundreds of thousands of fans, it was only in the last decade that they were—not without reluctance—officially recognized as great poets in the Soviet Union.

For almost half a century, from 1928 to 1973, not a single one of Mandelstam's books was printed in the USSR, and only a few of his poems made a brief appearance in periodicals from time to time. After years of effort by some intellectuals and false promises from officialdom, a selection of Mandelstam's literary heritage was published in Moscow in 1974 (and the limited edition was sold out immediately), although many of his verses continue to circulate throughout Russia in typewritten copies.

Akhmatova, who had enjoyed great popularity in the first and second decades of this century, was not allowed to publish from 1922 to 1940 when a reprint of her earlier works appeared in Moscow: it was followed by a book of *Selections* in 1943. But from 1946 to 1958 she was again condemned to "absence" from bookshops and the ban was lifted only in 1961. Full official recognition came only after her death in 1966. (The collected works of both

Mandelstam and Akhmatova, although by no means complete, can be found in the USA and Europe, in émigré editions.)

Tsvetayeva's case was more complex. She published two small books of verse in Moscow in 1910 and 1912, left Russia in 1922, and lived as an exile in Europe for seventeen years: all her major works were written abroad and most were partly published in book form or in émigré periodicals and banned in the Soviet Union. In 1939 she returned to Moscow, following her daughter and husband: he was soon executed and the daughter arrested and deported. Tsvetayeva committed suicide in 1941 in most tragic circumstances. Twenty years elapsed before a small selection of her poems was authorized in Moscow in 1961; a larger collection was published four years later.

Mandelstam, Tsvetayeva, and Akhmatova are extremely popular in the Soviet Union and have millions of readers, but large portions of their works are circulated in handwritten copies and learned by heart; at the same time, paradoxically enough, while hundreds of essays and research articles on each of the three poets do appear in magazines and academic journals, their correspondences and various other materials (including unpublished texts) are still under lock and key in the State archives. Moreover, Party pundits still prevent large printings of these three poets, who are still regarded as "not conforming to Communist mentality."

Ossip Mandelstam (1891-1938) was born in Warsaw into a family of middle-class Jewish merchants, but went through the formation of a typical Russian intellectual, attending school and university in St. Petersburg, studying literature and philosophy in France and Germany, and learning Latin and Greek. Physically, he was small in stature, frail, slightly eccentric, his head always thrown back, his manner often seemingly odd or ridiculous. He was almost unable to cope with daily life, let alone earn a living. Humble and ineffectual in his dealings with people, he displayed courage and moral stamina in defending his own ideas and the originality of his creations, or what he called "his truth." This sickly, neurotic youth was blessed with an extraordinary poetic gift and an innate power over language and rhythms. At the age of nineteen—with his usual fervor and sincerity—he joined the rapidly enlarging group of his contemporaries, who, under the

guidance of Nikolay Gumilev, called themselves "acmeists" (from
the Greek "acme," which they interpreted as the peak, summum,
or full flowering). They gathered in and around Gumilev's
"Guild of poets" and some avant-garde magazines, and opened
fire against the symbolists, the masters and rulers of Russian literature at the beginning of the twentieth century. They claimed
that symbolism, as a prevailing artistic current, had already
completed its cycle, was losing its vigor and beginning to decline. The acmeists rejected the priority of musicality in symbolist poetry, the obscurity of its vocabulary, the dimness of its
allusions and shadowy flights toward unknown worlds and unseen
signs of absolute. As a counterforce to symbolism they hailed precision in words and metaphors, concreteness in art and the acceptance of the objects and emotions of daily life. Instead of shadowy nuances, the acmeists tried to render clear meaning, plain
colors and plastic values. In general, they preferred the pictorial
over the euphonic. "We admire a rose because it is beautiful in
shape and coloration," wrote Mandelstam, "and not as a symbol
of mystical purity." The title of his first book of poems in 1913
was *Stone*; he loved to compare himself to an architect who carefully chooses each brick or rock for his building. His stanzas
merged verbal solidity with the lightness of full rhyme, his meters
were harmonically measured, and his poetic pace almost severe,
often grave and solemn. *Stone* and his second collection, *Tristia*
(1923), contained exquisite descriptive pieces of Dickensian London, the Mosque in Constantinople, a French landscape, or a
movie theater. It would, however, be an error to mistake them for
realistic portraiture. Acmeism was not a return to a faithful representation of reality: its partisans found the only palpable reality
in art itself. During his whole life Mandelstam was wedded to the
same aesthetic principles. "No word is yet written," he said, "but
the poem already has a sound, its inner image is alive and is heard
by the poet's ear." He argued that the rational, or the logos, is but
one side of the word, which includes many other elements—
sound, image, and hidden values—which can change according to
the context and meter.

Some critics emphasize the static character of Mandelstam's
early work. It is true that in *Stone* and *Tristia* one at first is capti-

vated by the almost sculptural perfection of meter and rhyme and by the concrete sensorial nature of his sonorous lines. But, between 1923 and his death, Mandelstam's poetry assumed a more emotional and dynamic tonality, often approaching lyrical confession. This writer always found symbolistic and futuristic strains in many poems of this acmeist who was a staunch opponent to both these literary movements of his times.

Mandelstam's remarkable prose (which also includes diverse theoretical articles on culture, poetry, Dante, and so forth) presents similar stylistic digressions. Clarence Brown, the American scholar, has rightly observed that Mandelstam, in his autobiographical sketches, "The Noise of Time" and "The Egyptian Stamp," mingles the procedures of poetry with those of prose within one body of discourse." This prose (like that of Khlebnikov) forms one of the most curious and interesting phenomena of Soviet letters in the 1920's.

In his poems he also achieves a peculiar kind of linguistic marvel by mixing the archaisms of Church Slavonic with common speech. As a rule, Mandelstam follows the declamatory tradition of Derzhavin and Tiutchev, and while Kuzmin, a precursor of acmeism, admired "Mozartian clarity," he hails the breadth and magnitude of Bach's oratorios. Despite his very skillful "poetization of colloquialisms," sudden sparks of humor, philosophical meditation, and almost surrealistic imagery, Mandelstam is basically a neoclassicist. His poems on St. Petersburg are excellent examples of this. It is common knowledge that, from the moment of its foundation, at the very beginning of the eighteenth century, St. Petersburg irresistibly attracted Russian writers, from Pushkin, Gogol, and Dostoevsky to Blok and Bely. Mandelstam's vision of the capital is quite different from the foggy mysteries of the symbolist poets. For him the proud glory of St. Petersburg with its sumptuous palaces and granite quays is that of the seat of a world empire. The Byzantine majesty of its domes and buildings is softened by the lovely proportions of Italian architects and the triumphant intensity of its cultural and artistic life. He celebrated the "Northern Athens" in the same way as the eighteenth-century French philosophers had hailed the great Russian city.

In general he believed in the Hellenistic roots of Russian civilization, and his theories enhanced the classic bent of his poetry. But he had the foreboding, which materialized during the revolutionary upheaval, that the city of Peter the Great was doomed: "We are going to die in the diaphanous Petropolis where Proserpina of the nether regions reigns over us." A whole series of his stanzas sound like a dirge: "Petropolis, your brother, is passing away. / Over the black Neva the spring is expiring, the wax of immortality is melting." Yet, in the days of destruction and famine, he exclaimed, "In the frost of Lethe we will recall that earth was worth ten skies," and he still hoped to meet his friends in Petersburg "in the black velvet of Soviet night, in the velvet of universal emptiness." In general, sorrow and melancholy prevail in the poems of the late 'twenties and early 'thirties; his famous pseudohumoristic tale about a poor Jewish musician, always playing Schubert, ends with poignant lines on failure and death.

What makes Mandelstam's poetry of this period so original and brilliant in diction, tone, and unexpected metaphors is not only his verbal magic and mastery, but also the fusion of sound, image, melody, and thought. He was not a philosophical poet, but in many of his poems there is a core of abstraction: it is not spelled out but only hinted at with the author's customary sobriety and restraint. On the other hand, Mandelstam had a keen sense of time and history and in his most striking poems he writes of the color, odor, and pace of various events of the past. But when he speaks of Homer or Dante he makes them live in the present, at our side. He liked to say about himself, "I am nobody's contemporary." But, actually he was not so indifferent to current events as he claimed, or pretended. "My century, my beast," he wrote in 1923, "Who will look into thy pupils? Who will cement with his own blood the disjointed vertebrae of the centuries?" He tried to remain outside of politics and, as a true introvert, avoided public activities. He consistently remained an alien in the midst of revolutionary explosion and literary squabbles—and this made him suspect in the eyes of the authorities and, finally, caused his ruin. He was disaster-prone, but could not keep himself from bursting out with a satirical jingle, for which he would pay dearly. Such was the case with his parody on Stalin which opened with these lines: "We live. We are not sure that we walk on our soil. Ten feet away no one hears us." But the secret police heard him and even though his authorship was not fully proven, Mandelstam was arrested in 1934. The intervention of influential friends, including Pasternak, saved him from severe punishment. With his wife, he was deported for only three years to a small northern town on the Kama river, where he suffered a nervous breakdown and, in an attempt to commit suicide, jumped out of the hospital window and broke his shoulder. After another intercession by well-known writers, the Mandelstams obtained permission to settle under police surveillance in Voronezh, five hundred miles from Moscow. Their material situation was desperate—he was not allowed to have a job and they lived in an unheated shack, like half-starved, miserable pariahs. Mandelstam however continued to write, and the collection of *Voronezh Notebooks*, published many years after his death, reveals new facets of his poetry. In 1937 the couple returned to Moscow, but in May 1938 Mandelstam was arrested in the clinic where he was trying to rest. After several months in jail he was sent, in December, in a prisoner's train to a transit center in the Vladivostok area: from there the prisoners continued their voyage to a Siberian concentration camp. The poet arrived at the transit point half-demented, suffering from persecution mania, and soon died from starvation and exhaustion. He was buried in a common grave, indicated as 1142, on December 27, 1938.*

ANNA AKHMATOVA

Mandelstam's lifelong friend, Anna Akhmatova, was another great poet of the era, and he often announced proudly: "I am her contemporary." Born Anna Gorenko in 1889, she belonged to the Ukrainian nobility; signed her poems with the family name of her grandmother and was always known as Akhmatova in Russian literature. Educated mostly in St. Petersburg and its fashionable suburb Pavlovsk, in 1910 she married Nikolay Gumilev, already a renowned poet and leader of the acmeist movement which she

---

* The date of his death had been kept secret, which explains why it was often indicated wrongly twenty-five years ago.

joined wholeheartedly. Two years later a son, Lev, was born to the couple, but the marriage was not a success and they separated and were divorced in 1918. (Gumilev was shot in 1921 as a counter-revolutionary.) Akhmatova's first collections of poems, *Evening* (1913) and *Rosary* (1914) were met by general acclaim and considered a challenge to symbolism and futurism. The subsequent slim volumes, *White Flock* (1917), *Plantain*, and *Anno Domini MCMXXI* (1921-23) increased her growing repute; she suddenly became one of the most beloved and widely read Russian poets.

All her books read like the lyrical diary of a passionate nun who fled the convent to partake in all the joys and sorrows of earthly love. Blok called Akhmatova "the Christian gypsy" because of her medley of prayers and erotic songs, but his definition failed to capture the true essence of her feminine poetry. Her epigrammatic, apparently simple, poems were construed as little dramas of a woman's life—from the bliss of fleeting happiness to the lover's indifference, separation and rejection and the sufferings of loneliness. All these experiences were told in colloquial language, but with restraint and devoid of rhetoric or beautified metaphors. Realistic details played a functional role in Akhmatova's poems: they served to reveal the hidden feelings of the "I" or the protagonist of each piece. In Soviet literary criticism such a personage is called the "lyrical hero or heroine." The recurrent theme of these concise stanzas is the disillusionment of unhappy love: the woman who yearns for tenderness meets the hungry look of lust; after the rupture with her lover she says, "It seems to me that there were so many stairs to descend—yet before there were just three." In another final parting the stunned girl complains of having put the right hand glove on the left hand. In another poem she meets her lover during a garden concert, he suggests that they should just be friends, and she hears the ironic voice of the violins: "Rejoice, for the first time you are alone with your beloved." There is no comfort in casual affairs, in easy intrigues, in the game of pretense, or even in dissipation. In the night club all the male revelers and wanton females seem bored and dull, and even the birds and beasts painted on the walls dream of the open skies. The humans also feel the same longing for

purity and fresh air, and after the frenzy of the senses and vagaries of the heart seek consolation in nature and God. Solitary
walks on the shores of a secluded lake or in the fields of a forlorn
countryside seem to heal the wounded soul.

In this mixture of passion and ascetic aspirations, of sin and
atonement, there is a strong religious undercurrent. The priestess
of acmeism and the refined poetess of the sophisticated intelligentsia employed Russian folk accents in her village ballads, in her
sketches of hamlets, humility, northern landscapes, and ancient
peasant rites. This national trend was emphasized in Akhmatova's
post-revolutionary poems. Behind the atrocities and privations of
the epoch she discovered a sort of light, of illumination. She felt
exhilarated even though everything is sold out, looted, and betrayed. She did not want to leave Russia, to emigrate, to be shel-
tered under a foreign wing. She remained in her country "where
my luckless people are condemned to stay," ready to share their
misfortunes and hardships. Yet her personal situation was hardly
enviable: to the authorities she still remained the widow of Gumilev, the executed enemy of bolshevism. She continued to write
but in the 'twenties and 'thirties her production diminished and
her excellent later poems seldom appeared in periodicals. She said
herself in one of her brief stanzas circulated in handwritten copies
by her admirers: "No one will now listen to songs; the world
ceased to be wonderful. This is my last song, do not break my
heart, do not resound any more." For eighteen years, between
1923 and 1940, no books by Akhmatova were printed in the Soviet Union. As mentioned above, only a 1940 anthology, *From the
Six Books*, came out in a small edition. One section, *Reed*, contained some new poems. A slim volume, *Selections* (1943), combined her usual lyrics of intimate emotions with patriotic songs
on war, on the tragedy of Leningrad—the martyr city where one
million people perished from starvation, epidemics, and German
bombs. These and various later poems showed her deep and unalterable love for the city in which she spent the longest part of
her life. During the blockade of Leningrad she was evacuated to
Tashkent, where she wrote a series of charming pieces devoted
to the capital of Uzbekistan, but after the end of the war and her
return home an unexpected blow struck the poetess. In 1946, dur-

ing the official attack by Andrey Zhdanov against "laxity and liberalism" in the arts and the announcement of the tightening of controls (see Chapter 27, "The Aftermath of War: The Era of 'Zhdanovism' "), Akhmatova was singled out together with Zoshchenko for an "exemplary lesson." She was accused of numerous sins, including mysticism and eroticism, and blamed in particularly sharp terms as an enemy of the people and a woman who had dedicated her art to the chapel and the bedchamber. She was immediately expelled from the Union of Soviet Writers, typesetting of her new book was stopped and its galleys destroyed. She was banned from the Soviet press, and her colleagues treated her like a criminal and avoided greeting her in the street. This political quarantine lasted until 1950 as far as periodicals were concerned, and until 1953 for book publication. Even her articles on Pushkin —the fruit of a decade of research—could not find a publisher. Essays on *The Golden Cockerel* (inspired by Washington Irving's *Tales of the Alhambra*), on Benjamin Constant, Pushkin's *Don Juan*, and others saw the light of day partly in the 'fifties (and partly posthumously). In the meantime she earned her living by translating (including the work of Korean poets). Only after Stalin's death did her own poetry begin to reappear in Soviet magazines—in the late 'fifties. This was her second comeback; from 1958 on her books continued to be published in several consecutive editions, their printing reaching 50,000 copies in 1961 and 1965. In 1964 numerous translations in foreign languages made her famous abroad. In the same year she was awarded the Italian Etna-Taormina Prize, and in the spring of 1965 was allowed to travel to England to receive an *honoris causa* degree of doctor of literature from Oxford University. She died the next year.

Some critics, analyzing Akhmatova's poetry from 1945 to 1965 consider it a new phase in her work. This writer does not see any fundamental change in her poems of that period. Of course, they show greater maturity, a natural growth which in some writers comes with age, but the technique, the intonations, the music of her verse remain the same as in her youth. The main difference probably lies in the expansion of the subject matter. The poet of individual destiny turned to the fate of her generation and that of her native land. This tendency reaches its highest aesthetic perfection and emotional potency in two poems, *Requiem*, written in 1938-40 (with some changes and additions in later years), and *Poem without a Hero*, which she is said to have worked on for twenty-two years. Both certainly belong to the greatest masterpieces of Soviet poetry.

Requiem was inspired by some tragic events of Akhmatova's personal life. Her son Lev, a historian, was arrested in 1934 by the secret police, liberated, then arrested again three years later, drafted during the war and sent from jail to the front where he fought through the whole 1942-45 campaign, but in 1949 was jailed for the third time and sent to a northern labor camp. His ordeal lasted seven years, and only in 1956 was he set free and allowed to resume his scholarly research. Akhmatova's second husband, the art historian Nikolay Punin, also fell victim to Stalin's terror and died in 1953 after imprisonment and deportation.

In the *Way of a Preface* (1957), Akhmatova says:

In the terrible years of the reign of Yezhov (head of the Secret Police) I spent seventeen months in the prison queues in Leningrad. Somehow, one day someone "identified" me. Then a woman standing behind me, whose lips were blue with cold and who, naturally enough, had never even heard of my name, emerged from that state of torpor common to us all and putting her mouth close to my ear (there everyone spoke in whispers) asked me: "And could you describe this?" And I answered her, "I can." Then something, vaguely like a smile, flashed across what once had been a human face.

Akhmatova fulfilled her promise, and *Requiem*, which tells the despair of a mother during the unjust and cruel imprisonment of her innocent son, became a poem of national, universal dimensions. "Stars of death stood over us, and Russia / In her innocence, twisted in pain / Under blood-spattered boots, there to crush her / And the Black Marias in their train." In the next chapter she makes an important confession: "For seventeen months my pleas, / My cries have called you home. / I have begged the hangman on my knees, / My son, my dread, my own." These lines refer to the poet's attempt to obtain Stalin's mercy by offering him adulatory poems, a series entitled *Glory to Peace*, in the customary form of pro-Communist eulogies. But her muse, instead of cooperating, refused such insincere effort and retaliated: these stanzas came out as the poorest and stiffest she had ever written. To the contrary, the twelve chapters of *Requiem* tell the truth with emotional intensity and genuine poetic might that transform them into an inimitable epic, a lay of the country's dark days. And Akhmatova exclaims: "And if they should silence my mortified lips / Let the hundred millions for whom my voice speaks / Let them take my place / and remember each year / Whenever my day of remembrance draws near." "I pray not for myself alone, my cry / Goes up for all those with me there—for all / In the heart of winter, heat-wave of July / Who stood beneath that blind deep-crimson wall." (Translation by Robin Kemball, 1974, *Russian Review*, vol. 33, No. 3.)

Of course, *Requiem* was never published in the Soviet Union; its copies printed abroad and smuggled into Russia were dubbed "dangerous 'anti-Soviet' items" and confiscated when found by the police.

The *Poem without a Hero* is a much more complex work, composed on several levels. Akhmatova calls it "a box with three bottoms," and it escapes purely rational interpretation. Without being esoteric, it contains rather mysterious passages and puzzling lines. She herself says: "I confess to sometimes using invisible ink or writing lines that could be read only in mirrors—and I cannot do otherwise; I am compelled to act this way." The theme of silence, present throughout the whole poem, obviously forms one of its main trends—and not only in practical terms (for many years she had been forced to still her voice).

The forty pages of the poem could be called a tale, but it is simultaneously an autobiographical memoir, a vision of a past epoch, a reflection on the nature of time and history, and a lament on human destiny. Its title should not be completely trusted. In fact, although the poem lacks one central figure, it brings in a whole cast of actors many of whom are perfectly recognizable, such as Blok, or the lovely actress and dancer Glebova-Sudeikina, appearing under different disguises—"Colombine," a "doll of St. Petersburg," a psyche, "the blonde marvel," a "muddled charmer," or the officer and poet Kniazev who committed suicide at the front door of her apartment, and many others. Not less factual are Akhmatova's numerous references to Western writers, from Dante and Shakespeare to Goethe, Byron, Shelley, Keats, and dozens of others; she also quotes biblical images and historical figures extending from Salome and Messaline to Mary Stuart.

The first part of the *Poem* opens on New Year's Eve with the carnival of fantastic masks, partly from the Italian Commedia dell'Arte and from Hoffman's *Tales*. Their motley procession evokes the past, more precisely the year 1913, and the foolish careless revelries of artists and intellectuals who did not guess that their world of amorous delights and sophistication was going to crumble, that 1914 was knocking at the door with an iron fist bringing in its wake war and revolution. "How could we be so irresponsible," asks Akhmatova, "failing to perceive the thunderous step that announced not a simple calendar year but the authentic and catastrophic twentieth century?" The masks of the carnival become menacing and diabolic, and fear is mixed with nostalgic reminiscences, interrupted by the terrible question: "How could we have been so heedless as to listen to false prophets and babblers and not feel that the last act was around the corner?"

The second part depicts New Year's Eve in 1941. In the form of an interior monologue, it reveals certain hidden tendencies of the whole poem, and links pre-revolutionary Russia and her literature with all of the Greco-Roman and European civilizations. In the third part, or the epilogue, there is a striking image of the Soviet Union in 1942. We are in the center of the great cataclysm; Russia is going through the cruelest ordeal of her history. The poem was written in Tashkent and later continued upon her return to Leningrad. She conceives the persistent image of St. Petersburg—unlike Mandelstam—in a much more populist and national vein—with a merging of fear and love.

This document of an era and creation of poetic fantasy calls for different interpretations, but all of them recognized its extraordinary verbal and formal beauty, and its passionate and stormy rhythm perfectly suited to its content. Prosodically, she combines anapestic feet with amphybrachian and iambic, and each chapter and part of the poem has its own original musical design. Akhmatova changes the measure of separate stanzas within the framework of the same meter, as Korney Chukovsky pointed out in his important essay, "Reading Akhmatova," in 1964. Fragments from the *Poem without a Hero* have been published in various Soviet periodicals, but its full text only appeared abroad in special *émigré* editions.

MARINA TSVETAYEVA

The poetry of Marina Tsvetayeva (1892-1941) is completely different from that of Mandelstam or Akhmatova, and it occupies a special and unique place in Russian twentieth-century letters. The daughter of a professor of art history and director of Moscow museums, Marina grew up in a highly cultured environment of scholars and artists and accompanied her ailing mother (a good musician) abroad, studied in Swiss schools, and acquired an excellent knowledge of French and German. According to her memoirs, she began "composing verse" at the age of six and had her first poem in print at sixteen. A couple of years later she published two collections, but kept them a secret from her family, *"The Evening Keepsake"* (1911) and *"The Magic Lantern"* (1912), noticed only by a few poets and connoisseurs. After 1912 Tsvetayeva wrote a great many striking poems reflecting her passionate temperament and a surprising mastery of technique. In 1922 the State Editions in Moscow brought out two books by Tsvetayeva, *The Czar Maiden*, a folk-tale in verse, and *Versty* (Pasternak said he was completely overwhelmed by the lyrical power of this slim booklet). In 1912 she married Sergei Efron, a student, and bore him a daughter, Ariadna, known as Alia. Another daughter was born later but died from malnutrition during the Revolution when Marina lived in misery and destitution; her husband was fighting with the anti-Communist armies in the south. After their defeat Marina succeeded in obtaining a permit to go abroad and the family was reunited in Berlin in 1922. At this time the Russian book trade fared well in Germany and Tsvetayeva published three small books, *Parting, Poems to Blok, Psyche*, and a collection of poems entitled *Craftsmanship*, which established her reputation as a first-rate poet among the *émigrés*. The family next moved to Prague. After a son (George, called Mur by his mother), was born in 1925, Tsvetayeva and her family settled in France and lived in the suburbs around Paris from 1926 to 1939.

Tsvetayeva arrived in Europe at the height of her creative development and during seventeen years of exile produced her best poetry and prose. The years of her sojourn in Czechoslovakia were particularly fruitful and affirmed the originality of her genius. The two long poems, *Poem of the Mount* and *Poem of the End*, both on love, its intricacies, emotional contrasts, and the anguish of tormented separation, written with fiery intensity, deep feeling, and extraordinary verbal brilliance, and the seventy-five-page tale in verse *The Pied Piper* belong indubitably to the most remarkable works of Russian twentieth-century poetry. *The Pied Piper*, based on a medieval legend, is partly a ferocious exposé of pettiness, banality, mediocrity, and meanness of the bourgeois of Hameln, a small town in Germany, plagued by an invasion of rats, and partly a romantic yarn on a mysterious young flute player, a symbol of poetry and magic. The rats abandon the town, following the sound of the Piper's flute, and in recompense he demands to marry Greta, the mayor's beautiful daughter. Snubbed, cheated, and vilified, he takes his revenge by abducting the town's children bewitched by his appealing tune. The Piper brings them to an imaginary paradise and they happily drown in an enchanted lake.

The form of this "lyrical satire," as Tsvetayeva called it, is completely its own. It has a succession of nervous rapid meters, of aphoristic lines, often reduced to one word, displays linguistic virtuosity united with the art of epigrammatic definitions and sharp maxims. *The Pied Piper* was printed in 1926 in its entirety in Prague by the Russian monthly *Volia Rossii* (*The Will of Russia*)* but *émigré* critics of the time failed to understand its unparalleled originality. Forty years later *The Pied Piper* was reproduced with some minor censorship cuts in the 1965 Moscow edition of Tsvetayeva's poems.

In 1928, thanks to friends' help, Tsvetayeva succeeded in bringing out in Paris a whole volume of poems, *After Russia*—it was the

* As literary editor of this monthly, this writer continued from 1922 to 1932 to publish Tsvetayeva's numerous poems, essays, and dramas in verse.

last book published during her lifetime, and here again the *émigré* press hardly paid any attention to this literary event. (Of course, it was not even mentioned in the USSR.) This was one of the typical aspects of her tragic fate: she was banned in the Soviet Union for thirty years and was appreciated during her exile in Europe by only a small group of enlightened readers. Even more terrible were the material conditions in which she had to work. For seventeen years she had to struggle for survival under the threat of want and destitution: she had two children and a husband in poor health to feed, clothe, and take care of. Marina was cook, laundress, nurse, and breadwinner. Whole months went by when the family's income consisted mainly of her small literary fees and occasional help from a few friends. In a letter of 1933 she says: "You cannot imagine the poverty in which I live, and I have no other way of making money except by writing. We are slowly perishing from starvation."

But the money problem was not the worst of Tsvetayeva's misfortunes—the others were solitude, isolation, and the bitter awareness of the poor response to her work. She never doubted the worth of her writings, but she resented being ignored both by the *émigrés* and the Russians. In the meantime her daughter Alia decided to return to Russia, and the political evolution of her husband Sergei led him not only to Communism but also to involvement in the assassination in 1937 by a Soviet secret agent of a former Party functionary, Ignacy Reiss. Marina did not know anything about this affair, and Efron's flight from France to Moscow was a sudden blow. She remained in Paris with her thirteen-year-old son who urged her to return home. Her position among the *émigrés* was almost untenable, and she finally was compelled to follow her husband and daughter to the Soviet Union. Although she considered it her duty, she departed with a heavy heart and without illusions. She said to a friend: "Here I am useless, there I would be unthinkable; here I have no readers, there, despite thousands of potential readers, I would not be able to breathe, which means to write and to publish." But what she found in Moscow surpassed her direst forebodings.

From her arrival in 1939 until her death, she was able to publish just one early poem, and worked only as a translator of foreign poets. A few months later her husband and daughter as well as her sister were arrested. Alia spent sixteen years in jail, concentration camps, and Siberian exile, was "rehabilitated" in 1956, and lived in Tarussa, near Kaluga, until her death in 1975. We still do not know the exact date of Efron's execution: he was probably shot either in 1940 or immediately after the outbreak of the war.

When the Germans marched on Moscow in 1941 Tsvetayeva and her son Mur were evacuated to Yelabuga, a village on the Kama River in the Tartar Republic. A few writers who lived in the neighborhood and whom she asked for assistance received her rather coldly. The only job offered her was that of a kitchen maid in an eating place. Her son, big for his age, wanted to volunteer for the Army. She found herself utterly alone, surrounded by indifference or hostility, with the feeling that everything was collapsing in a sort of universal catastrophe. On August 31, 1941, she hanged herself and was buried in a common grave. Nobody attended her funeral.

Posthumous glory came to Tsvetayeva two decades later, in the 'fifties and 'sixties in the Soviet Union as well as abroad and among the émigrés. In 1952 this writer, who had since 1923 promoted her works, expressed the conviction that "the day will come soon when Tsvetayeva's poetry will be rediscovered, reappraised, and given the place it deserves." In 1957 Pasternak wrote in his *Autobiographical Essay* that "the publication of her works would be a great triumph and a great discovery for Russian poetry, this belated gift will enrich it immediately and at one stroke." By that time the manuscript copies of her poems were arousing the enthusiasm of Russian youth who learned them by heart. New poets imitated Tsvetayeva and called her their master. Her popularity and influence grew with incredible rapidity, a number of her poems were reprinted in literary almanacs, the publication of selections from her verses in 1961 was followed four years later by an eight-hundred-page collection with notes and variants and by articles, reminiscences, and commentaries. It is universally accepted in both the East and the West that Tsvetayeva is one of the greatest Russian poets of our century.

Those who knew Marina Tsvetayeva, as did this writer, remember her as a slim, upright young woman, with a handsome, proud face framed by golden hair, and often illuminated by a whimsical smile and large myopic eyes. Her personality was as striking as her art (which Pasternak called "incomparable in its technical brilliance"). Fundamentally she was a romantic and seemed to incarnate and express the elemental forces of movement and restlessness, a perpetual surge upwards—"beyond the prison of existence." This trend, idealistic in essence, akin to the spirit of Hoelderlin and other German poets of the "Sturm und Drang" period, was, however, devoid of softness, sadness, and melancholy. Some critics spoke of her "masculinity" or virility. Despite her lyrical songs of love, she indeed possessed a vigor, an impetus and strength that her very feminine looks and shy and graceful manners seemed to belie.

Like all true poets, she was bent on sublimating reality, on transforming the tiniest occurrence into an emotional event, into something elevated, often mythical. She magnified objects, feelings, and ideas: whatever occupied her mind and heart at the moment was rendered—in verse or even in simple conversation—with such intensity as to leave her readers and listeners breathless. She was a master of repartee and greatly appreciated partners who were skilled in the game of lightning dialogue that resembled a tennis match, with words and sentences flying back and forth like balls. A woman of sharp intelligence and quick wit, she combined a sense of humor with the capacity of handling abstract concepts without ever losing the perception of concrete reality. Widely read in world literature, she was endowed with keen critical acumen and astonishing memory—they are quite evident in her essays and memoirs in prose. Although remote from metaphysics and leaving the problem of God to theologians (she disliked Dostoevsky), she searched for the divine spark on earth, in men and nature. This search was as excessive as her passion for poetry, for creative imagination or for great figures of the past. At various periods of her life she idolized Napoleon or Goethe and she would suddenly place on a pedestal isolated contemporaries and just as suddenly throw them down later: she often went from exaggerated glorification to bitter disappointment. Never neutral or indifferent, she loved or hated works of art or human beings to distraction. One of her favorite mottoes was: "Literature is propelled by passion, power, vitality, partiality." She was aware that her overflowing enthusiasms or aversions made her unfit for the routine of daily living. "What shall I do with my excessiveness in this world of weights and measures?" she exclaimed in one of her most revealing poems.

She cut a strange and solitary figure in *émigré* literary circles, where the predominant mood was either conservative or in the tradition of symbolism and acmeism. Tsvetayeva occasionally used symbolist metaphors and she loved Blok and Bely but did not belong to their or any other school. The whole tenor of her work and the daring of her linguistic experimentation place her close to Khlebnikov, Pasternak, and sometimes to Mayakovsky, and in general in the avant-garde of the 'twenties. Her style is precise, articulate, clear-cut, she prefers brass to flutes, her muse is violent, brisk, dynamic, the rhythm of her verse is a rapid vehement staccato, her diction is strongly accented, separate words and tone-syllables are scanned, and carried from one line or couplet to another (enjambement). The emphasis is definitely on expressiveness, on verbal stress, not on melody. She does not shout like Mayakovsky, her poetry is exclamatory rather than declamatory, she prefers to play percussion instruments instead of trumpets, and there is often harshness, almost shrillness, in her voice.

This poetic Amazon, as literary foes called her, was as exacting with herself as she was with others: she abhorred half-baked amateurs, empty redundance, and took time to find the right word and a fitting intonation. There was something ascetic in this sacrificial concentration on her work. When accused of being too egocentric she replied: "The only task of man on earth is the truth of self; real poets are always prisoners of themselves; this fortress is stronger than that of Peter and Paul."*

Tsvetayeva's poetry may seem difficult and obscure at first glance, but this superficial impression is caused mainly by her concise, almost telegraphic style, so different from the verbosity, elusiveness, and tongue-tied babblings of mediocre rhymesters. Her clipped sentences resemble sparkling flashes and pass through one like an electric current. Grammatical links between phrases are

* This fortress in St. Petersburg served as a jail for political prisoners.

often omitted and the verbal chain is constantly interrupted, while isolated words serve as signposts along the road the poet travels at an accelerated pace. With the exception of her folklore tales of the early 'twenties ("The Czar Maiden" and "The Lad"), the vernacular becomes but a part of her extremely vast vocabulary and blends with her refined metrics and language innovations.

Her favorite method was to dig into the very root of words. By cutting prefixes, by changing endings, one or two vowels or consonants (not unlike the French surrealists), she succeeds in baring the original meaning of various vocables. Playing on phonetics, she derives a new significance of words from the closeness of sound. For example, her long *Poem of the Mount* is structured on the parallelism of the words "mount" and "grief" in Russian (*gorà-gòre*) with an amazingly rich display of all the derivatives from the master word. This "game of phonemes" did not degenerate into mannerism and linguistic tricks. The search for the "core," the "truth" of words not only made them shine anew, but also gave them a deeper meaning, brought forth their emotional substance and ideational value, thus achieving a rare unity of form and spirit. The thrust of her short lines, the stormy and winged rhythms of her meters and alliterations, the high voltage of her exclamations express the poet's indomitable, rebellious nature.

The posthumous popularity of Tsvetayeva, leading to belated recognition from Soviet rulers, assumed tremendous proportions. When her sister Anastasia was released from labor camp she went to Yelabuga in 1960 and erected a simple wooden cross with Marina's dates of birth and death, in that part of the cemetery where Tsvetayeva's mortal remains were supposedly entombed. This is the only public memorial to the great poet in the Soviet Union. But her poems live on in the minds and hearts of hundreds of thousands of people. Innumerable readers were attracted by the fact that Tsvetayeva's verse was so completely different from the usual mass-produced Soviet poetry. Instead of thinly disguised propaganda, or Communist slogans and political and patriotic rhetoric, she offered perfectly authentic, purely lyrical and individual subject matter filled with sincere emotions, romantic dreams, the glorification of independence and visions of love and nature. The very titles of her series of verse seemed original: *Poems: of the Air, of Trees, of Clouds, Eulogy of Aphrodite, of the Red Steed, the Ode to the Pedestrians.* Her plays were devoted to Casanova and other eighteenth-century adventurers; her forceful, imaginative essays included fanciful reminiscences, interior monologues and portrayed writers and artists she had known. Her prose was published in the United States. In the USSR only minor sketches and the highly suggestive *My Pushkin* were allowed by the censors. Her letters form another important chapter of her work because of their high literary value, such as, for example, her correspondence with Pasternak about their platonic love affair.

The whole content of Tsvetayeva's work was completely unusual for the Party-conditioned Soviet audience because it lacked any link with current events and the realities of Russian social, economic, and political conditions. In the early 'twenties she hailed the anti-Communist "white armies" in the poems "The Swan's Camp" and "Perekop" (banned in the Soviet Union and published posthumously abroad),* and in 1939 she wrote a series of freedom-loving pieces on the occupation of her beloved Czechoslovakia by the Nazis. But in all the rest of her writings themes connected with the Revolution are completely absent. She lived, dreamed, and created outside of history, and being aware of this, said once: "I and my century missed each other." And paradoxically this poet so aloof to the life around her, used the most revolutionary poetics and the most challenging innovations and therefore represented more truly and impressively the spirit of her epoch than all those official bards of the Party line who vainly attempted the taming of poetry by using the shackles of political engagement and socialist realism.

---

* In 1938 or 1939 she also wrote a long poem on the atrocious murder of Tsar Nicholas II and the whole imperial family, probably as an answer and counterpart to Mayakovsky's "Imperator." This writer heard it in the 'thirties when she read it in Paris to a small group of friends. The original must have perished in the bombed archives in Amsterdam during World War II.

24

The Historical Novel

The enthusiasm for taking stock of the country and building it up were linked in the 1930's to a growing national awareness. The internationalism of the early revolutionary period, when even the name "Russia" was banned from the press and any Russian national aspirations were dubbed "shameful relics of the past," was definitely replaced by an official recognition of patriotic feelings. That nationalism could be used for the advancement of Communism in Asia and among colonial peoples had been acknowledged earlier by Lenin and his disciples and made part of their doctrine. But only in the 1930's was it accepted for Russia itself—and it was used in connection with the theory of building socialism in one country and the stress put on Russia's international role as the "leading country of mankind." Soviet citizens were told they should work to make their motherland mighty, rich and splendid—for their own benefit and for the sake of the world—and nationalistic feelings were used as powerful incentives for the masses.

The glorification of the Russian past became part of the government's program, and the study of history underwent a radical change. In the late 1920's the RAPP had been in a position to open a campaign against such prominent historians as Sergei Platonov and Evgeny Tarle, who had been arrested and exiled as "scions of bourgeois objectivity and anti-Marxism." Mikhail Pokrovsky (1868-1932), the head of the extreme Marxian historical school, considered history "a projection of politics into the past"; in all educational institutions his disciples were presenting historical material only as direct illustrations of the class struggle. The death of Pokrovsky in 1932 coincided with the beginning of a new era. His opinions were now condemned by the Party as a "deviation" and as "primitive sociologism." The study of historical figures was fully restored in the schools, and official celebrations tended to enhance the cult of national heroes, such as Peter the Great or Alexander Nevsky, the saintly prince who fought the Tartars. It was discovered that even Tsars and titled aristocrats had done some good for the country. Of course, the revision of the Party attitude was due to the pressure of the masses: together with a tremendous release of the people's energy, a sharpening of nationalistic emotions was a natural consequence of the Revolution.

The awareness of national continuity was preceded in literature by the idea of cultural succession. The first Soviet historical novel, even before the political changes, was written by Yury Tynyanov, the master of the biographical genre. A son of a petty noble, Tynyanov (1896-1943) was graduated from the university of Petrograd and took an active part in current literary debates. His collection of essays *Archaists and Innovators* (1929), in which he analyzed the Russian poets (chiefly Pushkin and Tiutchev) from a purely stylistic standpoint and challenged the academic standards, strengthened his already solid position among the formalists; at the age of 29 he became a university professor and was a distinguished scholar. He remained an educator to the end of his life, but it is as a writer of fiction that he won his great popularity.

A friend of Gorky and of the Serapion Brethren, Tynyanov matured as a novelist in the atmosphere of artistic experimentation that was so typical of the 1920's. He absorbed all the stylistic innovations of the times, enhanced them by his scholarship, and applied them to the historical narrative. It is not altogether accurate to call Tynyanov a Russian Lytton Strachey or André Maurois, as has often been done in the USSR and abroad, because he excelled not in essays or in romanticized biographies but in novels and tales. *Kukhlya* (1925), his first and probably best work of this kind, depicted the pathetic and odd Wilhelm Kuechelbecker, friend of Pushkin, political plotter and a romantic poet of the 1820's. The quixotic personality of this clumsy, short-sighted idealist, his pathetic love affairs, his role in the Decembrist uprising of 1825, and his trial and exile to Siberia where he died in blindness and misery, gave Tynyanov the opportunity to evoke the dawn of Russia's revolutionary movement and the peak of literary romanticism. He had a thorough knowledge of this exciting period and used vast documentation, but the scholar never gets in the way of the novelist: his fantasy and fictional inventiveness only gain from being based on authentic source material. The book was written in a stylized manner, which borrowed from Zamyatin's expressionism and Bely's symbolic composition.

Bely's influence made itself more apparent in Tynyanov's second work *The Death of Vazir Mukhtar* (1929); its English translation was published in 1938 under the title *Death and Diplomacy in Persia*. It tells the life story of Griboyedov, Russia's great dramatist, author of *Wit Works Woe*, who was one of the most intelligent men of the 1820's. He was a diplomat in Teheran where he was murdered by a fanatical mob. His inner conflicts, the frustrations of his brilliant worldly career, in which he played, in turn, the contrasting parts of a liberal, a satirist, and a high-ranking official—all the contradictions of Griboyedov's extraordinary existence were brought out by Tynyanov in a most subjective manner. The composition of the novel was fragmentary (the critics compared it to a broken mirror), many figures were introduced not as historical personages but as bearers and heralds of fateful tidings. In the bold psychological interpretation of his hero, in the dramatic exposition of the intrigues and machinations that led to Griboyedov's tragic end at the age of thirty-four, Tynyanov the novelist used symbolic devices and almost mystical overtones; this gave a special patina to the canvas. On the other hand, some parts of the novel were based on special research and literary discoveries made by Tynyanov the scholar.

The third great work by Tynyanov, his *Pushkin*, was written in a more realistic vein. It presents a marvelous panorama of the first two decades of the nineteenth century in Russia and a fascinating description of the poet's childhood and adolescence. Only two parts of the novel were published in a definitive version (1936-37); they were admired for the graceful ease with which the author handled such a wealth of historical data. He worked on this novel for many years but never finished it: an incurable illness had made him an invalid. Even on his death bed, however, with the stamina of a passionate lover of literature, he kept on dictating new pages of his *major opus*.

As literary achievements, Tynyanov's historical tales are no less valuable than his novels. "Second-Lieutenant Kizhe" (1930), which was made into an engrossing film and inspired Prokofiev's music, is an admirably told story about a double slip of the quill on the part of a harried army clerk which makes a ghost out of a real lieutenant and creates an incorporeal Second-Lieutenant Kizhe (Second-Lieutenant Likewise). Paul I, the mad Tsar, is induced to believe in the lieutenant's existence, has him flogged for a pecadillo and sent off on foot and under convoy to Siberia, but eventually brings him back, marries him off to a maid of honor in a church ceremony, promotes him to First-Lieutenant, Captain, Colonel, and General, bestows an estate and a thousand serfs upon him, and showers him with decorations. The general fulfills his duties as well as any other officer, his wife presents him with real children. But when Paul I decides that General Likewise is the one man in all the Empire whom he can trust, and demands to see him in the flesh, the general falls dangerously ill. Despite the efforts of the best physicians, he passes away and is given a magnificent funeral; as the cortege with the empty coffin passes by, the Tsar salutes and observes sadly: "My best men are dying off."

The descriptive accuracy and a Gogolian sense of whimsy and sarcasm makes this highly stylized grotesque a fine specimen of historical satire. Also fantastic but more gloomy, almost macabre, is "The Wax Figure" (1932). It depicts the last hours of Peter the Great and the modeling of the deceased Tsar's wax effigy, which the sculptor Rastrelli (father of the famous architect) was commissioned to make. The main symbolic thread running through the tale is the comparison between the Tsar's court filled with awe-inspiring or ridiculous dignitaries and the exhibits in Peter's Kunstkammer, a museum of freaks and monstrosities, including the lopped-off heads of the Tsar's enemies preserved in alchohol. This tale, with its stylization of speech, sentence structure, and spirit, shows one of Tynyanov's chief literary characteristics. He knew how to resurrect the atmosphere of a period through archaisms and verbal perculiarities; he also made meticulous use of significant details of dress, manners, and mores.

One might object that Tynyanov did not create characters out of his imagination, since his heroes were memorable historical figures. Of course, this was inherent in the genre he cultivated. His writings do bear the stamp of the serious artist. They are planned and laid out with the utmost care for proportions; they are shrewdly put together by a formalist greatly interested in the techniques of his trade. In the history of Soviet literature Tynyanov stands out as a first-rate craftsman, a good artist, and a successful initiator of the historical biographical novel. As head of a school he had many followers. Among them the talented Georgy Storm, author of *Works and Days of Lomomonossov*, *Tale of the Brothers Turgenev* (1931), and a biography of Radishchev. *Pushkin in Mikhailovskoye* and *Pushkin in the South* by Ivan Novikov (1877-1959) were united in the large novel *Pushkin in Exile* in 1947. His namesake Alexei Novikov (b. 1894) has been blamed by Communist critics for having committed "political errors" in his two novels on the great composer Glinka, *The Birth of a Musician* (1950) and *My Dawn Will Come* (1953), but the readers loved them and acclaimed the film made from the first book. Scores of novels on Russian nineteenth-century writers have been and still are published in the Soviet Union. Many of them deal with Lermontov's life and tragic fate (tales and plays by Pilnyak, Pavlenko, Sergeyev-Tsensky, Paustovsky, and others).

A separate chapter in the biographical novel was written by the prolific Olga Forsh (1873-1961), a noblewoman who studied painting and was associated with Populist socialism in her youth. The bulk of her writings discloses her admiration for the symbolists and the influence of Merezhkovsky's methods in the evocation of the past. She knew well and frequented the artistic avant-garde; her novels *The Mad Boat* (1931), later renamed *The Raven*, and *Symbolists* (1933), condemned by Communist critics, present an interesting record of Russian literary circles of the early 'twenties. But her success with the average reader was mainly due to her novels on the revolutionaries of the nineteenth century (*Iron Clad*, 1925), on Gogol and his friend the painter Ivanov (*Contemporaries*, 1928), on Radishchev, the liberal writer at the time of Catherine I (a trilogy, 1934-39), and on the panorama of the Decembrist movement of the 1820's (*The Firstlings of Freedom*, 1950-53). Her thrilling and colorful work always maintained a good literary standard combining exciting plots with solid historical background. Her genuine revolutionary feelings allowed her to link the biographical with the politically inspired historical novel.

In the late 1920's and throughout the 'thirties and 'forties, the purpose of Soviet historical novels was usually to show that the oppressed peasants and workmen had always nurtured revolutionary tendencies, and that Communism, therefore, had deep popular roots. Dozens of writers chose uprisings and movements of discontent as their favorite subjects. Only two fellow-travelers, however, were really successful in dealing with this popular theme: Shishkov and Chapyghin.

Vyacheslav Shishkov (1873-1945), friend of Remizov and Zamyatin, was the author of neo-realist novels on the Siberian peasantry (*Taiga*, 1916, *The Gang*, 1924) and on well-to-do merchants (*Ugrium River*, 1933). In *Emelyan Pugachev* (1938-45), a Stalin Prize book, he portrayed the eighteenth-century rebel, impostor, and leader of a huge popular movement in the southeast of Russia (Pushkin depicted him in his *Captain's Daughter*). In his monumental three-volume work Shishkov gave a broad panorama of Catherine I's reign emphasizing the suffering of the people oppressed by noble landowners and Imperial officials. He avoided, however, the false tone so typical of literature under Stalin and did not unduly idealize the peasants or denigrate the aristocrats.

This was also the case with *Razin Stepan* (1927) by Alexei Chapyghin (1870-1937), a writer influenced by Korolenko, Mikhailovsky, and other Populists. The very title of his remarkable work indicated the spirit in which it was conceived: instead of the familiar but deprecatory nickname "Sten'ka," which is also used in popular songs, Chapyghin employed his hero's full Christian name "Stepan." He made special studies for his broad canvas of seventeenth-century Muscovy, and particularly of the period when serfdom had been consolidated and a revolt of the oppressed, headed by Razin, the river pirate and the Russian counterpart of Robin Hood, flared up in the Volga region. His other novel, *The Rovers* (1937), depicted the ferment among the peasants in the years preceding the Razin rebellion. Gorky admired the originality of Chapyghin's carefully formed and slightly precious style, and compared it to a fine fabric woven with multi-colored silk.

To the names of Forsh, Shishkov, Chapyghin, and Alexey Tolstoy, whose *Peter I* was undoubtedly the best specimen of the historical genre, must be added that of Sergei Sergeyev-Tsensky

(1876-1958). A neo-realist, well known as a storyteller before 1917, and author of *Transfiguration*, a series of novels on contemporary Russia, he became a bestselling author with *The Ordeal of Sebastopol* (1937-39), which unfolds in its 1600 pages the Crimean campaign of 1854-55 and its Russian and international implications (with an obvious anti-British slant). Later Sergeyev-Tsensky's trilogy on World War I (*Brussilov's Breakthrough, The Guns Are Rolled Out, The Guns Began To Speak,* 1943-45) was the first important attempt in Soviet letters to vindicate the Russian Imperial Army (in which the author had been an officer), and to explain why despite all the heroism of the soldiers and talent of the commanders, Russia failed to win the war against the Central powers. As a work of patriotic self-assertion this trilogy expressed the general mood that prevailed in Soviet society during World War II. The same militant nationalistic spirit is strongly felt in the poetic plays *1812* and *Kutuzov* by Vladimir Solovyov (both 1939), in novels on Suvorov and other military heroes of the past, and, of course, in such famous films as *Alexander Nevsky* (1938) by Sergei Eisenstein with music by Prokofiev, *Minin and Pozharsky* (1939), *Suvorov* (1940), *Admiral Nakhimov* (1946) by Vsevolod Pudovkin, and *Peter I* by Vladimir Petrov (1937-38).

In the late 1930's and the 1940's the historical narrative followed two main roads. On the one hand, the explorers of the remote past centered their attention on the Middle Ages and the Asiatic invasions. Vassily Yan Yanchevetsky (1875-1954) gave an amazing picture of the Tartar Empire and of Russia under the yoke of the Golden Horde (*Genghis Khan,* 1938, *Batu,* 1942); Sergei Borodin (whose pen name until 1941 was Amir Sarghidzhan) extolled the fight waged by patriotic princes against the Mongolian hordes in his *Dimitry Donskoy* (1941), and in his *Stars Over Samarkand* (1953-62), a trilogy dominated by the figures of Tamerlane or Timur, gave a colorful picture of Central Asia and Trans-Caucasia in the fourteenth and fifteenth centuries; Konstantin Schildkreth in his *The Wings of a Slave* (1932) told the sad story of a peasant who invented a flying contrivance under Ivan the Terrible.

Meanwhile, a number of novels evoked events of the recent past in a semi-historical, semi-autobiographical manner. Most works in this category were spoiled by partiality and an annoying, monotonous political pattern; they represented revolutionaries as saints and thickened the dark colors whenever they wanted to paint Russian life under the last Tsar. A happy exception to this cliché is found in *Tsuchima* (1932-40) by Alexey Novikov-Priboy (1877-1944). A fellow-traveler and a former member of the socialist revolutionary party, Novikov-Priboy served as a sailor in the Russian navy during the Russian-Japanese war of 1904-05. In an unpretentious semi-factual narrative, adding firsthand experiences to the study of historical documents, Novikov-Priboy reported on the debacle of the Imperial navy on the shores of Korea. *Tsuchima* had a tremendous success and sold millions of copies. The popularity of another novel on the same period, *Port Arthur* (1944) by Alexander Stepanov, a 1000-page epic, was mainly due to the great vogue of patriotic novels during the World War II: otherwise it is long-winded and undistinguished.

There is no reason to include in this category of "historical novels" the innumerable potboilers about the 1917 revolution, civil war, Lenin, and (between 1937 and 1953) Stalin which flooded the Soviet market with distressing regularity. The vast majority of these works distorted history for the sake of Party slogans, and flattered dictators of the past and present.

It is extremely revealing that the highest honors in the development of the historical genre in Soviet Russia belong to the writers of the old generation. Alexey Tolstoy, Forsh, Sergeyev-Tsensky, Chapyghin, Shishkov, Novikov-Priboy, Storm, Ivan Novikov, and many other historical writers were fellow-travelers influenced by pre-revolutionary traditions. Moreover, none of them had anything to do with socialist realism. Equally alien to this formula were the younger writers of the biographical novel led by the formalist Tynyanov and his friends and disciples. In any event, all of them created a veritable school, and Gorky was right when he wrote in 1936 "we have genuine and highly artistic historical novels, such as we did not possess in the past." The same year the representative of the government made a significant statement: "The men and women of the Soviet have an ardent interest in the past of their socialist fatherland. The history of their people is near and dear to them. They see now that their love of their country had glorious traditions in the remote past."

The historical novel was, of course, utilized as a political weapon, but in most cases it offered to readers as well as to writers an escape from the pressures of the moment; it gave them the opportunity of making imaginary flights to safer shores than those of the USSR under Stalin's rule. It also offered an outlet to the newly developed and governmental-promoted Soviet patriotism which insisted on the continuity of Russia—the Russia of the red-blue-and-white flag as well as that of the red banner with the hammer and sickle.

25

The Pre-War Years

We can discover several trends in the literature of the late 1930's. The artistic diversity of the 'twenties was disappearing; literature had become more uniform; and despite all the debates on socialist realism, a single school was sanctified. The stabilization of the creative arts—as well as taste and style—coincided with the growing influence of such organizations as the Union of Soviet Writers, the Repertory Committee, the Union of Soviet Composers, and others which were national in scope and administered by the Communists. This signified a more planned and systematic pressure upon the artist and a perfected machine for exerting it. Another example of the bureaucratization of the arts toward the end of the 1930's was the increased activity of the Committee on the Arts attached to the Cabinet of Commissars (later the Cabinet of Ministers), and the establishing of Stalin Prizes for novels, poems, plays, critical essays, musical scores, and motion pictures, and the Government bestowed medals, honorary citations, decorations, and orders of various grades upon poets and novelists, playwrights and authors, scientists, and technicians. All practical issues of censorship, publications, circulation, and mass media were entrusted to official institutions, formally linked with the Ministry of Education and Central Committee *ad hoc* created bodies. Praise or blame in the Party press could make or destroy any artist's reputation. In general, problems of creativeness, style, tradition, or innovations became dependent on decisions of State councils. Theory also fell under central control: Party leaders affirmed the necessity for codifying Communist aesthetics and for raising socialist realism to the height of a doctrinary concept, incorporated in the political credo.

The expansion of literature and its great role in life having been recognized, the Party felt more than ever the importance of its integration into a planned society; channels and organs for that integration were more closely watched; aesthetic slogans lost their haphazard character and became more tightly interwoven with the over-all design. It may be argued that between 1932 and 1936 the controls were only receiving their final shape and still preserved a rather benign character. But the situation grew worse between 1936 and 1939, with the liquidation of Trotskyites and other real or imaginary enemies, the mass trials, and the hold of the secret police over the country. Fellow-travelers, and even Communists who had not been quick enough to get in line, were accused of connivance with the condemned groups and were in turn liquidated. Hundreds of writers and artists were executed or perished in jails and concentration camps: Babel, Pilnyak, Mandelstam disappeared during these dark years together with Meyerhold, Nikolay Kluyev, Pyotr Oreshin, Pavel Vasiliev, Ivan Katayev, Boris Guber, Artyom Vesely, Sergey Tretyakov, Nikolay Zarudin, Vladimir Kirshon, Mikhail Koltsov, Dimitry Sviatopolk-Mirsky, Abram Lezhnyov, Ferapont Sedenko-Vityazev, and many others. This list could be extended by hundreds of less familiar names, particularly of critics who were "suppressed" as "agents of Trotsky and world imperialism." Only a few writers were lucky enough to return ultimately from exile: Erdman, Zabolotsky, Galina Serebriakova (the latter, who wrote novels on Karl Marx, spent eighteen years in jail and exile).

This era of accusations and persecutions gave Communist theoreticians the opportunity for settling their accounts with the formalists who were hitherto influential in various literary groups and became the main challenge to official aesthetics.

Two of Russia's outstanding scholars had been, among others, the predecessors of the formalists. Alexander Potebnya (1835-91), a philologist whose explorations of the nature and evolution of the language have a truly modern ring; and Alexander Vesselovsky (1838-1906), who applied the comparative method to the study of poetics, folklore, and itinerant subjects in Russian and world literature, and whose brilliant and original research inspired a veritable school of ethnographers and literary historians. Before the Revolution the traditions of Potebnya and Vesselovsky were very much alive at the University of St. Petersburg and in what eventually became the cradle of the formalist movement—the Society for the Study of Poetic Language, which numbered in its ranks Andrey Bely, Victor Shklovsky, Roman Yakobson (b. 1896, later professor of linguistics at Harvard in the 1950's), Yury Tynyanov (1894-1943), Boris Tomashevsky (1890-1957), and those who later promoted formalism in scholarship and criticism: Boris Eichenbaum (1886-1959), Victor Zhirmunsky (1891-1971), and many others.

In the 1920's and the early 'thirties the study of literature in the Soviet Union was almost entirely in the hands of formalists. Their friends—such as the essayist and author of historical novels Leonid Grossman (1888-1965) and Alexander Dolinin (the pen name of Alexander Iskoz, 1885-1965), who specialized in Dostoevsky—and their disciples produced a great number of valuable monographs on the Russian classics and the literary currents of the nineteenth and twentieth centuries as well as treatises on various problems of prosody and scores of essays dealing with forgotten or minor authors. The most paradoxical fact was that the formalists flourished at the very time when the triumph of Marxian and sociological criticism would have seemed more appropriate. Here again their position under the Soviets and the many contributions they made to scholarship and criticism were the continuation of a trend that had begun with the Symbolists and had been projected into the revolutionary 1920's. And, of course, the Communists had nobody to oppose to the young formalists. It is amazing that a great country like Russia, placed under the Marxian banner, was unable in fifty years to produce a single truly Marxian literary critic or scholar of stature—while Hungary, for instance, could boast of a Georg Lucacz. This aggravated the hostility of sterile Communist dogmatists toward the talented formalists. Even later, despite wicked persecution campaigns in the press, most formalists remained quite prominent in linguistics and semiotics as well as in the other branches of philological discipline. They greatly influenced literary research in Russia and abroad, particularly in Italy, France, and the United States.

The formalists asserted that a work of art is primarily a sum of techniques and devices, that the order of the intellect or the order of morality exists only if it is organized in the order of artistic form—which in its turn represents ways of expression or "constructive diction." Renovation in language, structure, and genre have appeared in the past and continue to appear, not to translate new ideas but to replace old forms that have exhausted themselves and have ceased to excite the imagination and the emotions of the reader. The acceptance of this premise led to the conclusion that a succession of genres, schools, tendencies, modes of expression, fictional combinations, plot and story patterns, and poetic conventions had its own rhythm, determined not by the struggle of classes but by the laws of growth, maturation, decadence, and renewal. A similar approach was much later represented by the new criticism in the U.S.A. and structuralism in Europe. In the 1920's the formalists made a few concessions to the Marxians and accepted, at least officially, that stylistic devices depended on the general conditions of life; they attempted to place the changes of form within a larger framework of social transformation. Later they went even further (Shklovsky, for instance) and admitted that the class structure might be reflected indirectly in the means of artistic expressions. They would not, however, compromise on the basic principles—and this brought about their undoing. Formalist criticism challenged Soviet aesthetics in an era of theoretical codification that excluded the existence of independent criticism. The Communist doctrine asserted the predominance of ideological content as the organizing force of art, and this content necessarily had to reflect class consciousness and class struggle as the two determinants of value. The formalists never ceased to apply aesthetic standards and were mainly interested in the fulfillment of artistic intent (whether deliberate or intuitive), whereas the Communist critics spoke of ideational intent and educational utility as the highest criteria of achievement, and were concerned chiefly with the direct role a novel, a poem, or a drama could play in society. Good and evil in art were thus clearly delimited; and by the late 1930's "Formalist" had became a term of opprobrium.

The measures against the formalists indicated the final disappearance of the relatively liberal 1920's, almost in the same way as the trials and executions of Lenin's early comrades had marked the jettisoning of the political figures of the same period. The formalists were relegated to the limbo of academic journals and to obscure provincial universities. But they had to watch their step in whatever institutions of learning they were allowed to retire to, and some of them had to pay the usual penalty of recantation and take loyalty oaths to preserve their teaching positions.

With the suppression of the formalists the new line adopted by all critics was definitely that of the official doctrine: slight variations in appraisal seldom relieved the monotony of method and evaluation. The task of criticism was to compare literary figures and situations with the official image of real life. As in all other fields of Communist literature, a special jargon of slogans and formulas led to such a standardization of critical writing that it became hard to discover any difference of opinion. In general, with some rare exceptions, reviews of books and critical essays presented a dull picture of uniformity and censored statements. The campaign against the formalists was, of course, merely part of a broader movement for conformity in all fields of art, particularly in music and the theater. The bold experimentation of the avant-garde in theatrical production initiated by Meyerhold, Tairov, Vakhtangov, Evreinov, Kommisarzhevsky, Mikhail Chekhov, and their disciples or friends, the scores of Shostakovich, and eventually, even the routine of certain circus clowns were all stigmatized "decadent and bourgeois manifestations of the nefarious art for art's sake."

The situation in dramatic literature was rather complex. The Soviet repertory, aside from the repeat performances of classics and of plays by Gorky, started only around 1925 to include adaptations of current novels and dramas about the civil war. *The Storm*, a mediocre pageant by Vladimir Bill-Belotserkovsky, *Lyubov Yarovaya*, a pseudo-realistic melodrama by Konstantin Trenyov (1884-1945), *Revolt* by Boris Lavrenyov (1892-1959), and *Armored Train 14-69* by Vsevolod Ivanov, the best of all these romantic-heroic representations of revolutionary battles, were followed by *The Days of Turbins*, adapted by Mikhail Bulgakov from his novel *The White Guard*, and staged in 1926 by the Moscow Art Theater. It was the first serious attempt to reveal the idealistic and patriotic motivations of the anti-Communists. This play in the old realistic tradition had a great success, was then banned but finally allowed to be shown again in 1932.

By the end of the 1920's satirical comedy flourished briefly with Mayakovsky's *The Bedbug* and *The Bathhouse*, Katayev's adaptation of his *The Embezzlers* and *Squaring of the Circle*, a vaudeville. The farcical *Another Man's Child* by Vassily Shkvarkin (1894-1967) was a great hit. Nikolay Erdman (1902-70), a promising satirist, had a brilliant beginning with his *Credentials* staged in 1925 by Meyerhold; it ridiculed the last Mohicans of the old regime but at the same time cleverly exposed Soviet bureaucracy and the atmosphere of fear and suspicion endemic throughout the country. Erdman's comedy caused quite a stir because of its hints and humorous allusions about well-known figures and events. The play was vilified in the Party press and finally banned. The second Erdman play, *The Suicide*, a grotesque and biting satire, was banned after the dress rehearsal attended by Communist authorities. During the subsequent purges Erdman was imprisoned and sent to a concentration camp. He returned to Moscow twenty years later, in 1956, and earned his living by working as a scriptwriter for the movies. In the late 'sixties *The Suicide* was staged in German in Hamburg, Vienna, and Zurich.

Mikhail Bulgakov's *Zoika's Apartment*—a satirical description of Soviet citizens of the NEP period—pleased the audiences but displeased the Party critics, and was taken out of current repertory.

The comedies by Alexei Faiko (b. 1893)—*The Teacher Bubus*', produced by Meyerhold in 1925, and *Evgraf, The Seeker of Adventures*, staged by the Moscow Art Theater II in 1926, presented a curious mixture of fantasy and realism. Faiko's drama *Man With a Briefcase* (1928) deals with the moral problems of an intellectual caught by the revolutionary whirlwind.

In general, at the beginning of the 1930's satirical comedies were pushed aside by political dramas, usually inspired by Communist indoctrination and supplied mostly by young people, mainly Party members. Some of them were truly talented and achieved great popularity. This was the case of Afinogenov and Pogodin.

Alexander Afinogenov (1904-41) who started with *The Eccentric* and asserted himself as an excellent playwright with *Fear* (1926), a drama of ideological conflict between an old intellectual and the realities of the new order, later wrote two other hits: *Far Taiga* (1936), also devoted to the conflict between the old and the new, and *Mashen'ka* (1940), a play full of lyrical charm and humor. In general he followed the trend of psychological drama (as in *Fear*) but was also attracted by light comedy.

Nikolay Pogodin (the pen name of Nikolay Stukalov), a talented journalist (1900-62) , began his successful career with dramas and comedies devoted to the problems of industrialization (*Tempo*, 1929, *The Poem of the Axe*, 1930, *My Friend*, 1931) and reached great popularity with *The Aristocrats* (1934), a "serious comedy," as he called it: it represented the moral regeneration of former criminals through toil (actually, forced labor), a familiar theme in the literature under Stalin. In many works of the 1930's, the conversion of villains into good Communists, like the conversion of sinners into good Christians in old miracle plays, was largely used by clumsy hacks, but Pogodin was a good craftsman and knew how to relieve tendentious subject matter, such as the forced labor of prisoners, with jokes and humor (for example, his light sketch of Captain Kostya and his friends, builders of a canal between the White and Baltic seas). An excellent dramatist, he used cinematographic techniques, developing action in a sequence of short scenes and brittle dialogues. This method is most visible in his highly popular plays on Lenin and Stalin—which certainly stood out among the multitude of attempts to revive on the boards the "father of the Revolution" and his official heir. *Man with a Rifle*, staged in 1937 by the Vakhtangov Theater, showed a simple soldier who meets Lenin and Stalin in 1917. This encounter symbolized the union between Leninism and the aspirations of the half-awakened masses. *The Chimes of the Kremlin*, the second play in the Lenin series, mixed humor with mythmaking: while famine rages in the Russia of 1920, Lenin, helped by Stalin and Dzerzhinsky, plans the electrification of the country, but his talk with a little Jewish workman who makes the chimes of the Kremlin play the Internationale, is full of sharp wit and natural goodness. In 1955 Pogodin published *The Third Pathetic* depicting Lenin's death and conceived in a tragic mood, with the obligatory "hope in the future" motif at the end. None of Pogodin's later plays (which included among others a parody of President Truman called *Missouri Waltz*, 1950) equaled the suspense and humor of *The Aristocrats* or the Lenin cycle. The latter, however, contained distinct features of opportunism and of that inflated, pompous artificiality which contaminated the whole literary style of Stalin's era. Pogodin wrote many uneven plays, most of them simply carrying out Party ideas. In the 1950's, after Stalin's death, however, he tried to express himself freely in *Petrarch's Sonnets* (produced in 1957). It was undoubtedly one of his best works and it dealt with the role of poetry and fantasy in Soviet life and with the right of the individual to preserve his independent spiritual world. Some critics hailed him as a model of psychological portraiture, but the truth is that Pogodin's interpretation of human motivations is superficial and his description of emotions oversimplified.

Of lesser importance are two other playwrights of the period: Boris Romashov (1895-1958) and Vladimir Kirshon (1902-38). Romashov wrote a number of melodramatic works on the civil war and on problems of Soviet actuality. One of his better plays is *The Change of Heroes* (1931) on the problems of creative intellectuals. It was harshly criticized in the Party press—even though it represented Communists as intrepid and wise leaders in a melodramatic vein (a tendency which marred many of his works). Kirshon belonged to the same socio-political trend. But he showed some independence of approach in his controversial play *Bread*, about the Revolution on the village level. The same attempt to reflect reality with daring sincerity explains the success of *The Miraculous Alloy* (1939), a comedy of youth. A member of the Party, Kirshon was accused of "deviationism," executed in 1938, and his plays were banned. It took twenty-two years for them to reappear on the Soviet stage. In 1956 *The Miraculous Alloy* was produced in two hundred theaters of the Union. But otherwise Communist hagiography and a glorification of the Revolution prevailed under Stalin in theatrical literature. Vsevolod Vishnevsky (1900-51), a former admirer of Dos Passos and Joyce, expressed this tendency in his plays of the civil war: *The First Cavalry Army* (1929) and particularly in *Optimistic Tragedy* (produced by Tairov in 1933), a lyrical-heroic saga of turbulent marines who accept Party discipline and die in the battle against the Whites preserving until the last moment their faith in the final victory of the Bolsheviks. Vishnevsky was using avant-garde techniques, and introduced a Narrator who comments on the action and draws optimistic conclusions (hence the title of the play). It is sad that such a talented writer should end in 1949 with a thoroughly false piece, *The Unforgettable 1919,* in which distortion of history alternated with flattery of Stalin.

Despite the large number of playwrights nothing remarkable or of lasting value appeared on the stage on the eve of the war, except perhaps a few dramas and comedies by Olesha, Babel, and Leonov who were outside the main stream. But while dramatic literature was definitely second-rate and blazed no new trails, the staging was still magnificent in the avant-garde theaters and the acting good, and this often concealed from the public the poverty of dramatic inventiveness. The attacks on Tairov, and Meyerhold and on Vakhtangov's tradition, however, which had been so violent in the days of the On Guard group, were resumed in 1935-37 with renewed force, under the slogan "Down with Formalism, decadent Experimentalism, and Aestheticism." The liquidation of the 1920's heritage, which affected all the arts, destroyed the most original accomplishments of the Russian stage. Meyerhold was demoted, arrested in 1937, and executed; his wife, the actress Zinaida Reich, was stabbed to death, and Tairov's theater was practically finished even before the death of its director (1950). Other "heretics" were tamed or silenced. Most talented producers, such as Nikolay Akimov, Alexey Popov, Nikolay Okhlopkov, and Yury Zavadsky, had to submit to the Communist uniformity and march in step with the dull socialist realism, repeating oaths of loyalty to the Grand Chief. The same thing occurred in music and the fine arts.

In the field of motion pictures, which was flourishing in the 'thirties, conditions were much better. Not only did the film industry grow tremendously and became national in scope, and independent of European and American markets, but directors and producers who had been formed in the years of experimentation, such as Sergei Eisenstein, Dziga Vertov, Friedrich Ermler, Sergei Yutkevich, Grigory Kosintsev, Lev Trauberg, Vsevolod Pudovkin, Mikhail Romm, Georgy and Sergey Vassiliev, Mark

Donskoy, Alexander Dovzhenko, Vladimir Petrov and many others, maintained the Soviet film on a high level of artistry. The tradition continued even when experimentalism was officially banned and socialist realism became compulsory. On the whole, motion pictures followed the psychological and realistic trends; a strong Populist flavor and a "message" were part of the educational intent in most films. A bent toward monumentalism in style and bashfulness in representation came to the fore in the late 'thirties. As in all other arts, sex was treated on the screen in an almost shamefaced manner, thus reflecting the whole spirit of Soviet culture, in which manifestations of sensual excitement were frowned upon as bourgeois and decadent. The sexual morality of Stalin's era was that of "decency" and restraint, and marital fidelity and wholesome family life were enlarged upon by the Kremlin.

The anti-formalistic and anti-aesthetic trends, as well as the predominance of realism, were typical of the prevailing ideology. More than ever before, the Communist theoreticians stressed the fact that materialistic aesthetics should be identified with those of socialist realism: since a sense of the beautiful, they said, stems not from sensuous contemplation (as the idealists asserted) but from an active creative approach to reality and from man's desire to transform that reality, one can assume that art represents all the complexity of life, and not the beautiful alone, and thus coincides with social practices as a whole. The matter of aesthetics was thus, despite Hegel, transferred from consciousness to being.

The whole movement of socialist realism must also be regarded as a simplification of creativity, as "art-for-the-masses'-sake" (to repeat this writer's definition of many years ago). The new reader was not sophisticated and had no taste for literary tricks and complexity. Just as all the exegetic discussions of Marxian doctrine were reduced under Stalin to a few slogans, so art had to be made simple, easily digestible, and useful. It is difficult to determine to what extent this was deliberately promoted from above, and to what extent it actually corresponded to the wishes and needs of the multitude. At any rate the rising majority of the Soviet population formed a special brand of the middle class which, like every other middle class in the world, wanted no nonsense and aspired to conservatism and respectability. Thus the Communist critics, partly reflecting the moods of the masses, partly suggesting what the latter ought to demand, were rejecting the "mad," "bohemian," "individualistic" avant-garde in every province of the creative arts. They did so as smugly as any bourgeois philistine of Europe and America. Eventually this attitude turned into what may be called Soviet Victorianism.

In the late 'thirties the only interesting works of fiction in the USSR were those that succeeded in escaping or avoiding this simplification (Leonov, Fedin, Kaverin, Paustovsky, Prishvin, and some historical novels by Tynyanov and others). Many writers, however, felt earnestly that they ought to address the new reader in a simple accessible way; but only a few of them did so without betraying their art. An example of such a compromise can be seen in the novels of Valentin Katayev (b.1897), particularly his popular work *I Am the Son of the Working People* (1937). The title of this tale of adventures, love affairs, and underground activities of a young soldier during the German occupation of the Ukraine in 1918, sounded like an oath of allegiance to the regime. Of a much higher artistic standard is the *Lone White Sail* (1936), a delightful story of two young boys, Petya, whose father is a high-school teacher, and Gavrik, son of a fisherman. Both become involved in the revolutionary movement of 1905 in Odessa, help the socialists, play tricks on the police, and enjoy all their adventures in a manner reminiscent of Tom Sawyer and Huckleberry Finn. The humor, warmth, and realism of this semi-biographical novel endeared it to readers of all ages.

Among the host of authors who tried to write in the style and spirit of socialist realism, very few had any personal tone: Yury Gherman (1910-67) started with laudatory *Tales about Dzerzhinsky* (the head of the Tcheca in the first years of the Revolution), and portrayed simple folk and secret police officials in the full-length novel *Our Friends*, a picture of the NEP period; his historical and war novels of the 1950's and 1960's marked a higher degree of artistic achievement. Nikolay Virta (b. 1906) analyzed the anti-Soviet rebels from a psychological point of view in his *Solitude* (1936), a novel of the peasant uprising in the Tambov region. Most of his prolific production is nothing but an exaggerated glorification of Stalin's regime.

Works of "Communist persuasion" formed the bulk of Soviet

literature in the late 'thirties; these included novels by Ostrovsky,
Fadeyev, Makarenko, Pavlenko, Gladkov, and Sholokhov, and
plays by Korneichuk, Pogodin, and Vishnevsky.

Poetry in the pre-war years presented a confused picture. On
the one hand, the influence of the avant-garde was felt even among
Communist poets. Mayakovsky, Tikhonov, Bagritsky, and the
romantics, including the followers of Pasternak, made up the core
of Soviet poetry in the 1930's. On the other hand, the campaign
against formalism and experimentation led to the disappearance
of groups established in the 'twenties and to opportunistic changes
by their members. The case in point was constructivism and the
destiny of its leaders. At the opening of the first Five-Year Plan
constructivism, which made its appearance in 1924 as an offspring
of futurism, offered "a purposeful, motivated and Socialist art."
The Literary Center of the Constructivists, which was directed
in 1924 by Kornely Zelinsky (b. 1896), critic, literary scholar,
and the theoretician of the group, and included the poets Bagritsky, Selvinsky, Vera Inber, the storyteller Evgeny Gabrilovich,
and many others, was disbanded in 1930, but its former members
continued their activity, maintaining that subject matter determined the form of a poetic work, that its factual content "local-
ized" its choice of words, and solidified its whole structure. They
defended functionalism in art and aimed at the union of science
and poetry. They also claimed to represent the new Soviet intelligentsia and to create practical, technically minded heroes. Secret
romantics in literature and converted Bolsheviks in politics, they
had great individual diversity and could never form a school. Ilya
Selvinsky, a talented constructivist (1899-1968), was a native of
Crimea, who fought on the side of the Reds, changed professions
several times, and studied at the University of Moscow; he published *Records,* his first collection of poems, in 1926. During a
brief period it seemed as if Selvinsky would inherit Mayakovsky's
place; his poems were provocative and aggressive—and so was the
group of friends who were promoting his career. His "novels in
verse" attracted general attention. In *Ulyalayev's Band* (1927)
(or *Ulyalayevism*) he depicted the civil war in the eastern steppes
as it was fought by Cossacks and local guerrillas led by their anarchical, full-blooded commander. He rewrote the poem in 1956
and made Lenin its main figure. Most striking were Selvinsky's

Cossack ballads obviously inspired by gypsy songs, in which the changes in the actual beat of the rhythm and intonation were scored by special typographical signs indicating how to separate the syllables, prolong the vowels, and render phonetically the inflections of the voice or the melancholy drawl of the singers.

Ulyalayev's Band, as well as *Fur-Trust* (1929) which was a description of the Soviet fur trade, from the hunting or breeding of animals to the selling of skins, were both novels in verse with strong political intent. But while the ideological message of both works remained weak and hazy, and the narrative bombastic and inflated, Selvinsky revealed great descriptive qualities, and a brilliant verbal gift—particularly in rendering visual and auditory sensations. In the *Fur-Trust* the chapters on tiger-hunting and on reindeer mating are truly excellent. Earthy and exuberant, the Selvinsky of the early 1930's continued the line of verbal experimentation often bordering on Mayakovsky's "depoetization" of language. After his "lyrical play" *Pao Pao* (1932), the story of an ape, the symbol of bestiality and bourgeois corruption, who becomes almost human in the uplifting environment of a Communist factory, Selvinsky abandoned his attempts at creating a new style, and turned to epic narratives (*Chelyuskin*, 1937) and historical pieces of straightforward prosody (*Johann the Knight*, 1939, and *General Brussilov*, 1943). But his attempts at creating tragedies in verse resulted in dull, lopsided works, such as his historical trilogy *Russia*.

This change reflected the general tendency of the times. A narrative in verse, a long poem in traditional meter, or in a hybrid form partly derived from Mayakovsky, was considered a model of socialist realism. There is no doubt that the civic poetry of the 'sixties and particularly that of Nekrassov, had numerous disciples among Communist poets. Most of them produced insignificant illustrations of political slogans. There was, however, one young poet of the Nekrassov school who showed freshness and talent. Alexander Tvardovsky's (1910-71) long poem "The Land of Muravia" (1936) depicted Morgunok, a peasant who does not accept the Communist catchwords at first and seeks the land of his dreams on his own but finally joins a collective farm. The vividness of the images and the folk rhythms of the poem prevented it from becoming a mere paean to rural collectivization.

Tvardovsky with his poetic concreteness represented a step forward from the heroic abstractions of Bezymensky, whose "The Tragic Night" (1936), was devoted to the building of the Dnieper Power Station, and numerous lesser poets in their civic expositions.

Tvardovsky was a Communist, and his poems always carried a social message, but they did not try to make propaganda. These direct and single lines belonged to the post-revolutionary neo-populism which was strongly felt in the works of other poets of the period such as Alexander Prokofiev (1900-71), Boris Kornilov (1907-38), who perished in a concentration camp, Alexey Surkov (b. 1899), and the talented Vladimir Lugovskoy (1901-54).

Mention must be made of *Cinderella* (1935) by Semyon Kirsanov, a long fairy tale in a new manner. It had a definite social message but charmed its readers through its excellent lyrical passages and great metric diversity. Kirsanov's next collection of intimate poems, *Four Notebooks* (1940), was typical of a whole lyrical trend. Themes of love, tenderness, and the inner life became the *Leitmotif* in the poems of newcomers, they formed a counterpart to the "epic narratives on contemporary problems" which the supporters of socialist realism tried to impose upon Soviet poetry. In the late 1930's Margherita Aligher (b. 1915) sang "the little home, the little joys," motherhood, and the life of newly married couples. Konstantin Simonov (b. 1916) imitated Blok and the gypsy ballads in his verses of desire, unfulfilled passion, and *femmes fatales*. Evgeny Dolmatovsky (b. 1915) revealed in *Far Eastern Poems* (1937) that a young Communist can easily alternate patriotic subjects with love lyrics. Older proletarian poets, such as Yosif Utkin (1903-44), Sergei Mikhalkov (b. 1913), the official bard of the Soviet establishment and a mediocre writer, made hardly any contribution to literature. Nikolay Ushakov (b. 1899) also followed the "intimate" current which definitely tended toward an abolition of the exclamatory and a reversion to "small, personal" topics. Some Communist critics argued that lyricism was in keeping with the general scheme of things: "only a Western petty bourgeois and philistine could have the fantastic notion," they wrote, "that Socialism can be depicted without lyrical emotions."

It must be pointed out that whatever the direction and aims of Russian poetry may have been on the eve of World War II, it had reached a fairly high level of craftsmanship and poetic form. As a rule it revealed a greater knowledge of and consideration for advanced techniques than Russian prose did. This was confirmed not only by such a master as Pasternak but also by his followers (Tikhonov, partly Selvinsky) and by good poets of the older generation—the highly cultured, romantic, often philosophical Pavel Antokolsky (b. 1890), who began as an acmeist; the refined Vsevolod Rozhdestvensky (b. 1895) whose collected poems were published in 1934 and who was a novelist as well as a poet (*Goethe In Italy* and *The Corsair*, the latter based on Byron's life); Mikhail Zenkevich (b. 1886); Arseny Tarkovsky (b. 1907), a poet of perfect craftsmanship and great talent who published only a few collections in classical vein (the latest, *The Earthly to the Earth*, in 1966); and various minor figures. But Nikolay Zabolotsky (1903-58) towered over all of them.

In contrast to this "high poetry," mention should be made of low poetry if only to complete the picture: the lyrics for popular songs provided by a steadily growing number of poets who occupied physically a large place in the poetic production of the 1930's. This genre was successfully exploited by Alexander Zharov (b. 1904), to some extent by Mikhail Golodny (the "Hungry"—pen name of Epstein, 1903-49), author of "Guerrilla Zheleznyak," and Mikhail Svetlov (1903-64) whose greatly popular "Granada" and other civil war songs served as an early model for other lyricists. In all these popular hits the patriotic and the intimate were tightly knit. Most songs expressed either national feelings or the pains and triumphs of love; themes of toil, socialism, and struggle served only as orchestration for these two main motifs. Certain poets, such as Vassily Lebedev-Kumach (1898-1949) appealed to the multitudes by turning out military marches, songs of the motherland ("Vast is my native country"), or lyrics for musical comedies. Mikhail Isakovsky (1900-73) became famous for his songs of the village and the factory, while "Poliushko" and other patriotic songs by Victor Gussev (1909-44) crossed the borders of the USSR. The composers of tunes for these lyrics were initiating in the 1930's the simplified musical style which became practically official on the eve of the war with Germany.

26

War Literature

Between June 22, 1941, the date of Hitler's sudden invasion of the USSR, and May 9, 1945, V-E Day, Russia went through the most tragic and costly period of her history; and at first she seemed to be on the brink of total collapse. The retreat of the Red Army in 1941, the huge number of prisoners captured by the enemy, the steady progress of the Germans into the very heart of the country, and the enormous territory, up to the Volga river and the Caucasus, that fell under their yoke in 1941-42, all assumed the proportions of a national catastrophe. The Russians and other peoples of the Soviet Union were exposed to a terrible ordeal of indignities, starvation, bloodshed, and annihilation, before they gathered their full strength and unity for a successful defense of their land against the Nazis.

It is quite understandable that for five years Soviet literature should have been exclusively a war literature. The gigantic struggle provided all the subject matter needed by novelists, playwrights, and poets. In no other country did the war absorb artistic energies so completely, or find reflection in so many works.

Of course, the government and the Party encouraged this literary activity, and considered it part of the war effort. Writers were granted an exemption from military service: a novella on German atrocities or on the heroism of the fighters bolstered morale and was equal in value to any front-line duty. This, however, did not prevent more than a thousand men of letters from joining the army in various capacities—as combatant auxiliaries, war correspondents, and so forth. Two hundred and seventy-five of them were killed, including Yury Krymov, Arkady Gaidar, Vasily Stavsky, Yefim Zozulia, and Alexander Afinogenov. No official prodding was necessary to make the mobilization of literature general: the emotional impact of the war was sufficient incentive. The writing on the war was spontaneous; for novelists and poets could not concentrate on anything else. As the critic Victor Shklovsky put it: "Not to write about the greatest war while we are in it is simply impossible." Dostoevsky said that after the Lisbon earthquake of 1755 nobody could have the impudence to offer verses on the sweet trills of nightingales—and his words were often quoted in 1942.

Of course, the main problem was how to write about the staggering events. Writers wanted to give an immediate response to actuality, and therefore were deprived of the "psychological distance," the perspective, and mature inner growth, that true art usually requires. The whole literary output during the war was therefore hasty, and often lacked enduring artistic values, even though part of it was amazingly alive. Its emotional and documentary worth was superior to its aesthetic merits. It must be added that a great many works among the extremely large fictional output of the war years were made in a mechanical fashion and were little more than "patriotic trash."

At the beginning most writers felt that they ought to limit themselves to the modest function of chroniclers; they went back to "factography," depicting battles, bombardments, retreats, and offensives. Sketches, front-line diaries, and short stories lent themselves readily to naturalistic reporting. Only a few interesting books emerged from this welter of semi-journalistic records. Although gradually diminishing in quantity, they continued to appear for some years: *War Diaries* by Konstantin Simonov, *Stalingrad Letters* by Vassily Grossman, *In The Enemy's Rear* by Alexander Poliakov (1909-42), and *A Front-Line Diary* by Evgeny Petrov, who was killed in 1942 at the evacuation of Sebastopol, were published during the first years of the war, but many reports on guerrilla activities, came out after 1945: *People with Clear Conscience* by Pyotr Vershigora (1945), *A Partisan's Notes* (1945) by Pyotr Ignatov, *From Putivl to the Carpathian Mountains* by Semyon Kovpak (1946), and *In the Crimean Underground* (1946) by Ivan Kozlov. Articles and sketches in the daily press acquired unusual importance, particularly those by Ehrenburg, Alexey Tolstoy, Sholokhov, and Tikhonov. Ehrenburg's articles were highly popular among combatants and civilians alike because they expressed in violent terms the hatred of the invaders. His prose was an appeal to revenge, an incitement to merciless warfare, and it found a response in those Russian men and women who were suffering from the brutalities and tortures inflicted on them by the Germans. The success of *The Front* (1942), a drama by Alexander Korneichuk (1910-72), a prominent Party official, was due to the problems he raised in a primitive but effective manner. He set old commanders of revolutionary battles, men who relied on courage and enthusiasm, against young generals who understood modern warfare and knew how to use twentieth-century technology.

Although hundreds of Soviet writers went to the front as war correspondents, they did not approve of the purely descriptive and naturalistic trend. Psychological and interpretative fiction soon gained the most prominent place. At the Conference of the Union of Soviet Writers, held in April 1942, the speakers claimed that only through psychological realism and a humanistic approach could Soviet literature find a common language with the masses. "Humanness, humanism are the traditional and principal traits of our literature," affirmed Tikhonov; "it understands suffering and sympathizes with it because it has an intense interest in man's inner world and in changes brought about by the war—and this is the most important thing for us in Soviet arts."

Very indicative of this mood was *The People Are Immortal* by Vassily Grossman (1905-1964), whose first novel, *Stepan Kolchugin*, had been published in 1933. Despite its pretentious title, his epic tale of the first months of the war, brought out in 1942, is one of the best. Obviously imitating Tolstoy's method of "stripping the veils and showing things as they are," Grossman attempted to stress the purely human side of his characters: the members of the Soviet Supreme Military Council, before making a momentous decision, munch green apples to get on the right side of an army commander who likes "something rather sour"; the soldiers of a surrounded unit do not seem to think of their imminent death, but worry about the lack of cigarettes; before a battle a morose colonel takes infinite delight in listening to his orderly as the latter teases an old peasant woman and asks her whether she could make some fancy dishes and pies. At the same time Grossman glorified the simple man who sacrifices himself for his country, modestly and humbly without pathetic speeches and theatrical gestures. In portraying him Grossman adopted a lyrical style: "in vain do poets say that the names of those who fell on the battlefields would live for centuries, in vain do they compose poems trying to tell the dead heroes that they have not died, that they continue to live for ever in glorious memories. Human memory can not retain hundreds, thousands of names. Those who died, are dead. Millions went to war as they went to heavy work. Great is the people whose sons died simply, saintly, austerely on boundless battlefields . . . All those carpenters, miners, diggers, weavers, peasants who worked all their lives, they sleep soundly, eternally, like their forefathers. They had offered earlier plenty of sweat and hard, often unbearable toil. And now when the dreadful hour struck, they gave their blood and life."

The tendency to show war in its everyday aspects prevailed in 1942-44; it was linked with the exploration of some fundamental issues: What was the significance of the fateful clash with Hitler? What engendered and strengthened the heroism of the people—traditional patriotism or a new sense of national responsibility, awakened by the Revolution? Were they fighting simply for the land of their ancestors or for the land of social promise as well? And what conclusions about Russian character could one draw from the behavior of millions of men and women exposed to violent death, starvation, and the incessant strain of nerves, muscles, and will power? During the 900 days of Leningrad's siege 700,000 inhabitants perished from famine, Nazi bombing and shelling, and physical exhaustion. If a whole nation was capable of extraordinary feats of bravery and sacrifice, was it not an indication of its perennial qualities, of its "soul"? The interpretative answers to these questions went far beyond the prescribed formula of Marxian dialectics: the writers talked both of the Russian inexhaustible reserve of vitality, of the sheer physiological strength shown in the course of their history, as well as of their new found solidarity and common cause, which helped all tribes and nationalities cement the Union of the Soviets.

Most of the writers put their emphasis on the Common Man, on the average citizen. The hero in the war fiction was not necessarily a Party member, as he usually was in pre-war Stalinist literature. Peasants, workmen, humble clerks, and intellectuals were portrayed in sober tones, without eloquence. The very titles of the tales written at this time are revealing: *Simplehearted Men* (Lavrenyov), *Inspired Men* (Platonov), *The Russian Character* (A. Tolstoy), *A Naval Soul* (Sobolev), *Traits of the Soviet Man* (Tikhonov), and *The Unvanquished* (Gorbatov). In his collection of short stories Tikhonov related the unobtrusive heroism of ordinary people: of a photographer whose ship is torpedoed and who goes down clutching his beloved camera; of a young girl trembling with fear but courageously kicking away incendiary bombs; of a painter who is given a chance of being evacuated from Leningrad, but simply has not the heart to abandon the martyred city. In *Russian People* (1942), one of the most popular plays of the period. Konstantin Simonov glorified the simplicity and stamina of a doctor who says that "we Russians are visionaries, this is the reason we are fighting so bravely," the abnegation of Valya, a rather naïve girl who performs dangerous missions, and the daring of Globa, a rogue who leads a dashing life but sacrifices himself with humility. It has been noticed that Simonov and other Soviet writers revived in their writings the spirit of Tolstoy's *Sebastopol Tales* and of certain chapters of *War and Peace*.

One of the most successful examples of this literature dealing with the psychology of the Common Man was the highly popular poem, "Vassily Tyorkin" by Alexander Tvardovsky. Its hero is an "ordinary fellow," a private well liked by his comrades because he has a gay character, makes salty jokes, sings sentimental songs, and combines common sense with a naïve directness. Tyorkin looks at war as a dire necessity, as hard work that must be done as well as possible since the Russians are waging it "not for glory but for life on earth"; theirs is a deadly but just struggle—no use talking too much about it. The tragic and comic adventures of Tyorkin are described in a vernacular, folksy style which obviously derived from folklore, from the oral tradition of limericks and jingles, and from Populist poetry, particularly that of Nekrassov. Perhaps Hashek's good soldier Schweik served as a prototype for Tyorkin, but the latter was more warm-hearted and sociable than the Czech and was portrayed not as a grotesque but as a man of flesh and blood.

A different mood was struck by Andrey Platonov, a former member of the Pereval (or The Pass) group, in his folkloristic, almost legendary tales of soldiers who go to battle as peasants go into the fields to harvest and thresh. His humor shies away from Tvardovsky's slapstick, it is more subtle, and his heroes show great interest in religious and moral issues. Says one of them: "They say there is no soul. What is there, then? If we were but dry clay we would long since have been worn out and might even be dead. What is it that makes us go on and endure cold and hunger and death?" Platonov wrote in unusual prose which reflected, as he said, "this beautiful and furious world."

In many instances this glorification of national fortitude led to sentimentalism, verbosity, patriotic bombast, and a shrill style. A large part of the war fiction (even in the shorter forms which prevailed) was declamatory: the author addressed his audience directly and wanted to stir it. Such was the case with *The Rainbow* by Wanda Wasilevskaya (b. 1905), a Polish woman, and *The Unvanquished* by Boris Gorbatov (1908-54). Both books were awarded Stalin Prizes and enjoyed great popularity with readers, who found in these works, as in many similar ones, not aesthetic satisfaction but emotional release and a gratifying analogy to situations in real life. Gorbatov wanted to describe the ordeals of the Ukrainians in a town occupied by the Germans. The hero of his novel, an old workman Tarass (obviously a reminder of Gogol's Tarass Bulba), refuses to submit to the conquerors and goes underground to fight the enemy. Although built on authentic occurrences, *The Unvanquished* is marred by its hyperbolic style, primitive character portrayal, and romantic emotionalism. The same defects are to be found in many works of fiction about guerrillas, the sufferings of the population under the inhuman German yoke, and the Russian counter-offensive that finally dislodged Hitler's armies. "War eloquence," with strong overtones of nationalistic smugness and self-complacency, remained a weakness in Russian literature for a long time after the defeat of the Nazis. A typical example of this kind of false romanticism is represented by *The Standard-Bearers* (1947-50), a series of novels by Oles Gonchar (b. 1918), a Ukrainian acclaimed by Communist critics and awarded the Stalin Prize.

In accordance with Party slogans of 1945-53, quite a few writers attempted to create the "heroic Communist epic" of the war, but only produced long-winded and artificial works in many volumes, such as *The White Birch* (1947-52) by Mikhail Bubennov (b. 1909).

Among the best literary reflections of the "fatherland war," as the Russians called it, were certainly Leonov's *The Taking of Velikoshumsk*, a short novel, and his plays *Invasion* and *Lyonushka* (see Chapter 19). Two other outstanding works were conceived in completely opposed styles. *In the Trenches of Stalingrad* (1946) by Victor Nekrassov (b. 1915) which sold 1½ million copies, was a sober, expository novel of the "prose of the war," with objective reporting of daily incidents and psychological portraits of soldiers and officers done in a direct, unpretentious but very fine and skillful verbal manner, while *The Star* (1947) by Emmanuel Kazakevich (1913-62) was a powerful, highly romantic tale about a reconnaissance unit commanded by Lieutenant Travkin, a Communist. Surrounded by the Germans, the four days of the ordeal of the unit and the inevitable tragic end are rendered by Kazakevich in a highly expressive way, with a deft use of symbolic imagery and lyrical interludes.

A great many realistic stories, novels, plays, and poems were written by Konstantin (Kirill) Simonov (b.1915). His *Days and Nights* (1944), an epic of the battle of Stalingrad, showed the daily life and thoughts of average men thrown into the hell of raids, bombings, and deadly fighting for every inch of land. This slow paced, occasionally top-heavy, semi-factual, semi-fictional narrative has the ring of authenticity, and, without reaching a high artistic level, remains an impressive panorama of military events. After the death of Stalin, Simonov showed those aspects of the war one would look for in vain in novels published before 1953. In his *The Living and the Dead* (1961-62) and its sequel *We Are Not Born Soldiers* (1963-64) he told about the reverses suffered by the Red Army in 1941-42, and about the repressive measures and the atmosphere of suspicion that reigned at the front and behind the lines where security officials had the upper hand. The main hero of these revelatory works is an infantry officer who has gone through the ordeals of a concentration camp and is compelled, after a brief rehabilitation, to fight under an assumed identity. Here again the interesting exposition of facts and conditions is not matched by appropriate literary merits. All Simonov's novels could be classed as satisfactory second-rate literature which in all countries has a considerable appeal among mass readers.

In the same category is the evidently autobiographical *This Palm of Land* (1954) by Grigory Baklanov (b. 1923), which is a candid story of a small detachment holding a bridgehead on the river Dniestr after the German retreat from the Ukraine. The psychology of the 21-year-old commander and his men who find themselves in a dangerous predicament is depicted with dramatic simplicity. Vera Panova's *Companions* or *Fellow Travelers* (1946), which initiated the successful career of a talented woman writer, describes life in a hospital train with warmth, humor, and insight. Of lesser literary value were other popular works of the same period, among them the short novels *March-April* (1942) by Vadim Kozhevnikov, and *Division Commander* (1944) by Georgy Berezko.

While contemporary writers stressed the stamina and bravery of the combatants, Russians sought moral encouragement in historical works which evoked the country's glorious past and showed her gaining ultimate victories after excruciating ordeals. This explains the large sale of works by Sergeyev-Tsensky, Borodin, Golubov, and others, works which helped soldiers and civilians keep their faith in the future. In Leningrad, at the peak of the German efforts to seize the city, a 500,000 copy reprint of Tolstoy's *War and Peace* was made to bolster the morals of the besieged defenders.

The patriotic trend in war literature was accompanied by two other traits: a tendency to equate patriotism with "the defense of the new Humanism," and an effort to distinguish Soviet from pre-revolutionary nationalism. "Man is the object of all our efforts. Fascism is the decline of man," declared Alexey Tolstoy. And the poetess Vera Inber, in the *Meridian of Pulkovo*, a popular poem on the defense of Leningrad, exclaimed: "To save the world from the plague—that is true Humanism, and we are

Humanists." The soldiers were told that in defending Russia, their motherland and the land of the Revolution, they were protecting the highest achievements of mankind against medieval barbarism. In their orders of the day army commanders urged the fighters to launch an offensive "for the soil of Tolstoy, Pushkin, Chekhov, and Gorky." An enormous and genuine wave of national consciousness, mixed with idealistic visions, swept the country.

On the other hand, writers like Alexander Bek (1903-63), the author of *The Highway of Volokolamsk* (1944), a series of colorful but matter of fact tales about the Central Asiatic Division of General Panfilov which stopped the Germans at the gates of Moscow in the winter of 1941, endeavored to represent the USSR as a "family of nationalities," whose various tribes and peoples fought together in a solid phalanx for the liberation of their common country. This slogan was greatly emphasized in fiction and in numerous articles in the dailies and weeklies. Of course, no mention was made of the pro-German attitude of the Tartars in the Crimea, or the Chechentsy in the Caucasus, or of the ruthless treatment inflicted on them by the government. It is true, however, that such examples were scarce, and in the German occupied areas the number of "collaborators" and traitors was exiguous even among convicted foes of the Soviet regime. Despite the horrible conditions of life, forced labor and starvation, only a small number of prisoners of war followed the Soviet General Vlasov who defected to Hitler and tried to raise an anti-Communist army recruited from the Russians languishing in Nazi concentration camps.

The slogan of the "Union of Nationalities" was but part of a broader concept—a union of all patriotic forces. Stalin greeted audiences in his radio speeches as "Brothers and sisters"; Soviet citizens in England, Europe, and the United States fraternized with patriotic *émigrés*. This was the first time such a thing had happened in the Soviet Union—and while this interlude lasted (until 1945) it introduced a new political (and psychological) climate.

In literature it implied a relaxation of factional feuds and of external pressures, a softening of censorship, and consequently a higher degree of freedom in styles and ideas. Old writers who had been silent for years started to publish again and there were some timid signs of a literary revival. Poetry flowered during the war, as it had during the first stages of the Revolution; in some respects the production of verse exceeded that of prose, and it met with an enthusiastic reception.

As a rule Russia has always been, and still is, a country in which poetry is read more widely than anywhere else in the world (with the possible exception of Japan). During periods of upheaval and crisis the Russians are in particular need of an emotional outlet through poetry. Little wonder, then, that pocket-size collections of poems, which are so common in Russia, found so many readers on the battlefront and in the country. Many Soviet war poets certainly chose the line of least resistance and composed topical verses on the assumption that lofty themes—heroism, patriotism, suffering—made for lofty poetry. Russian periodicals were flooded with vapid exercises that followed the pattern of cheap emotionalism and grandiloquent nationalistic twaddle; and poetry of this sort continued to appear with monotonous repetition long after the end of the war.

Fortunately, even those who devoted themselves to panoramic representations of the war in poetic tales, understood the need for restraint. Lyrical, intimate notes prevailed in the period 1942-45. Novels in verse were constructed as lyrical diaries; among these were *Meridian of Pulkovo* by Vera Inber, a poetess of the older generation; *Blockade* by Zinaida Shishova; and the tragic *A Leningrad Poem* by the talented poet Olga Bergholz. Konstantin Simonov, a modest poet, rose to unprecedented popularity because he voiced the emotions of millions in his unsophisticated verse. His poems occasionally mixed the romantic tradition of Blok's love lyrics with poignant visions of war. Simonov's famous "Wait for Me" is an incantation, a prayer to the beloved whose image haunts the soldiers in the trenches; he implores her to remain faithful and worthy of all his sacrifices and sufferings. And this plea is enhanced by a mystical faith in the power of love: the woman's fidelity protects him from wounds and danger—even from death itself. Thousands wept over this poem, which was circulated in millions of copies at the front; seventeen composers tried to set it to music, and the author made the mistake of writing a mediocre play on the same subject and with the same title. Other well-known poems by Simonov express simple emotions: nostalgia, love of the motherland, or patriotic exaltation. One of the best of them, "Do You Remember the Roads of Smolensk?" evoking the tragic beginnings of the war and the initial retreat of the Red Army, has the poignancy of genuine grief. A journalist, novelist, and playwright, Simonov later adjusted to the policy of the Party by producing trivial and melodramatic plays and tendentious travelogues.

The theme of Russia—of her landscapes and her history, of her people and its rising national awareness—formed the inner core of poems by Alexander Prokofiev (Stalin Prize 1944), by Selvinsky, by Nikolay Rylenkov, and many others, including such older poets as Tikhonov, Pasternak, and Pavel Antokolsky (who dedicated a long and moving poem to his own son killed on the field of battle). At one point great popularity was attained by Margherita Aligher and Alexey Surkov. Aligher (b. 1915) started as a poet of unhappy love and motherhood in the Akhmatova manner. During the war she sang of those "who had been left behind," but her best known work was *Zoya*, a narrative in verse glorifying Zoya Kosmodemyanskaya, a young Komsomol girl who had fought in the underground and was then caught, tortured, and hanged by the Germans. Zoya became a symbol of martyrdom and moral rectitude—and the story of her short life is told by Aligher in a highly emotional and touching way. After the war she continued to portray young Communists as "heroes of our time" and to make lyrical feminine confessions. Alexey Surkov (b. 1899), a militant Communist, had been publishing verse since 1930 but came to the fore in 1942 with his passionate and politically oriented lyrics. His were patriotic songs of revenge. He described his own people roused by the invasion and made ferocious by German atrocities—a people brandishing the "sword of retaliation" and grown merciless in fierce loathing of the enemy. Surkov, like Ehrenburg, served the Muse of Wrath and Punishment, and for him the clarions of victory sounded like trumpets of indictment and judgment.

After the war, however, Surkov abandoned poetry and turned

into a literary official. Secretary of the Writers Union, Party representative in bureaucratic committees and at public festivities, he also became the leading member of all the delegations and semi-diplomatic missions sent abroad by Moscow for the betterment of cultural relations with the West. He might have been an efficient functionary, but stopped being a poet.

Some poets and novelists talked of "brotherhood among all freedom-loving peoples" and dreamt of a time when the alliance with the Western and American democracies, along with the rebirth of Slavophile tendencies, would expand the "national united front" into an association of the Soviets with the rest of the world. The liquidation of the Comintern and the reconciliation of the Communist State with the Greek Orthodox Church appeared to many observers as signs of a radical change in Party politics from which literature and art would be the first to profit. The events that took place immediately after the end of hostilities, however, showed that such hopes would have to be abandoned.

27

The Aftermath of War

The victory of 1945 put an end to the wartime easing of controls over literature. The signs of an imminent shift had become apparent by 1944, but its full impact was not felt until two years later. The causes of the change were the same as those that determined the foreign policy of the USSR. Instead of opening an era of peace and relaxation, the defeat of Germany was followed by an increase of tension among the former Allies. When this tension degenerated into the cold war that contained the seeds of an armed conflict between the Soviet Union and the United States, an ideological sort of alert was proclaimed in Russia; it led to cultural rigidity and isolationism. The writers who contributed so much to the war effort were now mobilized for a new task: they had to assist the Party in the consolidation of an ideological stability that had been somewhat undermined during the ordeals of 1941-45. The times of "loose patriotic unity and exultation" were over, the Party now required the stiffening of doctrine and the sharpening of Communist weapons in the USSR and in the satellite countries. The end of the war also called for great material and educational endeavors. According to official statistics, the country counted seven million killed and sixteen million wounded; millions more died of starvation and disease; there were four million orphans; 1710 Russian towns, 70,000 villages, six million buildings, 317 industrial plants had been destroyed, and 98,000 farms had been looted and ravaged, bringing the total damage to 679 billion rubles. The new Five-Year Plan, the new goals in agriculture, and the enormous task of the Second Reconstruction demanded fresh sacrifices and relentless work from the people, who had already been bled white by war. To whip up the energy of the masses and make them obey the commands of the state, literature and the arts were included in the vast plan of propaganda and psychological pressure, and disciplinary measures were put into action to compel writers and artists to fulfill their civic mission.

The new literary policy was officially formulated on August 14, 1946, in a resolution by the Central Committee of the All-Union Communist Party. It was written, following Stalin's "indications," by Andrey Zhdanov (1888-1948), member of the Politbureau and former secretary of the Party; his name has become identified with the whole post-war period in Soviet literature. Zhdanov made several speeches commenting on the Central Committee's resolution, and the latter was interpreted and supported by Fadeyev, Secretary General of the Union of Soviet Writers, and by hundreds of articles in periodicals. Another Central Committee resolution of August 26 dealt with the dramatic repertory and expressed the Party's surprise that out of 119 plays offered by Moscow's nine leading theaters, only 25 were devoted to contemporary themes, and even those were poorly written. On September 4 a new resolution on the subject of films criticized Eisenstein for having portrayed Ivan the Terrible as a "weak-willed Hamlet" and his special detachment (the *oprichniki,* often compared by the anti-Communists to the Soviet secret police) as "gangs of degenerates." Music was the last art form to be disciplined: the resolution of February 10, 1948, on *The Great Friendship,* an opera by the Georgian composer Muradeli, indicted the modernists and innovators and extolled "popular art" for the masses. Shostakovich was bitterly attacked in the press for his "modernism," a particularly disqualifying term.

Now that the state claimed to be the only middleman between the writer and the reader, it made clear its intentions not only to formulate the writer's ideas but also to impose on him the artistic methods by which they ought to be expressed. In literature as well as in music and in the graphic and plastic arts socialist realism became a "must," precluding any search for new forms: the Soviet writer had no other choice than to follow the obligatory patterns and stencils. This was amply illustrated by "exemplary lessons," which corresponded to political trials. Two monthlies, *The Star* and *Leningrad,* were accused of publishing harmful works; the former was reorganized, and the latter suspended. Anna Akhmatova and Mikhail Zoshchenko were singled out as scapegoats; both were expelled from the Union of Soviet Writers and were blacklisted. Akhmatova's deep influence on the younger generation was probably one of the reasons for Communist attacks. Akhmatova was dubbed "an exponent of the art-for-art's-sake heresy," of "eroticism, mysticism, and political apathy." Zhdanov spoke of her with disdain: "She divided her interests between drawing room, bedroom and chapel." Zoshchenko was blamed for his satirical tendencies, his inappropriate banter, and his story on the adventures of an ape which was interpreted as a calumny of the Soviet people. His old sins were also remembered: he had belonged in the 1920's to the Serapion Brethren, exposed by Zhdanov as an obnoxious center of bourgeois ideology; in recent years, instead of contributing to the war effort, Zoshchenko had written "pathological tales," such as *Before the Sunrise*, in a Freudian vein (see Chapter 10). In general his satire was blamed for undermining the official mood of optimism. Soviet citizens, particularly those whom the war brought into contact with Europe, were continually being told that they were a happy and fortunate lot, and whatever disturbed this euphoric state was ruthlessly eliminated.

The condemnation of Akhmatova and Zoshchenko put an end to certain undercurrents among writers, old and young, who had erroneously believed that the post-war era would be more tolerant than the years of stress. In any case, Selvinsky stopped talking of socialist symbolism as a possible substitute for socialist realism; Petro Pancho, the Ukrainian author, ceased to claim that the writer should be allowed to make mistakes; and a number of novelists preferred not to press the point that a time-perspective was necessary for an adequate interpretation of current events. Discussions either became confined to small groups of intimate friends, or continued, in various forms, on the periphery of debates in Communist circles. On the whole, these debates were indicative of the problems for the literary lawgivers, but they also revealed what was actually brewing among novelists and poets who tried to hide their true opinions behind the ready-made terminology of the Party.

The resolution of the Central Committee, the replacement of Tikhonov by Fadeyev as the head of the Union of Soviet Writers, and the repressive measures against dissenters marked the beginning of an ideological offensive which was soon in full swing. Literary critics, playwrights, painters, and musicians were successively called to order. Their shortcomings, their political aloofness, or dangerous formalistic tendencies were pointed out severely by Party pundits who also insisted on hailing "popular, simple, realistic art, suitable to the masses, as the only art befitting the great epoch of Socialism which is already looking forward to Communism." Never before had such a campaign combined ideological with formal intransigence. And although the promoters of what was called "Zhdanovism" emphasized their hostility to "left-wing deviation and vulgarization of Marxism-Leninism," the ghosts of RAPP seemed to have taken on new life. Nobody was safe from sudden attacks by Communist vigilantes. In 1950, for example, the Stalin Third Prize went to Hejdar Husseinov for his treatise *Social and Political Thought in Azerbaidjan in the XIXth Century*. But some new censors, after a more careful reading of the book, found in it "anti-Marxian trends," and the Cabinet of Ministers decided to cancel the prize.

In December 1948, a new raid was launched in the plenum of the Union of Soviet Writers "against formalism, aestheticism and groups of bourgeois cosmopolitans." This time the blow fell upon literary and theater critics particularly those of Jewish extraction (Gurvich, Yuzovsky, Altman). Very often nationalistic and "anti-cosmopolitan" slogans served as a poor cover for crass anti-Semitism, which was steadily gaining ground in government circles. It reached its peak in 1952 with the execution of Jewish writers, such as Bergelson, Feffer, Kvitko, Markish, and others. Together with numerous representatives of Jewish intellectuals and artists (among them the highly popular actor Michoels), they were arrested in 1948 and languished in prison under a frightful regime of torture and beatings. The Communist secret police were copying the methods of the Nazis.

In the field of literary history and criticism the remnants of the formalist school were struck at again—this time it was the "bourgeois liberalism" of Alexander Vesselovsky, as it was defined in

March 1948 by *Culture and Life* and *The Literary Gazette*. The great scholar and his followers (particularly Boris Tomashevsky) were rebuked for holding "cosmopolitan ideas on the interdependence of all literatures," and were accused of "formalistic illusions" about the specific character of literary genres. The main objective was to prove that Russia's literary tradition and her cultural heritage were free from Western influence. All those who worked in comparative literature and studied the foreign sources of Russian classics were continually denounced as "rootless, stateless cosmopolitans." It was even dangerous to sustain publicly that Pushkin's early poetry stemmed from French models or that Lermontov had been influenced by Byron.

In general the life of the Russian writer in the "Zhdanovism" era was far from being secure or enviable. Demoralized by malevolence and denunciations, forced to breathe in an atmosphere polluted by suspicion and slander, he was constantly obsessed by the menace of false accusations and impending arrest and exile. Fear caused the self-imposed silence of the strong and the recantations of the weak, but even these modes of self-defense did not guarantee security. Hundreds of members of the Union of Soviet Writers were "repressed"—a euphemism used in the USSR to designate people sent to jail or concentration camps or placed before a firing squad. After Stalin's death 617 of these political prisoners were "rehabilitated," but only half of them returned home: according to official statistics 305 had died in what was called the "Northern Hell."

The term "cosmopolitan" was employed extensively in the artistic and literary purges of 1946-52: whenever a composer, critic, novelist, painter, or even a circus performer had to be pilloried, he was dubbed a "cosmopolitan." This intimated that he was more interested in problems of form, in moral, psychological, or aesthetic issues than in Soviet actuality; it also denounced his reluctance to create in the style of socialist realism. The most heinous crime was to fail to assert Soviet superiority over the decadent West and imperialistic America. Soviet nationalists claimed that Russian inventors had been the first to discover all the technical gadgets that had been the pride and joy of Western capitalist civilization, including the radio and the electric light bulb. Moscow papers were constantly naming obscure Russians as the originators of most great currents of thought and art in the past and in the present. In the campaigns for the national and popular styles in all the arts, there was the same hodgepodge of chauvinistic boasting, Marxian theories, ignorance, and intellectual blindness. French Impressionists, for example, were taboo and considered inferior to some third-rate dauber of Lenin's and Stalin's portraits. This line often assumed such proportions and led to such insane or ridiculous exaggerations that even Party leaders finally recognized the necessity of putting on the brakes, at least in some areas of scholarship. In 1950 Stalin himself had to intervene in the logomachy of the philologists, throwing his weight against the school of the late academician Nikolay Marr (1864-1934), who considered language merely a superstructure of the economic basis. In his sensational pamphlet *Marxism and Problems of Linguistics*, the dictator spoke of language as a product of centuries and generations, as a universal phenomenon used by all social groups and not by a single one, and therefore not fitted to be judged as an outgrowth of economic conditions. But even in this rejection of "vulgar sociologism" Stalin sounded a strongly nationalistic note. And in the famous controversy about genetics, Lysenko was supported by the government because his theory of breeding new species of plants through change of environment not only fitted into general Communist doctrine but also served in the anti-Western campaign by demonstrating the superiority of Soviet science.

This was a period when distinguished scholars and academicians were arrested and sentenced to deportation, while research, even in biology, particularly in genetics, as well as in history, sociology, and statistics, was stopped, experiments were interrupted, and good specialists in high posts replaced by half-baked, often ignorant Party candidates.

The anti-Western and anti-American propaganda, which began in 1946 with official blessings, increased in intensity throughout the next two years and, by 1949, had assumed enormous proportions. To write a play or a tale against the "corrupted Europe and imperialistic USA" was the best proof of political loyalty, and opportunists did not miss the occasion to show their zeal. The uninterrupted flow of such literature was initiated in 1946 by Simonov's drama *The Russian Question*. It portrayed an American foreign correspondent who had been commissioned to write an anti-Soviet book. The hero, too honest to follow the orders of his boss, a publishing tycoon, is sacked and, what is worse, thrown over by his fiancée and abandoned by his friends. His journalistic career is ruined because he did not join the ranks of the red-baiters and Russophobes. In his novel *The Smoke of the Fatherland*, published a year later, Simonov portrayed a Soviet citizen who returns home after having spent two years in the United States and compares the American and Russian ways of life. As may be expected he acclaims the Soviet regime. Toward the end of 1948 Simonov published a collection of poems *Friends and Foes*, exposing reaction, racial discrimination, hatred of the Soviet Union, and imperialistic aggressiveness in the U.S.A., Canada, and Great Britain.

But these forays were relatively mild by comparison with a series of plays produced in 1948 and 1949; *The Voice of America* by Boris Lavrenyov (the sad fate of a left-winger in America); *I Want to go Home* by Sergei Mikhalkov (the story of a Russian child detained in Germany by American authorities); *The Foreign Shadow*, again by Simonov (a Soviet bacteriologist makes an important discovery and is almost trapped by American spies); and *The Ill-Starred Haberdasher* by Anatoly Surov (a thinly disguised parody of President Truman). In 1951 Alexander Sheiniss added to these; in *The Middle Ages* he told a fantastic story of a Norwegian physicist mistreated by the American police. All these vilifications of the West were crude and primitive potboilers. After a short and inglorious career they disappeared forever from the Russian stage, leaving no more trace than all the other literary trash of this sad period.

Popular writers like Ehrenburg followed the current and also exposed Europe and America. In *The Storm*, a full-length novel which was a best-seller in 1947, Ehrenburg unfolded the action simultaneously in France and the USSR. Even more tendentious and churlish is *The Ninth Wave* (1951-52), a sequel to *The Storm*. In this shameless, pseudo-literary concoction the protagonists are, on the one hand, the enemies—American "warmongers,"

French spies, Czech conspirators—and, on the other hand, highly moral, honest, loving Russians. Among other novels of the same type there was a vicious denunciation of Marshal Tito by Orest Maltsev (*The Jugoslav Tragedy*, 1951) and an exposé of Vatican intrigues by Dimitry Eremin (*Storm over Rome*, 1962).

Anti-Western literature had the task of picturing the corruption of Europe and America—but this vision of doom was always accompanied by a glorification of the "Soviet dream" and of the Soviet people. According to Zhdanov the purpose of literature was "to portray the Soviet man and his moral qualities in full force and completeness." In performing this duty it had to maintain its integrity and protect itself against the "poisonous miasmas of Western bourgeois art." The Soviet man was represented as a hero, as an idealized model of humanity, as a supreme flower of the new society. We know that this search for a Communist hero was obligatory for Soviet authors in the past, but only under "Zhdanovism" did it assume such ostentatious and artificial contours. The book hailed as a great achievement in this field was *The Story of a Real Man* (1947) by Boris Polevoy (Boris Kampov, b. 1908) which won the Stalin Prize. Its protagonist, Meresiev, a war pilot, has critically injured his legs in a forced landing; by a superhuman effort he crawls out of the forest where he has been lying, badly wounded, and later succeeds in sweeping away all physical and bureaucratic obstacles, to resume his active duty in the air force. A cripple with artificial limbs he displays iron will, endurance, contempt for suffering, and high moral virtues. While reproducing real events, the novel sounds false and stilted.

Other works in the same romantic and exaggerated vein brought forth characters endowed with civic fortitude; if some of them made a few mistakes, they recognized them and were converted to the true faith of social service. This literature represented life as a series of Communist successes; in colloquial terms its method was dubbed, "varnishing reality." It was responsible for the publication of mendacious platitudes that simply transformed contemporary Russian fiction into a morass of imbecility. For example, in a tale about a sick accountant, the reader was informed that the TB process in the lungs of the hero stopped when he was assigned to make budget charts for the sanitarium in which he was staying.

In a novel on a composer (*Sneghin's Opera* by Osip Cherny), the hero writes a "formalist" opera which is a flop because the proletariat does not need such sophisticated works. Sneghin asks his wife and her domestic help (who represents "the people") whether he should "feel the tragic and be, to a certain extent, its singer" and whether "such a vacancy exists in the arts." "No," answers the Marxian-Leninist wife, "there is no such vacancy in our times. One must be a great conscious artist and not fuss about your own self." The author fails to explain why self-expression is identified with the tragic element and why the latter is not appropriate to our era, but he sends the composer to a Party meeting where Sneghin listens to criticism of his work, sees the light, rejects his past, comes home regenerated, and begins to create in the vein of socialist realism.

Almost identical to this novel is *Ilya Golovin* (1949), a drama by Sergei Mikhalkov. It tells the harrowing story of a musician (a composite portrait of Prokofiev and Shostakovich) one of whose symphonies was criticized by the Party organs even as it was praised by American broadcasters. In the end, however, Golovin, distressed by the compliments from the rotten West, recognizes his errors, turns to the masses for further inspiration, and begins publishing scores in a popular, national, socialistic style, amid general satisfaction and with "Standing Room Only" signs at every performance.

In a tale written four years later called *Hello, Life* (1953) by P. Maliarevsky, the problem of the "artistic nature" is dealt with in the same expedient manner. Klava, a medical student, drops her studies because she wants to devote herself to the theater. A conversation with a famous actress (duly informed about Klava's case by the local Komsomol) makes her change her mind; consequently she leaves a note for her dormitory companion: "I am very, very stupid. Wake me up at nine. We shall study therapy."

Writers who dared to deviate from the prescribed road were quickly checked. This happened even for war novels, which continued to form a large section of Soviet fiction. The first volume of *For the Just Cause* (1952) by Vassily Grossman, depicting the battle of Stalingrad in the style of critical realism, was condemned as an "over-psychological work, permeated by hostile ideology and idealistic philosophy." Grossman was also accused of having portrayed his heroes as people with passive and contemplative natures, instead of building them up as dynamic fighters. Particular wrath was provoked by his assertion that times of crisis bring to the surface bad and destructive instincts in many people. After an attack from *Pravda*, *Novy Mir*, the monthly in which *For the Just Cause* was serialized, came out with a public statement admitting their "serious error" and promising a "reformed" editorial board. Publication of the novel was, of course, suspended. Its second part was confiscated by security organs and either destroyed or buried in some secret archives. The author, however, succeeded in hiding several chapters of the novel as well as the manuscript of an entire book, *Everything Flows*. The latter is a remarkable and moving testimony of Stalin's era: it describes the terrible famine of the 1930's in the Ukraine, the tragedy of female camps guarded by men wardens, and the terroristic practices of dictator's assistants, such as Yagoda, Beria, and Yezhov. The rescued chapters of *For the Just Cause* and *Everything Flows* were circulated by Samizdat and later published in posthumous editions in Europe by Russian *émigrés*.

A few years before Grossman's death (in 1964), he was viciously accused because of his play *If One Believes the Pythagoreans*, written in 1940 and published in 1946. Communist critics found the play dangerous and subversive because the author defended in it the idea that "the same human conflicts recur in different historical periods."

A similar fate befell Yury Gherman who depicted a Communist physician in the first chapters of his *A Lieutenant-Colonel of the Medical Corps* (1949) as an old bachelor, a highly nervous person afflicted with physical disorders and psychological complexes. This was sufficient to label the tale "morbid, individualistic, and decadent"; readers never learned how it came out.

All these restrictive measures were not due to the censor's whim but derived from a consistent policy: war had to be described in the context of the "new mentality" forged by Communism. Victory had been possible because Soviet man was so marvelous—and he was marvelous because the regime and the Party made him so. Novels and poems on war (or on any event of the past) had to extol the Party line. This meant that Stalin was always right and that no mention should be made of failures and defeats. It was but a part of a general "arrangement of history" for purposes of day-to-day propaganda; Soviet authors had to keep these purposes in mind whether they were describing the war against Hitler, the war against Napoleon, or revolutionary activities in Russia before and after the Revolution of 1917.

Alexander Fadeyev was forced to revise his highly popular *The Young Guard* in accordance with the official doctrine that anti-German resistance in Krasnodon, which he described as spontaneous, was not spontaneous but cleverly organized by Party leaders; his new 1951 version fitted into the prescribed mold. In 1949 Valentin Katayev had written *For the Soviet Power*, a full-length novel on the German-Rumanian occupation of Odessa and the underground activity of a small group of Communists and partisans who had fled to the city catacombs. The characters were well portrayed, but the critics attacked Katayev for not stressing the high moral qualities of the Communists, who were pictured as ordinary mortals rather than placed on a pedestal of infallibility, and for not emphasizing the leading role of the Party. So Katayev brought out in 1951 a revised and mutilated version of his novel. It was even more changed in the film, also entitled *For the Soviet Power*.

The "arrangement" of history involved first of all Stalin's role as the "father of the people, the builder of socialism and the great military genius, the winner of the war." The cult of the dictator became an authentic form of myth-making. His seventieth birthday in 1950 brought on a spate of poems and tales full of breathless adulation which had either a religious or a distinctly hypocritical flavor. As André Gide put it in 1937 after his travels in the USSR: "Even if it be genuine love for the leader, its manifestations are unbearable—since they are exaggerated, servile, and stupid." The cult was so infectious, however, that not only secondary writers such as Arkady Perventsev (b. 1905), the author of novels on the war and the Soviet navy, who glorified Stalin in a most subservient way, but also writers of higher caliber, such as Fedin and Pavlenko, followed it. The former expanded on the myth of Stalin as the hero of the civil war in his *An Extraordinary Summer* (1948); and the latter glorified him against the background of the Yalta conference in *Happiness* (1947). These two works were actually among the best of the period.

The same falsifications contaminated the historical novel which continued to fare rather well in the aftermath of the war. Even in the vast chronicle *Ivan the Terrible* (1943-46) by Ivan Kostylev (1884-1950), which was based on a serious study of the material, the interpretation of the Tsar's cruelty sounded like a justification of Stalinist terror. Only a few novels preserved a certain degree of objectivity: *The Birth of a Musician* was an examination of Glinka's childhood by Alexei Novikov; *Toward the Pacific*, a description of Nevelsky's expedition of 1848 by Nikolay Zadornov; *Fort Ross*, a novel about Russian settlers in California in 1812 by Ivan Kratt; and *Ivan the Third* by Valery Yazvitsky. Some authors believed it their duty to present non-Russians in a degrading manner. In his *Generalissimus Suvorov* (1947), Leonty Rakovsky is not particularly kind either to Austrian or German generals, while Marianna Yakhontova in *Potemkin* (1947), and other novelists who dealt mainly with the Russian naval and army commanders under Catherine the Great, did not spare ironical remarks about the French and the British. The Germans did not fare any better: Anna Antonovskaya and Boris Cherny represent them as robbers and morons in their joint novel *The Black Angel*, a chronicle of the German and British intervention in Georgia in 1918-19. In general, the closer the writers moved to our times, the more brazenly they rearranged facts and the more strictly they followed the official slogan: "history is politics applied to the past; historical events must be evaluated in relation to current Party policy." *The Soldiers of the Revolution* (1953) by Ivan Kremlev, a panorama of the civil war in the Volga region and of foreign intervention in the Northern Caucasus in 1919; *The Glow* by Yury Libedinsky (1953), a lengthy chronicle of the revolutionary movement in the early twentieth century, particularly in the Caucasus; *Faithful Friends* and *Engineers* (1950-52) by Mikhail Slonimsky, novels about Petrograd on the eve of World War I and in 1918-19, and dozens of other novels all presented a distorted view of the Russian revolutionary movement and of the role played by Stalin. The fiction devoted to contemporary life revolved mainly around the problem of reconstruction, particularly in the villages. The reader was constantly reminded that the USSR is a land of collective farms and the typical hero, just back from the front, was usually seen beginning a campaign for building a dam, or a local power station, or challenging the neighboring *kolkhoze* to compete in doubling the wheat harvest. Everyone has to face material obstacles and the opposition from backward or petty bourgeois elements of the village, and they all overcame them with the help of Party organizers. With some slight variations this forms, during the late 'forties, the story and the plot of almost every novel in this category. Most of them, including the two best-sellers by Semyon Babaevsky (b. 1909), *The Knight of the Golden Star* (1947-48) and *The Light over the Land* (1949-50) both awarded two Stalin Prizes, were lengthy, dull, and fundamentally untrue despite a plethora of naturalistic details. Slightly better but also falsely optimistic was *Harvest* (1951) by Galina Nikolayeva (died 1963), a woman physician and a hero of Stalingrad, describing the transformation of a backward *kolkhoze* into a model one.

One of the best books on "homecoming" was *With Greetings from the Front* (1945) by Valentin Ovechkin (1904-68), a talented middle-aged writer. His heroes discuss the future of collective farms and formulate the veterans' wishes: "we want plenty of beauty and joy, we gave our blood generously, and now we expect a great deal in return from life." Ovechkin actually initiated a series of works on the theme of post-war expectations, and his book became the object of heated discussions.

Novels on industrial reconstruction, such as *The Zhurbins* (1952) by Vsevolod Kochetov, a partisan of socialist realism, who showed a shipyard in turmoil; *The Days of Our Life* (1952) by Vera Ketlinskaya, who described the turbine section of a Leningrad factory; or *Far Away from Moscow* (1948), Vasily Azhayev's pedestrian best-seller on the building of an oil pipeline through the virgin forests in Siberia during the war, hardly had any literary significance, and their documentary value was marred by triteness and a tendentious "arrangement" of reality. Truth was not welcome in literature under Stalin, and writers who sincerely tried to communicate their own experience were severely reprimanded. Valentin Ovechkin was sharply criticized because in one of his fresh and colorful stories the second secretary of the Party Committee was more intelligent than the first secretary— and this was said to undermine the reader's faith in Party wisdom and justice. The fear of such discredit was so common that even such a Party favorite as Nikolay Pogodin confessed that he deliberately concluded his play *When Lances Are Broken* with a scene in which an "appropriate organ" dispenses rewards and punishments. "I was afraid," said Pogodin, "that if everything was not put in the right place, the play would not be passed by the censors." Often a critical article in the national press was sufficient to kill the production of a play. *New Times*, a drama by the Georgian Mdivani, was barred by the provincial authorities because it presented a chairman of a *kolkhoze* who lacked agronomical training and therefore felt unprepared for the tasks set by Soviet agriculture. The reasoning of the censors was very simple; since many *kolkhoze* chairmen were in a similar situation, the play might be taken as an affront by them.

In general the tightening of controls was particularly disastrous in dramatic literature. Communist critics of the late 1940's maintained that sharp conflicts should no longer exist in socialist society; if a writer depicted negative aspects of reality, such as clashes of interests and ambitions or contradictory emotional drives, he was immediately called "a slanderer" or "a secret enemy." In the best of cases he was indicted for depicting "the exceptional, the non-typical." The "conflictless" plays passed by the censors were dull ineptitudes that the public did not want. Between 1946 and 1952, comedies and dramas by contemporary Russian authors sank to their lowest level. The pompous statement that "the Soviet theater owes all its successes, all its achievements to the Communist Party and its wise, truly Marxian solutions of problems," which appeared in the opening article of an important collection of essays (*Stanislavsky's Heritage and the Practice of Soviet Theater*, 1953), sounded truly ridiculous, in comparison with the common joke of the Muscovites: "one finds the Soviet

theater at the cemetery, and the cemetery at the Soviet theater."
By 1952 plays on contemporary life dropped from 55 per cent to
41 per cent of the repertory; the number of their performances
was five to ten times lower than that of pre-revolutionary dramas
and comedies. Stalin and his advisers understood that a change of
policy was inevitable. "The reason for the poverty of our drama,"
wrote *Pravda* in the summer of 1952, "is that playwrights do not
base their plays on deep conflicts. If we judge life according to
their plays everything is ideal, marvelous ... and they think it is
prohibited to criticize the negative aspects of our life." "Let us
be frank," wrote Virta in his sensational article in 1952, "the playwright was surrounded by the barbed wire of obstacles," and the
"mortal fear of taking risks" made the censors and supervisors
hyper-suspicious of every word.

A place apart was held by Evgeny Schwartz (1896-1958), an
actor, a friend of the Serapion Brethren, and a highly talented
playwright. He wrote a great deal for the children's theater, but
his poetic fairy tales which are actually allegorical comedies and
dramas—particularly *The Naked King* (1934) and *The Dragon*
(1943)—charmed adults and have become, after his death, very
popular in the USSR and abroad.

The "conflictless drama" and the "comedy with a message"
ended up as complete theatrical failures. Similarly the attempt to
launch long narratives or novels-in-verse on such topics as collectivization, socialist emulation, and reconstruction resulted in pale
abstractions void of human significance and poetic excellence.
Typical examples of this imposed genre were *Spring in the Victory Collective* (1948) by Nikolay Gribachev, *The Flag over the
Village Soviet* (1947) by Alexey Nedogonov, *Pavlik Morozov*
(1950) by Stepan Shchipachev, *The Tale of Komsomol* (1952) by
Yakov Khelemsky, and *Fair Dale* (1951) by Margherita Aligher.
Slightly better was the latter's *Lenin's Hills*, about the construction of the 32-story university building in Moscow. The best
poems of the period continued the tradition of war literature,
either in works of seasoned authors such as Tvardovsky (*House
on the Road*, 1946) and Bergholz (*The Land of Stalingrad*, 1952),
or in shorter pieces by newcomers, such as Nikolay Dorizo and
Semyon Gudzenko (1923-53), some of whom were quite talented.

The true life of poetry, however, lay not only in what was being published, but in what masters such as Pasternak, Zabolotsky, and a few of lesser stature were writing in the seclusion of their studies, and what unknown young men and women who came to the fore in the next decade were dreaming or jotting down all over Russia.

In prose, only a very limited number of novels and tales enlivened the sluggish atmosphere of "Zhdanovism." The landscape of Russian literature between 1945 and 1953 looked like a monotonous plain, with just a few low hills under gray overcast skies. This rather desolate scene made it difficult to suspect that secret forces were active underground, awaiting a change of climate to burst into bloom.

28

The Thaw

Stalin's death on March 5, 1953, put an end to a regime of terror and opened a new era in the history of the Soviet Union. From that turning point the country developed under the banner of de-Stalinization—hidden in 1953, but more or less apparent in the next two years. Following the Twentieth Congress of the Party in 1956, de-Stalinization was intensified, especially after 1958 when Khrushchev consolidated his dominant position as the head of the government and the Party. Although the Russian Communists are reluctant to admit it, in these years, between 1953 and 1963, Soviet social, economic, political, and cultural life underwent a thorough revision. This process, of course, was far from smooth. The return to legality which helped to dispel the atmosphere of fear and suspicion resulted in the execution of Beria and other chiefs of the secret police. The rise and fall of Malenkov, Bulganin, Molotov, and many old-guard dignitaries were episodes in the furious fights and Byzantine intrigues among the rulers. The dismissal of 750,000 officials, mentioned by Khrushchev at the Twentieth Congress, and the reforms in the economy provoked strong opposition and discontent. And various dramatic events after Khrushchev's ascension to power indicated that the struggle between the revisionists and the Stalinists, or between the liberals and the conservatives, as the West called it, was actually a continuing contest between opposing factions. Each used technologists, professionals, intellectuals, and artists as allies or scapegoats in personal and political vendettas. An interminable series of moves and countermoves, of compromises, victories, and defeats accounts for the alternation of progress and reaction in all areas of Soviet life and particularly in literature and the arts. What happened in the community of writers in the decade following Stalin's demise corresponded to the changes within the Party and the government. Literature mirrored the general situation, offering a disturbing picture of thaw and freeze, as it was usually labeled in the Western press. The question was whether all these turns and oscillations pointed toward a growth of artistic independence and a release of controls. In the following decade, particularly after the Soviet intervention of 1956-58 in Hungary, the fragility of great expectations and exaggerated hopes became rather clear: the basic structure of the regime did not change, and what prevailed were minor concessions and cautious reforms.

The effects of Stalin's passing were felt almost immediately: numerous writers, released from prisons and concentration camps, returned home; censors' attitudes became less rigorous; forbidden themes made a timid appearance in the press; discussions flared up in writers' gatherings; for the first time in many years well-known artists came out with bold statements. "Creative problems cannot be solved by bureaucratic methods," declared Aram Khachaturian, the composer. Ehrenburg reminded his readers in the October issue of *Znamia* (The Banner) that "in art statistics do not play the same role as in industry" and that Chekhov and Gorky wrote what and when they pleased without being prodded by functionaries and Writers' Unions. From all parts came evidence of the writers' dissatisfaction with the present state of affairs and with current literary production.

A great stir was caused by Vladimir Pomerantsev's article in the monthly *Novy Mir* of December 1953. It stated in plain words that Soviet literature lacked honesty and sincerity, that most contemporary works resembled gramophone records and repeated worn-out slogans *ad infinitum* without ever trying to represent truth and real life. "Even about love they talk as if they were making speeches in a public meeting," complained Pomerantsev. And he rebuked the foes of "subjectivity": "The history of literature shows that writers made confessions and not only sermons." In the summer of 1953 Olga Bergholz claimed in her *A Talk About Lyricism* that poetry is impossible without the author's self-expression as an individual. Excerpts from Tvardovsky's new poem "Afar Farther Yet," although written in traditional style, had "liberal" overtones. *Volga Mother River* by Fyodor Panfyorov (1896-1960), serialized in August-September, contained a direct assault on bureaucracy and the "stultified" Party bosses who erected pompous public buildings instead of housing for the poor: "Forget about planning and think of people's needs," exclaims the hero of the novel. Panova's *The Seasons* pictured a member of the Communist upper crust as an egoist and profiteer driven to suicide by his own misdeeds; it also showed the moral confusion of Soviet youth and the rift between fathers and sons. And to climax all these signs of change, a new production of *The Bathhouse* by Mayakovsky was given on December 6 in the Moscow Theater of Satire, after an absence of a quarter of a century.

The new year 1954 came forth in an atmosphere of violent clashes between the "liberals" and the "conservatives." The latter, still occupying all the strategic administrative positions, opened fire against Pomerantsev, Panfyorov, and Ovechkin—the latter's *Weekdays of a District* being an unadorned report on the defects and miseries of provincial and village life. But all the efforts of the Stalinists to turn the clock back often proved to be ineffective.

The liberal campaign against "red tape," for example, continued with increasing zest, particularly in a number of new plays acclaimed by the public. *The Guests* by Leonid Zorin showed the moral decline of the bureaucrats: old Kirpitchev is an idealist and an upright revolutionary; his son Pyotr is a power-conscious "boss," remote from the people, a typical member of a reigning caste; and his grandchild is a "daddy's son," the idle and smug offspring of an upstart generation. After two performances the play was suspended. But then came another literary sensation: in May the magazine *Znamia* printed the first part of *The Thaw* by Ehrenburg (the second part came out in April 1956), and the title of this short novel served as the emblem of the whole period. Though far from being a masterpiece, it was avidly read by thousands and thousands because it mirrored their hopes for a milder climate after long years of tyranny. Readers got so enthusiastic about it that when it was released in book form on September 23, by the evening of that day all copies were sold out in Moscow.

Instead of focusing its attention on industrial and agricultural achievements, *The Thaw* deals with problems of love and personal happiness. The common trait of several couples of men and women in the novel is their inability to communicate and their reluctance to yield to their instinctual drives. Products of an era of constraint and repression, they all seem frozen, afraid of becoming frank and spontaneous. The disappearance of taboos and prohibitions, and the sentimental breakthrough of a warped and unhappy Soviet people represent figuratively the unfreezing of Russia. No less symbolic is the drama of Pukhov, a conformist painter who has won money and recognition for his canvasses of smiling pioneers and joyful cow girls. When he encounters Saburov, a true creator who is starving in obscurity, he understands his own failure. The opposition of Pukhov's artificial potboilers to Saburov's deeply felt, semi-clandestine art was interpreted by the readers as a request for a complete revision of accepted aesthetic dogma. Other topical elements added to the popularity of *The Thaw*: the famous "doctor's plot" engineered by the secret police; the old men returning home after fifteen years in prison and exile; the creeping anti-Semitism, and various other indignities and wrong-doings. The topical and political impact of the novel apparently redeemed its obvious literary shortcomings: it lacked any depth and originality of characterization, its structure was loose, and its style journalistic, with the sharp black and white strokes so typical of Ehrenburg; but as a novel of ideological importance within a specific historical context, it remains a document of the period, and evidence of the turmoil Russia was passing through in the middle 'fifties.

The Stalinists, who were still strong in the Party hierarchy and in literary organizations, launched a counter-offensive the moment *The Thaw* (and Pasternak's poems) was published. In May Surkov, the poet and functionary, attacked Pomerantsev in *Pravda* for his "anti-Marxian revision of basic principles and Party decisions of 1946-1948." In other words, the diehards continued to defend Zhdanovism. Panfyorov was dismissed from the editorial board of *October* in June, and Tvardovsky from that of *Novy Mir* in August (for having published "harmful critical articles by Abramov, Shcheglov, and Lifshitz"). Four novelists and playwrights, including Nikolay Virta, were expelled from the Union of Soviet Writers; Ehrenburg. Pomerantsev, Panova, and Zoshchenko got "public reprimands," and Victor Mokrousov was thrown out of the Composers' Union "because of his careless attitude toward creative work." These restrictive measures were aimed at curbing the growing unrest of the intellectuals on the eve of the Second Congress of Soviet Writers, scheduled for December 1954, the first such reunion in twenty years. This fact alone was of tremendous importance, and the solemn reception offered by the government to the delegates, indicated the Kremlin's desire to establish a better relationship with the "engineers of human souls."

But of much greater significance was what the debates of the Congress revealed to participants and observers. Like all Soviet public gatherings it followed the inevitable ritual—invocation of Lenin, recitation of the Communist credo, sermons by the high priests of the state religion, and ecclesiastic jargon of the celebrants. But what went on behind this official facade showed confusion, discontent, and the rumbling of an approaching thunderstorm. Once given the opportunity to speak up, even within imposed limits, delegates poured out an amazing amount of complaints and "self-criticism." "Writers do not and cannot think all in the same manner," said Marin Franicevich, the guest from Yugoslavia. Several themes prevailed in the ten days' discussions. There was an almost unanimous condemnation of bureaucratic methods in literature. "Our Union of Soviet Writers," said Ketlinskaya, "resembles a ministry, with this difference that at the head of it are placed poets and novelists who have no administrative abilities and dream with nostalgia of their writing desks." And Ovechkin proposed fewer meetings on how to study life and how to write, more actual living and writing. No less unequivocal was the charge against the insincerity and the artistic poverty of current fiction. Caution prevented the speakers from criticizing the sacred theories of educational art and socialist realism, but they turned their guns on the discrepancy between the growth of the reading audiences and the inadequacy of the literary nourishment offered to them. In 1954 the USSR printed 231 million copies of fiction, declared one of the "revisionists," and had 380,000 libraries; the love of reading was universal, first printings of novels were sold out in a week—and what did readers find in all this avalanche of printed matter? "Communal apartments painted in gold, workshops in factories looking like laboratories, *kolkhoze* clubs resembling palatial mansions—a world of stage properties, of tinsel trinkets inhabited by primitives or model children made of wax"—this was Ehrenburg's description of contemporary literature. And the poet Lugovskoy stigmatized raw, uncouth works, hailed by the critics and honored by state awards, but essentially false or insignificant (Simonov called them "pastry-shop fabrications"). "Literature must return to great human problems," said Lugovskoy. "I am speaking of high and eternal things common to every man. The tragedy of jealousy and betrayal, disappointments in love and friendships, grief over the loss of dear ones—all this exists for us as for all human beings . . . Where is it in our fiction? On our path we find the black shadows of stereotypes, coldness, incontestable thousandfold repeated ideas, all sorts of dull rot."

When it came to drafting final resolutions, such heretical voices were of course drowned in the usual babble of Communist phraseology, yet the writers did say that literature was lagging behind the impetuous development of Soviet society, that it did not satisfy the rapidly growing spiritual needs of the readers, that it did not create significant images of its contemporaries, and that many of its works ignored the contradictions and the difficulties of the times.

The writers pleaded for an expansion of the "permissible," for more latitude in the choice of themes and their treatment, and for less rigidity in official controls. In a way the Congress served as a catalyst. It is true that it did not weaken the Party's decision to maintain its hold over literature and to leave intact the organizational structure of the Union of Soviet Writers. But, on the other hand, the writers were assured that in the future they would be treated with more understanding, that their errors would not be considered crimes against the state, that the threat of arrests and repressions was definitively over, and that literature would henceforth be free to "present conflicts and contradictions that still exist in Soviet life." Certain facts seemed to confirm this attitude of the administration: Tvardovsky, Panova, Grossman, and other writers who had previously been reprimanded, were elected to the new Executive Board of the Union; Anna Akhmatova was re-instated as a member of the Union and ostensibly took part in the proceedings of the Congress. But the aftermath of the Congress was even more spectacular. The fall of Malenkov, the growth of the de-Stalinization movement, the humanization of the regime were felt throughout the country. In literature the speech by Mikhail Sholokhov at the Twentieth Congress of the Communist Party, published in *Pravda*, February 21, 1956, had a special impact. The honored dean of Soviet letters asked the delegates not to attach great importance to figures: the fact that the Union of Soviet Writers comprised "3773 members armed with pens should neither frighten nor rejoice the Congress," because the membership included a large number of "dead souls." And the high number of books printed in the last years should not be taken as proof of the great achievements of Soviet literature. "We must recognize," said Sholokhov, "that during the last twenty years we had but a handful of good, intelligent books, and huge piles of gray trash." He attributed this dearth to the alienation of the writers from life and the masses. But his main attack was against the Union of Soviet Writers. The latter, Sholokhov claimed, had been conceived as a creative collective but degenerated into an administrative organization, directed by Alexander Fadeyev, a power-hungry secretary general, who did everything except help writers to write. "Why nobody told him during the last fifteen years that a Writers' Union is not a military unit and certainly not a penal colony and that no writer wants to stand 'at attention' in front of Fadeyev, the general secretary?" "Prose writers did not go to Fadeyev to learn how to write because each of them had his own handwriting, his vision of the world, his style, and Fadeyev could not be and is not an infallible artistic authority." In the same way poets do not come to Surkov, the new secretary, to ask him how to write poetry because "he fails to understand that an orchestra is composed not only of drums and percussion instruments . . . We do not need such literary leaders to whom none of their colleagues ever come to solve creative problems."

Among Sholokhov's many cutting remarks one must have hit Fadeyev most painfully: "Neither as secretary general nor as a writer has he done anything in the last fifteen years." Fadeyev the bureaucrat held dictatorial power over literature, but Fadeyev the writer must have realized that by obeying orders from the Kremlin and revising his *The Young Guard* he had mutilated the

work and betrayed himself. After Stalin's death came his downfall as a Party functionary (he was demoted from a full fledged
member of the Central Committee to that of a candidate). But
loss of rank and addiction to the bottle were not the only causes
of Fadeyev's disintegration. He was obsessed with a thousand
doubts. Had he been right in following Stalin, in trying to regiment writers, in having participated in all the purges of the intellectuals? Now when the secret archives were dug up, the
rumors went around Moscow that there were documents proving
Fadeyev's role as a denunciator of Babel and Kirshon, probably
of other writers. His whole life's work was challenged, and at
the same time he, the man who wrote so many resolutions and
instructions, was incapable now of writing a good story. In a
moment of repentance and disgust, a bullet appeared to Fadeyev
preferable to a life of deceit.

Fadeyev's suicide on May 13, 1956, rocked literary circles all
over Russia but no explanation of his tragedy, except "illness,"
was ever given in the press, and standard text books (such as the
third volume of the semi-official *History of Soviet Literature*,
published in 1961) simply record that "he died" on such and
such a date.

The Twentieth Congress of the All Union Communist Party
and the "secret" speech by Khrushchev which gave a final consecration to de-Stalinization, and soon became known in the
USSR and abroad, served to encourage Russian writers. A great
many works published in the second half of the 'fifties were interesting and alive. Even though they were not masterpieces, they
compared favorably with the mass production of the Zhdanovism
era.

One of the best works was *In the Home Town*, a 1954 novel by
Victor Nekrassov. Its hero, a young officer, returns from the
front to find his wife with another man. His health is poor, he
wanders amidst the ruins of a severly damaged city looking for
a job, suffers from solitude and misery, is compelled to stay for
a long while in the hospital, and then tries to re-adjust himself
to civilian life. There is hardly any plot in this narrative, which
tells of relations between ordinary people who all have their

secret or manifest dramas, who lack food and fuel, but who crave above all human warmth, kindness, communication, and the modest niceties of existence. How different was this well written tale with its lyrical passages and muted tone, with its realistic portrayal of average Soviet men and women and their daily problems, from the "epics on heroes" made to measure a few years before. The Communist critics frowned at such a book, but readers refused to listen to them and brought the circulation of *In the Home Town* to one and a half million copies.

The main event of 1955 was the posthumous rehabilitation of writers who had been purged under Stalin and whose works and even names were proscribed for many years. The list included not only Babel, Bulgakov, Meyerhold, Vesyoly, Kirshon (executed in 1937 as a "Trotskyite"), but also members of The Pass, such as Ivan Katayev; Smithy poets, such as Kirilov, Gerasimov, Bakhmetiev; victims of the anti-Jewish campaign, such as Golodny and Bergelson (executed in 1952); and numerous Communist writers who were either killed or jailed during the trials and purges of the late 1930's, such as Koltsov, Yasensky, Serebriakova, and others. What was previously known only to a limited number of initiated through whispers and rumors was now revealed in the press. No details, however, were given about the fate of the martyrs: had they been shot, hanged, beaten to death, or had they died in prison and penal colonies? Of what had they been accused, had they been tried, what were the circumstances of their "elimination"? The reports on the writers who had perished offered only intimations, hints, euphemistic phrases which simply hid or veiled the horrifying truth.

In the meantime, rehabilitation served the purpose of the "posthumous homecoming." Special editorial boards were created for the publication of the "literary heritage of the deceased," and a series of their works appeared in new printings. (There were, however, significant exceptions, such as Pilnyak and Zamyatin, Mandelstam and Gumilev.) Bulgakov's plays were re-issued along with the poems of Pavel Vasiliev (1910-37) and novels by Artyom Vesyoly. Moreover, the stories by the expatriate Ivan Bunin, who always had strong admirers among Soviet authors (particularly Paustovsky, Lidin, Katayev), were offered to Soviet readers in large printings, with very mild expurgations. Other *émigré* writers who had died abroad (with the exception of Remizov and Zamyatin) were occasionally published in Soviet periodicals. Most spectacular was the official recognition of Dostoevsky as a great Russian classic, and the publication of his collected works for the 75th anniversary of his death. The living were also reinstated: Olesha returned to Moscow from Central Asia, Zabolotsky was published again, and Anna Akhmatova was hailed in the Literary Gazette as a "talented and noble creator of Russian poetry."

The rehabilitation of writers who had been banned since the 1920's and 1930's raised the problem of their place in Russian letters, and this, naturally, provoked a debate on the true evaluation of a period which the dogmatists rejected merely as an obnoxious survival of the Tsarist-capitalist tradition. In 1956, Simonov contended at the Moscow Congress of Teachers of Literature that the rehabilitation led logically to a revision of literary history; surveys of post-revolutionary prose and poetry could not ignore writers such as Babel, Olesha, Akhmatova, and others whose names had been hushed up for political reasons.

The "new look" in literature was also manifest in a changed attitude toward Western literature. Hemingway, whose works had been condemned for over fifteen years, made a comeback with *The Old Man and the Sea*, and translations of other American and European novelists were promised by *Foreign Literature*, a newly established monthly. Other new magazines (*Neva, Youth*), diverse publishing enterprises, literary panels, informal gatherings, and public discussions of best-sellers which attracted thousands of listeners, as well as a constantly increasing number of novels, tales, and poems by young authors, were among the signs of a cultural revival. An event of great resonance was the miscellany *Literary Moscow*. In its first volume it published poems by Akhmatova and Pasternak's essay on translating Shakespeare. The second volume contained poems by Marina Tsvetayeva, the great *émigré* poet who had returned to the USSR in 1939 and committed suicide in 1941. There were also stories conceived in the spirit of critical realism and several daring essays. In one of them the playwright Alexander Kron wrote: "a writer is an inventor, he works for the future, but a bent head cannot look forward." But the third volume of *Literary Moscow* never saw the light.

There is no doubt that by 1955 a large part of Soviet literature was breaking away from the official mold. The changes were wide-ranging and various. There was greater diversity of style, more inventiveness in plot, more freedom in the unfolding of a story. Such dangerous subjects as personal tragedies brought on by Stalinist terror were now treated. Since 1955-56 Soviet novels became populated by innocently condemned Communists, by non-Party convicts returning from exile, and by daughters and sons whose parents one night had been taken away for ever by the secret police. From *The Running Battle* by Galina Niko-layeva and *Not by Bread Alone* by Vladimir Dudintsev, to the novels of the 'sixties, such as *The Silence* by Yury Bondarev, *Kira Georghievna* by Victor Nekrassov, *The Living and the Dead* by Konstantin Simonov, *The Wild Honey* by Leonid Pervomaysky—to mention only a few—the figure of the former inmate of a concentration camp or retrospective scenes of unjust, iniquitous arrests made their entry into Soviet fiction.

The general movement toward a critical representation of life was a reaction against the laudatory falsehoods and the "varnish-ings" of reality. Old and young writers competed with each other in exposing the concrete shortcomings of the system; only on rare occasions did their hints seem to touch the very foundations of the regime.

The main targets of this literature were the bureaucrats and the new ruling class, the Soviet aristocrats who had denatured the very ideals of the Revolution. Some short stories on this sub-ject were so explicit that they obtained a huge success not com-mensurate perhaps with their artistic worth. In "Personal Opin-ion" Daniil Granin portrayed a Soviet engineer, the director of a research laboratory, who is afraid to form his own opinion; he is a coward and prefers to betray the truth rather than argue with his superiors and jeopardize his high position. "The Journey Home" by Nikolay Zhdanov depicted a high official of peasant extraction who, on a short and useless visit to his native village, is shocked by its poverty and deprivations, so leaves again in a hurry. The same theme is repeated in stories by Kazakov and other writers: the successful son or daughter returns home and feels the gulf between the city dwellers and the backward villagers who repeat Party slogans but live in primitive conditions. In "The Levers" by Alexander Yashin, *kolkhoze* administrators talk like human beings as soon as they are alone; they complain that Party bosses who come from the city keep on shouting "carry on" and are more interested in displaying high statistical indicators than in finding out how people live. The same men, however, themselves use the tired phraseology of the bosses as soon as they appear at a public meeting—because they are assigned the role of "levers" in the mechanism of the system. Yashin (1913-68) was also a master of lyrical prose, and his "Vologda Wedding," published in 1962, remains one of the most interesting descriptions of ancient rites and folklore in northern Russia.

The Twentieth Congress of the Party in February 1956 and the secret speech by Khrushchev, with his outright attack against Stalin, marked a watershed in the literature of social criticism. It reached its climax in the fall of that year when *Not by Bread Alone* by Vladimir Dudintsev (b. 1918) was serialized in *Novy Mir*. It did not rate very highly from a purely aesthetic standard; its structure was loose, its exposition was verbose, and its style was pedestrian, but it became a sensation and provoked riotous discussions and hundreds of articles. It was attacked and defended in special sessions of the Union of Soviet Writers, and it was talked about in Party councils and government meetings. Like *The Thaw* it articulated common moods and thoughts; it represented a whole movement within Soviet society. Khrushchev, in one of his speeches, dubbed Dudintsev "a calumniator who took a malicious joy in describing the negative side of Soviet life ... in an unhealthy, tendentious, and obnoxious work." The leader failed, however, to explain why such a corrupt novel fascinated millions of readers and remained the focus of general attention for such a long time.

Not by Bread Alone has a complicated plot with twists and ramifications but its main theme is simple. It revolves around Lopatkin, a former physics teacher who became an inventor after the war and worked on a machine for the centrifugal casting of iron drainpipes. A single-minded lonely man, obsessed by his

project, he does not belong to the "gang," lacks the "right connections," and seems a dull nuisance to pedantic experts and
ministry employees. His project is buried by red tape, while he
is reduced to poverty and isolation. The only support he has
comes from another.defeated eccentric and from Nadia the wife
of Drozdov, his chief enemy. At one point Lopatkin's invention
interests the military, but this brings upon him the accusation
of "divulging State secrets," he is arrested and sent to a concentration camp in the Arctic. His case is reviewed, however, thanks
to an honest trial judge puzzled by some legal incongruities, and
after Stalin's death Lopatkin returns to Moscow. He is rehabilitated, the army accepts his machine; yet all the functionaries who
snubbed or crushed him are still around and Drozdov is about
to become deputy minister. The evil is unpunished, the struggle
goes on, and the "happy ending" is by no means a satisfactory
and terminal solution.

Unlike other negative characters in Soviet fiction, Drozdov
and the whole clique he represents are neither villains nor paid
agents of American imperialism. They are Party members, solid
citizens, and first-class business men. "I belong to the producers
of material values," says Drozdov to Nadia who speaks about the
importance of relationships among people: "matter comes first.
Let us have things, we do not need to worry about relationships
and then you will begin to hang little pictures and china plates
on the walls." He dismisses all "ornaments," all superfluous "rubbish." He sees in Lopatkin one of those undisciplined idealists
who are pitted against the collective, take fantasy for reality, and
mumble "not by bread alone." Behind Drozdov stands a whole
army of Party leaders, academicians, generals, experts, functionaries—all that "apparatus of the state" which has replaced the Old
Guard of Communist intellectuals exterminated by Stalin. This
officialdom consists of "monopolists," who have vested interests
in the administration of the country, who form a sort of pale, a
restricted area, and who curb mercilessly talented non-conformists such as Lopatkin.

By depicting Drozdov as the end result of the Communist regime, the novel goes beyond the "little defects of the mechanism."
Within the limits of this kind of criticism permissible in the

USSR, Dudintsev indirectly questions the whole system. At a discussion of the novel among Soviet writers Paustovsky declared that it signified the first round in the battle against the Drozdovs, "whom literature should fight until they are completely exterminated . . . the book expressed the anxiety we all feel about the moral aspect and purity of the Soviet man and our culture." The same critical spirit that made *Not by Bread Alone* so popular was in evidence in a steadily increasing number of stories and novels in the late 'fifties.

The rejection of the puritanism that was so typical of the previous period, formed another important trend in 1955-57. It colored most novels of social criticism. In *Not by Bread Alone* Lopatkin and Nadia, who leaves her husband, become lovers out of wedlock. In *The Running Battle* (1957), a very typical novel of the period, Galina Nikolayeva depicts the love affair between engineer Bakhirev, a married man and a Communist, and Tina, a young woman whose first husband has been "repressed." Their relations form a large part of the story which includes a great variety of material, from an impressive picture of Stalin's funeral, to the struggle between Bakhirev and Valgan, a factory director whose authoritarian ways have separated him from his comrades.

Family life, marriage and divorce, the deceptions and joys of love ceased to hover ashamedly in the background of Soviet fiction; they came boldly to the fore and were treated as extensively as the professional activities of heroes and heroines. Themes and figures completely ignored for twenty years suddenly erupted into novels and plays: there were illegitimate children, unfaithful wives and husbands, flirting young women, highly sexed men, and drinkers and gamblers. Personal problems, emotional conflicts, erotic troubles now took priority in numerous works. The success of such mediocre, rather dull novels as *Ivan Ivanovich* and its sequel, by Antonina Koptiayeva, or of *Elena* by Xenia Lvova, who alternated scenes of passion with quotations from Lenin, was due to the large role given to the private lives of their protagonists.

A heated debate was provoked by "A Long Conversation," a half-narrative poem by Paruayra Sevak, an Armenian poet, translated into Russian by Evgeny Evtushenko. It was a lyrical protest against Party interference in the intimate life of the hero, who has fallen in love with a married woman. The local Party organization tells the young man to stop, but he questions the right of the collective to make decisions in such matters. Finally his beloved comes to live with him—and he defends her action because her marriage was not based on real love. Many readers sided with the hero, others accused him of violating the very principles of Marxism, and an avalanche of enthusiastic or irate letters descended on the monthly that published the poem.

Nikolay Pogodin's drama *Petrarch's Sonnet* stirred up a similar controversy: it represented an aged Communist whose romantic love for a young girl is desecrated by the vulgar interventions of Party officials and the gossip and malice of "virtuous" citizens.

This more human and realistic approach to the problems of love and marriage was not by any means comparable to the freedom and bluntness with which they are treated in modern Western literature. It would be an exaggeration to say that Soviet fiction is the least erotic in the world, but the writers of the USSR prefer to ignore sex or just talk of it in a naïve and sentimental way: if they take it seriously they use allusions, symbols, and lines of dots. But the "unfreezing" of literature in the 1950's included not only love but all sorts of drives and emotions. In general, man's inner feelings were given more attention—hence the success of *The Turbulent Youth*, a romantic and psychological autobiography by Paustovsky, of *Serezha*, a delightful story of a child by Vera Panova, of *Probation* and *Cruelty* (in English, *Comrade Venka*) by Pavel Nilin, who raised problems of individual conscience in short novels that were alive with action. The tendency was to get away from dry rationalism, utilitarianism, and the whole negative attitude taken by "strong, dynamic, and scientifically oriented Communists" toward the "stuff and nonsense" of fantasy and intimate feelings. This explains why Semyon Kirsanov's long ballad "The Seven Days of the Week" was so widely read and discussed: in sharp satirical verse laced with mordant irony and thrusts that recalled Mayakovsky's manner, it told of an invention acclaimed by the Communist "organizational men"—the industrial production of hearts which could easily replace those in human breasts and eliminate the troublesome diversity and surprise of individual emotions.

Among the factors that seemed to indicate various changes in Russian letters of the 1960's, some hope was placed on encounters between Soviet and European writers in Venice, Zurich, and later in Rome, but all these meetings brought few satisfactory results and did not promote an end of Russia's cultural isolation. Translations of contemporary Western novelists and poets were avidly read, and though important authors were often submerged by inferior "representatives of progressive literature," in whom Communist critics tried to discover a counterpart to socialist realism, readers were quick to make the right choice. Of course, preference was given by Soviet publishing houses to American and European writers who were considered more or less safe ideologically—Theodore Dreiser for example—but large printings were also authorized of Sherwood Anderson, O. Henry, Steinbeck, Erskine Caldwell, G. B. Shaw, Richard Aldington, Galsworthy, Stefan Zweig, Thomas and Heinrich Mann, Saint-Exupery, Mauriac, Roger Martin du Gard, Sartre, Moravia, Levi, and many others. In some instances an author with no reputation at home would become a best-seller in the USSR for some special reasons (for example, the American Mitchell Wilson who writes about American physicists falling in love with Soviet women scientists). On the other hand, writers like Camus were not translated until the 1970's, and then mainly in periodicals, and Kafka's works appeared in a limited edition only in 1965.

In the theater, adaptations of stories by Stendhal, Balzac, Galsworthy, and Jack London alternated with plays by Shaw, Brecht, Lillian Hellman, and even Agatha Christie: *Dial M for Murder* and Christie's *The Witness for the Prosecution* were box-office hits in Moscow for two years. This is not surprising in a country where thrillers and detective stories are just tolerated, without being officially approved.

And, finally, the chief source of Western influence in Russia was the satellite countries, chiefly Poland and Hungary. The Russians may not have traveled extensively in Western Europe, but they did go very often to Poland, Hungary, Rumania, Czechoslovakia, Bulgaria, East Germany, and to a lesser extent to Yugoslavia. The impact of their contacts with poets, novelists, and artists of those countries was tremendous. Not only in private conversations, but in public conferences, congresses, and public discussions they were confronted with concepts that hailed creative freedom and unhampered search for new forms of expression. Even more shattering to the Russians was their hosts' low opinion of the theory and practice of socialist realism. The foreign visitors, who came to Russia from the "people's democracies," also brought with them forbidden books and ideas. All this sustained in the USSR a skeptical attitude toward the native brand of socialist realism.

In 1954, during the Second Congress of Soviet Writers, the definition of the official school was reduced to one sentence: "Socialist realism being the basic method of Soviet literature and literary criticism, requires from the artist a truthful, historically concrete representation of reality in its revolutionary development." The fact that the Congress dropped the embarrassing extension of this ambiguous formula, was of course, extremely significant but it did not help greatly.* Simonov in a daring article (in the December issue of *Novy Mir*) recommended a revision of all the works published in the last decade, and criticized the very concept of the "Basic Method." An article by Netchenko in a specialist journal stated that 550 doctoral dissertations on Soviet literature in the last decade were little more than padded newspaper articles and shed no light on the obscurities of socialist realism. Other rebels scorned the requirement of "truthful representation of reality." What criteria, they asked, were offered for judging the degree of this truthfulness—and who wanted a "false representation" anyway? What did all this rigmarole about historic concreteness and revolutionary development have to do with artistic accomplishment? And why is it that some words of Lenin in his "Party organization and Party literature," which belonged to a definite pre-revolutionary period and were written more than half a century ago, were not viewed now in their historical concreteness? Were they not applicable only to

* This is what was judged superflous by the Congress: "Moreover, truthfulness and historical completeness of artistic representation must be combined with the task of ideological transformation and education of the working man in the spirit of socialism." The ideas expressed in these requirements have never in fact been abandoned by the Communist Party in the USSR.

a given situation? Was it reasonable to proclaim them today as an unchangeable law? Some defenders of socialist realism emphasized its "particular content" and quoted again Lenin's words about "Party-mindedness." Others insisted that socialist realists possess a Communist outlook on reality and their creation was founded on a revolutionary, Marxist-Leninist approach to life. In this interpretation the stress was on the *Weltanschauung*, on the general philosophy of the writer, and not on his literary method. Since all Communist authors were supposed to have the same philosophy, not only did their works threaten to become terribly monotonous but the whole concept of socialist realism was rendered superfluous. This, by the way, was the argumentation of Soviet novelists such as Simonov and Ehrenburg (the latter wrote quite pertinently on the subject in his essay "Stendhal's Lessons"). Very close to them was the position of prominent European Communists. Georg Lucacz, the well-known Hungarian critic, expressed serious doubts about the Kremlin's cultural policy. He wanted socialism to become more humane and to favor free discussion. He disapproved of Soviet literature under Stalin and recognized that "the general public identified socialist realism with those mediocre mechanical works that Party critics praised to high heaven." Italian and French left-wing literati also attacked the intellectual ineptitudes and artistic failures of socialist realism. Never before was this "method" exposed in the West and in the USSR with such frankness, nor criticized with such energy. Whatever the Moscow press kept repeating in its declarations in the years 1955-58, and then again in the 1970's, the theory of socialist realism was dealt a mortal blow in Russia; and it never operated as a determining factor in the satellite countries of Europe or in Latin America (not even in Cuba).

29

The Unstable Equilibrium

It is very difficult to trace the tortuous roads of Soviet literature in the decade after 1956, without keeping in mind one basic fact: despite all the zigzags, advances and retreats, ups and downs, the ruling group of the Communist Party never renounced its hold on the arts and the whole cultural life of the USSR. This is true not only of conservatives and avowed or hidden Stalinists, who did not want to budge from their intransigent positions, but also of Khrushchev, Brezhnev, Kosygin and of those who understood the necessity of granting some leeway to writers and artists. Everybody in the Kremlin agreed that the Party had to maintain its supreme authority over all creative activities and to promote socialist realism as the only school proper to the State. This was the common ground, the meeting place of various factions in the Central Committee. They could (and did) differ in their opinions over practical conclusions, over ways and means to apply the controls, but they all shared the same dogmatic convictions and they used the same terminology. The main novelty, however, was that coercive and harsh measures were used less frequently.

The range of freedom and the character of the concessions granted to writers depended, of course, on the fluctuations of "high politics" and the distribution of forces within the governing group. But they were also contingent on the overriding problem Khrushchev and his successors had to face on all levels of Soviet life: how to preserve the cohesion of the Party and the integrity of its doctrine while declaring fallible and even criminal the man who had dominated both Party and country for twenty-five years and whose supreme authority in all matters had been undisputed. In literature, the question was how to preserve Party aesthetics, how to defend the theory of Party-mindedness and of socialist realism, while condemning the products of these theories and rejecting the whole practice based on these aesthetics. Was it possible to obtain better novels, stories, plays, and poems without changing the requirements imposed on the authors and without revising the principles and slogans used since 1934?

To solve this the Party was compelled to employ all sorts of ideological and verbal falsehoods. The result was ideological confusion and a permanent controversy within the Party; in literature it led to constant clashes of opposing camps. Ultimately it provoked the great division of the 1950's and 1960's—the most important event in Russian history of those years—and although the Communist press denied the existence of a rift between fathers and sons, the liberals naturally recruited their supporters among the young, and Stalinists and conservatives mobilized the old. Neither the liberals nor their foes could ever claim a complete victory, and for almost a decade the thaw alternated with freezes, precluding a true change of season. In 1956 it might have looked different because the revisionist movement gained much ground and became so influential that it spread all over the Soviet Union and the satellites. The government was surprised by the range and dynamism of the movement. A Kremlin dignitary told a Western visitor at that time: "we opened the door a little to let in some fresh air, but such a stormy wind came through the aperture that we have to take protective measures." In August-September 1956 came the big warning—a highly publicized collection of Khrushchev's speeches under the general title "For a close link between literature and art and the life of the people," which gave a modernized version of Zhdanovism and repeated the same old slogans of "representing life and helping Communism." Servile pens immediately dubbed it "a decisive factor in the fight against revisionist tendencies," but it failed to have a sobering effect on the writers. In October, however, the Hungarian revolt was crushed by Soviet tanks, and the pendulum swung back again. The conservatives regained the upper hand, and the first months of 1957 were marked in Russia by a strengthening of censorship and a tightening of controls. At all public gatherings the Old Guard attacked Dudintsev and the authors of critical stories in the second volume of *Literary Moscow*. They

were parried by the liberals, among them Dudintsev himself and
Kaverin. At the Congress of Painters young artists dubbed works
by prominent "masters" of socialist realism as "colored photographs." In March at the Congress of Composers the accusations
against the pernicious influence of jazz and "diseased" Western
music were received with sneers of contempt.

Despite this resistance, governmental pressure during 1957 and
1958 became very strong, and the diehards' offensive was officially supported. All sorts of turncoats joined forces with the
dogmatists and hastened to write novels and stories in the official
vein. The conservative leaders even attempted some polemical
thrusts in fiction. Very typical of this genre was *Brothers Yershov* by Vsevolod Kochetov (1912-74), a spokesman of Party
dogmatists. The action of this full-length novel was located in a
provincial Southern town: it followed the pattern of the trivial
industrial story—the struggle between "good" workmen and "bad
engineers" in a metallurgical plant—but the plot was enlivened
by many sidelights of contemporary Soviet life, including political
and amorous conflicts. The main theme of the novel, however,
was the biting criticism of "decadent bourgeois tendencies in the
arts" and of "the corrupted intelligentsia." Kochetov intimated
that the consequences of freedom in literature would be "events
such as those in Hungary," and warned the panicked Party leadership of how dangerous liberalization might prove. As a counterpart to *Not by Bread Alone,* Kochetov also portrayed an inventor but made him a shallow, scheming individual unable to
adapt himself to the socialist collective. He is opposed by one
of the Yershov brothers who is a true, honest proletarian, a
model of Communist devotion. What Khrushchev told writers
at a meeting in 1957 on an estate near Moscow, was not very
different from Kochetov's denunciations and threats.

Despite all the obstacles and insidious campaigns, the best part
of the literary production of 1957-58 showed the vigor of the
critical current. On the one hand novels on the war, such as
South of the Main Push by Grigory Baklanov, dwelt much more
on the miseries and absurdities of the giant bloodletting than on
its uplifting and heroic character; on the other hand, narratives
of village life refused to represent it as a sort of Communist picnic.

Steep Mountains, by Nikolay Virta (b. 1906), a loosely knit, rambling, but colorful novel, contained a panoramic treatment of a badly organized *kolkhoze* which gets a new lease of life through rational management and human friendship. Daniil Granin's *After the Wedding* begins with an amusing personal story of newlyweds and then expands into a picture of economic conditions in a poor agricultural district. Fyodor Panfyorov, unafraid of negative criticism by the diehards, presented in *Reflections* (a sequel to his *Volga Mother River*) a shocking description of a collective farm in which everything is sacrificed to building up a false facade of prosperity and happiness. While Panfyorov's critical realism was expressed in undistinguished, often trivial language, the straight and poetic sketches by two very talented newcomers, Yefim Dorosh (*The Dry Summer*) and Vladimir Soloukhin (*By-Roads of Vladimir District*), vividly combined realistic matter-of-fact portraiture of peasants and their backwardness with a strong feeling for nature.

The new spirit was also patent in the short story. Moral problems facing ordinary Soviet citizens became the main theme of Vladimir Tendryakov's (b. 1923) tales; his "Three, Seven, Ace" (1960) provoked the indignation of the Party custodians because he told how a community of timber floaters in the north of Russia, was corrupted by a former convict, a gambler and a drunk. It showed the fragility of moral norms in average human beings and therefore was considered "a calumny on the Soviet people." More ambitious was his "A Short Circuit" (1962), in which he attempted to reveal the secret life and thoughts of a group of men and women during a breakdown of electric power on New Year's Eve. In this story there were various symbolic overtones in the picture of life suspended in darkness and finally restored to normalcy through the efforts of both staff and workmen. His 1964 novel, *A Date with Nefertiti,* dealt with the formation and destiny of the artist.

Other works of the period were Vera Panova's *A Sentimental Novel,* in which she wrote semi-autobiographical scenes from the first years of the Revolution, and *The First Acquaintance* (1958), a lively travelogue in France and in Italy by Victor Nekrassov.

Even more symptomatic events were in evidence in the theater and poetry. Obviously tired of Communist morality plays, audiences applauded any comedy which made them laugh and relax, particularly if it had some cracks about bureaucrats and allusions to current controversies. This explains the success of mediocre plays of Anatoly Sofronov (*The Cook* and *The Cook Gets Married*). Sofronov, as a good Communist, justified all his farcical situations by putting "Leninist" sentiments at the end, but the audience took these just as a part of a boring but obligatory ritual. In the same category, but of slightly better quality, was *The Factory Gal* by Alexander Volodin (or Lifshitz). His heroine, a weaver, is reprimanded by the Party councils and by other well-intentioned citizens because she provokes scandals at dances, laughs at the dogmatics, and fights routine. In her the image of an impulsive, rough, and difficult person came alive and has endeared her to spectators all over the country since 1956.

The anti-liberal comedy *Why Do the Stars Smile?* by Alexander Korneichuk, which was directed against young boys and girls who dream of Paris, jazz, fashion, modernist poets, and other poisonous "miasmas" of capitalism, was short-lived on the stage.

In general, a change in the repertory took place between 1956 and 1969. The Communist, heavy-handed comedy of the Stalin era was replaced by a lighter genre; the dramas of the revolutionary period (by Ivanov, Leonov, Pogodin, Vishnevsky) continued their successful careers alongside the nineteenth-century classics—mainly Chekhov, Gorky, and Ostrovsky. Schwartz's fairy tales finally conquered the Soviet stage.

Of greater scope and artistic significance was the renascence of poetry. A new generation of poets, both men and women, captured the imagination of crowded audiences, while collections of poems by the older masters, from Aseyev to Tikhonov, without counting Mayakovsky and Essenin, were in short supply despite large printings (between 20,000 and 75,000 copies). In 1956 the Day of Poetry was established with immense success throughout the country; it included the usual autographing sessions in bookshops, and evenings where poets read their new works in large halls. Hundreds of thousands of listeners came to those meetings in various cities of the USSR; in Moscow alone, ten to fifteen thousand of all ages would sit for hours in some huge stadium in religious silence to enjoy their favorites reciting; in summer, poems were read in Moscow public squares, mainly in Mayakovsky Place. A collection of some one hundred poets entitled *Day of Poetry* was published. Among the contributors were poets of the older generation, including Leonid Martynov (b. 1905), an excellent craftsman with a strong philosophical bent; and representatives of the middle-aged group who came to the fore only after Stalin's death: the terse, analytical, often aphoristic Boris Slutsky (b. 1919); the more lyrical, sensitive, and emotional Evgeny Vinokurov (b. 1925); and Victor Bokov (b. 1914), interpreter of the "back to nature" tendency. These and many others emerged as a well-defined group. All of them emphasized the intimate self. They wrote on social progress, labor, constructive effort, or patriotism in a more delicate and restrained way than their predecessors; they all abhorred declamatory rhetoric and sermons in verse. It was becoming quite clear that the new generation was formed not only in the school of Mayakovsky but also of Pasternak and Tsvetayeva (whose poems circulated widely in manuscript copies). A new avant-garde was marching; other newcomers, such as Evtushenko, Voznesensky, Akhmadulina, and Okudzhava, were soon to emerge from its ranks. Lyric poetry gave an outlet to emotions and dreams repressed in preceding years; it answered the yearning for imagination, fantasy, inner warmth, self-expression—all of which had been crushed by Communist rationalism and utilitarianism. It also gave form to hidden aspirations for novelty and freedom.

In Russia's history a flowering of poetry has often heralded a new trend in prose: this was the case in the Pushkin period and in the symbolist era at the turn of the century. It looks as if a similar phenomenon was originated by the new poetic flourishing of the 1960's and 1970's.

The most sensational event of 1958 was linked with a poet. In the fall of 1957 Boris Pasternak's *Doctor Zhivago* was published in Italian, initiating numerous translations of the novel in all European languages. Soviet authorities tried to prevent its appearance in Europe, but diplomatic pressure and the personal intervention of Communist dignitaries failed to impress Feltrinelli, the Milan publisher, who held the world rights for the book. All these efforts as well as the huge success of Pasternak's work in the West were never mentioned in the Soviet press. But the awarding of the Nobel Prize to Pasternak on October 23, 1958, could not be kept secret and it provoked an unparalleled explosion of vilification against the poet. Special meetings in Moscow and other cities denounced Pasternak as a "traitor," a "malevolent philistine," a "decadent formalist"; his novel was labeled "reactionary hackwork," "a shameless falsification," and there were attempts to stage an anti-Pasternak "popular movement." Except for a few friends and the editorial staff of *Novy Mir* which refused to print *Doctor Zhivago* and explained its position in a long critical letter, nobody in Russia had read a line of the incriminating book, but this did not stop dozens of "indignant citizens" from sending wrathful but suspiciously identical letters to dailies and weeklies. "I never read this lout Pasternak but I demand his expulsion from the USSR, ... This knave should be thrown out of the country which he betrayed in his lying disgusting novel, ... I am a doctor, I come from a family of physicians, I protest against Pasternak who is slandering our corporation"—these and similar ineptitudes filled entire pages of the *Literary Gazette* and other periodicals. It looked as if the rulers were preparing the ground for "Yielding to the pressure of the masses" and expelling Pasternak from the USSR.

The poet, who had at first "joyfully" accepted the Nobel Prize, was compelled to inform the Swedish Academy on October 29 of his "voluntary refusal of the award" because of the political storm it had aroused. Threatened with deportation he addressed a letter to Khrushchev in which he said: "Leaving my motherland would be equal to death for me. And that is why I ask that you do not take this final measure in relation to me. I can honestly say that I have truly done something for Soviet literature and can be useful to it in the future." He was too optimistic about the future—he could not publish a line until his death; and for the present he was expelled from the Union of Soviet Writers and had to witness all the excommunication rites conducted by Surkov and Tikhonov, the latter a man whose poetic growth owed much to Pasternak's influence.

The vast repercussions of the Pasternak affair throughout the world were probably responsible for the government's decision to cancel the poet's deportation and to leave him in peace at his home, at Peredelkino, a Moscow suburb. His friends and even foreign visitors were allowed to come and talk to him. This showed to what extent times had changed: Khrushchev and his supporters had no desire to create a martyr of a writer who had suddenly won a tremendous international reputation. They were also aware that the whole campaign against Pasternak was very unpopular in the satellite countries and miscarried within Russia: it simply had made him more popular than ever, especially with the younger generation. They well recalled what had happened at one of Pasternak's rare public appearances: he had hesitated for a moment while reciting one of his poems, and the whole audience had acted as a collective prompter, chanting in chorus the missing lines.

On the heels of uproar over Pasternak, the Russian section of the Union of Soviet Writers (which includes members of all the nationalities of the USSR) met in December 1958 with the purpose of "repelling the onslaught of reactionary revisionists," but it accomplished little, and showed the Communist leaders that leniency might be a better policy than reprimands. By this time Khrushchev, who had rid himself of all his competitors, had become the "first man" of the Soviet Union and could afford friendly gestures toward the intelligentsia. They were, however, accompanied by all sorts of reservations and the usual quibbling. A typical example of this casuistry was the revocation by the Central Committee of the resolution adopted by the Party in February 1948 against Muradeli's opera *The Great Friendship*. It began by paying respect to Zhdanov's strictures which "played, on the whole, a positive role in the development of Soviet music," then called his evaluation of individual composers "groundless and unjust," and finally rejected the condemnation of Muradeli and of most prominent Soviet musicians such as Shostakovich, Khachaturian, Prokofiev, Shebalin, Miaskovsky, and others. The leaders of 1958 attributed the earlier blunder to Stalin's subjectivity, which they said, was encouraged by Molotov, Malenkov, and Beria.

This was the attitude adopted by Khrushchev at the Twenty-First Congress of the Party which met on January 27, 1959. Stalin was made a bogey-man, a whipping boy for everything that was wrong in the USSR. Khrushchev was to go as far as changing the name of Stalingrad to Volgograd (to the great discontent of all the veterans who defended that city) and of removing Stalin's mummy from the Mausoleum in Moscow where it reposed next to Lenin's; but he had no force or desire to start radical reforms of the State and the Party and could not break the persistent grip of the Stalinists over many vital positions in administration, industry, and culture. This inevitably created ambiguity and outright contradictions in diverse situations. Thus the Third Congress of Soviet Writers, May 18-23, held again in the Big Hall of the Kremlin and greeted by a flourish of trumpets in the press, failed to fulfill the expectations of the optimists who hoped it would mark the beginning of a new thaw. It petered out into a sort of a compromise between the Party leadership and the writers. In its message to the Congress, the Central Committee formulated for the Nth time the rules of good conduct: "Soviet writers must inspire the people in their struggle for Communism, must educate them according to Communist principles, must develop in them high moral virtues and intransigent rejection of bourgeois ideology and morals . . . writers must become passionate propagandists of the seven-year plan and bring cheerfulness and vigor into the hearts of man . . . We need art capable of inspiring millions and millions of builders of Communism . . . Life showed the fruitfulness and stability of creative principles of socialist realism." This was the same old story of literature as the servant of the State, with the tedious repetition of "must" and the praise of socialist realism.

In practice, there were some secondary compromises: in his speech to the Congress, Khrushchev was rather mild, he used cautious language and assumed a benevolent and paternalistic attitude, acknowledging that writers can settle their own professional problems and their literary quarrels. The part of the speech in which he asked the writers to decide themselves whether a book was good and useful, without expecting a decision from above and "without bothering the government," actually contained a promise of greater freedom, and an indirect relaxation of controls. As a pledge of this agreement Konstantin Fedin was elected secretary general of the Writers' Union instead of Surkov. Smirnov replaced Kochetov at the head of *Literary Gazette,* and Tvardovsky and Panfyo-rov were not only re-instated as editors of *Novy Mir* but also elected as assistant secretaries of the Writers' Union. At the same time the conservatives got a pat on the head: "Soviet writers," declared the Central Committee, "evinced maturity and firmness in fighting bourgeois ideology and weak revisionist incursions."

Like many adjustments this one did not fool or satisfy anybody. The absence at the Writers' Congress of such personalities as Sholokhov, Ehrenburg, Panova, Leonov, Simonov, Ovechkin, and many others and the ominous "strike of silence" pursued by most of them was probably one of the factors leading to a further "softening" of official policy between 1959 and 1962. Some observers believe that in 1960-61 the encouraged liberals were again on the crest of a new wave, and that there was a stir in literature: more freedom in themes and techniques, more independence, more spirit in the rebuttal of Stalinists. This movement was evident mostly in the short story which attracted a steadily increasing number of writers.

It would be preposterous to speak in this connection of a crisis of the novel but it is symptomatic that no Soviet full-length narrative of significance has been published in the early 1960's. The second part of *The Virgin Soil Upturned,* which Sholokohov finally brought to a conclusion after an interval of 30 years, can hardly be said to disprove this claim. Particularly striking was the decline of the industrial novel, of which not a single work of average literary worth was produced. A typical example of the latter was the long, ambitious, but greatly muddled novel by Very Ketlinskaya, *It Is Not Worth Living Otherwise,* in which the author hardly succeeded in organically joining a story about coal gasification with the criss-crossing love affairs of her protagonists.

The novels portraying the "new Communist hero" did not fare any better: their low level was represented by *Meet Baluyev* by Vadim Kozhevnikov (b. 1909). Baluyev was a literary mixture containing all the ingredients of the exemplary man—vigor, devotion, sense of duty and sacrifice, enough eccentricity to pepper the dish, and enough kindliness combined with roughness to make it attractive—but utterly failing to project a living image. A certain substitute to the traditional industrial novel was offered by

Daniil Granin who explored the world of scientists, of laboratories, of research, and experiments in *The Searchers* (1961) and *Attacking the Thunderstorm* (1962), both interesting narratives. The only novels that were more or less palatable were sciencefiction narratives by Ivan Efremov (1907-72), the head of a whole group of writers in this genre, which became very popular in 1950-60; it charmed both young and old and gave the Russians the only kind of entertaining reading that Soviet writers were allowed to produce (it is not worth mentioning a few badly written "patriotic spy novels"). The brothers Strugatsky (Arkady b. 1925 and Boris b. 1933) at the beginning of their literary career in the 1960's seemed to have followed Efremov's road in science fiction and "cosmic themes." They showed, however, a much deeper interest in the psychology of their protagonists and displayed a great deal of humor. In later works they shifted toward social fantasy with a definite stress on "anti-utopia." In their sharp novels *Snail on the Hillside* (1968) and *Bad Swans* (1970), and in various short stories they drew pessimistic visions of the future of mankind and portrayed the state of the following centuries as a grotesque machine bent on man's bondage. In general they emphasized the elements of satire and irony, as well as their strong protest against any forms of man's spiritual oppression. The Strugatskys have been severely assailed by Communist conservatives for their liberal and libertarian tendencies, and some of their works, serialized in periodicals, were not authorized to appear in book form.

Among many reasons for the decline of the novel was the fact that a large work of fiction was more open to criticism because it was expected to present all sorts of things according to official requirements—a large panorama of social life, positive heroes, a happy ending, and other clichés of socialist realism. The shorter literary form was naturally more limited in scope, and therefore presented a reduced surface for criticism.

In any case, whether for reasons of safety, or simply following a prevalent literary current, a whole group of excellent writers, mostly liberals, chose the medium of the short story. Their manner definitely derived from Chekhov: they also wanted to describe without making a judgment or drawing a moral conclusion. In the

1880-90 period Chekhov was accused by radical critics of a lack of ideas and principles. The appearance of tales in his tradition in the 1960's was in itself an answer to the official insistence on "Party-mindedness" and the educational aims of literature. The most talented representative of the short story school, Yury Kazakov (b. 1927), succeeded in describing small incidents in the lives of lonely, non-heroic people without ever raising his voice. He conveyed a melancholic, at times bitter mood and a certain sense of the Russian nature which recalled Turgenev and Bunin. It would be difficult to find political hints in his unadorned, almost plotless renderings of love and parting, of contrasts between youth and old age, of daily joys and sorrows. A village carpenter dreams of living in the city, he goes there to put his moribund wife into a hospital and in doing so anticipates all the urban pleasures he will enjoy. A plain young girl is ready to fall in love with a lad who does not care for her and who acts like a knave. A greedy old woman who rents rooms in an old country house spoils the life of her daughter by avaricious nastiness. An engineer, who goes fishing on a few days' vacation, fails to understand the suffering of a young girl, his travel companion, and abandons her ruthlessly. A middle-aged official comes for an inspection visit to a Northern island, meets a woman who would have given him all the happiness in the world, and parts from her to return to his daily chores. These and similar stories of solitude and defeat form the main bulk of Kazakov's work. No wonder he has often been blamed for "pessimism" and "morbid interest in weak passive creatures."

In general, the short story writers of the 'sixties who have broken away from compulsory cheerfulness are often gloomy and do not hesitate to bring out the folly, cruelty, meanness, and lust of ordinary humans: until very recently such defects were attributed in Soviet fiction only to villains and foreign agents. The departure from the artificial mythology of the "positive hero" re-introduced a realistic note into the short story, particularly in the works of young authors. A reader might come across some of these tales in Moscow's and Leningrad's literary magazines during this period: a poor peasant father comes to visit his prosperous, well-established son in the city, but no communication is possible between the two, both belong to different social and human categories. A widow of a war hero is re-married and appears to the friend of her late husband as she is in reality—a petty, egotistical female (both stories by Kazakevich). A man of conscience who sticks to truth gets into trouble with opportunists and go-getters (Voinovich). A man of humble origin pretending he comes from a princely family meets a true aristocrat posing for safety's sake as a hereditary proletarian (Valeria Gherasimova). Perhaps a more affirmative note is struck by Yuri Naghibin (b. 1924), author of some excellent tales. One of his heroes, a weak, spineless youth grows and matures in the ordeal of the war and dies a man. Vas'ka the hunter loves his wife so passionately that the villagers call them the newlyweds although they have been married for six years—and their love is opposed to the emotional sterility of a city official.

Kazakov, Kazakevich, Naghibin, and their colleagues are representative of a whole group of writers who have brought genuine emotions, psychological insight, humaneness, and a careful objective rendering of reality into contemporary Soviet literature. They belong to a generation which had not been corrupted in Stalin's school of fear and handicapped by dogmatic blinders. Their young contemporaries do not resemble the well-behaved boys and girls portrayed by the "varnishers of reality." *Youth*, the Komsomol monthly, dared to publish in 1961 *The Ticket to the Stars* by Vasily Aksyonov (b. 1932, the son of Communist parents executed during the Stalinist purges), who depicted the Soviet teenagers without any flattery. The naturalistic precision, with which he rendered the coarse slang used by the young people among themselves, incensed conservative critics. Aksyonov's heroes, three boys and one girl, are bored by Party controls, by official slogans, by mandatory political jargon, so they ardently dream of freedom and adventure. In his other long tales "Oranges from Morocco" (1962) and particularly "Halfway to the Moon" (1963), Aksyonov focused on the mixture of churlishness and romanticism which he found so typical of his generation. He did it in a terse, almost naturalistic manner, reproducing the ribald speech of his protagonists, filled with profanities and unprintable words; the "code" language they employed in talking to each other was a sign of their alienation from adults, from the world of falsehood and rhetoric they hated intensely. Aksyonov's works enjoy enormous success among the readers and they were discussed in the press at length; to the Stalinists he was a "pessimist" and "slanderer." He provoked their furor in 1968 because of his new novelette, *Tare of Barrels*. Aksyonov himself defined it as "a work with exaggerations and dreams." This highly imaginative and profound tale describes a motley company of people who, while traveling together on a lorry loaded with empty barrels, discuss their own lives, conflicts, moods, and aspirations in unconventional and by no means Marxian terms.

Aksyonov's attempt to compile a historical novel on Krasin was certainly a flop.

The labels of "detractors" were affixed to the whole group of young authors who spoke of their contemporaries in the same frank fashion, using crude and colloquial language. Most of the group were published in *Youth*, but the Stalinists failed in their 1965 campaign against this magazine: the latter's circulation in 1967 went over two million copies. This popularity, however, brought about stricter control of the magazine by the Party: by the autumn of 1969 Evtushenko and Aksyonov were dropped from the editorial board which was re-shuffled in the same way as certain other regional and Moscow publications had been.

30

Posthumous Revivals

BULGAKOV, PLATONOV, ZABOLOTSKY

The words "arrest, execution, labor camp" are rarely mentioned in the Soviet press and are banned from literary encyclopedias. These blunt expressions are usually replaced by the current euphemism "illegally repressed." No other information is given about the imprisonment and death of many hundreds of novelists, poets, and critics, victims of Communist terror. We are still ignorant of the circumstances in which Babel, Pilnyak, Koltsov, Kirshon, Meyerhold, Tretyakov, and many, many others were "repressed." The official formula is usually followed by a brief notice: "posthumously rehabilitated." This does not apply to all writers and their works: *Doctor Zhivago* by Pasternak, Zamyatin's writings, Pilnyak's tales, and so forth, are still on the black list. And legal rehabilitation resulting in the closing of the political case does not mean an immediate reprint of the innocent victim's works. The most important posthumous revivals have been delayed for several years. This happened with Mikhail Bulgakov, Andrey Platonov, and Nikolay Zabolotsky.

In 1967, a year before his death, Paustovsky complained that

negligible books are presented [in Soviet Russia] as masterpieces . . . whereas excellent works are hidden and only see the light of day a quarter of a century after they were written. The damage done is irreparable. Had the works of writers like Platonov and Bulgakov been made available soon after they were completed, we all would have been immeasurably richer in spirit.

Bulgakov's literary road was especially thorny. Born in Kiev in 1891 into the family of a theology professor, Bulgakov studied medicine and practiced in the Ukraine until he moved to Moscow at the age of thirty and devoted himself to literature. From the beginning of his career he revealed himself as a satirical storyteller and playwright with a strong bent toward the fantastic and a keen interest in moral conflicts. His stories of 1925—"Devilry" and "Fatal Eggs"—were sharp grotesques; in particular, the latter describes how the peasants of a State agricultural farm mistakenly receive, instead of hens' eggs, some strange ovoids imported for zoological experiments, which turn into monstrous reptiles. The huge snakes multiply with lightning rapidity, devour and destroy everything around them, spread through the country, menacing Moscow until a polar winter cold freezes them to death. This Wellsian anti-utopia is at the same time an exposure of bureaucracy crammed with precise almost naturalistic details. There was a moment when critics labeled Bulgakov a realist mainly because of his novel *The White Guard*, published in 1925 and transformed into a play, *The Days Of Turbins*, the year after. Its subject matter was treacherous and politically dangerous; it was the chronicle of a military family of country gentry whose members join the White armies, fight the Communists, and either perish or have a change of heart after terrible defeats and disappointments. However, the Moscow Art Theater staged it with clamorous success. Its fate was decided by the fact that Stalin saw the play, liked it very much, and let it run for hundreds of performances. Then it was banned, authorized again in 1932, and repressed for the second time. Other plays by Bulgakov (*The Run, Zoika's Apartment*) exposing the doubtful morals of the NEP period, and his parody *The Purple Island* were severely criticized by the Communist dailies.

Bulgakov was chosen as a whipping boy by the diehards and reduced to isolation and starvation. He was condemned to silence; his works were declared unfit for the "programmed literature of Communist persuasion," and Bulgakov said that they were only useful to pile up in the drawers of his desk. A typical example of such unpublished writings was his half-fantastic, half-symbolic *The Heart of a Dog*, a tale about a famous surgeon engaged in a daring experiment: he transplants into a stray dog the brain cells and vital organs of an average, recently killed Soviet youth. The dog acquires the speech and attributes of a biped but becomes so coarse, vulgar, and obnoxious that the desperate surgeon resorts to a reverse operation and returns the dog to his primary canine status. The doctor draws bitter conclusions from his failure: "Scientific experiments are useless for producing a higher type of man, human nature can be changed only by compassion and kindliness; terror, constraint and all kinds of violence, be it red, brown or white, are completely futile." No wonder that this story, banned in the USSR, saw the light of day only forty-three years later—and, of course, abroad.

Bulgakov had even less luck with his plays: most of them were considered subversive because their main theme (as in *Molière*) was the conflict between the writer and the totalitarian regime denying the freedom of creation. The same theme reappears with particular eloquence in *The Master and Margarita* where repressive society destroys an imaginative artist.

When Bulgakov and his family found themselves in desperate poverty, help came unexpectedly from Stalin: one night he phoned the writer and offered him a job as artistic adviser at the Moscow Art Theater. It saved Bulgakov from destitution, but his works were still refused publication. He wrote thirty plays, but his *Molière*, staged in 1936, was soon banned. *The Last Days* (on Pushkin) was produced three years after his death (he died in 1940), his sparkling (unfinished) novel *Theatrical Romance* appeared twenty years later, and his biography of Molière was printed only in 1962. Five years later, and more than a quarter of a century after it had been written, his chief work, *The Master and Margarita*, finally was offered to Soviet readers (at first with cuts; the complete version was printed in the USSR only after having been issued abroad). It is undoubtedly a major masterpiece of contemporary Soviet literature. *The Master and Margarita*, a large (over 400-page) multi-level novel, succeeds in preserving a perfect unity of creative intent and a subtle coordination of different, often contrasting themes. This inner coherence and coalescence of various parts of the narrative present a real obstacle for academic dissection and analytical exposition—a critic is compelled to consider separately what actually forms an organic artistic whole.

Bulgakov worked on this novel for nine years and wrote not less than eight versions: he completed the final text just a few weeks prior to his death. A fantastic plot runs like a unifying thread through the complex, multicolored story: the Devil, called Woland, Professor of Black Magic, comes to Moscow with his assistants, including a black cat, who can take many aspects and speaks excellent Russian. Satan and his retinue play all sorts of insane and obscene tricks and jokes on the ordinary Muscovites, on the crowded audience of a variety theater, on pompous bureaucrats and ungifted writers. At first glance, this hilarious extravaganza with a number of comic episodes turns into a merciless exposure of the Soviet system, of the stupidity of arrogant rulers and the prejudices of their inefficient underlings. Alternating snappy scenes, shifting action from ridiculous situations to tragic events, the author maintains unflagging suspense and a fast pace, to the reader's enjoyment. Highly amusing are the chapters on Massolit, an easily recognizable parody of the Union of Soviet Writers with thinly disguised portraits of popular novelists and playwrights and with sarcastic descriptions of their business meetings and drunken revelries in a privileged restaurant. *The Master and Margarita* in general draws a caustic picture of Russia in the 1930's and reveals the unpleasant reality behind the official facade.

But the realistic painting is blended with supernatural happenings and symbolic images. In the opening chapter Woland, the Prince of Darkness, meets in a park the poet Ivan and the smug literary functionary Berlioz, for whom he predicts an imminent violent death. Both Russians are atheists and believe neither in God nor in Satan. Woland laughs at their naïveté, tells them about the confrontation between Pontius Pilate and Jesus Christ, and affirms having witnessed Christ's trial, crucifixion, and burial. Woland's story—beautifully written in restrained and impressive prose—becomes the leading subject of the book. Berlioz is killed by a speeding trolleybus; Ivan, who understands that he has met the Devil in person and tries to alert people to the Evil One and his dangerous doings, is taken for a madman and put into a psychiatric clinic. The doctors diagnose as hallucinations Ivan's tales about Satan and the latter's vivid report of what had happened in Jerusalem two thousand years ago. For a while, the only positive thing Ivan gains from medical care is his decision to stop writing bad verse. But suddenly Ivan is supported in his pronouncements about the Devil by the nightly visits of a neighboring inmate who calls himself the Master. Without revealing his name, he tells his misfortunes: he wrote a novel on Pontius Pilate but it was rejected by Moscow publishers who were frightened by the biblical subject of the book and the introduction of Jesus' image into Soviet letters. The Master burnt part of his manuscript, abandoned Margarita, his beautiful mistress, and finally landed in an insane asylum. He believes in the existence of Satan and ignores the fact that Margarita, on the brink of suicide, had met Woland. She secured the Devil's help, freed the Master and obtained for him the reward of eternal peace. The scenes of her flying through the air as a witch, the intercession of the apostle Matthew and his dialogue with Woland form the summit of Bulgakov's fantastic visions. Some of these scenes are reminiscent of the Valpurgis Night and Goethe's Faust.

When *The Master and Margarita* was serialized in the monthly magazine *Moskva* at the end of 1967, twenty-seven years after the death of its author, it became a literary sensation. Soviet readers were not accustomed to the abundance of fictional richness, to the mixture of imagination, satire, and black humor, to a rotation of moving and frightening episodes—and to such a daring emphasis of the theme of Christianity. To read a story which does not pretend to be a philosophical work and seemingly only entertains, but is actually profound, serious, and raises the problems of universal good and evil, was a new and exciting experience for the Russian public. The name of Bulgakov, especially after the appearance of *The Master and Margarita* in book form, became widely known in the Soviet Union, and his earlier works have been eagerly read and discussed in a number of critical essays and more or less sophisticated attempts to discover and comment on the true meaning of his fantasies.

It was certainly a most startling posthumous revival of an author who had been banned during his lifetime as an "antipolitical" storyteller and light humorist. Entirely different was the case of Andrey Platonov whose present popularity seems less complete and less dramatic.

The son of a railway worker, Andrey Platonov (1899-1951) fought during the civil war as a Red Army private, then earned the degree of agricultural engineer at the Technological Institute, worked in this capacity in the provinces, wrote poems and stories, and settled as a journalist and writer in Moscow in 1927, when his first collection of sketches, *The Sluices of Epiphany*, was published. Other works followed, bringing him some modest recognition. *Chevengur*, a tale on which he worked more than two years and which is now considered his best novel, could not pass the censor, with the exception of the first chapters entitled "Origins of a Master" (later published as a separate work of fiction). *Chevengur* tells the adventures of a group of proletarians, mostly eccentrics and queer characters, who dream of building a Socialist society overnight, and, after roaming across the country, choose a forlorn little town for their great experiment. They are animated by the best intentions, but have no idea how to translate them into reality. They begin by exterminating the bourgeois and eradicating all outspoken opposition, but neither cruelty nor goodwill suffice in organizing the production of commodities or even supplying the population with food. Their failure is complete, and a brawny blacksmith sums up the situation: "People who shout about the Revolution make people die from hunger, and the Party is filled with wretched wastrels." *Chevengur*'s implications are quite clear: Communist ideas have been developed by sophisticated minds who have lost any organic connection with nature and therefore have provoked havoc and confusion without achieving anything durable.

The prevalent feeling in *Chevengur* is compassion: Platonov pities all his protagonists—the innocent victims and their executioners—the naïve dreamers and narrow-minded officials. In general he cannot hide his sympathy for all human beings.

Chevengur was banned in the Soviet Union. It was published abroad in 1973, forty-three years after Platonov finished its last chapter. After reading the novel in manuscript, Gorky wrote to the author:

Willingly or unwillingly, you have presented reality under a lyrical and satirical light. Despite your commiseration and tenderness toward people, your personages are treated ironically, the reader sees them not as revolutionaries but as maniacs and lunatics. All this, of course, is unacceptable to our censors.

Even benevolent friends pointed to the absence of a definite plot and a certain vagueness of psychological characteristics, and some critics spoke of the mixture of basic unreality with down-to-earth details as a proof of Gogol's influence.

Akin to *Chevengur* in spirit are two other outstanding short Platonov novels, *Djann* and *The Pit* ("Kotlovan" in Russian, which means an excavation dug for a building foundation). Here again we are dealing with an anti-utopia: the inhabitants of a village want to raise an enormous community house for brotherly cooperative living—sort of a Fourier "phalanstery" (even though they have never heard of the French social reformer). But the project does not advance beyond the deep excavation hole and everything gradually peters out in mud and desolation. (*The Pit* was published only in the West.) And still mankind seeks happiness and looks for a better life. This theme underlies the tale of *Djann,* about a hungry, destitute tribe in Russian Central Asia, between the Sea of Aral and the Iranian border. These imaginary nomads ("Djann" in Persian means soul or spirit) roam the terrible desert of Sary-Kamysh, a depressed land several feet below sea level. They search, like the Jews led by Moses, for a promised land but never reach it. Famished, unhappy, and miserable they lose faith, and their chief, the young Tchagatayev, who has made them advance up until the end, sees how they disperse and how the last wanderers head off toward all four points of the compass. The drive for bread and water, the urge for peace and a parcel of land to settle on are irrepressible in men, but Platonov seems to hint at the failure of human aspirations—be it revolution or the Djanns' primitive wanderings in a dusty and salty wilderness, or in any other abysmal region. Despite its gloomy, nightmarish mood *Djann* was published in the posthumous editions of Platonov's tales, which also included many more cheerful stories on "little people" and their daily lives and strange attitudes toward the problems of existence. Most of Platonov's heroes are workmen, artisans, and semi-literate eccentrics. These simple, ordinary individuals are always beset with basic questions: who are we, where do we come from, and where are we going—and what is our relationship to our neighbors, to the state, to nature, to God? Their love of life is deep and strong, and one collection of Platonov's stories has a revealing title: *This Fierce and Beautiful World*. Everyone, in his opinion, possesses an inherent need for beauty, justice, equality, and humanity. His characters approach revolutionary events from the inside, and Platonov's originality consists exactly in his capacity to render the common people's attitudes, to describe their torments and painful clashes with ugly reality. Platonov himself was afraid that the popular revolutionary outburst had been subdued and deformed by the stiff dogmatists and their useless projects, by a rationalistic bureaucracy alienated from the natural sources of life, by "giantomania" and by falsification of noble slogans. This anxiety caused the ironic and skeptical mood of his tales—and the Communist critics bombarded him with reproaches and insults. One of them dubbed him "the enemy," and Platonov was forced to hide his identity and sign his articles with various pen names.

Moreover, the conservative reviewers were irritated by his unusual style. Platonov wrote just like his protagonists talked, employing the idiom—and also the slang—of the proletariats and the peasants, and reproducing the crude ungrammatical turns of their speech. In many cases the hazy thoughts of a simpleminded man were reflected in his quest for the right phrase and gave the impression of the painful birth of the right word. The book's terms, borrowed from the Communist press, radio, and television and usually disfigured, are mixed in Platonov's stories with the stuttering efforts of an uneducated person trying to invent a new, hardly adequate locution. What at first appears as the speech of the inarticulate, a kind of mumbling monologue, becomes—on further reading—a highly individualistic style and a rare linguistic achievement. But it was only in the 1970's, twenty years after his death, that Platonov was recognized as one of the most original writers of his time and his comeback in Soviet literature was accepted as an act of justice. Yet many of his manuscripts are still kept in State archives and it is not known when Platonov's complete collected works will be published in the Soviet Union.

The life story of the poet Nikolay Zabolotsky has some traits in common with that of Platonov. Born in 1903 in Kazan, Zabolotsky came from peasant stock and grew up in a village, studied in a small northern town, discovered Moscow and Leningrad at the age of seventeen, studied in a teachers college, and began to write and publish verse. His literary formation in the first years of the Revolution was influenced by Khlebnikov, Mayakovsky, and Pasternak. He was close to the futurists and belonged in the late 1920's to the group "Oberiuts." His first collection of poems, *Printed Columns* (an approximate translation of the Russian title "Stolbtsy"), published in 1929, was an excellent example of expressionism. Initiated in Germany, this trend acquired some national traits in Russia and a set of stylistic conventions: parody turning into a rough grotesque, strange metaphors based on the systematic distortion of objects and nature, whimsical images rejecting rationality and musicality, and a representation of objects as live creatures, humans and animals as inanimate matter. Zabolotsky said that "words fly into the world and become objects." His poems were erroneously mistaken for the descriptive abundance found in the Flemish school because he depicted markets, feasts, gargantuan repasts, drunken revelries, mountains of meat and fowl, the corporality of food, as well as wide-hipped females and red-faced trenchermen. But all his representative pieces are sheer exaggerations and their colors too garish. Besides, there is a realistic intent in his expressionism: he started by drawing business rogues, speculators, and their fat wives of the NEP period, and only gradually, in a sort of a poetic inebriation, created a whole museum of monsters and freaks enjoying "barrels of beer and kegs of toasts and boozy speeches."

Printed Columns came out in 1929 in a limited edition of twelve hundred copies, but most of them were immediately confiscated because influential critics dubbed the book "a calumny on socialism." It was thirty-five years before the censors allowed the poet's first book to be included in a 1965 collection of his works.

Already in the poems of the late 1920's Zabolotsky used not only the four-foot iambic verse, with sudden interruptions and shifts of measure, but also the ponderous measure of the eighteenth-century odes. The passage from expressionism to what is called "pseudo-classicism" became quite obvious in his long poems, *The Triumph of Agriculture, The Bowels of the Earth, The North,* and others—their majestic pace was solemn and full, rhythmic and consistent, without ever becoming inflated. Zabolotsky definitely changed from the elaborate grotesque to a more simple structure and from a parody to lyrical reflection and the poetization of natural phenomena. His poetry between 1930 and 1936 bears a resemblance to brass sonority and the wide-measured stride of Derzhavin. Their formal beauty and aesthetic perfection, however, left the Soviet critics cold, and they accused Zabolotsky of hiding from contemporary life in an antiquated past and a pernicious pantheism. It should be stressed that Zabolotsky's feeling toward nature is quite different from that of Tiutchev (with whom he is often mistakenly compared). He does not see the abyss, the chaos, the frightful cosmic mysteries as Tiutchev did. Animism prevails in Zabolotsky's mature poetry of his second period; he spiritualizes plants and rocks, converses with birds and beasts, and his universe resounds like a marvelous temple harmonium. His philosophy is summed up in *Metamorphozisi*: "Everything changes, but the circular rotation rules the world. What once was a bird, is now a written page in front of me, my thought in times of yore existed as a simple flower, and what was myself, is perhaps growing somewhere in the realm of plants."

But these and similar lines seemed suspicious and politically harmful. When *The Triumph of Agriculture* (1933) was published in the Leningrad magazine (Star) *Zvezda*, printing of that issue was stopped and the original text, accused of anti-*kolkhoze* tendencies, was replaced by a censored one. For years Zabolotsky was not permitted to publish a book. In 1938 he was arrested, submitted to interrogation with torture, and, after many surprising coincidences and interventions, was—without trial—sentenced to eight years in a concentration camp. He spent them building roads in Oriental Siberia and Asiatic Karaganda. During all this time he could not write, and only a few poems after 1946 have some hints of what he had endured when—as he said later—"The stars, symbols of freedom, did not look any longer on men."

Until his death in 1958 Zabolotsky earned his living by translating foreign poetry into Russian. He was an outstanding translator and, among other excellent works, was particularly praised for his transposition into modern Russian of the medieval *Lay of Prince Igor*. He also began to write poetry again. These verses—philosophical meditations, lyrical confessions of a belated love—were mostly tainted with mystical allusions and often reached an elevated degree of inspiration and poetic intensity. At the same time he composed a remarkable and linguistically brilliant tale in verse, *Rubbruk in Mongolia*, about the travels of a thirteenth-century monk into Mongolia to convert its population to Catholicism. But despite all these achievements, Zabolotsky's spirits and health were crippled (he was often sick as a result of the cruel experiences of imprisonment and camp). He told one of his friends that the blossoming of his talent had been violently and forcibly blighted at its very apex. But what he did write and leave us is sufficient to rank him as one of the most unparalleled poets of the Soviet era. This became quite clear in the late 'sixties and 'seventies during his posthumous revival, when his works could finally reach the large masses of Russian readers.

31

Alexander Solzhenitsyn

THE GREAT CHALLENGER

The year 1962 in Moscow ended with a literary sensation: the monthly magazine *Novy Mir* (New World) published in its November issue *One Day in the Life of Ivan Denisovich* by Alexander Solzhenitsyn, a novel which was destined to throw the USSR and later the West into an uproar. In 1963 it was also published in Moscow in book form (first printing of 700,000 copies, followed by another one of 100,000).

The author's name was completely unknown but the subject matter of his short novel was stunning: for the first time in Soviet literature the full truth was told about what went on behind the barbed wire of Stalin's concentration camps, which by 1953 held four million inmates and 250,000 guards. Solzhenitsyn's work was a sensation; newsstands were besieged; one Moscow bookshop with an allotment of ten copies of *Novy Mir* had 1200 subscriptions between noon and dinner time. In two days 94,000 copies of the magazine were sold.

Solzhenitsyn did not try to shock the reader. He presented the most gruesome details in a matter of fact way without exaggeration or indignation, with sparks of humor; and this probably intensified the impact of his restrained and stylized narrative.

The hero of the novel, Ivan Denisovich Shukhov, is a humble hard-working peasant with native shrewdness and a practical mind. During the war his unit had been encircled, and he had been taken prisoner by the Germans. He escaped and made his way back to the Russian lines, where he was arrested, accused of spying for the enemy, and sentenced to eight years of hard labor. He has accepted his fate with resignation and is only trying to survive. This struggle for survival is the main theme of *One Day*.

Solzhenitsyn follows in minute detail the daily routine of Shukhov's life: reveille at 7 A.M. with the risk of three days in solitary
confinement if one is late in jumping out of a bug-ridden bunk;
breakfast in the crowded mess hall—mashed and boiled gruel with
fish skeletons floating next to rotten cabbage leaves; roll call in
the arctic frost, the prisoners lined up waiting to be frisked by the
guards. Then departure for work, in slow procession, under the
escort of police dogs and wardens who shoot at anyone who steps
to the right or left of the ranks; the desolation of the snowy, icy,
northern steppe where prisoners mix cement and build walls and
roofs; short intervals for soup, and again roll call, search of each
inmate, and heavy slumber in cold barracks, 240 men in each of
them piling up everything they find to warm their frozen limbs.

At the end of a day of hard labor and minor incidents Shukhov
feels that he has been lucky: he has not fallen ill, he has escaped
the detention cell, managed to eat an extra bowl of soup, got a
pinch of tobacco, hid from the guards a piece of wire and a
string. The story ends: "Almost a happy day. There were 3,053
days like that in his sentence, from reveille to lights out. The
three extra ones were because of the leap years."

Shukhov is a "simple heart," a beloved type in Russian literature from Turgenev to Tolstoy. Adverse critics reproached the
author of *One Day* for having offered another version of Platon
Karatayev (in Tolstoy's *War and Peace*). But Solzhenitsyn also
gives excellent portraits of other inmates, mostly innocent victims
of absurd denunciations and abuse.

One Day had tremendous political impact: it opened the flood-
gate, thus allowing other revelations of Stalinist terror to rush
out. During 1964 and 1965 these were mainly recollections and
factual reports without any artistic pretensions: Alexander Gorbatov, an old Communist and Red Army general, told in his *Years
and Wars* how he was beaten and tortured by the secret police
and how he worked as a convict in Siberian mines. *What I Went
Through* by Boris Diakov, *Notes of Kolyma* by Georgy Shelest,
Men Remain Men by Yury Pilar, and many others, gave accounts
of indignities, humiliations, and starvation endured in concentration camps and penal colonies. Among the works of fiction published between 1963 and 1966 there were numerous references to
the terrifying aspects of Stalin's regime.

After 1966, however, this trend was more strictly controlled by the censors as a consequence of the increasing influence of hard-line Stalinists in the ruling institutions. Various authors were therefore compelled to secretly send their memoirs and confessions abroad, publishing them in Europe and the United States. Among them were pathetic and terrifying books by Eugenia Guinzburg, Lydia Chukovskaya (*The Deserted House*), Anatoly Marchenko (arrested four times), Galina Serebriakova (an old member of the Party), and particularly the stark realistic and gloomy short stories by Varlam Shalamov (b. 1907), a poet who spent many years in northern labor camps.

One Day was not only a political sensation, its publication being authorized by Khrushchev after the intervention of Tvardovsky, it also has great literary merit because of its stylistic originality. The events of the story are seen through Shukhov's eyes, his thoughts and impressions are rendered in a blend of popular speech and prisoner's slang. The realistic crudeness of dialogue is skillfully mitigated by the rhythm and tone of the narrative. Its masterfully controlled racy language, which recalls that of Remizov, its rich texture and its ring of authenticity, which was such a relief after the false pathos of most Soviet fiction, show an artistic maturity quite surprising in a newcomer. Born in 1918 into a family of Cossack intellectuals, Solzhenitsyn was brought up by his mother, a secondary school teacher; he graduated in mathematics from the University of Rostov on the Don and took correspondence courses in literature at the University of Moscow. He fought in World War II reaching the rank of artillery captain. In 1945, while advancing with his unit in Germany, he was arrested and after months in Lubianka jail in Moscow, was, without investigation or trial, sentenced to eight years in a concentration camp for having spoken in a letter about the military shortcomings of "the whiskered one," obviously referring to Stalin. His correspondent, also an army officer, got ten years. Solzhenitsyn spent four years in Karaganda, the desert region of Kazakstan, where the convicts had their numbers painted on the front, chest, back, and knees. At the end of his stretch, his term was prolonged by another three years of exile. Solzhenitsyn was released in 1956 and the following year his case was reviewed by a military tribunal. During his first confrontation with the judges, he read them excerpts from *One Day* and was finally "rehabilitated." He was then allowed to settle in Riazan, a provincial town in Central Russia, where he worked as a mathematics teacher. Almost immediately he began to write.

The short stories he published in 1963 confirmed the impression that Solzhenitsyn was an excellent writer, perhaps the most interesting and promising one of the post-Stalin era. Particularly impressive was *Matryona's Homestead*, a moving tale about a poor unassuming woman in a miserable backward *kolkhoze*; she is kind, helps everybody, and falls victim to a catastrophe brought about by the greed and dishonesty of certain villagers. Solzhenitsyn concludes his story by evoking a popular saying: "no village can exist without one righteous person." Matryona, the simplehearted one, a descendant of Turgenev's Lukeria in "The Living Relic," is conceived as a true Christian model of self-sacrifice with love of one's neighbor. No wonder that Solzhenitsyn was accused by the diehards of praising "bourgeois virtues." He was also attacked because of his *For the Just Cause* (1963), an ironic and sharp exposé of narrow-minded insensitive bureaucrats acting like junior Stalins.

With the exception of a short story ("Zakhar-Kalita," 1966), no works by Solzhenitsyn were published in the Soviet Union between 1963 and 1967. This was obviously an enforced silence. The authorities were resentful of Solzhenitsyn's strong influence on the younger generation and of the enthusiastic acclaim his writings received from the Russian literary world.

Solzhenitsyn's situation worsened after the fourth Writers Congress in 1967 to which he addressed a courageous letter, attacking censorship and bureaucratic restrictions and hailing cultural freedom. The Presidium of the Congress did not dare to read it in the plenary session, but it circulated widely in manuscript copy and Solzhenitsyn became the symbol of moral integrity and fearlessness for the Russian intellectuals. In his book of memoirs *The Calf Butts the Oak*, published in 1975 (English translation 1976), he tells about his subsequent wrangles and litigations with the Union of Soviet Writers and describes his desperate attempts to have his works published. He also discloses the foul play and machinations of the KGB (State Security Agency) which confiscated many of his manuscripts.* He won a unique position in Soviet society as an independent liberal and defender of human rights. Opposed by official hostility and threatened with administrative repression, he made a final decision to publish his novels in foreign countries. By the end of the 'sixties his two major novels—*The First Circle* and *Cancer Ward*—appeared abroad not only in Russian but also in numerous translations. Hailed as outstanding works in the best tradition of Russia's great classics, they became best-sellers in Europe, America, and Asia and made the author's name world famous.

Written between 1955 and 1964 in the mode of critical realism and based on personal experiences, *The First Circle* (the title obviously refers to Dante's description of hell in *The Divine Comedy*) offers an incisive and often astonishing, almost fantastic picture of Mavrino, a special prison in the vicinity of Moscow. Its inmates, scientists and technicians brought together from different places of detention, are compelled to work on government projects, usually connected with secret police activities. Because of this particular kind of research they are granted better food and some milder rules (figuratively they find themselves in the first of hell's nine circles). There are jails such as "the Sukhanov Villa"—so named, ironically, because of its torture-like treatment which leads the inmates either to death or to a psychiatric ward. While still alive they have the "Sunday privilege" of free access to the toilet. "Only those," writes Solzhenitsyn, "who have passed through this kind of prison can appreciate all the value of this immortal 'Sunday freedom.'"

The 281 prisoners of Mavrino guarded by fifty wardens and surrounded by spies and voluntary informers, are better off than other prisoners and they are visited once or twice a year by their relatives—although they can neither kiss nor even touch them. The action of the novel covers four days, at the end of 1949, and it unfolds a whole gallery of characters, from the mathematician Chelnov, who had spent eighteen years in jail and camps, to the linguist Rubin, a convinced Marxist, or the revolutionary of the 'twenties, Adamson, who like the engineer Nerjin, considers himself a victim of "the tortuous flow of history that went astray."

* And gives a vivid portrait of Tvardovsky, the editor of *Novy Mir*, his supporter.

The author also describes a few protagonists belonging to the ruling class and living outside the mad world of barbed wires and prison walls, although one of them, the young diplomat Volodin, makes a mistake and is caught in the cruel game of the security organs.

A separate chapter draws a remarkable portrait of Stalin at the age of seventy. The psychological depth and carefully chosen realistic details make these pages on Stalin a unique, unprecedented achievement in Soviet literature, perhaps more profound than that which Stalin's daughter, Svetlana Alliluyeva, who fled from Russia and became an *émigrée* in the United States, revealed to us in her two extremely interesting books (*Twenty Letters to a Friend* and *One Year Only*). *The First Circle*, a vast narrative of 660 pages, maintains the classical unity of place, time, and action and shows Solzhenitsyn's art of composition despite occasional prolixity, slowing of pace, and overabundance of minutiae. Although it is often called a "political novel" and compared to Dostoevsky's *Notes from the Underground*, it has symbolic and allegorical overtones as if Solzhenitsyn saw his native land as a huge concentration camp, directed by a united Communist penitentiary system.

The First Circle has a more pointed and ironical form and stands in more direct relationship to current events than *Cancer Ward*, written between 1963 and 1969. In my opinion, however, the latter possesses a superior fictional quality. It also is partly autobiographical: Solzhenitsyn himself was struck by cancer and in 1955 was sent to a provincial hospital in Tashkent, capital of Uzbekistan. Kostoglotov, the hero of the novel, a man of thirty-five, spent seven years in the Army and seven years in camps and exile in Soviet Central Asia. His tormented past is evoked in opposition to the easy life of another patient, Rusanov, a stiff and successful Party functionary who sees the world through a maze of orders, papers, and regulations. He simply cannot admit his being treated as an ordinary person and refuses to accept that rank and privilege have no bearing on disease and death. Kostoglotov, although hardened and embittered by his previous sufferings and declared incurable by the doctors, still preserves yearnings for life, beauty, and truth. In this overcrowded clinic in which new patients lie in corridors and stairways and often die there, in this abode of pain and annihilation, Kostoglotov falls in love with a medical worker, Vera Gangart, and her name shines as a star before his eyes. This romantic adoration gives him strength and hope, helps him to survive and to begin a miraculous recovery. He is surrounded by a procession of ghost-like invalids, by living corpses—but he talks to them, as well as to nurses, doctors, and staff employees. Most interesting are his discussions with Party members. Here again Solzhenitsyn portrays a variety of personages, including the orthodox lecturer who gave thousands of conferences explaining everything in terms of dialectical materialism and is now dying from throat cancer. Kostoglotov tries to understand what makes people tick, what forms the essence of each existence. A seventy-five-year-old physician tells him that the meaning of life is not in practical activities—be it science or commerce, art, or manual work—but in some feeling of eternity that illuminates our souls just like a moonbeam on the surface of a pond. Kostoglotov and his friend Shulubin understand that everything is empty without love and a moral idea and socialism must have both. True humanism demands a warm approach to people, the real sense of fraternity and the ethical principles we find in the wisdom of the Greek philosophers and the teaching of Jesus Christ. This concept is firmly opposed to the horrible reality of the Communist regime, which is based on cruelty, mendacity, intolerance, and physical and moral violence. *Cancer Ward* not only shows the individual actually facing death, but also raises problems of broad ethical significance—offering pages of delicate lyrism devoid of cheap sentimentalism, without ever becoming didactic or abstract.

Written in free, rich, and imaginative language, *Cancer Ward* is better structured and more concise (446 pages) than the over-expanded *The First Circle*. Both novels, however, indicate Solzhenitsyn's propensity toward large canvases. While occupying a first place in contemporary Russian fiction, they also are documents of an epoch.

To a much greater extent this is also true of the three volumes of *Gulag Archipelago*. These two thousand pages called by the author "an experiment in artistic exploration" were secretly assembled in Russia and completed abroad. They offer the extraor-

dinary combination of research based on the testimony and memoirs of several hundred former convicts, of tomes of printed
materials and the personal reminiscences, confessions, and comments of the author himself. The whole is an astounding chronicle
of the concentration camp empire, of the ferocious repression of
millions exposed to starvation, torture, beatings, and to hard labor
in arctic regions or Asiatic deserts. Hellish jails, a complete lack
of justice, falsified trials, mass executions, unlawful deportation,
barbarous terror, initiated by Lenin, fully applied by Stalin, and
still continued—although on a smaller scale—by his successors—all
blend in Solzhenitsyn's descriptions into an apocalyptic vision of
maddening proportions. Written in a masterful style with indignation, passion, polemic ardor, mordant sarcasm, and with passages of brilliant humor, *Gulag Archipelago*, published between
1974 and 1976 in dozens of translations, exploded like a bomb
everywhere (except, of course, the USSR, where possession of a
single Solzhenitsyn work can lead to arrest and to a prison sentence of at least five years). The political impact of this unique
literary monument and historical testimony was tremendous, shattering the public opinion of five continents, including the Left
wing. *Gulag Archipelago* has been on the bestseller list and sold
millions of copies in numerous countries, and many critics and
writers expressed the opinion that the book is Solzhenitsyn's masterpiece and assures him a unique place in twentieth-century literature and history.

In 1970, four years before the publication of *Gulag Archipelago*, the Swedish Academy awarded Solzhenitsyn the Nobel
Prize for his novels and tales, mentioning in its citation "the ethical force with which he had pursued the indispensable traditions
of Russian literature." Thus his reputation as a writer of fiction
was universally re-affirmed. But the Moscow official press dubbed
the event "political provocation." Solzhenitsyn did not go to
Stockholm to receive the prize; he was afraid that he would not
be allowed to return to his native land. In the USSR his situation
worsened greatly; he was denied the right to reside in Moscow
with his second wife and children and was compelled to find shelter
in the country house of his friend Mstislav Rostropovich, the famous musician.

Because of the authorities' ban, Solzhenitsyn's new novel, *August 1914*, could not appear in Russia and had to be published abroad. This 570-page epic is devoted to the early battles between the Russian and German Armies in World War I and lacks any reference to contemporary post-revolutionary life; its publication, however, was forbidden in the Soviet Union—an arbitrary act both shocking and stupid.

The work, the first of a projected trilogy, depicts the beginning of hostilities and the Russian invasion of East Prussia, which, after initial success, turned into a rout. With vigor, historical accuracy, and moral wrath, Solzhenitsyn denounces the High Command's inefficiency and exposes the fatal blunders of the incompetent Tsarist generals and courtiers. A fourth of the novel describes civilian life, the rest is packed with military scenes which many readers and critics find too detailed and heavy, although most of them—particularly the suicide of General Samsonov and the funeral of an army colonel arranged by his devoted soldiers—are excellent artistically and psychologically.

In the meantime, Solzhenitsyn, despite the official ostracism, continued his courageous struggle for freedom. His Nobel lecture, published by the Swedish Academy yearbook in 1972, condemned the persecution of intellectuals "as a danger to the whole of mankind." As a Christian Greek Orthodox believer, he sent an open letter to the Russian Patriarch Pimen and accused the church of being a servile tool in the hands of the Communist government.

In 1973 the harassment of liberal writers and dissidents became particularly obnoxious and it influenced Solzhenitsyn's living conditions. The Kremlin considered him the main enemy of the regime and the authorities could not let him continue his undaunted fight for freedom and human dignity. They understood, however, that harsh measures against him, such as deportation or imprisonment, might provoke a tremendous storm of protest in the West and harm the policy of foreign détente. The Politbureau therefore decided to get rid of this dangerous man by expelling him from Russia, and depriving him of Soviet citizenship. In February 1974 Solzhenitsyn was arrested and then put on a plane under the escort of police agents and flown to Germany. First he was welcomed by the famous novelist Heinrich Böll, but later he settled in Zurich, Switzerland, awaiting his family: his wife, children, and mother-in-law arrived after a few weeks.

His numerous interviews in the world press, appearances on radio and television, travels in Europe and North America, special reception in Stockholm as the Nobel Prize laureate, and his public speeches, pamphlets, and articles made him the most talked of and admired man of that year. The simultaneous publication of *Gulag Archipelago* naturally doubled his popularity and reinforced the weight of his criticism of Communist totalitarianism. However, Western intellectuals did not meet all of his forcefully expressed opinions with full approval; his general views on the theory of progress, which he finds wrong and unreasonable, his hostility toward all brands of socialism, and his insistence on the necessity of a religious revival in general and of the Greek Orthodox faith in Russia in particular as the only remedy against the sickness of contemporary civilization, led to heated discussions and many objections.

In 1975 Solzhenitsyn published a small book (140 pages), *Lenin in Zurich*, containing several chapters he had not included in *August 1914*. It offers a striking analysis of Lenin's character, of his complete dedication to revolutionary ideas, and a realistic description of his poor, ascetic existence as an *émigré* in Zurich between 1914 and 1916, on the eve of the Russian Revolution and during its early days.

The third colorful and lively volume of *Gulag Archipelago* was published in 1976, bringing to completion this gigantic and highly factual work.

A number of Western critics consider Solzhenitsyn's extraordinary popularity the result of the political situation; they see him as a writer bent on the exposure of "Communist evil," as a leader of underground Russia. They seem to avoid an aesthetic evaluation of his work. This is a fundamental error because the writer is a literary phenomenon, and must be judged as such. It would be ridiculous to deny the importance of his denunciation of Soviet reality or his social and moral message, which presents a mixture of conservatism, revolutionary aspirations, religious beliefs, and a realistic approach to daily life. He also reveals his search for truth in the tradition of great Russian classics, and uses linguistic innovations, partly inspired by the populists of the nineteenth century and partly originating from the vernacular of the Soviet era. But all this complex conglomerate holds together because it is expressed with the power and the craft of an accomplished story-teller.

It would be erroneous, however, to relate Solzhenitsyn to Tolstoy—even though they may appear to have much in common, namely the epic bulk of their novels and the tendency toward raising essential problems of human existence. I think that the roots of Solzhenitsyn's style and his particular interest in Russian national characteristics go back to the "writers of the soil" of the mid- and second half of the nineteenth century, namely to Melnikov-Pechersky, Ertel, Leskov, and other "narodniki."* This becomes obvious when we compare their style and diction with Solzhenitsyn's attempts to revive archaisms, regional locutions, and the speech of peasants and workers: this seemed odd, shocked many *émigré* readers, and presented insuperable difficulties to foreign translators, especially when they were confronted with convicts' slang.

The epic frame of Solzhenitsyn's novels do not resemble the chronologically slow pace of Tolstoy's chronicles and their river-like conception of time. Because *Cancer Ward, The First Circle,* and *August 1914* depict events happening over a very short span of days, weeks, or a few months, their action is condensed and has the same dramatic thrust and polyphonic structure as in Dostoevsky's novels. There are also other quite original traits in Solzhenitsyn's works which make them different from those written by the author of *Crime and Punishment.* Solzhenitsyn is firmly entrenched in existing reality, in the present instant which he describes in its fullness and autonomy. Despite their gloomy subjects and tragic plots, his novels breathe such a vitality, such an attachment to the process of being, that they never leave a somber impression. Yet their main themes are jail, concentration camp, war, and hospitals, and their protagonists are thrown face to face with the implacable monsters of the inhuman state, bloodshed, terror, torture, sickness, and death. Each of these themes is con-

* See Marc Slonim, *From Chekhov to the Revolution: Russian Literature, 1900-1917* (New York: Oxford University Press, Inc., 1962).

nected with the problem of Russia's destiny. Jails and camps have become the main foundations of the Soviet system, the cancer gnawing at man's vitals is the symbol of evil, corruption, and infection which threaten to destroy nation and society. It must be underscored that Solzhenitsyn's characters are shown in crisis and danger situations and that he draws the factual material of his narratives from personal experience. He himself went through war, prison, hard labor, and exile and was close to dying from cancer. The merging of his artistic imagination and creative intuition with the various occurrences of his own life, accurately retained by his prodigious memory, convey such authenticity, intensity, and spontaneity to all his writings that they never fail to awaken a strong emotional response in readers—and this is one of the secrets of his magical dominance over huge "captive audiences." All his images, characters, and scenes are deeply felt and expressed with contagious inner fire.

Marcel Proust compared Dostoevsky with Rembrandt because he usually seemed to pluck his heroes from the darkness and show them in the bright light of a penetrating analysis. Solzhenitsyn also uses a similar device: he brings the different actors into the spotlight one by one. In this alternation of people and circumstances, Solzhenitsyn is trying to uncover the true, often hidden, essence of each individual. This is done in a manner which some French critics—rightly or wrongly—call "existentialist."

In any case, the Russian excels in painting simple men and women, mostly from the lower classes (Matriona persecuted by the cruelty of bad men and by destiny, the guardian of the battlefield of Kulikovo, where Russians defeated the Tartars in the Middle Ages, the half-blind veteran of bondage, Spiridon, in *The First Circle*, and Ivan Denisovich, the convict and victim of Communist terror). These humble folk and many other superbly sketched types give in their totality a true image of Russia. Their sufferings, toil, and capacity for survival serve as elements for a solid understanding of the present and perhaps of the future of this immense land. Solzhenitsyn is its painter, chronicler, witness, and interpreter. Time will show whether we are justified in calling him one of the greatest men of the age, but we need no further proof to admire in him a genuine master of fiction, "tremendous in vision, heroic in spirit, unimaginably enduring," as Edward Crankshaw says, rising over all contemporary Soviet writers as one of the brightest luminaries of Russian literature.*

* And yet his name is taboo and officially ignored in the USSR and never mentioned in the eight volumes of the *Short Literary Encyclopedia* published in Moscow between 1962 and 1975.

32

Samizdat

THE UNDERGROUND PRESS

From the time when the free press was forbidden and pre-revolutionary publishing houses were shut in the 1920's, state pressure on literature and arts grew more restrictive every year. As a result, many poems, articles, and short stories had no chance of being printed in "legal" periodicals because of their "subversive" or ambiguous content, and they began to circulate mostly among intellectuals in typewritten copies. But such "publication" only occurred occasionally, on a small scale and in widely dispersed areas until Stalin's death. From that time on, however, it assumed the character of a vast and organized activity, an outlet for free expression, and acquired the name of Samizdat (which in Russian means "self-publication"), a well-known term used not only in the Soviet Union but also in the West.

Centered in Moscow and Leningrad and to a much lesser extent in provincial towns, Samizdat expanded into a true underground press, typewritten, mimeographed, and photocopied. There were also tapes and cassettes of labor camp songs, and unrestrained satirical ballads by Okudzhava, Galitch, Vyssotsky, and other minstrels. Samizdat became an important cultural factor and a subject of worry and investigation for the security organs. Samizdat activities reached their summit between 1955 and 1965, and later, covering not only poetry and fiction but also politics, philosophy, and religion.

When Pasternak's *Doctor Zhivago*, over 560 pages long, was banned in the USSR in 1957 but published in the original language and in dozens of translations in the West, it was smuggled into Russia and reproduced in large excerpts by Samizdat. This was the opening of a two-way exchange: many works initially circulated by Samizdat and secretly sent abroad would return in printed book form as contraband, "a prohibited commodity," and be reproduced again by homemade devices. Such was the case of Solzhenitsyn's writings, systematically reproduced by Samizdat. Often the authors themselves dispatched their works abroad by roundabout ways.

It is impossible to give here an exhaustive list of Samizdat's publications, but among them are certainly dozens of works still unknown outside Russia. Some prime examples would be *The Golden Century* by the geologist Grigory Podyepolsky (1926-76), *On the Sharp Edged Facet* by Yuly Aikhenvald, and poems by a few minor but original poets who are in their fifties (Sapghir, Aigi, Nekipelov, and so forth). Samizdat circulated the poems of dissident poets, and when one of them, Yury Galanskov, died in a labor camp in 1972 at the age of thirty-three, published a collection of his poems and letters as well as appeals from his family and friends—including those that came from prisons or labor camps. It also organized the circulation of underground almanacs (Phoenix, Sintaxis, Sphinx, Boomerang, and others) which contained works by non-conformist poets. The poems by Yosif Brodsky appeared in Samizdat long before his exile, although they were never printed officially in the USSR; his collection *Verse and Long Poems* was issued in New York in 1965. The same happened to Naum Korzhavin, poet and author of numerous articles published after his emigration in various Russian periodicals abroad between 1973 and 1976. There are important (and often bulky) books first distributed by Samizdat, and which then obtained great success abroad, for example, *Hope against Hope* by Nadhezda Mandelstam, a memoir by the widow of the poet, an extraordinary document of Russian life and literature in the 1930's interspersed with sharp philosophical and historical comments.

Sometimes a work circulated by the Samizdat was published in the West after a long delay. This happened with Grossman's *Everything Flows* and with the outstanding short novel by Georgy Vladimov (still living in Moscow), *The Faithful Ruslan*. Samizdat publication made it known in the USSR in the early 1960's, but it was printed in Europe in book form only in 1972

and acclaimed by *émigré* critics as a masterpiece. It is the story of
a police dog splendidly trained to keep the columns of convicts
in order. They march, in ranks of five, to their "work zones" under the surveillance of dogs and armed guards who shout repeat-
edly: "If you make one step to the left or to the right, we shoot."
Ruslan, a good intelligent dog and an unconscious agent of the
Communist system, is totally wrapped up in his duty. When the
camp to which he belongs is shut after Stalin's death, Ruslan, suddenly confronted with a crowd gathered in the neighboring village for a celebration, tries to keep people in orderly ranks, barks
furiously, bites, and is killed. The tale has numerous symbolic references, brilliantly unveiled by Siniavsky in his fine article "Men
and Beasts" in the fifth issue of *Continent*.

Alexander Beck's *New Appointment* had a similar fate. This
excellent novel about bureaucrats and the Communist "nomencla-
ture" or the special rotation of functionaries for important posts
was announced for publication by *Novy Mir* in 1965 but was
banned by the censors and never appeared in the Soviet Union.
Circulated by Samizdat, it was finally printed in Germany in
1971. A list of identical instances would be quite long.

Samizdat's role was, however, not only the circulation of fiction but also the spreading of political and factual information on
internal events in the country. Whenever a courageous writer's
open letter was addressed to the Union of Soviet Writers or to
Party organs and was passed over in silence by the officials and
kept in secret archives, Samizdat would publish it—together with
materials on political and religious prisoners, on psychiatric clinics
turned into jails for non-conformists, on members of Christian
sects and representatives of minorities fighting for national autonomy, and on all the troublemakers the police wanted to send away
without legal proceedings. Samizdat continuously distributed
hidden data on labor camps and on their populations submitted
to the so-called "severe or harsh regime." Some of this material,
for instance, on the punishment of dissidents by pseudo-medical
treatment has been published abroad in book form (*Sentenced to
Be Treated as Lunatics* in 1971, Frankfurt).

It was between 1965 and 1975 that the dissidents came into the
open, organizing public demonstrations and issuing challenging

speeches at political trials. Reports on those trials and denunciations of the KGB's unlawful methods and persecutions of free thought were fully publicized by Samizdat. It followed the history of the whole opposition movement step by step. One of the many and perhaps most efficient of Samizdat activities was the so-called "Chronicle of current events," issued periodically and providing accounts, notes, documents, and abstracts. For a certain time Samizdat served as an exclusive source for foreign correspondents who transmitted the "Chronicle" to the international press. Moreover, Samizdat propagated all the interviews, declarations, and writings by Andrey Sakharov, the distinguished scholar, academician, and initiator of the committee for human rights and the recipient of the Nobel Peace Prize in 1975. Samizdat revealed the arrests and deportations of all his companions (mostly prominent scholars and intellectuals). At the same time Samizdat made known the pronouncements and interviews of Solzhenitsyn and other members of the third emigration in Western and American newspapers, radio, and television, thus breaking the silence imposed on them in Soviet dailies and weeklies. One can say that in this field Samizdat reached its greatest expansion between 1969 and 1975. The security organs, irritated and worried, decided to crack down on Samizdat's several groups. Mass arrests and trials followed, in which people like Litvinov, Yakir, Gorbanevskaya, and many others were sentenced to imprisonment and deportation; some of them were later authorized to emigrate. Despite these repressions, Samizdat was not extinguished. In fact, its information enabled the publication in Russian and English of regular issues of *A Chronicle of Human Rights in the USSR* by Valery Chalidze in the United States, and made possible the *Annals of Samizdat: Uncensored Thought in the USSR*, printed in Great Britain in English and Russian and published for the Alexander Herzen Foundation in Amsterdam.

These types of publications, all called by the general term of Samizdat, presented a great variety of opinions. Some of them were anonymous, others were signed by courageous authors. Among those who came to the fore in the 1960's was Grigory Pomeranz, an Orientalist, whose numerous Samizdat writings could have easily formed a large volume. His central theme was the problem of the Russian intelligentsia—its past and present. What is the difference between the nineteenth-century idealists and revolutionaries and the contemporary class of technologists, teachers, holders of all sorts of university degrees, artists, and intellectuals? Being a part of a huge state apparatus, they had lost their humanism, independence, and creativity, and became "brain robots." Solzhenitsyn believes that this is the main trouble, or even calamity of the USSR: people who come out of institutions of higher learning lack, in comparison to their pre-revolutionary predecessors, moral values, high aspirations, and truly humanistic aims. They accept and seem satisfied with dogmatic slogans and the narrow doctrines of dialectical materialism. He even coins the term "obrazovantchina" (untranslatable, sounding like "educationism" in English) to designate those whom sheer instruction and specialization did not make better men and women. They have replaced the old intelligentsia, but are devoid of its positive traits and belong to the "subculture." The essays by Solzhenitsyn on "educationism" and his 1970 polemical criticism of *Reflections on Progress, Peaceful Coexistence and Intellectual Freedom* by Andrey Sakharov can be found in *From under the Clouds*, a collection of articles initially circulated by Samizdat and then presented as a book in 1974 by Parisian publishers in Russian and in translation. It provoked a considerable stir and heated discussions in the third emigration and—to a lesser degree—in the international press. Solzhenitsyn holds Sakharov in great esteem and admires his heroic efforts in defense of human rights, but he does not share the academician's optimistic belief in the possibility of a future "convergence" of such basically opposing political and social systems as capitalism and Communism. Neither has he any faith in the continuity of material and institutional progress and in the real "détente." The Communist ideology, formulated by Lenin as an implacable one-party dictatorship, is, according to Solzhenitsyn, intolerant, fanatical, cruel, and totalitarian, and since its seizure of power in Russia, has not, despite all its tactical fluctuations, yielded an inch of its basic principles. It is therefore organically unable to compromise. Stalin was applying Lenin's dogma in perhaps a more ferocious manner than his successors, but there is nothing accidental or abnormal in his policy of terrorism: it derives from the inner core of Communism. The hope in Soviet goodwill and in its rebuttal of Red imperialism is a fatal, colossal mistake that might cost the West, including America, its very existence. Other contributors to the book support Solzhenitsyn's thesis. Three essays by Igor Shafarevitch, a distinguished mathematician, laureate of several scholarly prizes, and articles by Michael Agursky (son of an American Communist, a cybernetics scientist, and now an émigré), by Vadim Borisov, and others, go even beyond Solzhenitsyn's affirmations and formulate an absolute indictment of socialism, of any socialism, in all its versions. They accuse it of atheism, of contempt for ethical and religious values, and of underrating the importance of individual freedom and spiritual aspirations. All the uncensored authors of *From under the Clouds* see Christianity and first of all Greek Orthodoxy as a source of inner awakening and the only firm way for salvation. They also deplore the religious indifference of the old intelligentsia as its worst sin, hail the role of great saints such as Sergei Radonezhsky, Serafim Sarovsky, John of Cronstadt, and of philosophers such as Florensky, Sergei Bulgakov, and other "pillars of faith." They are also aware of the present difficult and humiliating conditions of the Orthodox Church, dominated by Soviet functionaries.

An entirely different point of view is expressed by the group of dissident Marxists, also reaching their followers by Samizdat. In their front line stands Roy Medvedev, a historian, author of an important treatise on Stalin's era (of course, not printed in the Soviet Union) and of many pamphlets discussing the current events and criticizing Solzhenitsyn's declarations as well as Sakharov's attitudes. His brother, the biologist Zhores Medvedev, belongs to the third emigration, lives in the United States and seems more liberal and open-minded.

A group apart, composed of Russian nationalists, is also using Samizdat methods for popularizing their ideas, even though some of them appear in disguise in the legal press. Their most conservative wing is called "Russits." In the early 1970's they had a sort of a periodical, *Veche*—this title revived the word which in the Middle Ages designated the people's assembly for the discussion of public affairs and the election of the local princes and the ruling state and church hierarchy in the ancient cities of Novgorod,

Pskov, and Vladimir. Some Russits saw in *Veche* the model of the
contemporary soviets, and in general idealized the old customs,
speech, way of life, and civic spirit of Russia before its Western-
ization by Peter the Great. It is quite obvious that they followed
in the steps of the Slavophiles who in the 1840's opposed the "true
ancient country" to the depraved and rationalistic West, and that
they had strong ties with populists and the writers of the soil.
Some of their "legal friends" such as Soloukhin,* did an excellent
job in the defense of Russian historical monuments, icons,
churches, and all the artistic treasures and relics of the past. Apparently the authorities tolerated this movement for some time,
seeing in it a mood rather than an ideological menace, but then decided to eradicate this dangerous explosion of nationalism. Vladimir Osipov, the editor of *Veche*, was arrested and in 1976 was
still in jail. He fell victim to the vast KGB operations between
1972 and 1976 against all shades of dissidence and particularly
against Samizdat: in fact, the activities of the latter have been
greatly reduced since 1975.

* See his popular book, *Letters from a Russian Museum* (1966).

33

The Newcomers

In the 1960's a surprisingly large number of plays, novels, and stories tried to catch the salient traits of a new generation. Some authors maintained that young Soviet men and women were morally and physically healthy, good workers, and loyal Communists (the best example of this literature was *The Young Leaves* by Alexander Rekemchuk). Others found their young contemporaries amazingly similar in many ways to their opposite numbers in the capitalist countries (hence the enormous success in Russia of Salinger's *The Catcher in the Rye*). There was a stir, a feeling of discontent among youth, a critical attitude toward society, a growing interest in fresh ideas, an impatient rejection of boring formulas—all of which made them the natural allies of the liberals. While fathers sided with the conservatives and the Stalinists, their sons supported political reform and the artistic avant-garde, acclaiming as their accredited representatives the poets who had begun to voice the anxieties and yearnings of their generation. This explains the terrific response the poets of the "new wave" (mostly in their twenties) drew from their audiences. In 1962, 100,000 copies of Evtushenko's *The Sweep of the Hand*, and 50,000 copies of *Encounter*, a collection of poems by two dozen newcomers, were sold out in two days.

This extraordinary popularity of the poets gave special meaning to their work: from a literary phenomenon it grew into a social-political event. A case in hand was Evtushenko whose tempestuous career reflected the contradictions and aspirations of his generation (in his poem on Galileo he says: "I make my career by trying not to make one"). A native of Siberia, Evgeny Evtushenko (b. 1923) moved with his family to Moscow. He was twenty-three when he made a brilliant debut in 1956 with his long poem "Station Zima" (*zima* in Russian means winter). It was a

"soul searching" lyrical confession with strong patriotic overtones
—"glorious deeds, not weaknesses Russia expects from us"—but
also possessing a spirit of daring, a drive for independence, and a
consciousness that "the writer is not a ruler but a guardian of
thoughts."

Within a few years he had become famous not only in Moscow,
but also in Paris, London, and New York. He was permitted to
travel extensively and was received everywhere as an unofficial
delegate of post-Stalinist Russia. Foreign audiences in Europe,
America, Asia, and Cuba were entranced by this tall, handsome,
outgoing Siberian, an athletic, devil-may-care fellow, who personified youth and poetry. There was rebellion and hope, something
exotic and yet something still highly familiar in this messenger
from the Communist world. He was outspoken in his talk, and he
surprised the French and the Americans by his seemingly independent judgments. Slightly intoxicated by his international success and his ever increasing influence at home, Evtushenko made
the mistake of overestimating his possibilities as a free agent.
In 1962, while in Paris, he published a French version (never
submitted to censorship and never printed in the USSR) of his
Precocious Autobiography in which he wrote daringly about
himself and conditions in Russia. Summoned back to Moscow at
a moment when Party controls were being tightened again after
the Cuba crisis, Evtushenko was officially blamed and indicted by
Khrushchev, his former friend; his speeches during the encounters
between Party leaders and artists at the beginning of 1963 finally
made him lose his privileged position of "darling firebrand," and he
underwent a temporary eclipse. He made a comeback early in 1964
and was authorized to resume his travels abroad, although on a
reduced scale.

His vertiginous rise and the ups and downs of his career as a poet
were the result of a conjunction of political pressures and personal characteristics. Evtushenko was endowed with an almost
animal vitality, a zest for life, a passion for new experiences, for
love, for travel, for action. In his "The Prologue" he wrote: "I
greet all that moves! Ardent desire and eagerness, triumphant
eagerness! Frontiers stand in my way. . . . I bite into books and
carry firewood . . . With no thought of death I sing and drink,

fall on the grass with arms outspread, and if I should die in this wide world, then I'll die most happy to have lived." *

His general outlook and his poetics were basically Communist, but his rebellious nature prevented him from becoming a slave of the Establishment. He defied the accepted Communist norms and shocked the congregation with his behavior. Sincerely interested in other countries and cultures, he was strongly attracted by the diversity and innovations of modern European art. His own verse is abrupt, expressive, filled with jokes, jingles, and ironical hints. The scanning of the lines, the loud orchestration of broken rhythms, the vernacular used for the de-poetization of the language, come from Mayakovsky; like other poets of his age, he learned from Pasternak how to believe in the "truth of the word" and how to look for unusual metaphors; yet, he could never forget Blok's "harps and violins" and Essenin's melancholic complaints: they recur in his pieces on love, parting, and solitude. But above all, he is a declamatory poet, possessed of the same "oratorical passion" which engendered Mayakovsky's "civic odes." Evtushenko also wanted to have a dialogue with his epoch, to take part in political struggle, to employ poetry as a weapon, to put lyrical sensitivity at the service of a cause. Whether he criticized France or praised Cuba, his revolutionary hymns turned into blatant slogans. This was his main weakness and also the reason for his popularity. Some of his poems were like explosions; this was especially true of "Babyi Yar" published in the *Literary Gazette* in September 1961. He depicted the ravine in Kiev, "unmarked by any monument" where thirty-four thousand Jews were exterminated by the Nazis. In a highly emotional way, he evoked the horrors of the massacre and launched a fierce attack against the anti-Semites in the Soviet Union. His concluding lines challenged: "there is no Jewish blood in my veins. But all enraged anti-Semites should hate me as if I were a Jew: and for that reason I am a true Russian."

"Babyi Yar" was very embarrassing to the Party leaders who kept denying the existence of anti-Semitism in their own ranks and in the Soviet Union, and they blamed the poet for his "exaggera-

* This poem was translated by George Reavey.

tions." But everybody knew that Evtushenko was exposing a
hushed up aspect of Communist society. There was almost complete silence about Babyi Yar in Soviet literature until the end of
1966, when Anatoly Kuznetsov's documentary novel appeared
in *Youth*. In the spring of 1969 the same magazine published *Fire*,
another Kuznetsov (b. 1929) novel about the installation of a new
smelting furnace in a provincial town, during which activity the
narrator meets his old schoolmates and hears their confessions of
disillusionment and loss of faith. Two months later Kuznetsov
arrived in London and asked for political asylum in England. He
revealed to the press that "Babyi Yar" and *Fire* had been mutilated by Soviet censors. An unexpurgated version of the former
appeared in 1970 in the original and foreign translations.

No sooner had the polemics about "Babyi Yar" subsided than
Evtushenko came out with "Stalin's Heirs" (1962). This time he
certainly received preliminary blessings from the Kremlin because
the poem suited the Party line of the moment. Evtushenko demanded that the guards around Stalin's grave be doubled and
tripled lest the dictator rise from the dead and bring back the past
with him. A direct line from his tomb connects Stalin not only
with the Albanians but also with his Russian followers; he gives
them instructions while lying in the coffin. "Some people revile
Stalin from the podium but at night, left alone, they cry for old
times ... they do not like the era in which concentration camps
are empty and halls where poems are read, are crowded ... as long
as Stalin's heirs are alive on this earth, I can't be calm."

No less explicit is "The Dead Hand" which Evtushenko read
at one of his last public appearances in Paris in 1963. "Some
people write in the old manner and want to stab the new ... some
people look at everything like Stalin and frown at youth.... This
is the dead hand of the past that clutches the living and threatens
to strangle them."

Evtushenko responded favorably to the Party's demand for
social and political commitment and for his participation in the
life of the country. He believed in continuing the tradition of
Russian civic poetry, personified by Nekrassov, and his great
ambition was to become a tribune, a spokesman for the whole
generation. He lacked, however, the intellectual capacity, depth

and ideas for such a task. This is quite evident in his long work *The Power Station of Bratsk* (1965)—a collection of poems which presents a broad view of Russian history and of today's opposing ideologies, hails faith and condemns modern skepticism, and finally celebrates the creative efforts of Soviet builders of Communism.

While the poetic value of his topical works is dubious, their political impact was shattering. They provoked numerous rebuttals in verse, the most typical among them being "Our Years," a sequel of poems by Evgeny Dolmatovsky published in Kochetov's *October* (November 1962). Dolmatovsky (b. 1915) reflected the feelings of that "middle" generation which worked under Stalin, and was now shocked by the brutality of de-Stalinization. Dolmatovsky reminded those who enjoyed trampling over the fallen god that for a quarter of a century he had been the symbol of revolution and progress and that political prisoners, coming back from the torture chamber, wrote on the walls of their cells "Long Live Stalin." Another poet, Nikolay Dorizo, in a poem evoking the arrest and execution of his own father, an old Communist, remembered also how thousands upon thousands died with the name of the chief on their lips in the foxholes of that very Stalingrad that was renamed Volgograd by governmental order. Dolmatovsky identified the literary anti-Stalinists of recent vintage with the philistines who love cocktails and jazz, long for bourgeois calm, and replace revolutionary drums by "lute, harp and guitar."

This was equally the opinion of Vsevolod Kochetov who published in 1962 his second polemical novel *The Secretary of the Regional Committee*. He divided Communist officials into "good" and "bad." His hero Denisov follows the "right party line," and Artamonov, a petty tyrant, the "wrong" one and misuses his power. But Kochetov's main thrust was directed against the "modernists." Denisov's sister-in-law Yulia, a provincial vamp, a woman-painter working in a theater, gets rid of her "decadent inclinations" only when she meets a rational 100 per cent Communist. The erotic poet Ptukhov (a vicious caricature of Evtushenko) recognizes the futility of his poems only when he retires to a *kolkhoze* in order to forget his abortive affair with Yulia.

In *The Angle of Incidence* (1967), a half-historical, half-detective novel on the 1919 civil war, Kochetov either totally ignored, or portrayed as criminals and dangerous villains people like Trotsky, Kamenec, and other revolutionary "heretics." His next work, *What Do You Finally Want?* (1969) is a coarse political pamphlet doubling as a third-rate thriller—with blond spies, former Nazis disguised as Soviet friends, American secret agents trying to corrupt innocent Russian boys and girls by contaminating them with "decadent avant-garde art," while a luscious Negro musician seduced writers and painters, introducing them to surrealism and jazz. Many of Kochetov's heroes and heroines were well recognizable caricatures of living persons, such as an American woman journalist and an Italian Communist essayist. The serialization of the novel in Kochetov's magazine *Oktiabr* provoked a scandal and embarrassed Party officials to such an extent that it has not been published in book form.

What incensed all the Kochetovs of the USSR was not only the anti-Stalinist mood among the young but the "modernistic" direction of an entire literary current. With Evtushenko another idol hailed by Moscow youth was Andrey Voznesensky, perhaps the most remarkable poet of the Soviet avant-garde. Born in 1933, son of a scientist, reared in a highly cultured and sophisticated environment, he graduated in 1957 from the Architecture Institute, where he became an admirer of Le Corbusier and Frank Lloyd Wright. He started publishing poems the following year. A disciple of Pasternak, Tsvetayeva, and Mayakovsky, he represented in Soviet poetry a renovated version of surrealism, challenging all the approved clichés. His first small collections *Mosaic* (1960) and *Parabola* (1961), his much discussed "Thirty Digressions from the Poem *A Triangular Pear*" (1962), his selected lyrics of the *Antiworlds* (1964), and his poems in periodicals surprised readers with their formal daring and the blend of fervor, wit, and intellectual subtlety. With dazzling dexterity he used constantly changing rhythms and meters, alliterations, sound associations, and assonances in heavily accented broken lines. Beneath this verbal facility lay a tempestuous temperament, an original vision of reality, and a personal interpretation of the poet's destination—all of which are revealed allegorically in "Parabolic Ballad." "Fate like a rocket describes a parabola, usually in darkness, seldom over a rainbow.

... Each one goes to his own truth in his own way—the worm through a chink, a man by parabola ... Art, love, history, fly the parabolic trajectory." A worshipper of dynamism and speed, he declared that there is "no finish for a poet, creation always is a start."

In contrast with Evtushenko, Voznesensky's poetry is exclamatory rather than declamatory. He puts stress on single words making them linguistic and semantic centers of a whole poem. The main theme of his highly subjective work is the exploration of self through a variety of experiences. External objects and ideas alike furnish material for this self identification. In "The Triangular Pear" (devoted to his impressions of the USA) he wrote: "I discovered Americas in America—and myself; my portrait—a neon retort." In a similar way are conceived his long poems, "Longjumeau" (1963), devoted to Lenin's life in France and to Russian revolutionaries, and Oza (1964) particularly, one of Voznesensky's most complex and multi-level compositions. Oza is partly autobiographical, partly philosophical, with stanzas on history, modern civilization, love, and current events (including a striking and symbolic description of Stalin). Rhymed lines filled with visual imagery alternate with meditations and commentary in rhythmic prose. Not all the experimentation is successful, but Voznesensky's verbal inventiveness and originality are at their best in Oza.

He was often accused of being a "formalist," of using weird similes ("Airport, this Apostle of Celestial Gates"), and of attaching more importance to the metaphor than to the fact it describes. But his poetry is more revolutionary in its spirit (in the sense that Zamyatin understood revolution) than the dull expositions of a Dolmatovsky. Voznesensky hates the "bourgeois" just as the Romantics of the early nineteenth century did. He idealizes Lenin, whom he calls "the shatterer of the world." He also dreams, like many of his colleagues including Evtushenko, of a purification and renovation of the official doctrine. This sociopolitical tendency is quite complex: it coincides with Voznesensky's faith in freedom and his complete dedication to art ("art cannot accept abuse and tyranny" is the meaning of his "Masters," a pseudo-historical poem). Moreover he accepts science, technology, the "atomic age." For him there is no rift between science and poetry, between the world of measure, quantity, and weight, and the world of quality, values, and fantasy. But to march together the poet and the scientist must both belong to avant-garde in their fields—innovating, experimenting, breaking new ground, discovering untrammeled paths. This was Voznesensky's response to the debate on the relationship between physics and fiction, knowledge and imagination, that flared up in Russia in the 1960's and aroused immense interest among scientists, writers, and the general public.

A cryptic, often whimsical poet, who blends lyricism and irony, and writes puns to hide his intimate convictions, Voznesensky remains a major representative of the Russian poetic avant-garde. It must be added that his production of the 'seventies disappointed his friends: he continued to repeat himself, without bringing anything new in his last poems.

Another important poet of the "new wave" is Bella Akhmadulina (b. 1937), first married to Evtushenko, then to Yury Naghibin, a prose writer. As she says in her long poem "My Genealogical Table" (1964), she has mixed Tartar, Russian, and Italian blood but is a native of Moscow. There is, however, hardly any trace of exoticism in her main, remarkably mature, formally perfect collections *String* and *Music Lessons*, and numerous works in various periodicals. Her verse offers beautiful specimens of rare, almost precious, poetic virtuosity. More traditional than Voznesensky in her meters, she is equally inventive in her alliterations and metaphors. Whatever she chooses to describe—a village wedding, a Northern landscape, a machine for automatic distribution of soft drinks, a trip to the virgin lands, or the pains and delights of love—she does in a restrained manner with symbolic allusions that make every image resplendent with verbal freshness. In each poem she arrives at that "emotional displacement" of things and feelings Pasternak believed to be the mark of true art. For her the content *is* form, the world begins with the word; language is not a means or a device but a self-contained essence, a new assemblage of words that has the magic power of creating a new reality. This attitude and indeed Akhmadulina's whole vision of life are not abstract or intellectual (despite her keen intelligence), they are spontaneous and all-embracing, like faith—and this gives great unity to her harmonious, vigorous, yet delicate work. Her voice has such a purity of tone, such richness of timbre, such individuality of diction, that she certainly occupies today the first place among the living women poets of the Soviet Union.

Akhmadulina's belief in the word as a constantly renascent miracle is also found in the "eldest brother" of the avant-garde, Evgeny Vinokurov. Born in 1925, he did not publish his first collection of verse until 1956; his output is small but he is a refined and talented poet with distinct personal traits and a strong philosophical bent. He relates small facts to ideas (in a poem he speaks of "eternity's book of complaints") but does it in a calm, balanced way. A retiring man, he is not attracted by the hubbub of his age. At the international Conference of Poets in Belgium in 1962, he defended artistic independence, and stated that "Rublev's * paintings and the head of Nefertiti are much closer to us than many works that chronologically are quite near."

To the same generation belongs Bulat Okudzhava (b. 1924 in Moscow) author of a very good war story (*Good Luck to You, My Pupil*), a poet, and above all an extremely popular singer of ballads which he accompanies on the guitar. His poems are occasionally published in periodicals, mainly in *Youth*, but there are few recordings of his songs and they are not mentioned by the press. Okudzhava is officially ignored, but this has not prevented his becoming the most famous and beloved performer of his own words and music. His ironic topical ballads, as well as his songs on love and the joys and sorrows of daily life, have endeared him to millions. There is no rhetoric or sentimentality in his lilting lines which charm huge audiences throughout the Soviet Union with their humanity, kindliness and strong pacifist spirit.

But Okudzhava is also an original and talented novelist. In 1969 he published in a magazine with limited circulation his historical novel *The Poor Avrosimov*. Situating the plot in 1826, after the so-called Decembrist Uprising, Okudzhava unfolds the fascinating adventures of a young court clerk who works at the Tsarist Investigation Committee, appointed to prepare the trial of the

* Rublev is Russia's greatest religious painter (fifteenth century).

unsuccessful military rebels. At one moment Avrosimov is so sub-
jugated by the personality of Colonel Pestel, one of the revolutionary leaders, that he dreams of organizing his escape. The author makes oblique and disturbing comparisons between the past
and the present. The style, texture, and tonality of the novel are
reminiscent of Gogol and Andrey Bely and appear unique in contemporary Soviet fiction. Another satirical narrative, *Merci or
Shipov's Adventures*, is based on a historical fact—a house search
made by the police at the estate of Leo Tolstoy during his absence in 1862. This disquisition was the consequence of a fantastic report by Shipov, a secret agent, police reformer, scoundrel,
and drunkard. Many passages of this gay, amusing, picaresque tale
contain unmistakable allusions to the modern Soviet scene. These
and other prose writings by Okudzhava led to his expulsion from
the Communist Party.

Among other talented poets of the 1960's were Yaroslav Smeliakov (1913-73), a Romantic bard of youth, genuine emotions, and
social togetherness (which saved him from being "illegally repressed" for some time); Robert Rozhdestvensky (b. 1932), who
follows Mayakovsky's poetic style; Victor Sosnora (b. 1937), a
factory worker, influenced by Khlebnikov and greatly interested
in linguistic experimentation; Novella Matveyeva (b. 1935),
whose good collection *The Soul of Things* gives further proof of
her progress; and many beginners, are all part of the new school.
Together with painters and sculptors such as Radin, Zverev and
Niezvestny (now an *émigré*); musicians such as Volkonsky (now
an *émigré*); and dancers, actors, and theatrical or cinematographic
producers, they form the lively and ever-growing artistic avant-
garde. It has many admirers among young intellectuals, particularly scientists: the latter are the most independent, open-minded,
and progressive group in Russia. A great many gifted young men
and women who knew that in other areas (mainly the humani-
ties and art) they would have been held in bondage to the Party
turned to science—and this has resulted in the natural formation
of an "elite."

Daring, often experimental production of old and new plays
and shows, with strong stress on the satire and grotesque, made
famous two small theaters in Moscow: "On Taganka" and "The
Contemporary."

Substantial encouragement was given to the avant-garde in the 1960's by the liberals of the older generation. In his widely read memoirs *Years, People, Life,* serialized in 1961-64 in *Novy Mir* before appearing in book form, Ehrenburg wrote with admiration of European "modernists," and he reappraised the 'twenties. Paustovsky edited *Tarussa Pages,* a collection which printed laudatory essays on the *émigré* Bunin and on Meyerhold, a victim of the purges; it also contained poems by Tsvetayeva and Zabolotsky, a long story by Okudzhava, tales by Kazakov and Naghibin, and other fictional and critical material. Published in Kaluga, a provincial town, in 75,000 copies which were sold out immediately, *Tarussa Pages* became a nation-wide event, a challenge to "socialist realism," and a manifesto of "revisionism."

Such a publication was made possible by the general atmosphere of 1962, which resembled another thaw. The speeding up of de-Stalinization at the time of the Twenty-Second Party Congress aroused new hopes among the liberals. Expectations reached a climax by the end of the year when *Novy Mir* published *One Day in the Life of Ivan Denisovich* by Alexander Solzhenitsyn.

34

Fluctuations and Trials

Just one month after the publication of Solzhenitsyn's *One Day*, an event that cheered the liberals, the thaw gave way to a new freeze. In December 1962, Khrushchev, following his visit in Moscow to an exhibition of paintings and sculptures erroneously dubbed abstract (in Western terms the exhibition would have been labeled simply "post-impressionist"), launched a violent campaign against modernism in all the arts. Then in highly publicized "encounters" between leading government officials and intellectuals there was a return to the rigid line in literature. Between November 1962 and May 1963 the literary thermometer indicated a severe drop in temperature: it remained unchanged for the next decade.

There were several causes for such a sudden change. One of them was the spread of the liberal movement and the aggressiveness of an avant-garde emboldened by the withdrawal of coercive measures. When attacked by the dogmatists, writers and artists fought back and answered their critics—unimaginable under Stalin when the victims of Party indictment and denunciations were compelled to accept the blows in silence and recant in public. Moreover, the majority of young Soviet intellectuals sympathized with the liberals. As it had done under the Tsarist regime, the liberal opposition formed a sort of free masonry, and its ranks remained intact even when lightning and thunder descended from the heights of the Kremlin. Quite a few members of the Party Presidium naturally saw in such a situation danger for the future.

On the other hand, the attitude of the USSR during the Cuban crisis in the fall of 1962 provoked resentment among Khrushchev's comrades. The conservatives insisted that "softness" and concessions to the liberals would be interpreted by foes, particularly by the Chinese, as an ideological surrender following on the heels of a political one. A spectacular re-affirmation of doctrinal integrity was necessary, and it had to begin with a tightening of Party controls. A campaign which began with the plastic arts soon extended to prose and poetry. In January and March 1963 Khrushchev and Leonid Ilyichev, the official theoretician, made new thrusts against the "modernists" in public gatherings, accusing them of aiming at "ideological co-existence with the capitalist world"—a most heretical idea which had nothing in common with the Party slogan of "pacific international co-existence." Evtushenko was pilloried and so was Victor Nekrassov. The latter was threatened with expulsion from the Party because of his *Kira Georghievna* and especially on account of his letters from the USA, in which he dared to express an objective, and at times favorable, view of American life and art. Ehrenburg was taken to task for his defense of the 'twenties. Changes were made in editorial boards (*Literary Gazette* got the conservative Alexander Chakovsky as editor-in-chief) and in the administration of the Moscow Union of Soviet Writers.

In May 1963, however, things began to look brighter. The diatribes against the "decadents and revisionists" in the press lost some of their virulence, the project of lumping writers, painters, musicians, actors, and film producers together into a single, centralized union was postponed indefinitely, and literary monthlies resumed publication of stories by some critical realists. In August during the Leningrad meeting of the European Community of Writers, official Soviet speakers, including Fedin, extolled socialist realism as the only "fruitful literary trend" and dismissed Joyce, Proust, and Kafka as "decadent bourgeois formalists" whom Russians have no use for. Yet the floor was also given to Ehrenburg and other "subversives" who openly defended the right to creative experimentation.

At Gagry, Khrushchev's summer residence, foreign guests, including Sartre, Simone de Beauvoir, Alain Robbe-Grillet, Giuseppe Ungaretti, and others, were treated to a reading of "Tyorkin in the Other World," an anti-Stalinist satire by Alexander Tvardovsky, a leading liberal. His hero discovers after death that the other world has the same secret police, stupid censorship, bureaucratic abuse, and unjust rule of bosses that he suffered from in his life on earth. The poem is written in an easy, folksy, and humorous style and compares the common sense of the warm-hearted, simple minded private Tyorkin to the shenanigans, casuistry, and machine-like efficiency of the administrators of the nether regions. Copies of "Tyorkin in the Other World" circulated in Moscow in manuscript for two years, and one of its versions was reproduced at the beginning of 1963 by the *émigré* journal *The Bridges* in Munich. Finally the decision, a significant one, was made to print it in *Novy Mir*. "Tyorkin in the Other World" had great success with the readers and later was 'staged in one of the Moscow theaters. Capacity audiences applauded it for two years.

In general, 1963 ended in Moscow with the skies not so heavily overcast as they had been a few months before. This did not mean that the situation had radically changed. The battle between the liberals and the dogmatists went on as usual, and open or disguised Stalinists still held dominant positions on editorial boards and Party cultural institutions; but a sort of a stalemate had again been established between the two camps.

Less lucky was Vladimir Voinovich, one of the most promising and brilliant writers of the 1960's. Considered a non-conformist by the authorities, magazines and publishers refused to bring out his works; in 1974 he decided to publish his stories and his main work, *The Life and Unexpected Adventures of the Soldier Ivan Chonkin*, outside of Russia. He was immediately expelled from the Union of Soviet Writers and practically ostracized. *Ivan Chonkin* is a delightful, hilarious tale about a Russian simpleton, almost a double of the famous Private Schweik by the Czech humorist Hašek. It would not be an exaggeration to say that this still unfinished novel is the merriest and most meaningful Russian satirical work of the last decade.

Khrushchev's fall from power in October 1964 and his replacement by Leonid Brezhnev as Party secretary, and Alexey Kosygin as premier, brought little change in the disposition of conflicting and often clashing forces in literature and the arts. But during 1964 and 1965 it looked as though the conservatives and the Stalinists had gained several points over the liberals, both in Leningrad and in Moscow, and the stalemate between the two camps had come to an end.

In the spring of 1964 writers in the Soviet Union and in the

West were surprised by the unusual trial that took place in Leningrad. Yosif Brodsky, born in that city in 1940, was accused of being "an idler and a parasite" without "any socially useful work." His reply that he was a poet and a translator provoked sneers and jibes from the judges. The entire trial, so senseless and vulgar, was a caricature of justice. Although Brodsky had not committed a crime or a transgression, this Kafka-like tribunal sentenced him to five years of forced labor in the North.

He had begun serving his term, loading and carrying manure in a *kolkhoze* near Arkhangelsk, when rumors of his fate brought forth energetic protests in both the Soviet Union and the West. Under this double pressure the government decided to suspend his sentence. In the meantime his poems had been smuggled abroad and printed in the United States and Europe in the original and in translation. They revealed the uniqueness of the poet's diction and themes. Unlike the forceful poets of the podium, Evtushenko and, in part, Voznesensky, Brodsky remained aloof from the outside world and concentrated on inner visions. His individual stanzas, as well as his long poems ("The Great Elegy to John Donne," "The Procession," "Abraham and Isaac"), contain many concrete details but are basically dreamlike and fantastic, almost surrealistic. At twenty-four this "Stepchild of the Century," as he called himself, found his own language, sarcastic and tender, with highly personal intonations and changing meters.

Brodsky was freed in September 1965, the same month in which two writers, Andrey Siniavsky and Yuli Daniel, were arrested in Moscow and accused of having published their works —in the original and in numerous translations—abroad under the names of Abram Tertz and Nikolay Arzhak. Siniavsky-Tertz, a contributor to *Novy Mir*, was known as a literary critic and the author of books on Picasso and on Soviet poetry of the 1920's. He had also written an excellent introduction to a volume of Pasternak's poems (after his arrest this was removed from subsequent editions). Daniel-Arzhak was a translator. Both men, who were in their early forties, belonged to the new generation of the Soviet intelligentsia, and their arrest was interpreted as a blow to the liberals. During the trial of the two writers, in February 1966, no foreign correspondents were allowed in the courtroom, and no exceptions were made for representatives of the Communist press. The trial was called public, but those who attended it by special authorization were not permitted to stay in the courtroom for more than one session. The outcome of the pseudo-legal proceedings had been decided in advance by the Kremlin, and the debates resembled a dialogue of the deaf. The prosecutor, members of the court, and the well-chosen "witnesses" spoke in strictly political terms, while the two writers referred to their tales as literary works and claimed the freedom of artistic expression—a move that stunned the magistrates with its daring.

The harshness of the judgment was obviously due to an ulterior motive: to teach a lesson and give warning to the liberals and rebels among the Russian intellectuals, and to reaffirm the rigid line in literature, thus giving some satisfaction to Party dogmatists. Siniavsky was sentenced to seven, and Daniel to five, years of hard labor in a "severe regime camp." This penalty provoked a storm of protests in the West, and even prominent Communists, among them Louis Aragon, the French poet and novelist, raised their voices in favor of the convicted writers. More significant yet were reactions within the Soviet Union. The White Book prepared by the poet Alexander Guinzburg in Moscow, and sent to the authorities in 1966, contains 185 documents, including letters to the Presidium of the Supreme Soviet by sixty-two prominent writers who offered to bail out Siniavsky and Daniel, and letters by members of the Party who emphasized the harm to Communism this unprecedented and badly conducted trial had caused. The fact that these writers were punished not for a crime or a transgression of the Soviet law, but for their fiction, raised anger and resentment throughout the world, including the USSR. This was the beginning of a long procession of Soviet trials against writers, intellectuals, political dissidents, religious believers, and sectarians, and, in general, all sorts of non-conformists. For more than a decade this mockery and violation of legality provoked indignation in civilized countries and was condemned in the Soviet Union by such true defenders of justice and the rights of man as the academician Andrey Sakharov and his noble friends, who have been arrested and deported because of their protests.

Both Siniavsky and Daniel wrote in a free, imaginative manner, which shocked the conservatives as being too provocative and modern. Siniavsky, the more talented, builds his stories on a deliberate use of the grotesque. His "The Trial Begins" (1965) depicts purges of the Stalinist era, the dramatic clash of a Party prosecutor and his young son, whom he will condemn for his alleged non-conformism, all this in dreamlike sequences which reveal the intimate life of the new ruling class and the inner conflicts of its members. His favorite literary device is hyperbolic metaphor. In "The Tenants," the maddening conditions of a crowded communal apartment bring out supernatural features in the lodgers, who are shown as ghosts, ghouls and witches. The frightening confessions of an intellectual ("The Icicle") sound like a nightmare; the writing passion becomes quite pathological in the hero of "Graphomaniacs"; and Soviet citizens, haunted by imaginary informers and hidden secret agents, are affected by a persecution mania ("You and I"). Every comic situation in Siniavsky's stories has pathetic accents and a tragic essence.

A highly cultivated, widely read man, Siniavsky looked at Soviet reality from a personal angle and represented it subjectively, in a deliberately whimsical and satirical form. His idealistic outlook, his preoccupation with the psychological roots of human behavior and with universal problems, are best expressed in "Thoughts at Random," a sort of fragmentary diary. Siniavsky's fascinating tales, partly influenced by Dostoevsky and Kafka, abound in realistic details which enhance the satirical vision of life. At the Moscow trial the chief justice, Lev Smirnov, quoted this writer's statement that Soviet society was pictured in Siniavsky's stories as a madhouse. He omitted, however, the rest of the statement, which goes on to say that the unbelievable, presented in the light of brilliant metaphors, is taken as the norm by heroes. Siniavsky's very style was interpreted as proof of political subversion; the judges simply dismissed the last words of the defendant who tried in vain to make them understand that his exaggeration, similes, irony and allusive symbols were but tools for the poetic transformation of facts and characters. It was this clash, between a creator claiming his liberty and a bureaucrat reducing everything to political categories, which formed the real background of the Tertz-Arzak affair.

In his brittle and stimulating essay on socialist realism, Siniav-

sky thus formulated his literary credo: "Right now I put my
hope in a phantasmagorical art, with hypotheses instead of a purpose, an art in which the grotesque will replace realistic description or ordinary life. Such an art would correspond best to the
spirit of our time. May the fantastic imagery of Hoffmann and
Dostoevsky, of Goya, Chagall and Mayakovsky . . . teach us how
to be truthful with the aid of the absurd and imaginary." Siniavsky's figurative, allegorical style, and his view of life as grotesque,
a dream, can be traced back to Gogol. However, Gogol was not
brought to court because he depicted imperial officials as fools
and knaves in *The Inspector General,* or presented, in *Dead
Souls,* a gallery of provincial gentry as loathsome, grimacing
creatures.

Siniavsky's short novel, "Liubimov" (which this writer does
not count among the best works of Abram Tertz), represents a
mythical dictator who rules over a forlorn town and mesmerizes
its population into blind obedience, but who finally loses his hyp-
notic power and is overthrown by loyal Soviet troops. This is
pure satire, obviously inspired by the famous Russian nineteenth-
century novelist Saltykov, particularly by his *History of a Town,*
which ridicules a whole procession of Russia's tsars and their
ministers. But again, Saltykov was not sentenced to hard labor
because of thinly veiled hints and allusions to emperors and courtiers, while his literary follower was treated as a criminal for a
similar impudence toward his contemporaries. The Communist
state can accept only toothless, insipid satire, and reacts violently
against satire that is biting and aggressive; this is one reason why
Siniavsky and Daniel found themselves prisoners in a concentration camp.

Yuli Daniel-Arzhak, a minor figure in comparison with his
friend, also writes satirically. His stories include: "This Is Moscow
Speaking," about a fantastic day of legal murder established
throughout the USSR by Supreme Soviet decree but leading to
little bloodshed; "Man from Minap," in which the Party tries to
channel a young man's presumed ability to determine the sex of
his children. Perhaps less successful is "Hands," a dramatic tale
about a henchman with trembling hands, haunted by the memory
of his victim, an old priest. Daniel, nevertheless, undoubtedly has
remarkable literary talent, and the works of both Siniavsky and

Daniel are part of the outstanding Russian fiction of the 1960's. It is quite obvious that Siniavsky and Daniel are not unique phenomena, and that other talented writers are creating valuable work which is still concealed in their native country. The discovery and publication of these stories, novels and poems must be left to a more or less distant future. Some of these works circulate in manuscript in Moscow, some are smuggled abroad. It must be said, however, that those published in Europe and the United States in the 1960's and 1970's do not comprise the best specimens of the so-called "clandestine Soviet literature." Some poems, particularly by university students, are interesting as documents of moods and inclinations of the new generation but not as valid literary achievements.

The case of Valery Tarsis (b. 1902) may be interesting from a political standpoint, but his works follow the well-worn track of tendentious prose and do not rise above the level of second-rate Soviet fiction. A former Communist and later a rabid adversary of the regime, Tarsis published abroad—mostly under his own name—*The Bluebottle, Red and Black,* and *What a Gay Life,* all of which are satirical exposés of Stalinism and bureaucratic abuses. Apostolov, the hero of *What a Gay Life,* can easily be taken as a physical and moral caricature of Khrushchev. Following the publication of his novels in England, Tarsis was taken into custody in 1962, and then incarcerated for a year in a mental institution. (This latest measure prescribed by Soviet authorities for rebellious artists was also applied to M. Naritsa-Narymov, a sculptor, whose *Unsung Song,* a lyrical protest against injustice and violence, was published in Munich in 1962). Valery Tarsis was set free after intervention from the West, and he wrote of his experiences in *Ward 7* (1965), an outspoken attack on the philosophy and practices of Communism. In 1965 Tarsis was permitted to go abroad, but a few days after his departure Moscow announced that he had been deprived of Soviet citizenship. He lived in Europe as an expatriate and visited the United States, but his public appearances and 1966 writings revealed, unfortunately, such a queer combination of megalomania, pretense and vulgarity that, instead of helping, he only harmed the foes of the Communist regime.

Unlike Siniavsky and Daniel, most authors, including Tarsis, whose works cannot be published in the Soviet Union, belong stylistically to the conservatives and by no means mirror the new tendencies. But what makes the so-called "clandestine literature" symptomatic, is the fact that it does represent the general desire for truth and honesty. In the 1960's and 1970's the reaction against officially approved stereotypes, the "correction of history," the varnishing of reality, stock characters, and false, inflated language, acquired an unparalleled impetus. Its effects can be traced in fiction and—to a lesser degree—in criticism. The chief aim of the decade was to tell the truth, but the rejection of consecrated patterns was not easy and met with stubborn resistance. Some works on war, for instance, without being outstanding aesthetically, became popular because their authors showed courage and integrity. In 1965, the twentieth anniversary of the fall of Germany occasioned *The Last Two Weeks* by Alexander Rosen, which depicts the period preceding Hitler's sudden attack without hiding the fact of the Soviet's lack of military and psychological preparation. *July 1941* by Grigory Baklanov deals with the same theme and unfolds a sad, moving panorama of conditions in Russia the first month after the Nazi invasion. *Hot Snow*, Baklanov's 1974 war novel, sold two million copies. In general, war continues to be the main theme of Soviet literature, which explains the popularity of Simonov's novels and even his diaries of the war years.

The Dead Feel No Pain, by the Byelorussian Vasil Bykov, provoked the ire of Communist critics and was sharply censored in the spring of 1966 at the Twenty-third Party Congress as a "work filled with subversive tendencies and distortions." Bykov (b. 1924), was eighteen when he joined the army, and he recounts, in the first person, the adventures of a junior lieutenant and his companions, wounded and pursued by the Germans. His story deals primarily with the unglorious aspects of war—the bungling of incompetent commanders, the stiffness of bureaucrats at critical moments, the suffering of common soldiers—but above all, the inhuman activities of the secret police and their sadistic, power-hungry agents who look for subversion even on the battlefield, and do not hesitate to torture and kill. Although Bykov's descriptions may appear crude and too naturalistic, their emotional intensity has appealed to thousands of readers. The protagonist of *The Pack*, one of his last works, says that he is not a hero, and in general Bykov depicts humble privates and represents their inner fears and apprehensions, without glorifying the "heroic deeds of the Soviet people" in that typical rhetorical style which had become a "must" in war literature. The Party press attacked Bykov because, in their words, he "offended the honor of the glorious Soviet Army." This is typical of Russian practice today. In the fall of 1966 *The Red Star*, the organ of the Defense ministry, angrily denounced the story "On Home Leave" by A. Makarov, which portrays a soldier on leave drinking and carousing in his native village. In a similar way, truck drivers protested against a novel in which a Crimean member of their group was shown taking bribes; and steel workers in Siberia felt that a literary figure in another novel was damaging their good name.

The *kolkhoze* theme is another sensitive area. Although everyone knows that Soviet agriculture is not doing well, a novel telling the truth about work and life in the village is called "pessimistic and revisionistic." Such was the case with Fyodor Abramov's *Round and About* (1964), a frank documentary of a poor and badly administered rural community. *From the Life of Fyodor Kuzkin* by Boris Mozhayev, a short novel published by *Novy Mir* in the fall of 1966, fared no better with the zealots of orthodoxy. The novel's witty, earthy language, the crisp dialogue and the peasant flavor remind one of Solzhenitsyn. Mozhayev's hero, a "little man," does not want to sing in tune with the cowed majority of a despotically ruled *kolkhoze*, and falls victim to bureaucratic machinations and repressions. He finally quits the community and tries to make a living by his own wits, outside the collective.

Two Siberians, Vasily Shukshin (1929-74) and Valentin Rasputin (b. 1937), are probably the best representatives of rural prose in the 1970's. Shukshin was a prodigiously talented man, a poet, storyteller in the Chekhovian vein, film producer, actor, and the author of two moviescripts—*The Lubavins* (1965) and *I Came to Bring You Freedom* (1971)—about Razin, an eighteenth-century peasant rebel. A man of extraordinary artistic possibilities, Shukshin died at the summit of his creative career. He wrote, directed, and acted as the hero of his last, extremely popular picture, *The Red Snowdrop Berry* (1974), in which a released criminal looks for inner peace and a normal life in his native village and is killed by members of his former gang.

Rasputin's tales are not as amusing or psychologically convincing as those of Shukshin but they often have a more tragic character—for instance, his short novel *Live and Remember*, about a war deserter and his unhappy wife. The young writers Vassily Belov and Alexander Bitovalso belong to the group of storytellers devoted to the description of village folk.

A general survey of Soviet letters between 1965 and 1975 offers a rather mournful picture. No change had occurred in the relationship between the rulers and the ruled: the dogma and the practice of the Party remained unalterable, the machine led by bureaucrats and security police, continued to crush inexorably any shade of opposition, while the cringed majority of writers went on adapting themselves to the Establishment and trying to extract from it the maximum of material benefits—often at the price of painful compromises and hypocrisy. The thin layer of various dissenters or simply honest men who raised their voices in defense of freedom and justice have been banned, arrested, and exiled, and the wheels of the gigantic mechanism did not slow down their monotonous and inhuman rotation and grinding. It did not spare even such well-known members of the Party as Alexander Tvardovsky: his name was dropped from the list of candidates to the Central Committee, and then in 1970 he was forced to resign his post as editor-in-chief of *Novy Mir*, which thanks to his efforts had become the mouthpiece of liberal and more independent literature. All his assistants were dismissed, and the magazine, under new leadership, was swiftly transformed into a faded and subservient publication. Tvardovsky died a year later (December 1971).

Despite the impressive statistics registering the huge output of books, the results of the last decade in terms of literary value were rather meager. It would be impossible for any observer to find memorable works of prose and poetry in the 1970's—with the exception of Solzhenitsyn's novels. The most striking illustration of this fact was the grandiose celebration of Lenin's centenary in 1970. Thousands of volumes, ranging from scholarly treatises and personal memoirs to collections of poems and tomes of fiction, flooded the market. The balance sheet of this manifestation, however, was recognized as unsatisfactory by even the most loyal Communists. To present a relatively objective report on today's situation means simply to list a selection of works which seem to be above the usual level of uniformity and banality.

Among the writers of the older generation, Valentin Katayev, born in 1897, surprised readers and critics by publishing in 1966 *The Holy Well*, a modernistic narrative completely lacking any social preaching. It included an amazing vision of the United States, treated the problem of time and space in a free avant-garde manner, mixing dreams and reality. His next work, *The Grass of Oblivion*, offered reminiscences on the first years of the Revolution and an excellent portrait of Ivan Bunin, whom Katayev recognizes as his master. In *A Broken Life, or Oberon's Magic Horn* (1972) Katayev returns to humorous and sentimental evocations of his childhood and adolescence, and hails the colorful port of Odessa, the lively Ukraine city.

In opposition to the revival of Katayev stands the decline of one of the relatively young—Evgeny Evtushenko (b. 1933). He had a meteoric and brilliant career as a lyrical poet but wanted to become a social bard and, after some success, failed in this ambitious attempt in the 1960's. His poetry in the 1970's was repetitious and shallow. His popular image has also been tarnished. The ambiguity of his relations with the "bosses," his noisy, strange contradictory public statements in prose and verse, and his apparent acceptance of being used abroad as a medium of propaganda, saddened and disappointed his former fans.

Voznesensky, at least, did not pretend to become a loudspeaker of the nation and limited his revolutionary zeal to linguistics. His political pronouncements were rare and cautious (even though in "The Prologue to a Poem" (1967) he fiercely denounced the Chinese and stressed the destiny of "eternal Russia to shield the West from oriental hordes"). His last collections, such as *In Shadow of Sound*, do not bring anything new but continue to show his verbal mastery and art of poetic acrobatics.

In prose there are quite a few talented young and middle-aged writers, such as Vassily Belov, Alexander Bitov, Yury Trifonov, Vladimir Voinovich, Vassily Shukshin, Valentin Rasputin, Chinghis Aitmatov, Vassily Bykov, and many others. The war seems to continue to form one of the main subjects in Soviet literature.

A characteristic of recent literary production is the emergence of "peripheral" writers, natives of Asiatic regions of the country. Among them the first places are attributed to Fazil Iskander and Chinghis Aitmatov. Iskander (b. 1929), a poet and humorist, writes cheerful stories about the people and old customs of his native Abhasia, a small Caucasian republic federated with Georgia. His satirical *The Kozlotur Constellation* is a fantastic, ironic, and very funny story of a stubborn Party official who foisted upon the *kolkhoze* on the Black Sea shore an incredible hybrid of the argali and the goat. Written in the same folklore vein with verbal mastery and genuine wit are Iskander's *The Man with the Shriveled Arm* and particularly the 1974 novel *Sandro from Tchighima*, serialized in *Novy Mir*. The latter is filled with benevolent humor and exotic flavor.

Another exotic author, the Kirghiz Chinghis Aitmatov, wrote interesting, well-constructed stories about his Mongolian kinsmen. His short novel, *The White Steamer*, depicting the dreams, trials, and suicide of a lonely boy in Soviet Asia, provoked heated discussions in the 1970's because of its symbolic allusions. Most critics praised the poetic and psychological qualities of the novel, but others accused it of pessimism—considered almost a crime in the land of compulsory optimism.

Central Asia is also the location of *The Custodian of Antiquities* by Yury Dombrovsky, serialized in *Novy Mir*. Written in the first person, it relates the adventures, thoughts, and feelings of a young man in the late 1930's who has joined the staff of a State museum in Alma Ata, capital of the Kazakh Republic. The hero dislikes various aspects of his environment, particularly the vulgar propaganda and ineptitude of militant Communists, and, seeking escape from the harsh realities of "collectivistic" life, turns to nature and archeology. Despite the non-political character of his interests, the secret police suspect him of subversion, and he gets involved in dark intrigues and will probably be purged. Unfortunately, obvious cutting by censors has marred the second part of this rich and unusual narrative. A special niche should be reserved for Dombrovsky's *The Dark Lady*. Printed in 1970 in a relatively small edition, it became quite popular among young artists and intellectuals. In three novelettes it evokes Shakespeare's love for Mary Fitton (presumably the "dark lady" of his sonnets), his family life, and his death. The book welds fact and fantasy and offers a relief from the stereotypes of current Soviet fiction.

Also to be singled out is the magnificent *The Life and Unexpected Adventures of the Soldier Ivan Chonkin*, a highly comical satire by the very talented Vladimir Voinovich. He wrote it in the late 'sixties but could not publish it in the Soviet Union, was expelled from the Writers Union, and sent the manuscript abroad where it was published in 1974 and obtained an ever-growing success. The story of Chonkin, a Russian simpleton, victim of formalism and military bureaucracy, has common traits with the famous soldier Schweik by the Czech humorist Yaroslav Hašek.

It is impossible to anticipate the next series of fluctuations in Communist literary policy or in the development of Russian arts and letters. In both areas changes will inevitably occur and their direction depends on so many factors, including the international situation, the possibility of war and peace, the degree of tension or relaxation between the Communist and non-Communist states, relations between the East and the West, and the internal evolution of Communism itself. In any event the course Russian literature has taken in the late 1950's and early 1960's points toward greater independence and creative freedom. This overall trend is irreversible—even though it may take years to develop and though many young men and women will suffer from external pressures and from the forced imposition of antiquated aesthetics.

The Third Emigration

In the first decade after the 1917 Revolution, nearly one million Russians abandoned their homeland and moved to various countries around the world, mostly to Europe and North America. This first emigration included the remnants of the vanquished White armies—several hundred thousands—and a large number of people from the "suppressed" social classes, the aristocracy, the gentry, and the upper bourgeoisie. But this huge human wave also carried on its crest a multitude of intellectuals, poets, novelists, journalists, scholars, academicians, musicians, and artists. They formed a lively Russian diaspora with their daily and weekly papers, monthlies, scientific journals, publishing houses, schools, universities, theaters, and all sorts of cultural enterprises. Future historians will be amazed by the multiple activities of these émigrés, but we can already emphasize the important part played by their writers. Quite a few of them shifted to writing in a foreign language—the most striking examples of this group being Vladimir Nabokov who became a world-famous American novelist, and Henri Troyat, elected to the French Academy of "Immortals" for his works of fiction. However, the great majority of older émigrés, led by Ivan Bunin, the first Russian to receive the Nobel Prize in literature (1933), continued to write in their native language. In the 1920's and 1930's the first emigration counted many prominent pre-revolutionary novelists, such as Remizov, Merezhkovsky, Zaitsev, Kuprin, Shmelyov, and others, and a host of excellent poets—among them Khodassevich, Hippius, Georges Ivanov, and Tsvetayeva. Writers of the younger generation were soon added to the old guard. A similar phenomenon took place in the field of philosophy, represented by Berdiaev, Shestov, and their friends, and in all the other branches of art, particularly in music, where Stravinsky and Rachmaninoff were the leading figures.

It is common knowledge that the Russian emigration had a strong impact, until World War II, on the culture of various countries in which it settled. That catastrophe destroyed the existing Russian colonies in Europe and forced many émigrés to look for refuge on the other side of the globe, mainly in the USA, where they contributed greatly to American cultural life.

In the wake of World War II and the Nazi atrocities, former Russian prisoners of war, national minorities from the Baltic states, and refugees from countries shattered by Soviet invasions and annexations formed the so-called second emigration. Their group was closer than its predecessor to Soviet realities but contained only a limited number of the intelligentsia. On the whole, however, it infused some new blood and brought a fresh outlook to the aging members of the older generation of émigrés.

The third emigration in the 'seventies had a completely different composition. It should not be confused with the thousands of Russian Jews who, after years of waiting, struggle, and efforts, finally obtained visas to Israel and went there. A small group of these émigrés, identifying themselves as members of the Russian intelligentsia, joined the true third emigration whose main bulk— socially and psychologically—was formed by dissidents leaving the USSR for political reasons or even being forced out by the authorities. Many of them were granted official permits to go abroad because the Soviet government wanted to get rid of troublemakers. Most settled in Paris, Munich, Vienna, and the USA, a few in the Scandinavian countries, England, and Switzerland, and founded a closely knit society of men and women with a common past, common experiences in the homeland, and a basic opposition to the Communist regime. They represented various shades of opinion and faith but were unanimous in the rejection of totalitarian ideology and united in their craving for free expression.

The central figure of the third emigration was indubitably Alexander Solzhenitsyn, expelled from Russia and deprived of Soviet citizenship in February 1974. He has settled with his wife and children in Zurich, Switzerland, working hard and steadily, and has never missed an opportunity to say what he thinks on the problems of the day. Not all his views on the decline of the West and the aggressive policy of the Kremlin, on the "ethical revolution," and the role of the Greek Orthodox Church, have been shared by all the dissidents and the old exiles, but his courage, moral intrepidity, international fame, and genius have given him a unique position as a spiritual and literary leader.

Among other prominent writers, mention should be made of Andrey Siniavsky-Tertz, Vladimir Maximov (deprived of Soviet citizenship), Victor Nekrassov, laureate of two Stalin prizes, Alexander Galitch, a highly popular Soviet troubadour, Efim Etkind, a literary scholar, and a number of younger poets, writers of prose and criticism (Vassily Betaki, Natalia Gorbanevskaya, Vladimir Maramzin, Leonid Chertkov)—all living in France.

Another group of dissidents went to the USA: the poets Yosif Brodsky and Naum Korzhavin, the mathematicians Essenin Volpin, Valery Chalidze (deprived of Soviet citizenship and a friend of Andrey Sakharov, the head of the Moscow movement for human rights). A few of the young writers stayed in New York. Lea Vladimirova (b. 1938), a follower of Akhmatova, published a book of very good poems, *The Connection Of Time Periods*, in Jerusalem.

After his release from prison camp a year and a half prior to the end of his term, Andrey Siniavsky (b. 1925) was invited by the Sorbonne to give a course on Russian literature and in 1973 was authorized to go abroad with his wife and their little son. Since his establishment in France, Siniavsky has shown himself a brilliant lecturer and critic, and published several books in Russian, which were rapidly translated into foreign languages. The first was *A Voice from the Chorus*, based on the monthly letters he had sent to his wife from the Potma (Mordovia) labor camp. He was not permitted to write about camp conditions and his daily existence as a convict, and could give free vein only to his meditations and theoretical discourses. *A Voice from the Chorus* is therefore an unusual, thoroughly original confession; it reveals the religious and philosophical thoughts of an exceptional individual who in the darkness of a penitentiary preserved the sharpness of his mind and the intimate aspirations of his soul. Written in the form of an interior monologue, alternating moral humility with intellectual sophistication, it resembles the writings of Vassily Rozanov, the Russian existential thinker, and should be read slowly, like the fragments of Pascal or maxims of Montaigne. In France it was chosen as "the best foreign book" in 1974.

Before his arrest Siniavsky was already well known as a literary critic and author of excellent essays on Pasternak, Evtushenko, and modern poetry. In the first two years of his emigration he published two books, *In the Shadow of Gogol* and *Walks with Pushkin*, under his old pen name of Abram Tertz, probably using it to make clear that they were not historical treatises but subjective, sometimes fantastic interpretations in a free anti-pedantic style.

The book on Gogol, a volume of over 500 pages, shocked conservative specialists not only by its unconventional language but also by its approach to Gogol's inner duality and contradictions, analyzing psychologically and metaphysically the writer as a sorcerer, attracted and terrified by demons and witchcraft. What captivates the reader in this work, as well as in the smaller book on Pushkin, is Tertz's verbal flow with its interplay of scholarship, sarcasm, humor, independence of judgment, and daring conjectures.

Tertz's manner also prevails in *Walks with Pushkin* where the writer appears as a satirist and practitioner of fantastic realism, who is fed up with official monuments, laurel wreaths, and academic orations; he prefers a familiar slightly coarse speech filled with parody and comedy devices. But Siniavsky the critic stands just behind Tertz, offering penetrating revelations on Pushkin's masterpieces, particularly on *The Bronze Horseman, Don Juan, Eugene Onegin*, and on his unrestricted devotion to "pure art," which was akin to a religious cult. In all these books Siniavsky-Tertz displayed his rich, outstanding qualities as critic, philosopher, and artist and added to them the sharpness of a polemist. His essay "The Literary Process in Russia," published in October 1970 in the quarterly *Continent*, is probably the best analysis on this difficult theme. At the same time he obliquely explains the reasons which compelled many of his friends to choose the road of exile. "A Russian writer," says Siniavsky, who does not wish to write at the behest of the State is in the highly dangerous and fantastic situation of an underground author . . . exposed to harsh measures of suppression and punishment. Literature has become something forbidden, risky, and . . . all the more enticing, a sort of double-edged game or adventure which itself could constitute the plot of a fascinating novel.

The periodical *Continent*, where Siniavsky's article had appeared, became between 1974 and 1976 one of the most important publications of the third emigration (together with the already existing *New Russian Word*, the oldest *émigré* daily in New York, the Parisian weekly *Russian Thought*, the Frankfurt magazines *Facets*, *Posev* (Sowing), and the New York quarterly *New Review*). *Continent* was founded under Solzhenitsyn's aegis and with the financial aid of Germany's Ullstein Verlag. Its aim was to make it a common organ of dissidents from Russia and from the East European satellite countries. Sustained by its energetic editor-in-chief Vladimir Maximov and projected to appear not only in Russian, but also in German, French, English, and Italian, it called itself "a literary, social, political, and religious journal" and defined its program as based on "unconditional religious idealism, anti-totalitarianism, democracy, and non-partisanship." Each issue of over 400 pages contained fiction, essays, and articles by Soviet, Czech, Polish, Rumanian, and Hungarian publicists. It printed *With No Hands and No Feet*, a novel on the Russian youth of the war and post-war years by the talented Vladimir Kornilov (b. 1928), a poet living in Moscow, as well as other writers who sent their short stories to the quarterly. But the main contributors are the third emigration poets and prose writers. Solzhenitsyn gave *Continent* an unpublished chapter from *The First Circle*; Andrey Sakharov sent it his greetings from the Soviet Union, and the writings of many foreign *émigrés* appeared in various issues of the quarterly. Not all the material printed in *Continent* has been translated into its foreign language editions: the most complete of the latter is the German one; the French presents an extract, while the English and Italian editions are published with two years' delay. It is difficult to tell whether the journal has accomplished its initial purpose of serving as a bridge between the East European dissidents and publishing meaningful fiction and important information. It is also rather doubtful whether it has succeeded in making clear what the vague term of "religious idealism" signified.

It is true that the third emigration had the merit of bringing invaluable material to the West about the real conditions in the Soviet Union and about the complete degradation of revolutionary ideals by a tyrannical totalitarian regime—but these revelations based on personal experience appeared principally in books, memoirs, articles in periodicals, and interviews on the radio and television.

Perhaps Maximov, the initiator and guiding spirit of *Continent*, has done more by his novels and public appearances than by his quarterly, even though the latter has had the merit of uniting a large group of international anti-Communists on the same rostrum. He was born in 1932 into a proletarian family; his mother died, his father was imprisoned for seven years as a Trotskyite and was killed on the front during World War II. Brought up in orphanages and reform schools for young delinquents, Maximov learned the trade of stonemason, worked from the age of fifteen on various building projects, mostly in Siberia, roamed all over Russia, often associated with hoboes and thieves, and in general had a very checkered career, described later in his autobiographical *Farewell from Nowhere*. He started writing when toiling as an artisan in the Ukraine, published his first poems in 1956 and a short novel in 1961. He was soon acclaimed as a truly proletarian writer originating from the working class and as a talented self-taught man. In Moscow he was appointed to the editorial board of *October*, the hard-line Communist monthly. But after the revelations of the Twentieth Party Congress on Stalin, Maximov went through an ideological and religious crisis, was secretly baptized, then, horrified by the 1968 military invasion of Czechoslovakia and the suppression of the "Spring of Prague" by violence, he joined the dissidents, published his novel *Seven Days of Creation* in Germany (1971), and was expelled from the Union of Soviet Writers. He asked for an authorization to go abroad, and after many refusals, received it in 1974 on the day of Solzhenitsyn's banishment.

His main work is the five-hundred-page *Seven Days of Crea-*

tion. It contains six separate tales based on his own experience. They also form the chronicle of a proletarian family, the Lashkovs, and their trials and suffering during the war and the Revolution. The old Pyotr Lashkov, a Communist, appears directly or obliquely in each tale and unites them all. He undergoes a complex and painful psychological re-examination at the end of his life, being tormented by doubts about Party methods, conditions of life in the provinces, and the destiny of his relatives. The peregrinations of various members of the family offer Maximov the opportunity to describe different social strata and the changes in the Soviet morals between the end of the civil war and the 1960's. Particularly impressive is the third tale, "The Courtyard in the Middle of the Sky," telling the story of Vassily Lashkov, the janitor, his misfortunes, his confrontation with the police, his attempts to drown his inner troubles in vodka, and his utter loneliness. The fourth tale, "The Late Light," represents a psychiatric hospital that serves also as a prison for Vadim, Pyotr Lashkov's grandson, who had joined the dissidents and the Orthodox Church (Maximov himself had been thrown into such an institution for several months).

The novel is certainly one of the outstanding works of fiction in the 1970's: it proves the great imaginative gift of the author and his capacity to draw psychological in-depth portraits of numerous protagonists. He is a forceful storyteller who likes to represent inner conflicts and tragic situations. There is power and sweep in Maximov's picture of contemporary Russia, of its contradictions, woes, and spiritual quest. He is at his best when depicting clashes of opposite emotions and scenes of turmoil and violence. In general he is attracted by somber moods and shattering, negative events. Although Maximov's prose has its own, rather heavy rhythm, its style is uneven, and he often repeats Gorky's mixture of realistic, almost naturalistic details with romantic rhetoric and high-pitched exaggerations, and his language sometimes reminds one of the pseudo-impressionism of a Gladkov or the nineteenth-century populist "writers of the soil." While many chapters of his chronicle, especially the scenes of physical and moral disintegration, do have an intensity and persuasive directness, Maximov was not able to avoid some prolixity and overweight in composition—so that the abundance becomes heaviness. He has a strong feeling of drama and knows how to communicate it to the reader, but it is hardly ever expressed with artistic restraint. These negative traits are most visible in his second large narrative, *Quarantine*. Its plot is rather unusual: a train from Odessa, where a sudden outburst of cholera is discovered, is stopped midway to Moscow in forlorn countryside, encircled by a cordon of troops and submitted to six days of medical quarantine. The central figures are thirty-year-old Boris Khramov, an army captain, and his girl friend Maria; their mutual passion seems to cool but they feel some kind of spiritual awakening, under the influence of a mysterious Ivan Ivanovich, the bearer of a Christian message. The novel follows the old pattern of "the tale within a tale," with the emotions and thoughts of the couple constituting the inner core. On a second level, the passengers of the immobilized train sink into a gigantic orgy of drinking, make surprising confessions in a sort of delirium, and narrate to each other various realistic or fantastic stories. These anecdotes and fables are different in content and render the particular speech or slang of single narrators: the intellectual economist whom his unfaithful wife has simply thrown out of their apartment, tells of his homelessness and his nights in station waiting rooms in the company of bums, thieves, and prostitutes. A Jewish youth recounts in the idiom of the ancient "pale" the strange funeral of his uncle, an old Bolshevik who died forgotten and poor. An Estonian speaks of his dream of a universal language, like Esperanto, to bring brotherhood to mankind. Some stories are comic, some are tragic. Khramov's drunken reveries go back to his ancestors, from the pagan pre-Christian founder of the family to the grandfather who joined the Party and was executed during the Stalinist purges. Here Maximov expresses his ideas and constant visions of Russia's fate and the meaning and distortion of the Revolution.

The allegorical character of the novel is quite obvious: the epidemic of cholera is the image of evil and particularly of the disease that struck Russia (it reminds one of Camus' *The Plague*). One's soul needs a quarantine to achieve, like Khramov and Maria, a moral rebirth. This part of the novel might appear less convincing than its colorful pages describing Russia, but the didactic trend is very strong in Maximov, deriving from his sincere religious faith. It must be added that the use of parody and satire, the dramatic sense and the skill in portraying widely different human types, counterbalance the author's tendency toward preaching and redeem his occasional lack of taste and proportions. His artistic temperament often exposes him to verbosity.

Victor Nekrassov is the dean of the Soviet writers in exile. Born in 1911, the son of a Ukrainian physician, he studied architecture and dramatic art, and has been active as an actor and a theatrical designer. From 1941 to 1944, as a deputy commander of a sapper battalion he took part in the battle of Stalingrad, was wounded, joined the Communist Party, and published *In the Trenches of Stalingrad* in 1946. One of the best war books, it attracted millions of readers by its sincerity, lack of rhetoric, and a lyrico-psychological approach to events and people, and was awarded the Stalin prize; so was his next novel, *In the Home Town*. In the 1960's his objective travelogs on Europe and the United States and his articles about thousands and thousands of Jews and Ukrainians who had been massacred by the Nazi occupants brought down the thunder of Party officials on him. The situation worsened when Nekrassov refused to sign letters against Pasternak and other non-conformist writers and openly condemned the military pressure on Czechoslovakia in 1968. Nekrassov was then accused of anti-Soviet feelings, expelled from the Party and the Union of Soviet Writers in the 'seventies, was interrogated by the KGB (Russian abbreviation for Committee of State Security), and submitted to long disquisitions at his home in Kiev. One search lasted three days. He decided to leave Russia and in 1974 settled with his wife in Paris. He published "Notes of a Gawker" in the fourth issue of *Continent*, of which he became the assistant editor. "Notes of a Gawker" is written in a light rambling familiar autobiographical manner, ranging from childhood reminiscences to an evaluation of Kievan architecture, from a humoristic praise of vodka called epithalamium (Greek nuptial song) to descriptions of walks through Paris, and to cross-examinations by the secret police. What transpires from these apparently disconnected sketches and gives them an inner unity is the personality of their author—a candid man of great vitality, honesty, spontaneity, and devotion to truth, an enemy of false slogans and inhuman actions. Nekrassov accuses the rulers of the Soviet Union not only of Red imperialism and tyranny but also of lack of humanity, compassion, and of any nobility of feeling and actions. He never complains, keeps himself aloof from the wrangles and quarrels of his fellow *émigrés*, and remains for them the image of kindliness and moral integrity.

Alexander Galitch (b. 1918), has been a successful playwright and movie scenarist: his comedies and films made him widely known in the Soviet Union. But his true fame came in the 1960's when he devoted himself to lyrical and humoristic ballads that he sang, accompanying himself on the guitar—poet, musician, and performer. The modern troubadours in the Soviet Union had quite a vogue after the war, starting with the romantic and intimate songs of Bulat Okudzhava, who also accompanied himself on the guitar. But Galitch, despite his qualities as a poet, reached an unprecedented popularity both as a creator and performer of a special type of artistic production. Endowed with a satirical bent and the tremendous capacity for catching the funny details of Soviet life, from the lower classes to the Party rulers, he inaugurated as troubadour short sketches in verse, accentuated on stage by simple musical tunes and rendered with an amazing efficiency of intonation, pronunciation, accent, linguistic oddities, and slang of the concentration camps. On the one hand, his songs reflected trivialities of daily routine—drinking, scenes of love, lust, and jealousy, snobbery of the bosses and humility of the "offended and humiliated." On the other hand, they laughed at pretentious slogans, at mass brain washing, at the cowardice of small employees, and at the abomination of corrupted functionaries. He did not spare the treachery of writers and the murderous attacks of Party leaders against talented dissidents. After his epigrammatic ballads on Czechoslovakia and the exposure of "timorous souls," he was forbidden all public appearances in 1968. Then began a period of harassment and persecution: the authorities could not forgive Galitch for expressing in his ballads what so many were afraid to spell out. In 1971 he was expelled from the Union of Movie Craftsmen as well as from the Writers Union and forbidden to follow a treatment for his heart disease in a Moscow private clinic. Feeling ostracized and in permanent danger, Galitch decided to go abroad with his wife but obtained a visa only after having "renounced" his Soviet citizenship, and paying a five-hundred-ruble tax (per person) and four-hundred for exit visas (per person). Galitch and his wife arrived in Norway with only ninety rubles as their capital, and stayed with friends. Then Galitch undertook a series of public recitals and was acclaimed by enthusiastic Russian and foreign audiences in Geneva, Paris, London, Frankfurt, and other European cities. In 1974 he left Norway to live in France and Germany where he published his memoirs and a play, *General Rehearsal*, a book of poems, and recorded some of his songs.

It is impossible in this book to give a list of the young writers of prose and poetry belonging to the third emigration who came to the West between 1973 and 1976 and who have begun to publish their works in *émigré* periodicals. There are also numerous painters, such as Chemiakin, Gleser, and so forth, sculptors such as Ernst Neizvestny, Zlotkin, ballet artists, such as Baryshnikov, Makarova, Panov and his wife, and musicians such as the famous cellist and conductor Rostropovich, and numerous scholars and intellectuals. As a social phenomenon, the third emigration represents the reaction of the intelligentsia to the totalitarian government that denies individual freedom and tries to control all the creative endeavors of its citizens. It also reflects the sweep and the various currents of the opposition or dissidence which had become a new and significant phenomenon in the USSR in the 1960's and 1970's.

Index

Abramov, F., 323
  Round and About, 403
Afinogenov, A., 282-83, 292
  Eccentrics, The, 282; *Far
    Taiga*, 283; *Fear*, 282;
  Mashen'ka, 283
Agursky, M., 381
Aigi, G., 377
Aikenvald, Y., 50
  On the Sharp Edged Facet, 377
Aitmatov, C., 406
  White Steamer, The, 406
Akhmadulina, B., 343, 390-91
  Music Lessons, 390; "My Ge-
    nealogical Table," 390;
  String, 390
Akhmatova, A., 4, 9, 98, 248, 249,
    253-60, 302, 306, 325, 329, 410
  Anno Domini MCMXXI, 254;
  Evening, 254; *From the Six
    Books*, 255; *Glory to Peace*,
    257; *Golden Cockerel, The*,
    256; *Plantain*, 254; *Poem
    Without a Hero*, 257, 258-60;
  Reed, 255; *Requiem*, 257-58;
  Rosary, 254; *Selections*, 248,
    255; *Way of a Preface*, 257;
  White Flock, 254
Akimov, N., 285
Aksakov, S., 110
  Notes of a Rifle Hunter, 110
Aksyonov, V., 350-51
  "Halfway to the Moon," 350;
  "Oranges from Morocco,"
    350; *Tare of Barrels*, 351;
  Ticket to the Stars, 350
Aldington, R., 335
Aligher, M., 290, 302, 318

Fair Dale, 318; *Lenin's Hills*,
    318; *Zoya*, 302
Alliluyeva, S., 368
  One Year Only, 368; *Twenty
    Letters to a Friend*, 368
Altman, I., 307
Anderson, S., 335
Andreyev, L., 4, 176
Annals, 20, 70
*Annals of Samizdat: Uncensored
    Thought in the USSR*, 379
Antokolsky, P., 291, 302
Antonovskaya, A., 315
  Black Angel, The, 315
Aragon, L., 218, 398
  Bells of Basel, The, 219
Artzybashev, M., 176
Arzhak, N. *See* Daniel, Y.
Aseyev, N., 22, 30, 224, 342
  "Vladimir Mayakovsky," 30
Avdeyenko, A., 242
  Fate, 242; *I Love*, 242
Averbakh, L., 160, 162, 163
Azhayev, V., 247, 316
  Far Away From Moscow, 247,
    316

Babaevsky, S., 316
  *Knight of the Golden Star,
    The*, 316; *Light Over the
    Land, The*, 316
Babel, I., 54, 57, 58, 59, 60, 69-74,
    118, 169, 171, 222, 278, 285,
    327, 328, 329, 352
  "Beginning, The," 69; "Dante
    Street," 69; "Death of Dol-
    gushov, The," 73; "Di
    Grasso", 69; "First Love,"

69; "Gapa Guzhva," 69;
"History of my Dovecote,"
69, 70; *Marie*, 69; *Odessa
Tales*, 73; *Red Cavalry*, 69,
70-72, 73, 74; *Sunset*, 69;
Velikaya Krinitsa, 69
Bagritsky, E. (Dziubin, E.), 57,
59, 106, 118, 132-33, 288
"Fowler, The," 132; *Last
Night, The*, 133; "Lay of
Opanas, The," 133; *South-
west*, 132-33; *Victors, The*,
133
Bakhmetiev, V., 328
Baklanov, G., 299
Hot Snow, 402; *July 1941*, 402;
South of the Main Push, 340;
This Palm of Land, 299
Balmont, K., 4
Balzac, H. de, 335
Banner, The (Znamia), 52, 321,
322
Beauvoir, S. de, 395
Bedny, D. (Pridvorov, Y.), 16,
38, 39
Men of Might, 39
Bek, A., 300
*Highway of Volokolamsk,
The*, 300; *New Appoint-
ment*, 378
Beklemishev (Krymov, Y.), 242n
Belov, V., 404, 406
Bely, A., 9, 53, 55, 62, 82, 199,
251, 265, 270, 279, 392
At the Turn of the Century,
54; *Beginning of a Century,
The*, 54; *Between Two Rev-
olutions*, 54; "Christ is
Risen," 9; *Kotik Letayev*, 53;
Moskva, 53; *Petersburg*, 53;
Recollections of Blok, 53
Berdiaev, N., 50, 408
Berezko, G., *Division Com-
mander*, 299
Bergelson, D., 307, 328
Bergholz, O., 321

Land of Stalingrad, The, 318;
Leningrad Poem, A, 301;
Talk About Lyricism, A, 321
Beria, L., 238, 313, 320, 345
Bessalko, A., 34
Betaki, V., 410
Bezymensky, A., 30, 38, 290
"The Tragic Night," 290
Bill-Belotserkovsky, V., *Storm,
The*, 281
Bitov, A., 406
Bitovalso, A., 404
Blok, A., 3, 7, 8, 9, 31, 38, 64, 84,
147, 227, 251, 254, 258, 265,
290, 301, 385
Retaliation, 229; "Scythians,"
9; *Twelve, The*, 8, 9
Blucher, F., 238
Bobrov, S., 225
Bogdanov, A. (Malinovsky, A.),
35
Art and the Working Classes,
35
Bokov, V., 343
Böll, H., 371
Bondarev, Y., *Silence, The*, 330
Borodin, S. (Sarghidzhan, A.),
274, 299
Dimitry Donskoy, 274; *Stars
Over Samarkand*, 274
Bowen, E., 186
Borisov, V., 381
Braque, G., 218
Brecht, B., 335
Breton, A., 218
Brezhnev, L., 338, 396
Bridges, The, 396
Brik, O., 22, 172
Briussov, V., 4, 37, 53
Brodsky, Y., 377, 397, 410
"Abraham and Isaac," 397;
"Great Elegy to John Donne,
The," 397; "Procession,
The," 397; *Verse and Long
Poems*, 377
Brown, C., 251

Bubenov, M., *White Birch, The,* 298
Budenny, S., 74
Bukharin, N., 49, 182, 238
Bulgakov, M., 50, 54, 105, 328, 352-56
  Days of Turbins, The, 57, 281, 353; "Devilry," 353; "Fatal Eggs," 353; *Heart of a Dog, The,* 353-54; *Last Days, The,* 354; *Master and Margarita, The,* 354-56; *Molière,* 354; *Purple Island, The,* 353; *Run, The,* 353; *Theatrical Romance,* 354; *White Guard, The,* 281, 353; *Zoika's Apartment,* 282, 353
Bulgakov, S., 50, 381
Bulganin, N., 320
Bunin, I., 4, 18, 110, 118, 134, 328, 349, 393, 405, 408
  Hippius' Diary, 4; *Ungodly Days,* 4
Burliuk, D., 19
Burns, R., 132
Bykov, V., 402-3, 406
  Dead Feel No Pain, The, 402; *Park, The,* 403
Byron, G., 259, 308

Caldwell, E., 335
Camus, A., 231, 335
  Plague, The, 415
Chaikovsky, N., 147
Chakovsky, A., 395
Chalidze, V., 410
  Chronicle of Human Rights in the USSR, 379
Chapyghin, A., 273, 275
  Razin Stepan, 273; *Rovers, The,* 273
Chekhov, A., 73, 95, 134, 245, 321, 342, 348, 349
Chekhov, M., 281
Cherny, B., *Black Angel, The,* 315

Cherny, O., *Sneghin's Opera,* 312
Chernyshevsky, N., *What To Be Done?,* 185
Chertkov, L., 410
Chesterton, G. K., 215
Christie, A., 335
  Witness for the Prosecution, 335
Chukovskaya, L., 196
  Deserted House, The, 365
Chukovsky, K., 196
  "Reading Akhmatova," 260
Cocteau, J., 218
Coleridge, S., 132
Constant, B., 256
Continent, 378, 411, 412-13
Cooper, J., 180
Crankshaw, E., 375
Culture and Life, 308

Daniel, Y. (Arzhak, N.), 143, 196, 397-401
  "Hands," 400; "Man from Minap," 400; "This is Moscow Speaking," 400
Dante, 259
  Divine Comedy, 367
Day of Poetry, 343
Days to Come, The, 35
Deniken, A., 147
Derzhavin, G., 27, 251, 361
Diakov, B., *What I Went Through,* 364
Dickens, C., *Tale of Two Cities,* 137
Dolinin, A. (Iskoz, A.), 279
Dolmatovsky, 290, 387, 389
  Far Eastern Poems, 290; "Our Years," 387
Dombrovsky, Y., 406-7
  Custodian of Antiquities, The, 406; *Dark Lady, The,* 407
Donskoy, M., 286
Dorizo, N., 318, 387
Doronin, I., 38

Dorosh, Y., *Dry Summer, The,* 341
Dos Passos, J., 51, 62, 244, 284
Dostoevsky, F., 8, 62, 123, 182, 198, 202, 251, 264, 293, 329, 373, 374, 399, 400
Brothers Karamazov, The, 185; *Idiot, The,* 138, 185; *Legend of the Grand Inquisitor,* 87; "Notes from the Underground," 203, 368
Dovzhenko, A., 286
Dreiser, T., 335
Dudintsev, V., 331-33, 339-40
Not by Bread Alone, 330, 331-33, 340
DuGard, R., 335
Dumas, A., 51
Duncan, I., 14
Dürer, A., 132
Dzuibin, E. *See* Bagritsky, E.

Efremov, I., 247, 348
Efron, S., 260, 262
Ehrenburg, I., 22, 49, 52, 54, 58, 213-22, 293-94, 302, 310, 321, 322, 323, 325, 337, 347, 395
And Still It Is Turning, 215; *Autobiography,* 222; *Conspiracy of Equals, A,* 216; *Extraordinary Adventures of Julio Jurenito, The,* 215; *Factory of Dreams, The,* 215; *Fall of Paris, The,* 219-20; *In Protochny Lane,* 216; *Last Wave, The (The Ninth Wave),* 220, 310-11; *Life and Death of Nikolay Kurbov, The,* 217; *Love of Jeanne Ney, The,* 217; *Meditations,* 214; *Memoirs,* 222; *Moscow Does Not Believe in Tears,* 219; "Prayer for Russia," 4, 214; *Racketeer, The,* 57, 216; *Second Day, The,* 218; *Spring, The,* 221; "Stendhal's

Lessons," 337; *Storm, The,* 220, 310; *Summer,* 216; *10 HP,* 216; *Thaw, The,* 221, 322-23, 331; *Thirteen Pipes,* 215; *Trust DE,* 215; *Turbulent Life of Lazik Roitschwanz,* 217; *United Front, The,* 216; *We and the West,* 219; *Without a Breathing Spell,* 219; *Years, People, Life,* 222, 393
Eichenbaum, B., 104, 279
Eisenstein, S., 285, 305
Alexander Nevsky, 274
Eliot, T. S., 228
Encounter, 383
Engels, F., 182
Erdman, N., 54, 278, 282
Credentials, 282; *Suicide, The,* 282
Eremin, D., *Storm Over Rome,* 311
Ermler, F., 285
Essenin, S., 7, 10, 11-18, 19, 38, 49, 54, 59, 169, 223, 248, 342, 385
"Black Man, The," 16; "Comrade," 12; "Confessions of a Hooligan, The," 15; "Inonia," 12; "Moscow of Taverns, The," 15, 17; "Pugachev," 14; "Soviet Russia," 16, 17
Etkind, E., 410
Evreinov, N., 281
Evtushenko, E., 333, 343, 351, 383-87, 389, 390, 395, 397, 405, 411
"Babyi Yar," 385-86; "Dead Hand, The," 386; "Long Conversation, A," 333-34; *Power Station of Bratsk, The,* 387; *Precocious Autobiography,* 384; "Prologue, The," 384; "Stalin's Heirs," 386; "Station Zima," 383; *Sweep of the Hand, The,* 383

Facets, 412

Fadeyev, A., 58, 79, 151, 162, 168, 175, 178-81, 183, 288, 305, 307, 314, 326-27
  Against the Current, 178; *Last of the Udegs, The*, 179-80; *Overflow, The*, 178; *Road of Soviet Literature, The*, 183; *Rout, The (The Nineteen)*, 57, 168, 174, 178-79, 181, 183; *Young Guard, The*, 180, 187, 314, 326

Faiko, A., 282
  Evgraf, The Seeker of Adventures, 282; *Man With a Briefcase*, 282; *Teacher Bubus', The*, 282

Faulkner, W., 207

Fedin, K., 54, 58, 59, 88, 100, 101, 102, 105, 134-43, 287, 314, 315, 346, 395
  "Anna Timofeyevna," 134; *Arctur Sanitarium, The*, 141; *Bonfire, The*, 141, 142-43; *Brothers, The*, 137-38; *Cities and Years*, 57, 134-37, 139, 143, 200; *Extraordinary Summer, An*, 141, 142, 315; *First Joys, The*, 141; *Gorky in Our Midst*, 105; "Orchard, The," 134; *Rape of Europe, The*, 139-41; *Transvaal*, 137; *Vacant Lot, The*, 134

Feffer, I., 307

Feltrinelli, G., 344

Flaubert, G., 70, 73

Foreign Literature, 329

Forsh, O., 272, 273, 275
  Contemporaries, 272; *Firstlings of Freedom, The*, 272; *Iron Clad*, 272; *Mad Boat, The (The Raven)*, 272; *Symbolists*, 272

France, A., 86, 215

Franicevich, M., 324

Friche, V., 49, 182

From Under the Clouds, 380, 381

Frunze, M., 65

Furmanov, D., 58, 171
  Chapayev, 57, 171, 172; *Revolt*, 172

Gabrilovich, E., 288
  Year 1930, 244

Gaidar, A., 175, 292
  Timur, 187

Galanskov, Y., 377

Galitch, A., 376, 410, 417-18
  General Rehearsal, 418

Galsworthy, J., 335

Gastev, A., 37
  Hymn of Industrial Might, 37; *Poems of the Workers' Strike*, 37; *Proletarian Victories*, 37; *We Grow From Iron*, 37

Gerasimov, M., 37, 38

Gerasimov, S., 218

Gherasimova, V., 350

Gherman, Y., 245, 287, 313
  Lieutenant-Colonel of the Medical Corps, A, 313; *Our Friends*, 287; *Tales About Dzerzhinsky*, 287

Gide, A., 218, 314
  Counterfeiters, The, 202

Giraudoux, J., 218

Gladkov, F., 7, 58, 162, 168, 175-78, 183, 218, 288, 414
  Cement, 57, 58, 168, 174, 175-77, 178; *Energy*, 177; *Free Gang, The*, 177; *Oath, The*, 177; *Steed of Fire, The*, 175; *Tale of Childhood, The*, 177; *Wicked Year, The*, 178

Glinka, M., 272

Goethe, J., 259
  Faust, 225

Gogol, N., 62, 95, 251, 272, 297, 358, 392, 411
  Dead Souls, 67, 184, 400; *Inspector General, The*, 400

Golodny, M., 38, 106, 291, 328
"Guerrilla Zheleznyak," 291
Gonchar, O., 298
Standard-Bearers, The, 297-98
Goncharov, I., 184
Gorbachev, G., 53
Gorbanevskaya, N., 379, 410
Gorbatov, A., 364
Years and Wars, 364
Gorbatov, B., 297
Don Basin, 242n; Unvan-
quished, The, 296, 297
Gorbov, D., 106, 107, 182, 183
Gorenko, A. See Akhmatova, A.
Gorky, M., 4, 17, 20, 36, 47, 48,
49, 58, 69, 70, 74, 75, 80, 90,
96, 99, 109, 110, 111, 117, 120,
134, 138, 141, 150, 162, 164,
166, 167, 169, 174, 175, 178,
188, 194, 198, 200, 205, 269,
273, 275, 281, 321, 342, 357,
414
Lower Depth, The, 90; Mother,
186; Reminiscences, 29
Granin, D., 330, 348
After the Wedding, 341; At-
tacking the Thunderstorm,
348; "Personal Opinion,"
330; Searchers, The, 348
Gribachev, N., Spring in the
Victory Collective, 318
Griboyedov, A., 270
Wit Works Woe, 270
Grin (Grinevsky, A.), 58, 116-18,
132
Fire and Water, 117; On the
Slope of the Hill, 117; Red
Sails, 117
Grinevsky, A. See Grin
Grossman, L., 279
Grossman, V., 294-95, 312-13, 325
Everything Flows, 313, 377;
For the Just Cause, 312-13;
If One Believes the Pytha-
goreans, 313; People are Im-
mortal, The, 294-95; Stalin-

grad Letters, 293; Stepan
Kolchugin, 294
Gruzdev, I., 99
Guber, B., 106, 278
Gudzenko, S., 318
Guinzburg, A., 398
Guinzburg, E., 365
Gumilev, N., 46, 50, 102, 129,
132, 133, 250, 253, 254, 255,
328
Gurvich, A., 307
Gussev, V., "Poliushko," 291

Harms, D., 107
Harte, B., 246
Hashek, Y., 217, 296, 396, 407
Hellman, L., 335
Hemingway, E., The Old Man
and the Sea, 329
Herzen, A., 95
Hippius, Z., 4, 408
History of Soviet Literature, 68,
327
Hitler, A., 239, 292
Hoffman, E. T. A., 99, 103, 228,
400
Serapion Brethren, The, 99;
Tales, 259
Hugo, V., Toilers of the Sea, 245
Husseinov, H., Social and Politi-
cal Thought in Azerbaidjan
in the XIXth Century, 307
Huxley, A., 89

Ignatov, P., A Partisan's Notes,
293
Ilf, I., 98, 118
Little Golden Calf, The, 54;
Twelve Chairs, The, 54
Ilyichev, L., 395
Ilyin, Y., The Big Assembly
Line, 242
Inber, V., 288, 299
Meridian of Pulkovo, 299, 301
International Literature, 48

Irving, W., *Tales of the Alhambra*, 256
Isakovsky, M., 291
Iskander, F., 406
  Kozlotur Constellation, The, 406; *Man With the Shriveled Arm, The*, 406; *Sandro from Tchighima*, 406
Iskoz, A. (Dolinin, A.), 279
Ivanov, G., 408
Ivanov, Vsevolod, 54, 55, 59, 75-81, 88, 100, 101, 102, 171, 342
  Adventures of a Fakir, 80; "Amulet, The," 76; *Armored Train 14-69*, 57, 76, 77, 80, 281; *Child, The*, 76; *Colored Winds*, 76; *Exotic Tales*, 76; "Hops or To Meet the Autumn Birds," 81; *Iron Division, The*, 76; *Journey Into Never-Never Land*, 80; "Michael of the Silver Gates," 80; *Mystery of Mysteries*, 79-80; *Parkhomenko*, 76, 80; *Partisans*, 76; *Return of Buddha, The*, 76; *Seizure of Berlin, The*, 80; *Skyblue Sands*, 76; *Tales of Brigadier Sinitzyn*, 80
Ivanov, Vyacheslav, 4
Ivanov-Razumnik, R., 7, 11
  History of Russian Social Thought, 7; *Jails and Exile*, 7
Ivnev, R. (Kovalev, M.), 13

John of Cronstadt, 381
Joyce, J., 207, 284, 395

Kafka, F., 335, 395, 399
Kalmanson-Lelevich, L., 38
Kamenev, L., 43, 238
Kampov, B. *See* Polevoy, B.
Katayev, I., 106, 278, 328

"Milk," 106; "Poet, The," 106
Katayev, V., 105, 118, 287, 314, 328
  Broken Life, A, or Oberon's Magic Horn, 405; *Embezzlers, The*, 54, 242, 282; *For the Soviet Power*, 314; *Grass of Oblivion, The*, 405; *Holy Well, The*, 405; *I Am the Son of the Working People*, 287; *Lone White Sail*, 287; *Squaring of the Circle*, 282; *Time Forward*, 242-43, 244
Kaverin, V. (Zilberg, V.), 54, 58, 59, 88, 100, 101, 102, 103-4, 287, 340
  Artist Unknown, 103; *Brawler, The, or The Evenings on Vassily Island*, 103; *Doctor Vlasenkova*, 103; "End of Khasa, The," 103; *Fulfillment of Desires, The*, 103; *Illuminated Windows, The*, 104; *In Front of the Mirror*, 103; "Masters and Apprentices," 103; "Nine Tenths of Fate," 103; "Oblique Rain," 103; *Open Book, The*, 103; *Prologue*, 244; *Search and Hope*, 103; "Seven Pairs of Impure, The," 103; *Two Captains*, 103, 246
Kayden, E., 228
Kazakevich, E., 298, 350
  Star, The, 187, 298
Kazakov, Y., 330, 349, 350, 393
Kazin, V., 37
Keats, J., 259
Kemball, R., 258
Ketlinskaya, V., 324
  Days of Our Life, The, 316; *It Is Not Worth Living Otherwise*, 347
Khachaturian, A., 321, 345
Khelemsky, Y., *Tale of Komsomol*, 318

Khlebnikov, V., 39, 130, 251, 265, 306, 392
Khodassevich, V., 4, 408
Khrushchev, N., 196, 222, 320, 327, 331, 338, 339, 340, 344, 345-46, 365, 384, 394, 395, 396
Kipling, R., 116, 130
Kirilov, V., 37, 328
Kirsanov, S., 30, 290, 334
"Cinderella," 30, 290; "Comrade Marx," 30; "Five Year Plan, The," 30; *Four Notebooks*, 290; "Seven Days," 30, 334
Kirshon, V., 278, 284, 327, 328, 352
Bread, 284; *Miraculous Alloy, The*, 284
Kluyev, N., 7, 278
Kochetov, V., 316, 340, 346-47, 387-88
Angle of Incidence, The, 387-88; *Brothers Yershov*, 340; *Secretary of the Regional Committee, The*, 387; *What Do You Finally Want?*, 388; *Zhurbins, The*, 316
Koestler, A., 126, 213
Kogan, P., 49, 182
Koltsov, M., 214, 222, 278, 328, 352
Kommisarzhevsky, F., 281
Koptiayeva, A., *Ivan Ivanovich*, 333
Korneichuk, A., 288
Front, The, 294; *Why Do the Stars Smile?*, 342
Kornilov, B., 290
Kornilov, V., *With No Hands and No Feet*, 412
Korolenko, V., 175, 273
Korzhavin, N., 377, 410
Kosintsev, G., 285
Kostylev, I., *Ivan the Terrible*, 315
Kosygin, A., 338, 396
Kovalev, M. (Ivnev, R.), 13

Kovpak, S., *From Putivl to the Carpathian Mountains*, 293
Kozakov, M., 218
Kozhevnikov, V., 245
March-April, 299; *Meet Baluyev*, 347
Kozin, A., *Mountain and Night*, 247
Kozlov, I., *In the Crimean Underground*, 293
Krasnaya Nov' (*Red Virgin Soil*), 47, 51, 105
Krassin, L., 44
Kratt, I., 245
Fort Ross, 315
Kremlev, I., *The Soldiers of the Revolution*, 315
Kriukhov, F., 197
Kron, A., 329
Krupskaya, N., 120
Krylov, I., 39
Krymov, Y. (Beklemishev), 242n, 292
Tanker Derbent, The, 242n
Kuprin, A., 4, 408
Kusikov, A., 13
Kuskova, Y., 49
Kuzmin, M., 53, 251
Kuznetsov, A., 386
Babyi Yar, 386; *Fire*, 386
Kvitko, L., 307

Lardner, R., 93
Lavrenyov, B., 58
Break, The, 57; *Revolt*, 57, 281; *Simplehearted Men*, 296; *Voice of America, The*, 310
Lebedev-Kumach, V., "Vast is My Native Country," 291
Leger, F., 218
Lelevich, L., 49, 182
Lenin, V., 3, 13, 14, 25, 26, 29, 36, 41, 42, 43, 47, 48, 114, 167, 169, 182, 214, 229, 238, 268, 283, 309, 336, 337, 346, 370, 372, 380, 389

Leningrad, 98, 305
Leonov, L., 54, 55, 57, 58, 59, 79,
    105, 169, 182, 198-212, 285,
    287, 342, 347
  Badgers, The, 57, 200-202, 205,
    206; Blizzard, The, 208;
    "Breakthrough of Petushi-
    khino, The," 200; "End of the
    Little Man, The," 199-200;
    Evgenya Ivanovna, 211; In-
    vasion, 209-10, 298; "Kovya-
    kin's Diary," 199; "Legend
    of Kalafaat," 201-2; Locusts,
    The, 247; Lyonushka, 209,
    210, 298; Orchards of Polov-
    chansk, The, 209; Ordinary
    Fellow, An, 209; Russian
    Forest, The, 210-11; Skuta-
    revsky, 206-7; Soviet River
    (Sot'), 205-6, 242; Stories
    About Unusual Muzhiks,
    204; Taking of Velikosh-
    umsk, The, 210, 298; Thief,
    The, 202-4, 206, 209; "Tua-
    tamur," 199; Untilovsk, 208-
    9; Way to the Ocean, 207-8,
    211; Wolf, The, 209;
    "Wooden Queen, The,"
    199
Lermontov, M., 31, 130, 230, 272,
    308
Leskov, N., 90, 93, 115, 185, 199,
    373
Levi, C., 335
Lezhnyov, A., 106, 107, 183, 278
Lezhnyov, I., 107
Liashko, A., 37
Libedinsky, Y., 38, 51, 58, 162,
    183, 315
  Birth of a Hero, The, 183;
    Commissars, The, 183;
    Glow, The, 315; Tomorrow,
    183; Turning Point, The,
    183; Week, A, 53, 183
Lidin, V., 52, 328
Lifshitz, V., 323

Literary Gazette, 308, 329, 344,
    347, 385, 395
"Literary Heritage," 29, 32
Literary Moscow, 329, 330, 339
Literary Notes, 101
Literature of the Fact, 172
Litvinov, I., 379
Lobachevsky, N., 86
London, J., 246, 335
Lowell, A., 13
Lucacz, 279, 337
Lugovskoy, V., 290, 325
Lunacharsky, A., 29, 33, 48
Lunz, L., 100, 101
  "Go West," 101
Lvova, X., Elena, 333
Lysenko, T., 309

Makarenko, A., 175, 187, 288
  Pedagogical Poem, The, 168,
    187
Makarov, A., "On Home Leave,"
    403
Malenkov, G., 320, 326, 345
Maliarevsky, P., Hello Life, 312
Malinovsky, A. (Bogdanov, A.),
    35
Malraux, A., 126
Maltsev, O., The Jugoslav Trag-
    edy, 311
Malyshkin, A., 106
  Fall of Dair, The, 53, 58
Mandelstam, N., Hope Against
    Hope, 377
Mandelstam, O., 53, 222, 248, 249-
    53, 259, 278, 328
  "Egyptian Stamp, The," 251;
    "Noise of Time, The," 251;
    Stone, 250; Tristia, 250; Vo-
    ronezh Notebooks, 253
Mann, H., 335
Mann, T., 207, 335
  Buddenbrooks, 139; Magic
    Mountain, The, 141
Maramzin, V., 410
Marchenko, A., 365

Marienhof, A., 13
Markish, P., 307
Marr, N., 309
Martynov, L., 343
Marx, K., 16, 118, 156, 182
    Capital, 16
Maslin, M., 31-32
Matveyeva, N., *The Soul of
    Things*, 392
Maupassant, G. de, 73
Mauriac, F., 333
Maurois, A., 269
Maximov, V., 410, 412, 413-16
    "Courtyard in the Middle of
    the Sky, The," 414; *Fare-
    well from Nowhere*, 413;
    "Late Light, The," 414;
    Quarantine, 415-16; *Seven
    Days of Creation*, 413-14
Mayakovsky, V., 10, 17, 19-32,
    33, 34, 38, 39, 49, 54, 55, 59,
    104, 133, 169, 223, 224, 226,
    248, 265, 288, 289, 322, 334,
    342, 343, 360, 385, 388, 392,
    400
    "All Right," 24, 25; "At the
    Top of My Voice," 28;
    Bathhouse, The, 28, 31, 282,
    322; *Bedbug, The*, 28, 31,
    282; *Cloud in Trousers*, 20,
    27; *Imperator*, 267; "Letter
    from Paris Concerning Love,
    A," 28; "Man," 20, 21; "Most
    Extraordinary Adventure,
    A," 26; *Mystery Bouffe*, 23,
    33, 57; *New LEF*, 34; *150
    Millions, The*, 23, 29; *Spine
    Flute, The*, 20; "Vladimir
    Illych Lenin," 24, 25; "War
    and Peace," 20
Mdivani, G., *New Times*, 317
Medvedev, R., 381
Medvedev, Z., 381
Merezhkovsky, D., 4, 272, 408
Merimée, P., 116, 118
Meyerhold, V., 11, 28, 33, 54,

278, 281, 282, 285, 328, 352,
    393
Miaskovsky, N.. 345
Mikhailovsky, N., 273
Mikhalkov, S., 290, 312
    I Want to Go Home, 310;
    Ilya Golovin, 312
Minsky, N., 4
Mokrousov, V., 323
Molotov, V., 144, 320, 345
Moravia, A., 335
Moskva, 356
Mozhayev, B., *From the Life of
    Fyodor Kuzkin*, 403
Muradeli, V., *The Great Friend-
    ship*, 305, 345

Nabokov, V., 408
Naghibin, Y., 350, 390, 393
Napoleon, 159
Naritsa-Narymov, M., *Unsung
    Song*, 401
Nedogonov, A., *The Flag Over
    the Village Soviet*, 318
Neizvestny, E., 418
Nekrassov, N., 26, 31, 289, 296,
    386
Nekrassov, V., 298, 327-28, 395,
    410, 416-17
    First Acquaintance, The, 341;
    In the Home Town, 327-28,
    416; *In the Trenches of Sta-
    lingrad*, 298, 416; *Kira
    Georghievna*, 330, 395;
    "Notes of a Gawker," 416
Neva, 329
Nevarov, A., 58, 172
    Tashkent, City of Bread, 172
New LEF, 34
New Review, 412
New Russian Word, 412
New World. See Novy Mir
Nietzsche, F., 63, 124
Nikitin, N., 54, 88, 100, 101, 102
    Aurora Borealis, 102; *Baku*, 102;
    Flight, The, 102; *Fort Vomit*,

102; *Kirik Rudenko's Crime,*
102; *Stones,* 102; *Tales of
Oboyansk,* 102; *Third Alley,
The,* 102
Nikolay I, Tsar, 240
Nikolayeva, G., 316, 333
Harvest, 316; *Running Battle,
The,* 330, 333
Nilin, P., *Cruelty (Comrade
Venka),* 334; *Probation,* 334
Novikov, A., 272
Birth of a Musician, The, 272,
315; *My Dawn Will Come,*
272
Novikov, I., 275
Pushkin in Exile, 272; *Pushkin
in Mikhailovskoye,* 272;
Pushkin in the South, 272
Novikov-Priboy, A., 275
Tsuchima, 275
Novy Mir (New World), 52,
313, 321, 323, 331, 336, 344,
347, 363, 367, 378, 393, 396,
397, 403, 404, 406

"Oberiuts," 107-8, 360
October, 38, 49, 52, 87, 97, 323,
387, 388, 413
O. Henry, 102, 335
Okhlopkov, N., 285
Okudzhava, B., 343, 376, 391-92,
393, 417
Good Luck to You, My Pupil,
391; *Merci or Shipov's Adventures,* 392; *Poor Avrosimov, The,* 391-92
Olesha, Y., 57, 58, 59, 88, 105,
122-29, 285, 329
Cherry Stone, 122; *Envy,* 122-
27; *Excerpts from the Intimate Notes of Fellow Traveler Sand,* 122, 127; *List of
Benefits, The,* 122, 127; *Love,*
122; *Strict Youth, A,* 122, 128;
Three Fat Men, The, 122

On Guard, 38, 49, 51
On Literary Guard, 51
On The Eve, 148
Ordzhonikidze, S., 131
Oreshin, P., 278
Orwell, G., 89
Osipov, V., 382
Ossorghin, M., 50
Ostrovsky, A., 342
Ostrovsky, N., 58, 175, 185-87,
218, 288
Tempering of Steel, The, 168,
185, 186-87
Ovechkin, V., 171, 316, 317, 322,
324, 347
Weekdays of a District, 322;
*With Greetings From The
Front,* 316

Pancho, P., 306
Panfyorov, F., 58, 195, 322, 323,
347
Bruski, 194; *Reflections,* 341;
Volga Mother River, 321-22,
341
Panova, V., 299, 322, 323, 325,
347
*Companions or Fellow Travel-
ers,* 299; *Seasons, The,* 322;
Sentimental Novel, A, 341;
Serezha, 334
Pass, The (Pereval), 105-8, 133,
297, 328
Pass Almanacs, The, 106
Pasternak, B., 38, 39, 54, 57, 59,
102, 130, 132, 143, 169, 196,
223-35, 248, 253, 260, 264,
265, 267, 288, 291, 302, 319,
323, 329, 343-45, 360, 385,
388, 390, 397, 411, 416
Above the Barriers, 225; "Aerial
Ways," 225; *Autobiographi-
cal Essay,* 263; "Childhood of
Luvers, The," 225; *Doctor
Zhivago,* 4, 223, 225, 228,
230-35, 343, 352, 376; *Essay*

in Autobiography, An, 31;
"Letters from Tula," 225;
Lieutenant Schmidt, 225;
Life, My Sister, 225; *On
Early Trains*, 225; *Safe Con-
duct*, 225, 227; *Second Birth,
The*, 225; *Selected Poems*,
225; *Spektorsky*, 225, 229;
Tale, The, 225; *Tales*, 225;
Terrestrial Expanse, 225;
Themes and Variations,
225; "Tratto d'Apelle,"
225; *Twin in Clouds, A*, 224;
Year 1905, The, 225
Pasternak, L., 224
Paustovsky, K., 58, 79, 115, 118-
22, 128, 272, 287, 328, 333,
352
*Beginning of an Unknown Cen-
tury, The*, 121; *Birth of a
Story, The*, 120; *Black Sea*,
120; *Charles Lonceville's Fate*,
119; *Distant Years*, 121; *Glit-
tering Clouds, The*, 119;
Golden Rose, The, 121; *Kara
Bugaz*, 120; *Kolchida*, 120,
242; *Northern Story, The*,
119; *Restless Youth, The*,
121; *Romantics*, 119; *Tale of
Forests, The*, 120; *Tale of
Life, The*, 121-22; *Tarussa
Pages*, 393; *Throw to the
South, A*, 121; *Time of Great
Expectations*, 121; *Turbulent
Youth, The*, 334
Pavlenko, P., 105, 106, 218, 272,
288, 315
Happiness, 315; *Red Planes Fly
East*, 246
Perventsev, A., 314
Pervomaysky, L., *The Wild
Honey*, 330
Petrov, E., 98
Front-Line Diary, A, 293;
Little Golden Calf, The, 54;
Twelve Chairs, The, 54

Petrov, V., 286
Peter I, 274
Picasso, P., 218
Pilar, Y., *Men Remain Men*, 364
Pilnyak, B., 49, 52, 53, 54, 58, 59,
60, 61-68, 82, 102, 106, 153,
162, 169, 171, 201, 272, 278,
328, 352
Cow-Wheat, 62; *Diary*, 64; *Ma-
chines and Wolves*, 62; *Ma-
hogany*, 66-67; *Mother Earth*,
64; *Naked Year, The*, 57, 61,
62, 63, 64; *OK*, 68; *Ripening
of the Fruit, The*, 68; *Spilled
Time*, 65; *Tale of the Unex-
tinguished Moon, The*, 65-66;
Third Capital, The, 64;
*Volga Flows Into the Cas-
pian Sea, The*, 63, 66
Platonov, A., 106, 297, 352, 356-59
Chevengur, 357-58; *Djann*, 358;
Inspired Men, 296; "Origins
of a Master," 357; *Pit, The
(Kotlovan)*, 358; *Sluices of
Epiphany, The*, 357; *This
Fierce and Beautiful World*,
358
Platonov, S., 268
Podyepolsky, G., *The Golden
Century*, 377
Poe, E. A., 116, 118
Pogodin, N. (Stukalov, N.), 282,
283-84, 288, 317, 334, 342
Aristocrats, The, 283, 284;
Chimes of the Kremlin, The,
283; *Man With a Rifle*, 283;
Missouri Waltz, 284; *My
Friend*, 283; *Petrarch's Son-
nets*, 284, 334; *Poem of the
Axe, The*, 283; *Tempo*, 283;
Third Pathetic, The, 283;
When Lances are Broken,
317
Pokrovsky, M., 268
Polevoy, B. (Kampov, B.), 187
Story of a Real Man, The, 311

Poliakov, A., *In The Enemy's Rear*, 293
Polonskaya, E., 99, 101
Polonsky, V., 49, 183
Pomerantsev, V., 321, 322, 323
Pomeranz, G., 379-80
Pomialovsky, N., 173
Popov, A., 285
Posev (Sowing), 412
Potebnya, A., 278
Pound, E., 13
Pozner, V., 100
Pravda, 197, 313, 318, 323, 326
Press and Revolution, 52
Pridvorov, Y. See Bedny, D.
Prishvin, M., 58, 106, 109-15, 118, 121, 287
   Calendar of Nature, The, 110; *Chain of Kashchey, The*, 110, 113, 114; *Crane's Birthplace*, 110, 114; *Forest Drip-Drop*, 110; *Honey From Beyond the Pale*, 111; *In the Land of Unfrightened Birds*, 110; *Larder of the Sun, The*, 110; *Little Round Loaf, The*, 110; *Root of Life-Ginseng, The*, 112; *Springs of Berendey, The*, 110
Prokofiev, A., 290, 302
Prokofiev, S., 271, 274, 345
Proletarian Culture, 35-36
Proust, M., 207, 374, 395
Proyart, J. de, 224
Pudovkin, V., 285
   Admiral Nakhimov, 274; *Minim and Pozharsky*, 274; *Suvorov*, 274
Punin, N., 257
Pushkin, A., 31, 130, 251, 256, 269, 308, 343, 411
   Bronze Horseman, The, 411; *Captain's Daughter*, 273; *Don Juan*, 256, 411; *Eugene Onegin*, 411

Rachmaninoff, S., 409
Radischev, A., 272
Radonezhsky, S., 381
Rakovsky, L., *Generalissimus Suvorov*, 315
Rasputin, V., 403, 404, 406
   Live and Remember, 404
Reavy, G., 385n
Red Star, 403
Red Virgin Soil (Krasnaya Nov'), 47, 51, 105
Reich, Z., 11, 285
Reiss, I., 262
Rekemchuk, A., *The Young Leaves*, 383
Remizov, A., 4, 53, 54, 55, 62, 82, 112, 115, 199, 273, 329, 365, 408
   "Lay of the Destruction of the Land of Russia," 4
Renoir, J., 90
Reshetnikov, F., 173
Robbe-Grillet, A., 395
Rodov, S., 38, 49
Romains, J., *Men of Good Will*, 219
Romanov, P., 58, 173
   Comrade Kisliakov or Three Pairs of Silken Stockings, 173; *New Tablet, The*, 173; *Without Cherry Blossoms*, 173
Romashov, B., 284
   Change of Heroes, The, 284
Romm, M., 285
Rosen, A., *The Last Two Weeks*, 402
Rostropovich, M., 370, 418
Rousseau, J., 180
Rozanov, V., 62, 63, 104, 124, 411
Rozhdestvensky, R., 329
Rozhdestvensky, V., 291
   Corsair, The, 291; *Goethe in Italy*, 291
Rubinstein, A., 224

Ruge, G., 231
Runyon, D., 72, 93
Russian Review, 258
Russian Thought, 412
Rutko, A., *Immortal Earth*, 247
Rykov, A., 238
Rylenkov, N., 302

Sadofyev, I., "Dynamo Poems,"
37
Saint-Exupery, A. de, 335
Sakharov, A., 379, 380, 381, 398,
410, 412
Reflections on Progress, Peaceful Coexistence and Intellectual Freedom, 380
Salinger, J. D., *Catcher in the Rye*, 383
Saltykov, M., 95
History of a Town, 400
Samizdat, 376-82
Sannikov, A., 37
Sabgir, G., 377
Sarghidzhan, A. *See* Borodin, S.
Sarovsky, S., 381
Sartre, J., 335, 395
Savich, O., *Imaginary Interlocutor*, 218; *We and the West*,
219
Schildkreth, K., *The Wings of a Slave*, 274
Schwartz, E., 318, 342
Dragon, The, 318; *Naked King, The*, 318
Scott, W., 132
Scriabin, A., 224
Sedenko-Vityazef, F., 278
Seifullina, L., 58, 172-73
Four Chapters, 173; *Humus*,
173; *Lawbreakers, The*, 172;
Virineya, 173
Selvinsky, I., 288-89, 291, 302, 306
Chelyuskin, 289; *Fur-Trust*,
289; *General Brussilov*, 289;
Johann the Knight, 289; *Pao*

Pao, 289; *Records*, 288; *Russia*, 289; *Ulyalayev's Band*,
288-89
Semenov, S., 172
Hunger, 172; *Natalia Tarpova*,
172; *Typhus*, 172
Sentenced to be Treated as Lunatics, 378
Serafimovich, A., 53, 178
Serafimovich-Popov, A., *The Iron Torrent*, 174
Serapion Brethren, 49, 54, 59, 75,
88, 92, 99-105, 129, 134, 199,
215, 269, 306, 318
Serapion Brethren Anthology,
101
Serebriakova, G., 278, 328, 365
Sergeyev-Tsensky, S., 272, 273-
74, 275, 299
Brussilov's Breakthrough, 274;
Guns Are Rolled Out, The,
274; *Guns Begin to Speak,
The*, 274; *Ordeal of Sebastopol, The*, 274; *Transfiguration*, 274
Sevak, P., "A Long Conversation," 333-34
Severyanin, I., 4
Shafarevitch, I., 381
Shagynian, M., *Hydrocentral*,
242
Shakespeare, W., 225, 259
Shalamov, V., 365
Shaw, G. B., 335
Shcheglov, M., 323
Shchegolev, P., 149
Shchipachev, S., *Pavlik Morozov*,
318
Shebalin, V., 345
Sheiniss, A., *The Middle Ages*,
310
Shelest, G., *Notes of Kolyma*,
364
Shelley, P., 259
Shengeli, G., 118

Shershenevich, V., 13

Shevchenko, T., 133

Shishkov, V., 273, 275
  Emelyan Pugachev, 273; *Gang, The*, 273; *Taiga*, 273; *Ugrium River*, 273

Shishova, Z., *Blockade*, 301

Shklovsky, V., 99, 104, 172, 279, 280, 293
  About the Theory of Prose, 104; *Hamburg's Accounts*, 104; *Sentimental Journey, A*, 104; *Technique of the Writer's Craft, The*, 104; *Third Factory, The*, 104; *Zoo, or Letters Not About Love*, 104

Shkvarkin, V., *Another Man's Child*, 282

Shmelyov, I., 408
  Sun of the Dead, The, 4

Sholokhov, M., 55, 58, 122, 144, 151, 168, 175, 181, 184, 188-97, 223, 288, 293, 326, 347
  "Man's Fate," 195-96; *Quiet Don, The*, 152, 168, 188, 189-94, 197; "Russian Character, The," 196; *Tales of the Don*, 189; *They Fought for Their Country*, 194, 195; *Virgin Soil Upturned, The*, 194-95, 347

Short Literary Encyclopedia, 375

Shostakovich, D., 281, 305, 345

Shukshin, V., 403-4, 406
  I Came to Bring You Freedom, 403; *Lubavins, The*, 403; *Red Snowdrop Berry, The*, 404

Silone, I., 126

Simonov, K., 290, 296, 298-99, 301-2, 310, 325, 329, 336, 337, 347, 402
  Days and Nights, 298; "Do You Remember the Roads of Smolensk," 302; *Foreign Shadow, The*, 310; *Friends and Foes*, 310; *Lad from Our Town, The*, 187; *Living and the Dead, The*, 298, 330; *Russian People*, 296; *Russian Question, The*, 310; *Smoke of the Fatherland, The*, 310; "Wait for Me," 301; *War Diaries*, 293; *We Are Not Born Soldiers*, 298-99

Siniavsky, A. (Tertz, A.), 143, 166, 196, 397-401, 410-12
  "Graphomaniacs," 399; "Icicle, The," 399; *In The Shadow of Gogol*, 411; "Literary Process in Russia, The," 411; "Luibimov," 400; "Men and Beasts," 378; "Tenants, The," 399; "Thoughts at Random," 399; "Trial Begins, The," 399; *Voice From the Chorus, A*, 410-11; *Walks With Pushkin*, 411; "You and I," 399

Slavin, L., 118, 218

Sleptsov, V., 173

Sletov, P., 106
  Distant Republic, 106; *Mastership*, 106

Slonimsky, M., 88, 100, 101, 102-3, 315
  "Actress, The," 102; *Chairman of the Town Soviet, The*, 102-3; "Emery's Death Machine," 102; *Engineers*, 103, 315; *Faithful Friends*, 315; *Foma Kleshnyov*, 102; *Lavrovs, The*, 102

Slutsky, B., 343

Smeliakov, Y., 392

Smirnov, L., 399

Smirnov, S., 346

Sobolev, L., *A Naval Soul*, 296

Sofronov, A., 342
  Cook, The, 342; *Cook Gets Married, The*, 342

Sokolov-Mikitov, I., *Tales of the Motherland*, 115

Soloukhin, V., 171, 382
  By-Roads of Vladimir District,
    341
Solovyov, V.,
  1812, 274; *Kutuzov*, 274
Solzhenitsyn, A., 143, 196, 197,
  363-75, 377, 379, 380, 381,
  403, 404, 409-10, 412
  August 1914, 371, 372, 373; *Calf
    Butts the Oak, The*, 366; *Can-
    cer Ward*, 367, 368-69, 373;
    First Circle, 367-68, 369, 373,
    374, 412; *For the Just Cause*,
    366; *Gulag Archipelago*,
    369-70, 372; *Lenin in Zurich*,
    372; *Matryona's Homestead*,
    366; *One Day in the Life of
    Ivan Denisovich*, 363-66, 393,
    394; "Zakhar-Kalita," 366
Sosnora, V., 392
Sosnovsky, A., 49
Soviet Literary Encyclopedia, 69
Stakhanov, A., 242n
Stalin, J., 7, 18, 29, 31, 39, 43, 44,
  65, 74, 90, 107, 151, 155, 157,
  158, 159, 164, 165, 220, 221,
  222, 225, 236, 237, 238-41,
  252, 257, 283, 284, 286, 300,
  305, 308, 309, 314, 318, 320,
  328, 345, 346, 353, 354, 364,
  365, 368, 370, 380, 386, 389,
  394
  *Marxism and Problems of Lin-
    guistics*, 309
*Stanislavsky's Heritage and the
  Practice of Soviet Theater*,
  317
Star, The (*Zvezda*), 52, 98, 305,
  361
Stavsky, V., 292
Steam Whistle, 122
Steinbeck, J., 335
Stendhal (Beyle, M. H.), 335
Stepanov, A., *Port Arthur*, 275
Sterne, L., 104
Stevenson, R., 116, 118

Storm, G., 275
  Tale of the Brothers Turgenev,
    272; *Works and Days of
    Lomomonossov*, 272
Strachey, L., 269
Stravinsky, I., 409
Strugatsky, A. and B., 348
  Bad Swans, 348; *Snail on the
    Hillside*, 348
Stukalov, N. *See* Pogodin, N.
Subotsky, L., 180
Surkov, A., 290, 302-3, 323, 326,
  344, 346
Surov, A., *Il-Starred Haber-
    dasher, The*, 310
Svetlov, M., 38, 106, 291
  "Granada," 291
Sviatopolk-Mirsky, D., 278

Tairov, A., 33, 54, 281, 284, 285
Tarkovsky, A., 291
  Earthly to the Earth, The, 291
Tarle, E., 268
Tarsis, V., 401
  Bluebottle, The, 401; *Red and
    Black*, 401; *Ward 7*, 401;
    What a Gay Life, 401
Tarussa Pages, 393
Tendryakov, V., 341
  Date with Nefertiti, A, 341;
    "Short Circuit, A," 341;
    "Three, Seven, Ace," 341
Tertz, A. *See* Siniavsky, A.
Thing, The, 22, 23
Tikhonov, N., 39, 57, 59, 99, 101,
  102, 129-32, 133, 179, 288,
  291, 293, 294, 296, 302, 307,
  342, 344
  "Gardener's Dream," 130; *Geor-
    gian Spring*, 131; *Horde,
    The*, 129; "Kirov With Us,"
    131; *Mead*, 129; *Oath in the
    Fog, An*, 130; *Reckless Man,
    The*, 130; "Saga About A

Journalist, A," 130; "Sergo in the Mountains," 131; *Shadow of a Friend, The*, 131; *Traits of the Soviet Man*, 131, 296; *War*, 131; *Yurga*, 130

Tiutchev, F., 111, 251, 269, 361

Tolstoy, A., 4, 49, 52, 58, 144-54, 171, 275, 293, 299
    Adventures of Rasteghin, 146; *Aelita*, 148; *Azef*, 149; *Black Gold*, 149, 152; "Blue Cities," 149; *Bread*, 152; *Cagliostro Defeated*, 146; *Chinese Shadows*, 147; "Council of Five, The," 148-49; *Cranks*, 146; *Death Box, The*, 148; *Emigrés, The*, 149; *Garin the Dictator*, 148; *Hyperboloid of the Engineer Garin*, 148; *Ibicus or The Adventures of Nevzorov*, 149; *Ivan the Terrible*, 154; *Lame Squire, The*, 146; *Love, the Golden Book*, 147; *Moon Dampness*, 147; *Murky Dawn*, 150; *Nikita's Childhood*, 147; *1918*, 150; *Peter I*, 149, 152-54, 273; "Peter's Day," 153; *Rasputin or The Conspiracy of the Empress*, 149; *Road to Calvary, The*, 147, 149-52; *Russian Character, The*, 296; *Seven Days in Which the World Was Robbed*, 148; *Sisters, The*, 150; "Vassily Sushkov," 149; *Viper, The*, 149

Tolstoy, L., 14, 82, 113, 114, 115, 181-82, 183, 185, 189, 202, 224, 244, 364, 373
    Anna Karenina, 185; *Resurrection*, 185, 224; *Sebastopol Tales*, 296; *War and Peace*, 185, 189, 224, 235, 296, 299, 364; *What is Art?*, 182

Tomashevsky, B., 279, 308

Trauberg, L., 285

Trenyov, K., *Lyubov Yarovaya*, 57, 281

Tretyakov, S., 54, 160, 172, 278, 352
    Iron Pause, 160; *Roar China*, 57, 160

Trifonov, Y., 406

Trotsky, L., 3, 17, 43, 44, 47, 49-50, 105, 151, 155, 156, 159, 160
    "Dictatorship, Where is Thy Whip," 50; "Law of Combined Development," 156; *Literature and the Revolution*, 49

Troyat, H., 408

Tsvetayeva, M., 4, 222, 228, 248, 249, 260-67, 329, 343, 388, 393, 408
    After Russia, 261; *Craftsmanship*, 260; *Czar Maiden, The*, 260, 266; *Evening Keepsake, The*, 260; "Lad, The," 266; *Magic Lantern, The*, 260; *My Pushkin*, 267; *Parting*, 260; "Perekop," 267; *Pied Piper, The*, 261; *Poem of the End*, 261; *Poem of the Mount*, 261, 266; *Poems*, 267; *Poems to Blok*, 260; *Psyche*, 260; "Swan's Camp, The," 267; *Versty*, 260

Turgenev, I., 82, 110, 184, 349, 364
    Fathers and Sons, 109, 185; "Living Relic, The," 366; *On the Eve*, 185

Tvardovsky, A., 289-90, 296, 318, 321, 323, 325, 347, 365, 367, 404
    "Afar Farther Yet," 321; *House on the Road*, 318; "Land of Muravia, The," 289; "Tyorkin in the Other World," 395-96; "Vassily Tyorkin," 296

Tynyanov, Y., 58, 269-72, 275,
  279, 287
  Archaists and Innovators, 269;
  *Death of Vazir Mukhtar,
  The*, 270; *Kukhlya*, 269;
  Pushkin, 270; "Second-
  Lieutenant Kizhe," 270;
  "Wax Figure, The," 246

Ungaretti, G., 395
Ushakov, N., 290
Uspensky, G., 173
Utkin, J., 38, 290

Vaghinov, K., 107
  Song of the Goat, The, 107
Vakhtangov, E., 281, 285
Vardin, I., 38, 49
Vasiliev, P., 278, 328
Vassiliev, G. and S., 285
Veche, 381-82
Veressayev, V., 53
Verhaeren, E., 37
Verlag, U., 412
Verne, J., 116
Vershigora, P., *People with Clear
  Conscience*, 293
Vertov, D., 285
Vesely, A., 106, 278
Vesselovsky, A., 278, 307-8
Vesyoly, A., 53, 54, 55, 328
  My Native Land, 53; *Russia
  Washed in Blood*, 53
Villon, F., 14
Vinokurov, E., 343, 391
Virta, N., 287, 318, 323
  Solitude, 287; *Steep Mountains*,
  341
Vishnevsky, A., 183, 284-85, 288,
  342
  First Cavalry Army, The, 284;
  Optimistic Tragedy, 284;
  Unforgettable 1919, The, 285
Vladimirova, L., *The Connection
  of Time Periods*, 410

Vladimov, G., *The Faithful
  Ruslan*, 377-78
Voinovich, L., 350, 396, 406, 407
  *Life and Unexpected Adven-
  tures of the Soldier Ivan
  Chonkin, The*, 396, 407
Volia Rossii, 89, 261
Volodin, A., *The Factory Gal*,
  342
Voloshin, M., 9
Volpin, E., 410
Voltaire, F., 215
Voronsky, A., 17, 48, 49, 105, 106,
  183
Voznesensky, A., 343, 388-90, 397,
  405
  Antiworlds, 388; *In Shadow of
  Sound*, 405; "Longjumeau,"
  389; "Masters," 389; *Mosaic*,
  388; *Oza*, 389; *Parabola*, 388;
  "Parabolic Ballad," 388;
  "Prologue to a Poem, The,"
  405; "Thirty Digressions
  from the Poem *A Triangular
  Pear*," 388; "Triangular Pear,
  The," 389

Wasilevskaya, W., *The Rainbow*,
  297
Whitman, W., 25, 37
Wilson, M., 335
Wilson, W., 23, 26
Wvedensky, A., 107
  *Christmas Tree at Ivanov's,
  The*, 107; *Elizabeth Bom*, 107
Woolf, V., 207

Yakhontova, M., *Potemkin*, 315
Yakobson, R., 279
Yanchevitsky, V., *Batu*, 274;
  Ghenghis Khan, 274
Yasensky, B., 328
Yashin, A., 331
  "Levers, The," 331; "Vologda
  Wedding," 331
Yassinsky, Y., 4

Yazvitsky, V., *Ivan the Third*, 315

Yezhov, G., 238, 257, 313

Young Guard, 49

Youth, 329, 351, 386, 391

Yutkevich, S., 285

Zabolotsky, N., 107, 278, 291, 319, 329, 352, 359-62, 393
  Bowels of the Earth, The, 360; *Lay of Prince Igor*, 361; *Metamorphozisi*, 361; *North, The*, 360; *Printed Columns* ("Stolbtsy"), 360; *Rubbruk in Mongolia*, 362; *Triumph of Agriculture, The*, 360, 361

Zadornov, N., *Toward the Pacific*, 315

Zamyatin, E., 54, 59, 60, 67, 75, 82-91, 92, 93, 99, 101, 102, 112, 118, 162, 169, 199, 229, 270, 273, 328, 329, 352, 389
  At the World's End, 83; *Attila*, 90; "Cave, The," 85, 86, 199; "Dragon, The," 85; "Eyes, The," 85; *Fires of St. Dominic*, 87; "Fisher of Men, The," 84, 85; *Flood*, 85; *Fly, The*, 90; *Impious Tales*, 86; *Islanders, The*, 53, 84, 85; "Mamai," 85, 86; "North," 83, 85; *Tale of a District*, 82-83; "Tale of the Most Essential, The," 85; *Tales for Adult Children*, 86; *We*, 88-89

Zarudin, N., 106, 278
  Thirty Nights in a Vineyard, 106

Zavadsky, Y., 285

Zelinsky, K., 288

Zenkevich, M., 291

Zharov, A., 38, 291

Zhdanov, A., 98, 131, 165, 256, 305-19

Zhdanov, N., "The Journey Home," 330

Zhirmunsky, V., 279

Zilberg, V. *See* Kaverin, V.

Zinoviev, G., 43, 238

Znamia (*The Banner*), 52, 321, 322

Zorin, L., *The Guests*, 322

Zoshchenko, M., 54, 88, 92-98, 100, 101, 102, 256, 306, 323
  "Adventures of an Ape, The," 98; *Apollo and Tamara*, 95; *Before the Sunrise*, 97, 306; *Black Prince, The*, 97; *Frightening Night*, 95; *Gay Adventure*, 95; *Letters to a Writer*, 93; *Pale-Blue Book, The*, 96; *Restored Youth*, 96; *Tales by Nazar Ilich Sinebryukhov, The*, 93; "Tales of Lenin," 97; *What the Nightingale Sang Of*, 95; *Wisdom*, 95

Zozulya, Y., 88, 105, 292

Zvezda (*The Star*), 52, 98, 305, 361

Zweig, S., 335